Karl
Kautsky
and the
Socialist
Revolution
1880–1938

Karl Kautsky and the Socialist Revolution 1880–1938

Translated by

Jon Rothschild

Massimo Salvadori

VERSO

London · New York

First published as *Kautsky e la rivoluzione socialista 1880–1938* by
Giangiacomo Feltrinelli Editore, Milan 1976
First published in English 1979
This edition published by Verso 1990
© Giangiacomo Feltrinelli Editore 1976
Translation © New Left Books 1979

Verso
UK: 6 Meard Street, London W1V 3HR
USA: 29 West 35th Street, New York, NY 10001-2291

Verso is the imprint of New Left Books

ISBN 0-86091-528-X

Typeset in Monophoto Ehrhardt by Servis Filmsetting Ltd
Printed in Great Britain by Biddles Ltd, Guildford

Contents

Preface

Karl Kautsky was one of the leading exponents of Marxism from the last decades of the 19th century to the early decades of the 20th. It has been universally recognized that he played a major role (for good or ill) in the history of German Social Democracy and the Second International. He was perhaps the supreme target of the polemics of Lenin (and Trotsky) in the controversy over the political and ideological significance of the Bolshevik Revolution and the Soviet state. Despite all this, Kautsky has been singularly ignored as an independent figure for historical study, unlike his peers in the history of Marxism and socialism. This does not mean that much has not been written about Kautsky. For the most part, however, he has been in effect assimilated into the history of the workers movement and treated in relation to other figures – Eduard Bernstein, Rosa Luxemburg, Franz Mehring, or August Bebel, not to mention Lenin and Trotsky. These, unlike Kautsky, have themselves been the subjects of a considerable historiographic tradition. In sum, there is an enormous disproportion between the volume of references to Kautsky in the course of history itself and the paucity of critical studies devoted to him.

I have come to the conclusion that the main reason for this disproportion is that scholars have so far fundamentally confined themselves to the judgments 'for' or 'against' Kautsky that were pronounced in the thick of the political struggles between parties, ideologies, and movements in his own time. One might say that the image of Kautsky has remained fixed ever since in the forms it acquired in that epoch. A purely theoretical figure who lived a tranquil and 'anti-heroic', even a rather prosaic, life in an era of fire and steel, Kautsky has not proved an attractive subject for biography.

The general conception that long predominated, given the influence of Leninism and the judgment of Lenin himself, was that Kautsky was a distinguished Marxist theoretician (albeit somewhat 'tarnished') until he became a 'renegade', when he opposed the Bolshevik Revolution – indeed, 'the great renegade', precisely because of the 'positive' role he had played previously. This interpretation, which puts Kautsky in contradiction with himself, has never been substantiated by any comprehensive communist historical study. There is, however, another and very different interpretation which has also had significant influence: that advanced by Karl Korsch in his celebrated essay of 1929 on Kautsky and the materialist conception of history.[1] Korsch maintained that Kautsky had never understood anything of Marxism, either before he became a 'renegade' or after, and that he was always merely the exponent of a banal evolutionism, equally in his political theory and in his historical-philosophical outlook. The conclusions of the present work differ from both these views.

My interest in Kautsky goes back quite some years. I hope readers will pardon a brief explanation of it. My first contact with the veteran theorist dates from 1959, when his work *The Agrarian Question* (which, as we know, Lenin hailed enthusiastically when it originally appeared in 1899) was published in an Italian edition, with a long preface by Giuliano Procacci. This book made a deep impression on me. At the time, I was conditioned by the entire violent polemic of Lenin, leader of the Bolshevik Revolution and the Soviet State, against Kautsky the 'vulgar liberal' who upheld a conception of the state and of democracy that never went beyond the platitudes of a dreary, philistine secondary-school teacher, a man who was thoroughly incapable of understanding the role of finance capitalism in the interpretation of imperialism, and so on. I was struck in particular by one fundamental question. How could Lenin have described Kautsky as a revolutionary up to the eve of the First World War if *The Agrarian Question* already evinced a conception of the state in full accordance with the positions Kautsky later defined in his polemic against Bolshevism, and in complete contradiction with the 'model' of the Paris Commune?

Shortly after the appearance of the Italian edition of *The Agrarian Question*, Werner Blumenberg published *Karl Kautsky Literarische Werk: Eine Bibliographische Uebersicht*,[2] which furnished a precious instrument for research into Kautsky's work. I thus began a study of German Social Democracy and of Kautsky in particular, the fruit of which, after many interruptions, is represented by the present work.[3]

---

[1] K. Korsch, *Die materialistische geschichtsanffassung. Eine Auseinandersetzung mit Karl Kautsky*, Leipzig, 1929.

[2] Amsterdam, 1960.

[3] A part of this work, in very abbreviated form and dealing only with Kautsky's work up

The nature of my findings can be summarized under two headings: one 'formal', the other substantive. So far as the former is concerned, this book is not only not a biography of Kautsky in the complete sense; it is not even an intellectual biography dealing with Kautsky's work as a whole. I have not dwelt systematically on Kautsky's philosophical and historiographic production – I touch on this only insofar as it clarifies the specific field of my research. Neither have I gone deeply into Kautsky's ideological and philosophical formation.[4] My work does cover nearly all of Kautsky's output, but from a specific angle. For the substantive focus of this book is an examination of the way Kautsky approached the relationship between socialism and democracy in the course of his long political activity. Indeed, the title easily could have been 'Democracy and Socialism in Kautsky'. What I have sought to do is 1) to offer a concrete historical context for the analysis of Kautsky's positions, viewing them through the prism of the history of the SPD and the German labour movement; 2) to examine to what extent and for what reasons Kautsky did or did not change his positions; 3) to draw some conclusions about the central problem raised by Lenin as to whether there was a real 'break' in Kautsky's evolution.

It may be useful here to give a brief preview of some of the conclusions I have reached on the third of these questions and to stress in what sense the work of Kautsky appears important and significant to me, beyond the specific role he played in his time.

As I point out in the course of this work, Kautsky's evolution was indeed marked by a series of changes, even 'contradictions'. Could it have been otherwise with a figure who grappled with social developments over a period lasting from the years immediately following the Paris Commune to the eve of the Second World War? Nonetheless, throughout his activity, or at least from the beginning of the 1890s to his death in 1938, Kautsky maintained a 'consistent' conception of the modern state, of the role of parliament, of the function of the political and civil liberties bequeathed by bourgeois liberalism, of the indispensability of a central-ized bureaucratic-administrative apparatus (in open polemic against the

---

to the aftermath of the First World War, was published in AA.VV., *Storia del marxismo contemporaneo*, Milan, 1974, under the title: *La concezione del processo rivoluzionario in Kautsky (1891-1922)*.

[4] W. Holzheuer's study, *Karl Kautskys Werk als Weltanschauung. Beitrag zur Ideologie der Sozialdemokratie vor dem Ersten Weltkrieg* (Munich, 1972), is devoted to Kautsky's formation and to his philosophical conception of socialism. The reader may also consult several essays by E. Ragionieri in *Il marxismo e l'Internazionale*, Rome, 1972.

principle of 'direct legislation'), and of the importance of political democracy as an instrument for assuring knowledge of society and ascertaining the will of its citizens. Kautsky's point of view on all such problems remained remarkably constant. My answer to the question of whether Lenin was 'correct' to call Kautsky a 'renegade' because of his conception of the state and democracy is therefore clear: by the end of the 19th century, Kautsky held a view of them that would inevitably clash with Soviet theory and the practice of the government of the Bolsheviks. To be sure, Kautsky had spoken of socialist revolution and the dictatorship of the proletariat. Nonetheless, when Lenin and Trotsky accused Kautsky of having abandoned the perspective of the dictatorship of the proletariat which he had earlier long upheld, they were thoroughly mistaken, for they failed to note, or perhaps did not want to see, that Kautsky had always regarded the dictatorship of the proletariat as a regime which, although it would represent the power of the proletariat alone, would be established by free elections, would be committed to respect political and civil liberties, and would be based on the use of parliament for socialist purposes, and on constitutional control of a centralized administrative-bureaucratic apparatus of government. Undoubtedly, this was a standpoint in profound contradiction to the Marxist conception of the transitional state: on this point Lenin was correct. But it was nonetheless one that Kautsky had developed as far back as the turn of the century, and which he upheld constantly and openly even during the time when Lenin considered him a 'master of Marxism'.

Having made this point (the illustration of which is obviously one of the tasks of the present book), I would like to try to set out what appears to me the general significance of Kautsky's work. Firstly, of course, its historical importance is obvious. Kautsky was a central figure of the European workers' movement; to retrace his development is indispensable for a deeper knowledge of it. Secondly, and even more pertinently, Kautsky's work is preeminently representative of a type of awareness of the complex problems posed to the workers' movement by the social evolution of the developed capitalist countries, beyond the perspectives of Marx and Engels, and opposite in direction to that of the revolutionary heirs of Marx and Engels (Rosa Luxemburg, Lenin and Trotsky, to mention the major names). Kautsky's consciousness of these problems was anything but 'limpid'; it was partial and contradictory. But it was a consciousness which has nonetheless made its way, after many vicissitudes, into the Western Communist movement itself, after the crisis of Leninism as a model of theory and practice and of the Soviet state as a model of organized power. Indeed, the approach of the Western Communist Parties to these problems today has assumed a shape which in my view can be defined, without the slightest polemical provocation, as essentially 'Kautskyist'. In effect Kautsky developed an analysis of the relations between society, state, and parties which was representative of the Social Democratic approach to some of the same problems explored by Antonio Gramsci from the contrary standpoint of an original interpretation of Leninism. In this sense, Kautsky provides the terms for a comparison with the 'Gramscian road'. Both Kautsky and Gramsci were equally conscious of the importance of democracy for socialism; they arrived at conclusions which have 'exemplary' significance precisely as political opposites.

Arthur Rosenberg, the great historian of the labour movement and of Bolshevism, once made an observation which I consider a fundamental starting-point for an understanding of the sense in which Kautsky may be regarded as 'representative'. In his work *Democracy and Socialism* Rosenberg remarked that Marx and Engels failed to register the nature of the organization of modern parties, particularly socialist parties, in the context of capitalist development: 'In the first place, both men never completely understood the actual character of the new European labour parties that developed after 1863. They felt that these parties did not act in accordance with their own ideas. Yet they regarded the mistakes of the workers' leaders and the petty-bourgeois backwardness of their followers as the cause of this deviation. Marx and Engels mercilessly criticized individual actions of Lassalle and Wilhelm Liebknecht, yet this criticism hides the conviction that basically the socialist parties are, or at least should be, revolutionary parties like those of 1848; that it suffices to berate the erring leaders and to oppose the petty-bourgeois prejudices of their followers in order to set matters right again. But Marx and Engels failed to recognize that after 1863 they were not dealing with individual mistakes within the socialist parties, but rather with a new type of party, and that the average European labour party was basically different from revolutionary Marxism.'[5] Now I would say that Kautsky, on the contrary, expressed a different outlook on the nature and role of modern parties: with respect to the development of capitalism, with respect to the state, and even with respect to their internal structure. Central to Kautsky's analysis was the conviction that the model of 1848 and the Paris Commune could no longer serve to advance workers' interests in a social

[5] A. Rosenberg, *Democracy and Socialism, A Contribution to the Political History of the Past 150 Years*, London, 1939, pp. 296–297.

context dominated by large-scale capitalism; it could inspire neither greater offensive actions by labour, nor the construction of a socialist state. The coherence of his interpretation of this position led inevitably to his clash with Lenin's rehabilitation of the revolutionary spirit of 1848 and 1871. So far as the state, the civil service, and the nature of political parties were concerned, Kautsky arrived at conclusions which seem to me singularly analogous to those of Max Weber on the relationship between firm, state and parties. This emerges particularly clearly in his 1893 essay on parliamentarism and direct legislation. Kautsky maintained that any project of 'direct democracy' was doomed to failure in a society dominated by large-scale modern industry – that is, by a mode of production whose very essence requires not only central planning and coordination of the economy and the state, but also a bureaucratic apparatus as a professionally selected technical instrument for its implementation. He concluded that although the state apparatus and the technical-administrative apparatus constructed by the modern bourgeoisie could be used for different socio-political purposes, they could not be 'shattered' and replaced by an 'anti-bureaucratic' state and form of social organization. These are central theses which the Western Communist movement has recently come to accept. When Kautsky, convinced of all this, saw the Bolsheviks in practice abandon the model of the Commune and instead establish a super-centralized, bureaucratized state machine, he judged that force of circumstance and 'rationality' had prevailed, but in the worst possible form, so to speak. For he thought that the centralization and unified legislation characteristic of the modern bourgeois state had to be energetically 'corrected', on the one hand by bringing the bureaucracy under the control of parliament and of consumers, and on the other hand by creating a network of democratic and de-centralized local bodies circumscribing its centralized nucleus. These conditions, however, could only be established by full political democracy. He saw the super-centralized machine of the Soviet state as a one-sided triumph of un-bridled centralism and bureaucratism, the inevitable consequence of a despotic political system.

If we shift from the problem of the state to that of the socio-economic development of capitalism, Kautsky believed up to the years immediately preceding the First World War that the German and European workers' movement was on the way to the decisive show-down with the bourgeoisie and with the ruling classes in general. He then became acutely, even embarrassingly, aware that the enemy commanded rather greater reserves than had been suspected and that a new analysis was needed to prospect the future of capitalism. During the Great War itself he arrived at his theory of 'super-imperialism', which Lenin denounced (in *Imperialism, Highest Stage of Capitalism*) as a theoretical error and a political betrayal. From the beginning of the world conflict, Kautsky reiterated the penetrating judgment that it was quite possible that in itself the war would not lead to the end of capitalism and the inauguration of an international revolutionary process, but might rather consecrate the end of the primacy of Europe and the advent of the young and powerful United States as the dominant power on the world scene. This, he said, raised the possibility of a new global balance among the capitalist states. His analysis of imperialism held that it was *a* policy, but not necessarily *the* policy of capital, representing not an economic *necessity* but rather a *choice* by big capital determined by the influence of militaristic circles and business sectors with interests in armaments, under the direction of reactionary finance capital (here there was a strong similarity to Schumpeter's *Sociology of Imperialism*). Kautsky concluded that there were no objective limits to the operation and perpetuation of capitalism *per se* and that socialism could only be an expression of a will for a different social order. Socialism would thus no longer be a historical *necessity*, as Kautsky himself had long preached, but rather a *possibility* to be realized by political organization and practice. Such an approach, with all its oscillations and many internal problems (which I have sought to elucidate in this book), represented a picture of capitalist development and of the international relationship of forces of substantial realism.

Even though he came to hold this perspective, Kautsky continued to believe in the advent of socialism. Having reached the conclusion that capitalism retained possibilities of development, he held firmly to another conclusion: that through its development capitalism would increasingly augment the potential of the workers' movement, since it was constitutionally incapable of overcoming its class nature or of preventing the exploitation of labour by capital from creating the objective basis for socialism, along with the historical need for it. Nevertheless, having abandoned any faith in an automatic 'collapse' of the capitalist system, he considered political democracy of even greater importance as the supreme means by which the proletariat could express itself, become conscious of its exploitation, organize its own struggles, and breathe real life into the possibility of socialism. Thus in Kautsky's eyes political democracy assumed the character of a necessary and decisive condition for the growth of socialism. Hence when fascism made its appearance in Europe, Kautsky insisted that the supreme task of the labour movement was the reconquest of political democracy as the basis for a resumption of the struggle for socialism. Since he held that democracy was the indispensable general form of both the conquest of power and the construction of socialism, he opposed any strategy aimed at directly replacing fascism with the dictatorship of the proletariat in the form of class or party rule. It was for this reason that he argued that, given the negative model of Bolshevism, the European workers' movement should abandon the notion of the 'dictatorship of the proletariat', replacing it with that of the 'domination' of the working-class (the word he used for 'hegemony'). He meant by such a 'domination' a regime founded on three elements: 1) an established consensus in favour of socialism; 2) maintenance of political democracy; 3) the use of parliament for socialist purposes and the construction of a system of organs of rank-and-file democracy capable of lending the state and the central power a popular foundation.

A little noted aspect of Kautsky's theoretical activity which is analysed in this book are the positions he took on Stalinist Russia and on fascism. It is well known that he was an implacable opponent of Stalin's Russia, but the precise terms of his opposition are less familiar. Here again, Kautsky's standpoint was to acquire a representative significance. He was the originator of the theory that the Soviet regime had given rise to the rule of a 'new class', a theory that had a long future before it. He reached this judgment on the basis of criteria at which he had arrived during the period prior to the First World War. Kautsky never ceased to stress that the nationalization of the means of production was not in itself at all equivalent to socialism and that it could even become the most powerful instrument for the creation of another form of class rule different from capitalism. For him socialism was the product of an indissoluble combination of political democracy and the abolition of private property. Observing the development of the USSR, Kautsky concluded, well before Bruno Rizzi, James Burnham, or Milovan Djilas, that it represented a third form of society distinct from capitalism or socialism, yet which had in common with capitalism a class character expressed by the rule of a minority over the majority. In his view this type of class rule was even more oppressive than that of capitalism in its bourgeois-democratic form, under which the proletariat preserved the possibility of defending its living conditions.

As for fascism, here Kautsky developed one of his most significant theories. He argued that fascism could be but an 'interlude' which would be followed by a return to political democracy, for he was convinced that modern industrial society required that the relations among social forces be regulated through formal rules of free bargaining. Since he regarded democracy as the most 'rational' and normal form of industrial society, he considered fascism a 'deviation' brought about by exceptional circumstances. At first he harboured the illusion that a society like Germany could never fall victim to the virus of fascism. Then, when it did, he was convinced that fascism would expand no further and that it could in no way represent the destiny of capitalism. Hence his slogan: the struggle against fascism can only be the struggle for the reconquest of democracy.

Such is a rapid and concise summary of the major themes treated in the present book. I should make clear that my prime objective has been to present the thought of one of the principal exponents of post-Marxian socialism, who has been more vilified than read. I have been sustained in this objective by the conviction that for those who are interested in socialism today, in a historical situation that has changed much since the epoch in which Kautsky, Lenin, Trotsky or Luxemburg lived, mere passive repetition of old hates and loves is a futile exercise. In my view we need rather to reconstruct the history of socialism with greater depth and discrimination, and then to reflect on it in a spirit of critical independence.

If I had to offer an interpretation of Kautskyism, I would say that it cannot be defined in the manner of his son, Benedikt, who called it an organic systematization of Marxism,[6] nor in the manner of Korsch, for whom Kautsky was simply a mystifier of Marxism, nor in the manner of Erich Matthias who, in his noted and in many respects acute work *Kautsky und Kautskyismus*,[7] called it an 'ideology of integration'. I stand rather closer to the assessment of Hermann Brill, who is cited by Matthias. Brill noted that Kautsky, while considering himself the great 'orthodox' systematizer of Marxism, 'very rapidly went "further", into uncharted territory'.[8] Let me try to explain. Kautsky was certainly in no way a very original thinker, and 'Kautskyism' discovered no new theoretical

---

[6] Cf. B. Kautsky, introduction to the collection *Ein Leben für den Sozialismus, Erinnerungen an Karl Kautsky*, Hanover, 1954, pp. 8–9. For the viewpoint that Kautsky was the continuator of Marx and the man who systematized his doctrine, see the essays devoted to the relationship between Marx and Kautsky in the volumes published in honour of Kautsky's seventieth birthday: *Karl Kautsky zum 70. Geburtstage. Ein Sonderheft der 'Gesellschaft'*, Hrsg. von R. Hilferding, Berlin, 1924; *Karl Kautsky, der Denker und Kämpfer. Festgabe zu seinem siebzigsten Geburtstag*, Vienna, 1924; *Der Lebendige Marxismus. Festgabe zum 70. Geburtstag von Karl Kautsky*, Hrsg. von O. Jenssen, Jena, 1924.

[7] E. Matthias, *Kautsky und der Kautskyismus*, in *Marxismusstudien*, Second Series, Tübingen, 1957, pp. 151–97.

[8] H. Brill, *Karl Kautsky 16. Oktober 1854–17. Oktober 1938*, in 'Zeitschrift für Politik', 1954. The formulation is cited in Matthias, op. cit., p. 10.

horizons in the sense that it furnished no new 'categories' of thought. Kautsky's Marxism was a hybrid combination of influences deriving from Marx, Darwin, or Liberalism, and of reflections on the major products of German academic culture, with which he nonetheless polemicized constantly. But it was not only this. For Kautsky was a sensitive and sometimes very keen observer of new phenomena of social development, which could not simply be 'read' through the eyes of Marx and Engels. He was caught up in these developments, and sometimes led astray by them. What makes Kautsky remarkable, despite his monotonous, even tedious style, is that he, the most 'orthodox' of the orthodox, was able to grasp the real import of certain problems with an attention and sometimes an open-mindedness that even led him, where necessary, to question the tenets of his beloved Karl Marx. This process, regardless of its results, contains a lesson of no mean importance. Although he was not an original thinker in theoretical terms, there was an 'originality' in the representative character of his positions, which was not merely 'static', but anticipated with clear and solid analyses many problems over which polemics are raging today: the relationship between democracy and socialism, between the state and the workers' movement, between capitalism and the role of the proletariat as a class.

Finally, I would like to express my dissent from Matthias's study of Kautsky. The German scholar has interpreted Kautsky's role in German Social Democracy before the First World War as that of an advocate of integration into capitalist society, even while he remained in appearance a theoretician of 'socialist revolution'. Yet what should be the real object of his analysis is lacking in Matthias's essay. For to define Kautskyism simply as an ideology of integration tends to presume that Kautskyism was 'responsible' for this integration – in other words that a different ideology would have enabled German Social Democracy to avert such integration. What integrated Social Democracy into German society, however, was not an erroneous ideology; it was the product of real historical conditions. Between the end of the 19th century and 1914 the SPD experienced a situation completely unforeseen by the heritage of Marxism, which was nonetheless its official ideology. Its integration into the Second Reich was fundamentally determined by objective processes, which met with the active accord of some sectors of the party and the opposition of others: above all by the peculiar combination of a powerful and conservative state apparatus, based on an alliance of aristocratic militarism and elite bureaucracy, and an unprecedented industrial development dominated by a brutal finance capital. In these conditions, the real 'motor force' of integration was actually the trade-union move-ment. German Social Democracy was the first great workers' party that was compelled to deal, squarely and bluntly, with a capitalist system whose rapid end its theory had led it to expect, which instead exploded outwards in an imperialism that rallied wide mass support. Kautsky's reaction to this unforeseen development was contradictory, oscillating between optimism and anxiety that 'something had gone wrong'. His ideology was an expression of this situation more than a real and decisive cause of it. Indeed, if the constraints had not been so powerful in reality, in the abstract nothing would have prevented Social Democracy from ranging itself behind an ideology of non-integration, which was after all defended within the party, above all by Rosa Luxemburg.

I dedicate this book to the memory of Ernesto Ragionieri, in the full knowledge that he would not have shared some of its approaches and conclusions. I also owe a grateful debt to the memory of Theodor Pinkus, the noted librarian of Zurich, thanks to whom I was able to obtain precious materials that completed the results of inquiries conducted in the libraries of Leipzig, Dresden, Zurich, Munich, Amsterdam, and the Giangiacomo Feltrinelli Foundation of Milan.

M. L. S.

I
The Guarantees of History

1 The Emergency Laws and 'Revolutionary Violence'

'The Social Democratic workers' party has always emphasized that it is a revolutionary party in the sense that it recognizes that it is impossible to resolve the social question within the existing society. . . . Even today, we *would prefer*, if it were possible, to realize the social revolution *through the peaceful road*. . . . But if we still harbour this hope today, we have nonetheless ceased to emphasize it, for every one of us knows *that it is a utopia*. The most perceptive of our comrades have never believed in the possibility of a peaceful revolution; they have learned from history that violence is the midwife of every old society pregnant with a new one. . . . Today we all know that the popular socialist state can be erected only through a violent overthrow and that it is our duty to uphold consciousness of this among ever broader layers of the people.'

Thus wrote Karl Kautsky in *Der Sozialdemokrat* in February 1881. After affirming the historic necessity of preparing for a revolutionary process in which violence would act as the midwife of a new society, he continued by outlining the basis of this process. Popular suffering and despair, expressions of permanent social mechanisms of economic exploitation and political oppression, would not provoke a revolution by themselves. At most they could provoke revolt. 'Popular revolt is transformed into revolution only when the state and society are so rotten, so decayed, as to collapse under the shock.' This was the deeper reason why all the efforts of agitators and conspirators to conjure up revolutions were condemned to sterility. It was also the reason why not even a party can provoke a revolution by itself. 'No, the revolution cannot be the work of a party but must come from the people. No party can provoke it, and still less a secret sect. It must be the consequence of conditions which are

20

necessarily born of the organization of the state and society.'

This sort of plea to let things ripen, not to set conspiracies afoot, however, did not mean that the liberating birth of the new society was consigned to the distant future. Kautsky was convinced, at the beginning of the 1880s, that the old order had reached the end of its tether. 'Now,' he asserted, 'modern society and modern states are ripe for revolution; they are not in a position to survive any insurrection. Their own consequences, over-production and militarism, have brought them near bankruptcy. The next insurrection will turn into revolution, which will bring down the existing order. There can be no doubt of this.'

From these theoretical premises arose the practical task of the Social Democratic party. The party must not substitute itself for the people, for the masses, 'because it is false that revolutions are made by minorities'. Indeed, revolutions 'always arise from the *mass* of the people'. The task of the party, the organized and conscious minority, is to guide the masses: 'a well-disciplined minority, energetic and conscious of the goal' must 'guide the revolution, give it direction', saving the people from 'painful convulsions' and orienting their action in the direction prescribed by the course of historical development. 'Our task is not to organize the revolution, but to organize ourselves *for* the revolution; it is not to *make* the revolution, but *to take advantage of it*.'[1]

For Kautsky, to prepare the party for the revolution, especially in Germany, was a task that had to be undertaken promptly, precisely because bourgeois society 'is in the final stages of its malady' and 'the slightest shock should destroy it'.[2] The bourgeoisie as a class had demonstrated that it was incapable of self-renovation, as could be seen from the fact that its ideal was the protection of private property under the aegis not even of a republic but of a military monarchy. Hence the significance of the SPD's call for a republic, not a bourgeois-democratic, but a socialist republic: 'the republic we aim at is not abstract; it is a socialist republic, the red republic'.[3]

Kautsky saw the 'reforms' of Bismarck (accident insurance, tobacco monopoly, state ownership of the railroads) as no more than belated attempts to save a sinking ship. He compared the situation of the German bourgeoisie and monarchy to that of France on the eve of the revolution of 1789. Bismarckian 'state socialism' was no more than recourse to measures that confessed that capitalism was bankrupt; it was an attempt

---

[1] 'Verschwörung oder Revolution?', in *Der Sozialdemokrat*, no. 8, 20 February 1881.
[2] 'Die Vivisektion des Proletariats', in *Der Sozialdemokrat*, no. 39, 22 September 1881.
[3] 'Die Bourgeoisie und die Republik', in *Der Sozialdemokrat*, no. 17, 24 April 1881.

to use 'socialist ideas' by deforming them. 'State socialism' is 'a natural product of our time, just as the reformist ideas of Turgot, Necker, and Calonne were products of the previous century'. Like their predecessors, the present advocates of 'state socialism' would 'necessarily fail'. Reformism from above could perhaps postpone, but not avert the fall of the military monarchy, for the capitalist mode of production and the bourgeoisie had arrived at their 1789. 'State socialism is the declaration of bankruptcy of the modern state and modern society.'[4]

In this context, Kautsky concluded that 'Social Democracy harbours no illusion that it can directly achieve its goal through elections, through the parliamentary road'. Elections, 'as everyone knows, have a primarily propagandistic purpose'.[5]

On the question of the state, and the attitude of the proletariat toward it in the course of the revolutionary process, the young Kautsky affirmed that 'the first step of the coming revolution, whose goal is the abolition of class differences', would be to 'demolish the bourgeois state'; the second would be to 'create the state anew', in accordance with the interests of the revolution and its 'preservation'. It is necessary, he continued, that the future revolutionary government constitute itself so as to defend the proletariat: 'The victory of the proletariat does not yet entail the disappearance of all class contradictions. The coming revolution will first of all raise the proletariat to the position of the ruling class, but not the only class. The conflict between the rulers and the ruled will persist, and the proletariat will thus need a *government which, as an instrument of the ruling class, will curb the ruled with all the means at its command.* All this may sound very undemocratic, but necessity will compel us to act in this way.'

But although Kautsky explicitly referred to the use of 'violent' means to 'annihilate' the economic power of big capital and the large landlords, whose goods 'must immediately be transformed into common property', he took care to state immediately that the goal of the victorious proletariat would not be to turn the members of the defeated class into 'slaves'.[6] The political triumph of the proletariat meant, in the most complete sense, the replacement of the previous form of liberty for individuals and single classes by the commitment of all to common duties, superseding the bourgeois system. 'The socialist revolution, unlike the great French

---

[4] 'Der Staatssozialismus und die Sozialdemokratie', in *Der Sozialdemokrat*, no. 10, 6 April 1881.

[5] 'Wahlen und Attentate', in *Der Sozialdemokrat*, no. 23, 5 June 1881.

[6] 'Die Abschaffung des Staates', in *Der Sozialdemokrat*, no. 51, 15 December 1881.

Revolution, does not mean a further step in the development of the struggle for existence in the form which has held sway up to now, but the beginning of a completely different form of existence.' It was therefore a pure slander when the opponents of Social Democracy accused the party of wanting to 'replace the present rule of one class with the rule of another class', stamping out freedom of the press, speech, and association. On the contrary, what Social Democracy sought was the elimination of the state and society of particularist liberties and its replacement by full equality, accompanied by the necessary measures against the champions of the old social order. The model of the new state could not be 'bourgeois democracy', but proletarian order, founded on the only 'compulsion' that society could and should exercise over the individual: equality.[7] In imagining the 'free society' Kautsky assigned it one characteristic which was henceforward to be typical of the emphatically anti-anarchistic and anti-libertarian cast of his outlook on institutions: centralized organization. 'The free society,' Kautsky wrote, 'will be a federation of nations and not of groups or communes; production in these nations will be left neither to free choice nor to the spontaneous formation of groups, nor even to sheer force of social attraction; instead, production will be placed under the direction of a well-organized administration.'[8]

Imminent ruin of bourgeois society; conviction of the inevitability and invincibility of socialism, regardless of the repressive measures of the old society; mission of the party as the organizer of the proletarian masses, who must carry out their own historic task themselves; opposition to the spirit of conspiracy – all these elements of the young Kautsky's thought rested on a conception of social development that closely linked Marxism and Darwinism. Later, in 1924, recalling the period of his own formation, Kautsky was to say that when Darwinism 'conquered the ranks of culture', he also had accepted it 'with enthusiasm' and that his 'theory of history was intended to be nothing other than the application of Darwinism to social development'.[9] This fusion of Marxism and Darwinism served to inspire Kautsky with a conception of the revolutionary process as the development of an organic necessity. There was no room for illusions that anything which had been historically condemned by evolution could be conserved or that anyone could voluntaristically force the pace of evolution itself. The conservatives, he wrote in 1880, fear the revolu-

---

[7] 'Klassenkampf und Sozialismus', in *Der Sozialdemokrat*, no. 40, 29 September 1881. Cf. *Freiheit*, no. 37, 8 September 1881.

[8] 'Die freie Gesellschaft', in *Der Sozialdemokrat*, no. 1, 1 January 1882.

[9] *Das Werden eines Marxisten*, Leipzig, 1930, p. 120.

tionary implications of Darwinism, whose application to the domain of society teaches that 'the transition from an old to a new conception of the world occurs irresistably'; that 'the traditional institutions founded on the needs of the preceding epoch will fall into ruin, while new institutions will take their place'.[10] To the conservatives who sought to interpret the 'struggle for existence' in an anti-socialist sense, Kautsky replied that the direction of social evolution itself would lead to the exhaustion and therewith the end of this struggle as a conflict between the weak and strong, oppressors and oppressed. The rise of civilization found its completion in socialism, just as science was the affirmation of control over natural forces.[11] 'The cessation of the struggle for existence; this is precisely socialism.'[12] 'In the mind of a socialist, Darwinism signifies knowledge of the conditions of *social* life'[13] – a knowledge transformed into consciousness of the invincibility of socialism as a necessary stage in human evolution. 'The logic of things' would teach the reactionaries 'that neither prison, nor bullets, nor bayonets can kill socialism'.[14] When Darwin died Kautsky likened him to Marx in the gigantic stature and revolutionary value of his work;[15] when Marx died Engels was to take up the comparison again, asserting that just as 'Darwin had discovered the laws of development of the organic nature of our planet', Marx had been 'the discoverer of the fundamental laws that regulate the course and development of human society'.[16]

In Kautsky's view, the political party of the proletariat was the bearer of the social science elaborated by socialist theoreticians, and the organizer of the effort to translate the dictates of historical evolution into practice, at the lowest possible cost. 'Theoretical socialism,' Kautsky wrote, 'has the task on the one hand of clarifying for itself the direction in which the development of modern society is moving and on the other hand of discovering which of the present social institutions contain the germs of this development and which are incompatible with it. Practical socialism then has the duty to favour the former with all its might, while combating the elements that must be eliminated.'[17]

[10] 'Der Darwinismus und die Revolution', in *Der Sozialdemokrat*, no. 14, 4 April 1880.
[11] *Aus Oesterreich*, no. 8, 22 February 1880 and no. 16, 18 April 1880.
[12] 'Phäakentum', in *Der Sozialdemokrat*, no. 28, 6 July 1882.
[13] 'Der Darwinismus und die Bourgeois-Wissenschaft', in *Der Sozialdemokrat*, no. 41, 9 October 1881.
[14] *Aus Oesterreich*, op. cit.
[15] 'Darwin', in *Der Sozialdemokrat*, no. 18, 27 April 1882.
[16] Marx-Engels, *Werke*, vol. XIX, Berlin, 1962, p. 333.
[17] 'Der Uebergang von der kapitalistischen zur sozialistischen Produktionsweise', in *Jahrbuch für Sozialwissenschaft und Sozialpolitik*, 2 Häfte, 1880, p. 60.

Several years later he was to explain his opposition to utopianism, his conviction that socialism was fully inherent in historical development, in social and economic evolution itself. There was thus no need for 'projects' counterposed to reality, reducing socialism to preconceived schemas devised by some external will. Why, Kautsky asked, have we no need of any 'Icarus' or 'New Harmony'? He answered: 'Because we see the preconditions of socialism developing before our very eyes. To recognize this development and its course; to understand it and satisfy the demands which it poses to the elements striving for progress: this is the task of socialism in our epoch. On the other hand, whosoever has the State of the future ready in his own pocket will never be capable of judging the present with lucid and dispassionate eyes.'[18]

In Kautsky's view, Social Democracy, the party of the 'science of reality', possessed some of the characteristics of a new and higher *ecclesia militans* within which the best and most conscious individuals of society found the source of a normative mode of behaviour inspired by secular science in its most advanced form. In this fashion, socialism represented, for all society, the overcoming of the bourgeois principle of the raw struggle for existence as an eternal law of nature, just as the party constituted the crucible in which old individualistic 'instincts' were purged in favour of 'communist instincts'.

'What attracts us to the party,' Kautsky explained in 1881, 'what links us to it, is not a desire for gain, nor for glory and esteem, nor even a desire for recognition, nor any particular sympathy for the individuals who make up the party. What attracts us to the party is purely and simply communist instinct, the sense of duty, which tells us that the disinherited class has the right to our full personality, and not simply a limited portion of it, the limits being set by individual liberty. We belong to the party body and soul; with respect to the party we have only duties and no rights, save one: equality. We must be prepared to sacrifice everything for the party; the party, on the other hand, has nothing whatever to sacrifice for us.'[19]

These radical positions – denunciation of the bureaucratic-military state, use of parliament only for agitational and tactical purposes, expectation of a crisis of bourgeois society in the imminent future, summons to the party to prepare itself for the creation of a proletarian state, 'mystique' of the party as a new *ecclesia militans* – gave full expres-

---

[18] 'Brauchen wir ein positives Zukunfts-Programme?', in *Der Sozialdemokrat*, no. 34, 20 August 1885.

[19] 'Klassenkampf und Sozialismus', op. cit.

sion to a tendency within German Social Democracy which had been strengthened by the anti-socialist laws enacted by Bismarck. On the one hand, the defeat of the German bourgeoisie in 1848–9 and the subsequent triumph of the Hohenzollerns and the caste of Junkers, culminating in the formation of the Empire and the establishment of an 'emasculated' parliament, induced Social Democracy to expect little or nothing from 'bourgeois democracy'. On the other hand, the efficacious resistance of the SPD after the passage of the laws of 1878 gave the party secure confidence that only the working-class and socialism could assume the task of the historic renovation of society. Yet Social Democracy was itself caught in a sharp contradiction: on the one hand aversion to the Bismarckian state and the 'cowardly' German bourgeoisie, which induced the party to uphold revolutionary positions; on the other hand, fear that a head-on clash with the powerful military-bureaucratic apparatus erected by Bismarck could result in disaster. The German Social Democrats extracted themselves from this contradiction during the period of the Emergency Laws in two ways: first, by a radicalization of theory and a denunciation of parliamentary illusions, which appeared to be without prospects at the time; second, by a form of resistance to the emergency regime that resorted to illegality only for purposes of propaganda, avoiding any violent clash for the moment. The crisis of confidence in parliamentarism, rendered official at the Copenhagen Congress of the SPD and evidenced in Kautsky, as we have seen, had its objective basis in the sharp loss of votes in the elections of 1881. The Social Democrats had polled 493,000 votes in the elections of 1877 (9.1%); the total fell to 437,000 in 1878 (7.5%) and 312,000 in 1881 (6.1%). In spite of electoral disappointments and legal persecution, however, the party's organizational strength continued to grow, and with it that of the proletarian masses. The sense of the historic invincibility of socialism among theoreticians like Kautsky arose from this advance of Social Democracy and the working-class within the capitalist process of production.

2 The Erfurt Programme and the Polemic against Direct Legislation

In 1883 Kautsky took over as editor of *Die Neue Zeit*, the theoretical review of German Social Democracy. Three fundamental objectives were set out in the editorial statement of the journal, 'to our readers': democratization of science as an instrument for the socialist elevation of the proletariat; party commitment ('we will take part in the struggle of parties to the extent that this is compatible with the scientific character of our review'); devotion to the truth as the precondition for the 'fruitfulness of research'.[20] Thus began Kautsky's official politico-cultural activity. Because of the prestige of the review he edited, Kautsky was to appear to the ranks of international Social Democracy as the most eminent legatee of Marx and Engels for a whole historical epoch. In his celebrated history of German Social Democracy, Franz Mehring wrote that Kautsky's merit was to have continued 'the unitary and coherent conception of the world created by Marx and Engels' and to have done so critically and creatively: 'Far from asserting that Marxism was the last word of humanity, Kautsky was concerned that Marxism should be able to say *its* last word in *Die Neue Zeit*.' He went on: 'Steeped in varied studies and absolutely free of the traditional vanity of the literary man who schemes and intrigues for purposes of mutual adulation, Kautsky distilled with tireless care and inexorable criticism the real historical characteristics of Marxism, out of the confused all-purpose socialism which had grown up around it.'[21]

Among all the articles on the problem of revolutionary strategy written by Kautsky during his first several years of activity at *Die Neue Zeit*, in the period that preceded the end of the Anti-Socialist Laws and thus the 'new course' in the life of German Social Democracy that began in 1886, one stands out by its organic coherence and importance, and its relevance to Kautsky's future positions: *Das 'Elend der Philosophie' und 'Das Kapital'*. Kautsky's central concern in this article was the question whether the socialist revolution should be conceived, in an abstract ideological radicalism, as the pure and simple destruction of the existing order or whether it should be viewed as a united process of destruction-reconstruction. Defending the latter view, Kautsky argued that an adequate comprehension of the role of the development of the productive forces and therefore of the proletariat as a social class made it possible to establish a concrete historical connection between the terms 'destruction' and 'reconstruction'. He developed his argument by challenging the concept of revolution once upheld by Wilhelm Weitling, counterposing the SPD's concept of revolution to Weitling's. Weitling, it is true, had commendably linked socialism to the workers' movement, shedding its philanthropic cast for an avowedly proletarian and revolutionary character. But he viewed the labour movement as a mere instrument, the

[20] 'An unsere Leser', in *Die Neue Zeit* (henceforth cited as NZ), 1883, pp. 1–8.
[21] F. Mehring, *Geschichte der deutschen Sozialdemokratie*, Berlin, 1960, vol. II, p. 581.

hammer of the destruction of the established order, and not as the protagonist of 'reconstruction'. He therefore undervalued the 'precondition of both the political and economic struggle of the working class', namely political liberties, 'such as freedom of the press and the right to vote'. Weitling's idea had been that the worse things were the better.

'For Weitling, the elevation of the proletariat was not only not the precondition for its emancipation, but on the contrary was rather an impediment to it. He expected this emancipation to arise from the *deterioration of the proletariat's physical and moral level*. The reduction of the toiling worker to the position of sub-proletarian was, for Weitling, the most effective pressure for the overthrow of present society.'[22]

Hence, 'for him the masses were only a machine' to be exploited for the goal, a machine that would have to place its trust in a providential dictator, the 'messiah' of the proletariat, whose task would be to implement an authoritarian regeneration of society. The proletarian assault on the established order, according to Weitling's view, 'did not have the purpose of placing political power in the hands of the working class, but of creating room for the activity of the "just man", the beneficent redeemer, from whose head paradise on earth will spring'.[23] The Marx of *Capital* had posed the 'union of socialism with the workers' movement' on a completely different basis. He had demonstrated that the 'goal of socialism has nothing of the arbitrary, is not the work of a "great man" or an "eternal" principle' that must be revealed to the masses by an 'enlightened seer'. On the contrary, 'the goals of socialism are necessarily determined by the development of the modern mode of production and the class struggle and can be discovered only through the study of that mode of production, of its origins and development'.[24] In this sense the major teaching of *Capital*, in Kautsky's view, was that 'the goal of the workers' movement is in no way arbitrary, but is determined by social conditions'. Only an understanding of the relation between social conditions and goal could allow the task of the socialist parties to be achieved. Without it the workers' movement would be unable to determine the field of possible action and would fall into 'doctrinaire utopianism or opportunism', that is, into an empirical practice with no future. Kautsky concluded that the socialist parties 'can neither create the workers' movement nor prescribe its goals. They must instead recognize this goal

[22] 'Das "Elend der Philosophie" und "Das Kapital"', in NZ, IV, 1886, p. 12.
[23] Ibid., p. 13.
[24] Ibid., p. 15.

and assume the leadership of its fulfillment'.[25] He remained firm in his conviction that if socialists were able to read the objective tendencies of history correctly and to direct them, then the course of history would not disappoint revolutionary expectations. It was necessary, he said, to forge indissoluble links between the results of capitalist development: the growing strength of the proletariat as a class, the growing organization of the party and the trade unions, the growing inability of the bourgeoisie to deal with social and economic problems, the growing intensification of the class struggle. Still in 1886, Kautsky wrote: 'It is true that all progress within the capitalist mode of production bears within it the seeds of new prosperity and greater well-being. It does not, however, produce these automatically, but rather through such terrible contradictions that to overcome and resolve them becomes an inevitable necessity.'[26]

The end of the emergency Anti-Socialist Laws and the electoral recovery of the SPD – after the critical point of 1881 there was an irresistible and continuous surge in the socialist vote, which rose from 550,000 (9.7%) in 1884 to 763,000 (7.1%) in 1887 and finally to 1,427,000 (19.7%) in 1890 – seemed fully to confirm that the proletariat and Social Democracy, because of the very development of capitalism and the growing weight of the working class, could not be defeated by repression. Thus the fall of the 'Iron Chancellor', the failure of his internal policy, the resistance displayed by the workers in the factories with powerful strikes, and the very fact that the Emperor Wilhelm II became the advocate of proposals for reform that acknowledged the strength of the workers' movement appeared to justify the greatest hopes. Was it not now more than ever permissible to think that the constant development of political and trade-union organization and the increasing social force of the working-class could open the road to the conquest of parliament, now rendered a realistic prospect by the sharpening of class struggle and the ever greater support obtained by Social Democracy? If even the anti-socialist laws had ultimately failed to halt the electoral advance that culminated in 1890, did not the end of the Bismarckian regime authorize the greatest optimism? The sense of security with which the party emerged from legal persecution was fully expressed in the words of Mehring, who spoke, in his History of German Social Democracy, of 'incalculable successes', of 'the consciousness of invincibility permeating the party itself', which 'having thrown itself into struggle like a pre-

[25] Ibid., p. 165.
[26] 'Die chinesichen Eisenbahnen und das europäische Proletariat', in NZ, IV, 1886, p. 517.

cocious boy, his head spinning with a few wild ideas', had 'emerged from struggle . . . a vigorous man, tempered by storms, determined, prepared, conscious, always up to his tasks'.[27]

The tasks and perspectives of Social Democracy in the new historical phase found a sustained reflection, at this threshold in the maturity of the German socialist movement, in the Erfurt Programme. The first part of this document, the theoretical section, was drafted by Kautsky, while the second, dealing with the practical demands of the party for the 'democratization' of the German state, was written by Bernstein.[28]

Kautsky's theoretical survey, which took up themes from both the *Communist Manifesto* and *Capital*, opened with the affirmation that 'the economic development of bourgeois society necessarily leads' to the decadence of small enterprises and to capitalist concentration. It went on to highlight the contradictions of this development, which at once permitted a gigantic growth in the productive forces and divided the classes into two opposing camps: on one side the monopolization of social wealth in the hands of a few capitalists and large landlords, on the other side the workers and the 'decaying middle layers', for whom 'insecurity of existence, poverty, oppression, servitude, humiliation, and exploitation' were constantly intensifying. Meanwhile the inevitable numerical increase of the proletariat and the unemployed had the social effect of unleashing 'ever sharper conflict between exploiters and exploited', and the more clearly political effect of determining 'the ever more bitter class struggle between the bourgeoisie and the proletariat, which divides modern society into two enemy camps and constitutes the distinctive feature common to all the industrialized countries'. The guarantee – a crucial aspect of the document and its significance – that this socially and politically revolutionary process could not be halted or contained, lay in the essential features of the capitalist mode of production itself. Its ever more serious and generalized crises constituted the objective basis at once for the sharpening of social conflicts and for their solution by the socialization of the means of production. On such foundations rested the mission of the working class to liberate all humanity, the duty of this class to undertake the struggle for such a goal in the present society, the necessity of aiming at the conquest of political power, and finally, the specific task of the political party: 'to lend this workers' class struggle a conscious and united character and to point it towards its necessary goal'. The conclusion of Kautsky's analysis was an insistence on the universalist

[27] Mehring, op. cit., II, pp. 674–5.
[28] Cf. *Das Werden eines Marxisten*, op. cit., p. 131.

and humanist character of the goal of Social Democracy: 'The German Social Democratic Party thus struggles not for new class or private privileges, but rather for the destruction of class rule and of classes themselves and for equality of rights and duties for all, regardless of sex and origin.' For this reason, 'in the present society' Social Democracy 'fights not only against the exploitation and oppression of wage workers, but also against any form of exploitation and oppression'. The section of the Erfurt Programme devoted to the democratization of the state and society within the framework of capitalism, which was written by Bernstein, set out the task of fighting against the state that had emerged from Bismarck's victory, in the direction of a democratic republic and of the assumption of power by the SPD (although the republic was not mentioned, apparently so as not to provide pretexts for new laws against the socialists).[29]

The link between the first and second parts of the programme lay in the conviction that the objective dynamic of capitalist development would, so to speak, 'itself assume the task' of uniting the phase of democratic growth of the workers' and socialist movement and the phase of the seizure of power, as the class struggle and the crisis of bourgeois society qualitatively intensified. This assumption was the key to the constant references in the programme to the category of historical 'necessity', so cherished by Kautsky. In that sense the unity of the programme was quite real. Precisely because of this confident expectation in the direction to be taken by historical necessity, the programme left the 'form' of social change – whether it would be accomplished through legal or extra-legal, revolutionary means – unspecified. Since the SPD did not want to offer the ruling class new pretexts for repression and was convinced that the parliamentary struggle and the broadening of the scope of democracy were the decisive tasks in the current historical situation, it was determined to put the onus for the possible violence of a future clash on its adversary. An indication of the profound influence of the Erfurt Programme on the other European Socialist Parties and of the way in which it was read by revolutionaries elsewhere is furnished by Lenin's comment on it in 1899; 'We are not in the least afraid to say that we want to imitate the Erfurt Programme; there is nothing bad in imitating what is good, and precisely today, when we so often hear opportunist and equivocal criticism of that programme, we consider it our duty to speak openly in its favour.'[30]

[29] Cf. the text of the Erfurt Programme in *Revolutionäre deutsche Parteiprogramme*, edited by L. Berthold and E. Diehl, Berlin, 1964, pp. 82–6.
[30] V. I. Lenin, *Collected Works*, vol. 4, Moscow, 1960, p. 235.

Of course, the possibility that a gap could arise between the theoretical section of the programme, with its socialist objectives, and the practical section, with its struggle for democratic reforms within the existing order, certainly existed. But such a possibility was not automatically inherent in the programme itself. A contradiction could emerge in the concrete case of the growth of the workers' movement not being accompanied by an equivalent crisis of capitalism as a dominant social system – in other words, if capitalism conserved sufficient strength to assure the development of the forces of production while simultaneously maintaining effective control over the proletariat. In that event, the category of historical 'necessity', understood as the guarantee that the struggle for democracy would be transformed into a crisis of the dominant system, would inevitably lose its utility and potency. The result would then be an impasse for Social Democracy.

The mediation between the ultimate socialist goals and the daily practice of political activity of the party by the notion of historical necessity was illustrated with particular clarity by the famous commentary on the programme written by Kautsky himself – a commentary which, translated into many languages,[31] appeared to the European Socialist Parties of the Second International as a sort of new *Manifesto*, rewritten in the light of contemporary social developments. The ideological cornerstone of this famous text is undoubtedly the general thesis that capitalism was bankrupt, that only socialism could answer to social needs, and that the bourgeoisie had parted company with science because of its inability to understand the meaning of a history that was sounding its death knell.

'Capitalist society,' Kautsky asserted, 'has failed. Its dissolution is now only a matter of time; incessant economic development leads by natural necessity to the bankruptcy of the capitalist mode of production. The creation of a new social form to replace the existing order is no longer merely *desirable*; it has become *inevitable*. . . . Continuation of the civilization of capital is not possible; the alternative has sounded; either towards socialism or a return to barbarism. . . . No other party has a goal as definite and clear as the Social Democracy. . . . All the other parties live only in the present, from day to day. . . . Up to now there has never been a party that has so profoundly investigated and so well understood the social tendencies of its own epoch as Social Democracy.'[32]

---

[31] Cf. *Karl Kautskys literarisches Werk (Eine bibliographische Uebersicht von W. Blumenberg)*, Internationaal Instituut voor sociale Geschiedenis, Amsterdam, 1960, pp. 47–8.

[32] *Das Erfurter Programm*, Berlin, 1965; the quotations are from pp. 140, 141, 134, 135, 145, respectively.

It was this pervasive sense of the 'natural necessity of the final victory of the proletariat'[33] that inspired Kautsky to resort to religious terminology, comparing the most active and conscious part of the proletariat to a new '*ecclesia militans*' and the socialist doctrine to 'a new gospel'.[34] In Kautsky's writings the concrete action of Social Democracy appeared to fulfil a necessarily predetermined verdict of the laws of social evolution. Marxist science and political organization became instruments for the rational and practical realization of these laws. His warning of the possibility of a relapse of society into barbarism had the force not so much of a real historical alternative as of an evocation of the condemnation history had pronounced on the old order. The mission of socialism was universal. Kautsky indicated two essential axes for the expansion and realization of its 'new gospel': one pointed towards the 'necessity' of winning the workers' parties to socialist theory, the other warned militants and their adversaries of the no less necessary and inevitable destiny of the class struggle, which would never end until 'the goal of socialist production' had been achieved and state power had been conquered by the proletariat.[35]

In his commentary on the official text of the Erfurt Programme Kautsky approached the question of the revolutionary process in terms that were at least formally more explicit than those of the programme itself. Precisely because he strongly emphasized that the reforms of the bourgeoisie could not 'halt the social revolution'[36] and that its situation was now hopeless, he drew the conclusion that specific historic circumstances and the attitude of the old ruling classes would determine whether a resort to violence would be necessary or not. Significantly, however, he maintained that the possibility of a peaceful road was realistic because of the persuasive effect of the superiority and inevitability of socialism on the enemy. The ruling classes, he argued, mired in confusion and insecurity, would lack any alternative.

'Such an overthrow,' Kautsky wrote, 'can assume the most diverse forms, depending on the conditions in which it occurs. In no way is it fated to be necessarily linked to acts of violence and bloodshed. There have already been cases in world history in which the ruling classes were either clever enough or weak and craven enough to abdicate voluntarily in face of a hopeless situation. A social revolution is not something that must be resolved in one fell swoop. Indeed, it may be doubted that this

---

[33] Ibid., p. 228.
[34] Ibid., pp. 216, 230.
[35] Ibid., p. 231.
[36] Ibid., p. 115.

has ever happened. Revolutions are prepared in the course of political and economic struggles which last for years and decades and occur through continuous modifications and oscillations in the relationship of forces between the particular parties and classes, often interrupted by counter-attacks of long duration (periods of reaction).'[37]

Energetic affirmation of the 'goal'; equally energetic affirmation of the necessary direction of social history; confident assertion that the use of violence in the seizure of power was not inevitable – these are the fundamental features of Kautsky's discourse as we have examined it up to now. But what was Kautsky's attitude towards the state, and towards institutions more generally? He approached the analysis of this problem in a manner fully consistent with the general thesis that socialism holds the solution to the contradictions generated by capitalist *development*, economic, social, and political. Here again he rejected Weitling's claim that it was not possible 'to educate the mass of the population in socialist thought' as a symptom of infantile radicalism in the proletariat and insufficient development of the productive forces and the working class. Weitling had believed it necessary to take advantage of the desperation of the masses, according to the theory 'the worse, the better', to destroy the existing order and thus 'open the road for the socialists', who were envisaged as demiurgic liberators in whose eyes 'any form of class struggle not directed at the immediate overthrow of the existing order . . . was nothing but *a betrayal of the cause of humanity*'. This, Kautsky commented, was a form of petty-bourgeois anarchism that expressed 'aversion, even hatred, for any persistent class struggle and especially for its highest form, the political struggle'.[38] It culminated in a critique of bourgeois society that called for an enlightened despotism. Socialism, however – Kautsky stressed – is not barracks planning. Some opponents of socialism, seizing upon radical utopian projects, claimed that socialism not only 'destroys economic liberty, the freedom of labour' but also goes much further, since it 'introduces a despotism in comparison to which the most enlightened political despotism represents a condition of freedom, in the sense that the latter subjugates only a part of the man, the former the *entire* man'.[39] Kautsky combated this falsification, even while rejecting the infantile radicalism of Weitling. He insisted, on the contrary, that the accusation that socialism represents a new despotism rests on a total misunderstanding of its practice, which is founded entirely on the

[37] Ibid., p. 112.
[38] Ibid., pp. 235–7.
[39] Ibid., p. 168.

exercise of liberty, which Marxists regard as the supreme means first for conducting the class struggle and then for constructing the new society. Without freedom, Kautsky declared, socialism is perverted and cannot achieve its goal. The history of the labour movement and its achievements provides empirical confirmation that the working class has been able to make progress only by combining economic demands and the conquest of freedom of association, assembly, and the press:

'These freedoms are of prime importance to the working class; they represent *vital conditions of existence* without which the class itself cannot develop. These freedoms are light and air for the proletariat, and whoever restricts them, rejects them, or tries to divert the workers from the struggle to win and broaden them is among the worst enemies of the proletariat, whatever great love for the proletariat he may feel or feign.'[40]

Having established the vital necessity of political and civil liberties for the proletariat, Kautsky broached the question of parliamentarism in terms that are indicative of the change in his outlook that had occurred since the beginning of the 80's, when he had written that parliament could be no more than a tribune of agitation and not a means for the affirmation of proletarian power. Now, in his commentary on the Erfurt Programme, Kautsky developed two central themes: the indispensability of parliament as an instrument of government in great states, for all classes and therefore for the proletariat as well as the bourgeoisie; and the need to win a majority of parliament, treating elections as a fundamental strategic avenue of the labour movement. In this famous book, so deeply influential on German Social Democracy and on European socialism in general, Kautsky posed an indissoluble link between the conquest of the state and the conquest of a majority in parliament, between defence of the technical importance of parliament and a scientific and rational attitude towards institutions in general. For Kautsky, as early as his commentary on the Erfurt Programme, the democratic republic, the conquest of a parliamentary majority through the strength and influence won by the Social Democracy in its political and social struggles, and the use of parliamentary legislation for socialist purposes, constitute the very content of the 'dictatorship of the proletariat'. 'In a great modern state,' Kautsky wrote, the proletariat, like the bourgeoisie, can 'acquire influence in the administration of the state only through the vehicle of an elected parliament.' 'Direct legislation,' he said, 'at least in a great modern state, cannot render parliament superfluous' but can only represent a ramification of the administration. Hence the general thesis: 'It is absolutely

[40] Ibid., p. 219.

impossible to entrust the entire legislation of the state to it [direct legislation], and it is equally impossible to control or direct the state administration through it. So long as the great modern state exists, the central point of political activity will always remain in its parliament.' Now: 'the most consistent expression of parliament is the parliamentary republic'. The struggle for the conquest of parliament was therefore indispensable for Social Democracy. While defending parliamentarism, Kautsky also launched a frontal attack on anti-parliamentary tendencies. These, he argued, flourished among the peasantry and the petty bourgeoisie and were rooted in the sense of impotence that arises from social isolation, from the inability to organize a homogeneous political force. They were expressions of political sterility and nihilism.

'The radical petty bourgeois,' Kautsky asserted, 'who would like to put an end to capitalism, are thus led to regard parliamentarism as the principal cause of the maintenance and perpetuation of the servitude of the lower classes. They do not want to hear about parliaments and are convinced that the collapse of the bourgeoisie can occur only through the complete abandonment of parliamentarism. Some demand the complete replacement of parliament by direct legislation; others go further: recognizing that the modern political state and parliamentarism are indissolubly linked, they wholly condemn any political activity. All this may sound very revolutionary, but in fact it is nothing but a declaration of the political bankruptcy of the lower classes.'

Unlike the peasantry and the radical petty bourgeoisie, the proletariat, which is capable of forming its own independent party, strives to become a great force in parliament. Once the proletariat is present within the representative institutions, parliamentarism begins to 'alter its original essence' such that it 'ceases to be a mere instrument of the rule of the bourgeoisie'.[41] Since parliament was a technically indispensable means for the administration of society in a great modern state and it underwent a change in character once Social Democracy entered it, Kautsky concluded that parliament was not merely an essential avenue for socialists under bourgeois rule, but was also the necessary instrument for the exercise of their own power.

That Kautsky considered the relationship between Social Democratic strategy and the problem of violence, between the road to power and the question of parliamentarism to be the central issue for the future of the party is shown by the fact that immediately after his commentary on the Erfurt Programme he devoted his principal writings to an examination of

[41] Ibid., pp. 220–25.

these relationships, outlining ideas that were not only to become *de facto* official positions in the development of 'orthodox' Marxist theory within the party, but were also to sketch out the permanent features of Kautsky-ism. In the pamphlet *Der Parlamentarismus, die Volksgesetzgebung und die Sozialdemokratie* (1894) and the article *Ein Sozialdemokratische Kate-chismus*, which appeared in *Die Neue Zeit* in 1894, Kautsky spelt out the line of thought he had broached in his previous writings on the pro-gramme. In the first essay he took the field against Karl Bürkli, who had asserted in the 21 October 1892 issue of *Vorwärts* that 'just as the repre-sentative system, the constitutional state or the representative republic of the type that exists in North America constitutes the pure, precise *political instrument of the bourgeoisie*, so direct legislation through the people constitutes the typical and *best political instrument of the toiling masses*, and in particular of the organized proletariat' and therefore the most suitable legislative method for the social action of the masses. Kautsky replied that discussion of the problem of the use of direct legislation in the 'state of the future' was devoid of concrete value in the present, counterposing to it two major points: 1) that the parliamentary struggle fully corresponded to the needs of the proletariat in bourgeois society; 2) that the political revolution and the conquest of power by socialists could not be accomplished except through parliament, here defined expressly as an instrument with which to realize the dictatorship of the proletariat. In arguing that the problem of direct legislation was not on the agenda, Kautsky wrote: 'The question of whether direct legislation through the people in the so-called state of the future is possible, necessary, or desirable is one which is of little interest to us. Once in possession of political power, the proletariat will determine the institutions it needs and the measures it should take in accordance with specific conditions.'[42] He went on: 'Even today it is beginning to become clear that a geniune parliamentary regime can be as much an instrument of the dictatorship of the proletariat as an instrument of the dictatorship of the bourgeoisie.'[43]

Kautsky argued that it was a lesson of historical experience that direct democracy and the anti-centralism associated with it were products of a past that had been thrown into irretrievable crisis by the development of the modern state power and the rise of the classes linked to contemporary capitalism, the bourgeoisie and proletariat. It was no accident that the

[42] *Der Parlamentarismus, die Volksgesetzgebung, und die Sozialdemokratie*, Stuttgart, 1893, p. 3.
[43] Ibid., p. 118.

internal structures of modern parties, including the SPD itself, reflected the representative and centralist principles. The remedy for the negative effects of parliamentarism and centralism, Kautsky maintained, was control over the central representative institutions and not their negation in the name of outmoded and irrational ideals that could never resolve the problems of an advanced contemporary society. Direct legislation could play a positive role as a parallel instrument of control. But if it was conceived as an instrument for 'the abolition of the representative system',[44] it was a demand that ran counter to all the techniques of social administration proper to a developed society and the modern social classes, the bourgeoisie and the proletariat, and merely expressed the individualism and socio-political isolation of peasants who dreamt of doing everything themselves in harmony with their own 'individuality'.[45] While great parliamentary election campaigns educated the masses to a general view of national problems, direct legislation encouraged particularism.[46] Whereas parliamentary elections powerfully contributed to the fortification of modern political parties, direct legislation tended to eclipse them.[47] In this sense, for the 'fighting proletariat' the parliamentary-democratic state constituted the most suitable basis for the struggle against the other modern class, the bourgeoisie; parliament was the natural 'battleground' where the 'last decisive battle between the proletariat and the bourgeoisie can be fought'.[48] The modern character of the SPD was due to its ability to acquit the functions of a political party in the modern state. Since the modern state was defined by the representative system, it was no accident that the Social Democratic Party had its own system of central representation.

'Everywhere all the important decisions relating to the life of the Social Democratic Party are dealt with in congresses, in *assemblies of delegates* – congresses necessary to elucidate contradictions and settle misunderstandings; congresses to sanction splits or effect fusions; congresses to discuss and decide on all important questions of principle and tactics. . . . The representative system constitutes the only form in which the entirety of the party can come together, understand itself, and make its decisions. Only a congress makes it possible to bring to light the collective will of the party; only through congresses can the unity of the party be maintained.'[49]

[44] Ibid., p. 120.
[45] Ibid., pp. 124–5.
[46] Ibid., pp. 129–31.
[47] Ibid., pp. 131–2.
[48] Ibid., p. 123.
[49] Ibid., pp. 79–80.

The moment of democracy was maintained through the control exercised over delegates and was guaranteed by the representativeness of these delegates. Social Democratic members of parliament in particular were not and must not be special representatives of electoral committees, but of the entire party;[50] thus, even in this regard there was a correspondence between the rules of parliamentarism in general and the 'parliamentarism' that regulated the internal life of Social Democracy.[51] In sum, the centralization of Social Democracy corresponded to the centralization of parliament in the modern democratic state. Political and civil liberties, independent organization of the proletariat, class struggle, maintenance of the technical legacy of the institutions historically produced by the modern bourgeoisie, and conquest of power constituted a seamless whole with which the socialist movement could not dispense for an entire historical epoch.

In his essay on parliamentarism Kautsky maintained that all historical experience demonstrated that the relationship between the large-scale modern state and the proletariat could not be resolved otherwise than through acceptance of parliament and the transference of parliamentary techniques into Social Democratic organization itself. In *A Social Democratic Catechism* he asserted that the same lessons of history had taught the workers' movement to reject any theorization of violence and conspiracy and to accept the democratic method as the road to power, leaving the possibility of a desperate resort to violence to the adversary. Kautsky did not rule out the eventuality that the actual course of the class struggle might assume a violent and bloody character, but he stressed that a peaceful spirit was becoming an increasingly marked feature of contemporary society. This pacificist-humanist illusion was to become a distinctive feature of Kautsky's ideology; he did not fail to express it even in his assessment of the future character of wars between civilized nations. In 1888 he had innocently written that 'the conduct of war has been humanized to some extent in Europe' as a result of the increasingly international character of capitalist development, which gave states an interest in not waging wars of devastation.[52] To interpret this aspect of Kautskyist ideology, it is necessary to identify the factors that motivated it. In our view its explanation must be sought in a new articulation of the category of 'necessity' as it was applied by Kautsky to the contradictions of capitalist development. Since Kautsky was convinced that these would make the advent of socialism inevitable as though by natural law, he

[50] Ibid., p. 112.
[51] Ibid., p. 137.
[52] 'Kamerun', in NZ, IV, 1886, pp. 23–4.

concluded: 1) that revolutions cannot be fabricated; 2) that when their time comes there is no power on earth that can halt them; 3) that the progressive maturation of the revolution predisposed Social Democracy to harvest the fruits of its growing influence through respect for the rules of parliament, up to and including the conquest of power, without risings that would serve reaction; and 4) that the historically irresistible force of Social Democracy *could*, given a democratic and parliamentary state, induce the ruling class to accept the verdict of history peacefully. 'Social Democracy,' Kautsky wrote in the 'Catechism', 'is a revolutionary party, but it is not a party that makes revolutions.' He went on: 'We know that our objectives can be attained only through a revolution, but at the same time we know that it is just as little in our power to make this revolution as it is in the power of our opponents to prevent it. . . . The proletariat is constantly growing in numbers and in moral and economic strength . . . so its victory and the defeat of capitalism are inevitable. . . . Since we can know nothing about the decisive battles of the social war, we cannot say whether they will be bloody, whether physical violence will play a significant role in them, or whether these battles will be fought exclusively by means of economic, legislative, and political pressure.'

This said, however, Kautsky declared that he considered the latter alternative more probable; it was towards this variant that the German party and proletariat were orienting themselves in practice. 'It may thus be said that in all probability methods of the latter sort will prevail over those of physical force, i.e. over armed violence, in the course of the revolutionary struggles of the proletariat much more than they did in the course of the revolutionary struggles of the bourgeoisie.'

Kautsky noted that the immense superiority of the repressive arsenal commanded by the state militated against the success of violent revolutionary struggles. He also observed that in·states with democratic institutions the exercise of political and civil liberties tended to reveal the 'balance of forces between particular parties and classes', which in itself influenced the 'spirit' of these parties and classes in a direction increasingly favourable to Social Democracy. Kautsky seemed to assume that the ruling classes, however strong in military and police power, would be ever more demoralized and dispirited by political and social defeats. In his discourse democratic-parliamentary institutions acquire the character of common social values, respect for which would increasingly prevail. These institutions were becoming, he maintained, a general barometer for the various classes in struggle. It was correct to define them as the safety-valve of society, in the sense that they allowed society to pay the lowest possible price in suffering and convulsion, for fundamental change. At the same time, Kautsky had no fear that democracy could become a means of integrating the proletariat into the ruling system, since it 'could not abolish the class contradictions of capitalist society and prevent their necessary result, namely the overthrow of this society'. On the other hand, what democratic institutions could effectively do was 'to prevent premature and hopeless revolutionary attempts and render any revolutionary uprising superfluous', since they permitted an accurate knowledge of the real relationship of forces in society and the state, which was impossible under a despotism. In conclusion, the Social Democracy must 'avoid anything that could uselessly provoke the ruling classes and induce them to adopt a policy of violence'; any confrontation of that sort should be postponed until the proletariat 'becomes strong enough' to 'destroy and subdue' the supporters of reaction. Let the upper classes choose the terrain; let the proletariat respect democracy as a strategy, in the hope that such a strategy would be fully respected by all concerned.[53]

3 Against 'Staatssozialismus' and Von Vollmar

Kautsky, then, considered the peaceful and legal road to power within the framework of democratic representative institutions both possible and desirable. But he also held that in any event the full organizational, ideological, and parliamentary independence of the SPD had to be maintained and that the exploitation of any opportunity for peaceful advance should on no account induce the party to fall into a reformist strategy that would rely on the state to mediate social conflicts, or into an ideological illusion that the state could function independently in the socio-economic domain. In 1884 he had laid the basis for a theoretical analysis of this question by attacking the positions of Rodbertus. Kautsky began from the assumption that the Manchester doctrine was devoid of scientific value. The real choice was between Marxist socialism and the conservative 'socialism' of which Rodbertus had been a distinguished representative.[54] By the beginning of the 1890s the question of whether the Social Democracy could travel a certain distance together with the

---

[53] 'Ein sozialdemokratische Katechismus', in NZ, XII, 1893–4, vol. I, pp. 368–9, 402–5, 409–10.
[54] 'Das "Kapital" von Rodbertus', in NZ, II, 1884, pp. 337–8.

supporters of 'Staatssozialismus' (state socialism) had taken on great importance within the party. Georg von Vollmar, the influential leader of Bavarian Social Democracy, claimed that because of the strength of the Socialists in Germany an objective convergence was occurring between the workers' movement and bourgeois reformers, both of which were interested in economic and social reforms by the state. Consistent with this position, von Vollmar had written that 'the Social Democracy has no reason to combat the viewpoints of *Staatssozialismus* with any particular zeal'.[55] Kautsky launched a vigorous polemic against such an attitude. He stressed that it was important not to make a fetish of nationalizations, since their character was determined by the kind of state that implemented them. Although nationalization could generally be considered positive in states in which the process of democratization was advanced, in other states – the German Reich, for example – similar measures were a direct instrument of the ruling class against the proletariat:

'These measures of nationalization,' Kautsky wrote, 'would be in the interests of the proletariat only in states in which the very factor that constitutes the precondition and essential characteristic of *Staatssozialismus* is lacking: a state power independent of the mass of the population. The convergence of Social Democracy with *Staatssozialismus* in the sense recommended by Vollmar is possible only where there is no room whatever for the development of "Staatssozialismus" in the sense in which it is meant by its supporters.'

In Germany the theory of state socialism was the creation of Rodbertus, who advocated an independent initiative of the bureaucratic monarchic state, unacceptable to the Social Democracy.[56] Kautsky insisted that the logic of the bourgeois supporters of state socialism was always ultimately conservative, that the nationalization they championed would amount simply to the exploitation of the proletariat by the state instead of by private capitalists: 'the state itself remains a power that dominates the workers'. To be sure, the proletariat struggled for reforms; it did not share the theory of 'the worse, the better'. But the workers could improve their own conditions effectively only by winning, through class struggle, concessions that by their very nature could not be of a sort the state of the ruling class would be inclined to make. The working class struggled to achieve conquests that would alter the relationship of class forces. The objective of state reformism in Germany, on the contrary, was to yoke the

[55] G. von Vollmar, *Ueber Staatssozialismus*, Nurenburg, 1892, p. 8.
[56] 'Vollmar und der Staatssozialismus', in NZ, X, 1891–2, vol. II, p. 710.

workers to the chariot of the state. 'When we combat state socialism, we are also combating the measures it recommends, through which it seeks to attain its own ends.' The task of Social Democrats was to combat the illusions this reformism sought to generate among the masses, firmly maintaining that only the conquest of political power could emancipate the workers. Kautsky warned that 'reprisals and persecutions are not the worst weapons the enemy uses against us' but that 'the most dangerous' of these weapons is 'deception of the workers, winning them over through small concessions'. The principal aim of state socialism and its brand of reformism was to 'divide the proletariat', to separate the less conscious and combative sector from the most advanced.[57] Kautsky held that in the final analysis the emergence of the theory of state socialism was merely a symptom of the crisis of the capitalist system, which was seeking, in contradictory manner, to overcome its own limits. From the standpoint of Social Democracy, however, it was 'utopian' to believe that 'the capitalist mode of production can be reformed within the framework of the existing state and by means of that state'. The conservatives who sought remedies in state socialism were actually setting themselves the impossible task of 'acknowledging the legitimacy of the socialist critique' while trying to deny that it 'implies the conquest of political power by the proletariat'.[58]

Kautsky clarified his view of the function of the party programme and of the relation between struggles for partial objectives and the general goal of the SPD in his polemic with Rosa Luxemburg on the national question (which centred on the question of whether or not it was correct for Polish Social Democracy to pose the goal of the independence of Poland from Tsarist Russia). Elevating the debate to the level of general principles, Kautsky maintained that the practical demands of Social Democracy could not be gauged according to whether 'they are *realizable* in the context of the present relationship of forces, but rather according to whether they are *compatible* with the present society and whether their implementation would tend to facilitate or foster the class struggle of the proletariat and to clear its road to political power. . . . The programme must show what we *demand* from the present society or the present state and not what we *expect* from it.'[59]

For Kautsky, then, the criterion for assessing reforms and partial struggles was their effect on the organizational strength and ideological

[57] 'Der Parteitag und der Staatssozialismus', in NZ, XI, 1892–3, vol. I, pp. 214, 218–20.
[58] 'Der Breslauer Parteitag und die Agrarfrage', in NZ, XIV, 1895–6, vol. I, p. 111.
[59] 'Finis Poloniae?', in NZ, XIV, 1895–6, vol. II, pp. 513–14.

independence of Social Democracy. Some years after the polemic with Luxemburg, Kautsky returned to the question of the party programme, and specifically to the importance for it of parliamentary action. He denied that the realism of the Social Democracy consisted in striving merely for what could actually be attained. This, he said, was the road of empirical reformism, parliamentary compromise, and renunciation of practical and ideological independence.

'Genuine and productive influence by the Social Democracy in the legislative field,' he wrote, 'is still a thing of the future. For the present, propaganda and organization stand in the forefront. These are our most important "practical" tasks. From this it follows, however, that a programme of parliamentary action based solely on what is "realizable" without taking account of whether or not it compromises our future or endangers the unity and clarity of the party would be a highly impractical programme. For a party that pursues grandiose goals and presently finds itself in a minority, striving for the "unrealizable" can be more practical in the long run than seeking agreement over what is "realizable" under the rule of an imposing reaction.'[60]

According to Kautsky, however, programmatic clarity and organizational and ideological independence should not signify isolation but should be accompanied by a quest for social alliances to further the class struggle. He stressed that Marxism, as a method of investigation of relations among social classes, stood in contradiction to Lassalle's theory that all the opponents of Social Democracy constituted a 'single reactionary mass'. If this was the case, Kautsky said, 'why would we have to study the differences' among the various classes?[61]

The most important discussion by Kautsky of the question of alliances during the 1880s, before the polemic against revisionism, dealt with the role of the peasants and intellectuals and the attitude the party should adopt during the elections to the *Landtag* in Prussia, where the 'three-class' electoral system prevented the Social Democrats from achieving any significant results unless they formed an 'alliance' with the Liberals. His theory of the connection between tactics and strategy, between acceptance of the necessary compromises and the safeguarding of the theoretical and organizational independence of the workers' movement, emerges with particular clarity in these analyses. In his 1895 essay *Die*

[60] 'Das böhmische Staatsrecht und die Sozialdemokratie', in NZ, XVII, 1898–9, vol. I, p. 299.
[61] 'Die preussischen Landtagswahlen und die reaktionäre Masse', in NZ, XV, 1896–7, vol. II, p. 585.

Intelligenz und die Sozialdemokratie Kautsky declared that the Social Democracy could not resolve its strategic problems without a correct relationship with the peasants on the one hand and the intellectuals on the other. He wrote:

'It is impossible to ignore them [the peasants]; we must be clear about what we expect from them, to what extent their interests are compatible with those of the proletariat, to what extent they can join with the proletariat in the fight for specific goals, and to what extent they can furnish *party comrades* who can march shoulder to shoulder with the industrial working-class in all respects. Alongside the question of agitation in the countryside, we must pay particular attention to our position towards the intellectuals.'[62]

The central methodological principle to be applied to other social strata, Kautsky held, was that a common basis of organization and struggle could be established only with those groups that shared the most essential and decisive interests of the industrial proletariat, accepting the ideological and strategic perspectives of Social Democracy and agreeing to subordinate their own particular interests to them. Any other policy would 'stimulate deviation and disintegration within our own party'.[63] In particular, the position of intellectuals – some of whom had 'no direct concern for the class interests of the proletariat' but nonetheless 'often have no direct interest in capitalist exploitation either'[64] – must be measured directly by their willingness to consider the 'goals of proletarian struggle' disinterestedly and to understand 'the necessity of the victory' of the working-class,[65] subordinating every particular interest of their own to basic historical class interests. The importance of the intelligentsia derived primarily from its growing social weight, and secondly from its rising dissatisfaction. It was on this that the Social Democracy had to base its intervention among them.[66] In addition, another characteristic of intellectuals had to be considered. Although in a certain sense the intellectuals occupy a position in the struggle between capitalists and workers similar to that of the peasants and the petty bourgeoisie, they differed from these other layers in that intellectuals, by their very nature, possessed instruments of social analysis and lacked any real class interests of their own. Hence their frequent impulse to conceive ideas of sweeping

[62] 'Die Intelligenz und die Sozialdemokratie', in NZ, XIII, vol. II, pp. 11–12.
[63] Ibid., p. 44.
[64] Ibid., p. 75.
[65] Ibid., pp. 74–5.
[66] Ibid., p. 16.

social change. Among many intellectuals this took the form of an inclination towards social reformism and adherence to 'professorial socialism'.[67] It was the task of Social Democracy to intervene on this terrain, to link up with a sector of intellectuals, winning them away from bourgeois perspectives and drawing them closer to Social Democratic ideology and Marxist theory.[68] In reference to what he saw as an underestimation of intellectuals on Rosa Luxemburg's part, Kautsky exhorted party members to bear in mind that the intellectuals 'in capitalist society fulfil functions of maximum importance; they are completely irreplaceable'. For intellectuals, he said, not only 'possess a monopoly on knowledge in the present society', but also constitute, because of their theories, a fundamental element of mediation for the subordinate classes.[69] Indeed, even though 'they are not in a position to form a class or party of their own or to generate their own leadership', it is necessary to grasp the full importance of the fact that 'they furnish literary and political representatives for the other classes'.[70] Once they abandon their contradictory social position and range themselves on the side of the proletariat, joining it in the field of class struggle, intellectuals assume a necessary and indispensable political function as revolutionary social analysts.

Particular layers of peasants and intellectuals who agree to adopt the class interest and conception of historical development of socialist workers could thus establish an ideological and organizational link with the proletariat. This would represent an organic alliance. Another kind of alliance was also possible: tactical, but never strategic, agreements between Social Democracy and non-reactionary elements of the bourgeoisie, i.e. left liberals. In approaching the question of whether the party should establish electoral accords with the left liberals in Prussia against the prepotence of the Junkers, codified in the 'three-class electoral system' which forced Social Democracy into a position of absolute impotence if it was isolated, Social Democracy should not make the mistake of determining its policy on the basis of Manichean criteria. Instead, the party should seize upon any opportunity presented by the contradictions in the strategy of the other classes: its 'strength and possibilities of practical action rest on the lack of unity of its adversaries'. While it was true that the party should fear the introduction into its ranks of the viewpoints and interests of classes other than the proletariat, which

[67] Ibid., p. 76.
[68] Ibid., p. 77.
[69] 'Finis Poloniae?', op. cit., p. 518.
[70] 'Das böhmische Staatsrecht und die Sozialdemokratie', op. cit., p. 294.

feed 'the germs of division', it was also true that the party should not fear to make the necessary 'compromises', provided its full independence and unity were maintained, for to do so would be to exhibit infantilism and insecurity. 'It is not compromise in *action* that is dangerous, but compromise *in programme*.'[71] Kautsky held that in a case like Prussia, where the caste of Junkers held complete control of the government, the bureaucracy and the army, the Social Democrats, so long as they were too weak to achieve significant electoral results (given the restrictive voting system) and so long as they did not renounce the struggle against reaction, could make electoral agreements with the liberals, but only in a framework of tactical alliances that allowed the party full political and strategic independence.[72]

[71] 'Die preussischen Landtagswahlen und die reaktionäre Masse', op. cit., p. 586.
[72] Ibid., p. 590.

II

The Fight against Revisionism

1 The Debate on the Agrarian Question

Kautsky's polemic against Vollmar over 'state socialism' was one aspect of a wider struggle against coherent and organic 'reformist' tendencies centred in Bavaria and more generally in Southern Germany. This region, less industrialized than the North, had a strong small-peasant economy and a Catholic majority. Its governments and regional parliaments were generally more liberal than those of the authoritarian regime in Prussia, where the antagonism between a ruling class composed of big industrialists and eastern Junkers and a subordinate class composed of a strong industrial proletariat flanked by the agricultural workers of the large estates imbued the two opposing camps with a spirit of irreconcilable conflict, of struggle 'to the death'. In the South Social Democracy emerged from the period of the Emergency Laws convinced that socialism would be achieved essentially through a continuous reformist evolution; that to spur this evolution forward required an electoral consolidation unthinkable without a policy that defended the broad layer of independent peasants; and that the task of Social Democratic deputies in the regional parliaments was to obtain from the local governments social legislation whose positive effects would raise the prestige of the SPD in the eyes of poor and middle peasants, without whose support the electoral strength of the party would suffer inevitable crises, given the absence of a strong working-class. These positions led the Southern Social Democrats to maintain that they should vote for government budgets whenever they contained measures that corresponded to the economic interests not only of the working class but also of the peasantry (on questions of mortgages, loans, aid to cooperatives, etc.). Here lay the roots of the sympathy of party members like Vollmar for the *Staatssozialismus* Kautsky opposed. In a speech delivered in Munich in June 1891, which stirred a great deal of comment throughout the party, Vollmar had clarified his view of the tasks of Social Democracy. He saw the transition from the struggle for reforms to the struggle for socialism as a continuous process, in practice anticipating Bernstein's famous later formula: 'the movement is everything, the goal nothing'. Thus it was not fortuitous that the early signs of what was later to become a systematically reformist and revisionist theory first appeared during the discussion in the party on what line to take towards the peasants. The importance of the agrarian question was imposed on German Social Democracy by the dimensions of the economic crisis that had been racking agriculture in West-Central Europe for years, a consequence not only of American and Russian competition, but also of the difficulties of small and middle-sized producers, who lacked the capital necessary for the renovation of their techniques and modes of cultivation. In particular, it had become increasingly urgent for the SPD to define its response to the fate of small peasant farms in the course of capitalist development. It was quite obvious that the small peasant was the victim of the development of capitalist competition. Should the party give voice to the 'anguished cry' of these peasants, or should this cry be deemed an expression of the despair of a backward social layer falling into ruin as the result of the progressive laws of capitalist concentration?

The debate on the agrarian question occupied a central position in the party congresses of German Social Democracy held in Frankfurt (1894) and Breslau (1895). Vollmar assumed the leadership of the wing that considered it urgent for the Social Democrats to trace out a line of reformist intervention to support the small and middle-sized agricultural producers. The position of this current reflected the conviction that only a programme of immediate demands could enable the SPD to engage a victorious battle with the Catholic 'Centre' Party and its schemes. The small peasant, Vollmar asserted, suffered from mounting debt and the full weight of intolerable taxes, while there was no conclusive evidence that small and medium farms were economically any less productive than big farms. The model of industry could not be mechanically applied to the domain of agriculture, he argued. What small and middle-sized production needed was planned assistance from the state, promoted by Social Democracy. The poor peasants, Vollmar concluded, responding to the accusations of 'orthodox' party members, engaged in no relations of exploitation and 'differed from the modern proletariat only in that they were still in possession of their instruments of labour'.[1]

[1] G. von Vollmar, *Bauernfrage und Sozialdemokratie in Bayern 1895–96*, Nuremberg, 1896, p. 10.

In Frankfurt debate at the Congress flared up over a resolution presented by Bruno Schönlank and Vollmar which stated that it was an urgent task of the party 'to develop a specific programme on the agrarian problem' favouring the peasants and the agricultural proletariat,[2] to round out the Erfurt Programme. In his speech to the Congress Schönlank emphasized the political necessity of 'not repeating the experience of 1848' and of 'neutralizing' the peasants by lending support to their demands. 'We must prevent the hobnailed boots of the peasants and their sons from turning against us,' he said. 'We must neutralize them, pacify them.' This, he continued, could not be done through 'grey theory' but only through '*practical agitation*' free of 'pseudo-radicalism'.[3] For his part, Vollmar insisted that it was a historic fact that the population of the countryside was increasingly active on the political scene; Social Democracy must remain thoroughly faithful to its own programme, according to which the party 'fights not only against the exploitation and oppression of the wage workers, but against any sort of exploitation and oppression'.[4] But in order that the peasants might accept Social Democracy, it was necessary that the party convince them that it was prepared to fight for the immediate defence of their interests and did not intend to put everything off to the 'far future'.[5] The alternative was now: either to support a *de facto* 'Manchester' policy that left agriculture prey to the development of unchained capitalist forces, with negative consequences for the struggle of the workers in the cities, who would soon find themselves engulfed by a mass of proletarianized peasants seeking employment in industry under any conditions; or to abandon the 'Blanquist point of view' that it was possible to 'carry out a social overturn solely with a proletarian minority', a policy doomed to failure even in a country like Germany, and to develop a programme of practical and immediate intervention in defence of small and middle peasant farms.[6] This task was especially urgent, Vollmar concluded, since the situation in the countryside was 'most favourable' for the Social Democracy and 'the domination of our enemies over the population of the countryside is tottering'.[7]

The debate was pursued the following year at the Breslau Congress. In

[2] *Protokoll über die Verhandlungen des Parteitages der SPD. Abgehalten zu Frankfurt a.M. vom 21. bis 27. Oktober 1894*, Berlin, 1894, p. 135.
[3] Ibid., p. 141.
[4] Ibid., p. 143.
[5] Ibid., p. 145.
[6] Ibid., p. 148.
[7] Ibid., p. 152.

Frankfurt the party had recognized the importance of the agrarian question and established a special commission to deal with it. The two most outstanding leaders of the SPD, August Bebel and Wilhelm Liebknecht, were members of this commission. At the Breslau Congress it presented a report calling on the party to support concrete measures by the state in favour of the peasants and consequently to modify the introduction to the second part of the Erfurt Programme. In describing the fundamental practical objective of the struggle for reforms, the proposed amendment used the phrase 'democratization of all public institutions' and spoke of the need to improve the 'situation in industry, agriculture, commerce, and transport within the framework of the present social and state order'.[8] In the view of the intransigent current, whose most determined representatives at the Breslau Congress were Karl Kautsky and Klara Zetkin, the acceptance of this amendment was tantamount to a substantial change in the whole strategy and policy of the party. As we have seen, Kautsky had clearly set out the sense of the democratic demands contained in the Erfurt Programme: there must be no illusion that the class state could become an independent instrument with which to combat the dynamic of capitalist exploitation, in the interests of the oppressed classes. In regard to the peasants, Kautsky said at Breslau: 'We must go to the dispersed peasants and show them that their situation is in no way transitory, but rather necessarily flows from the capitalist mode of production, and that only the transformation of the present order into a socialist society will be able to help them. It is possible that this is not "practical", but it corresponds to the truth and is necessary.'[9] Kautsky's resolution opposing any modification of the text of the Erfurt Programme triumphed by a vote of 158 to 63.

The constant themes of Kautsky's writings on the agrarian question, traceable from his articles on the subject at the beginning of the 80's through the debates at the Frankfurt and Breslau Congresses, can be summarized in the following thesis: the small peasant farm was a historically doomed institution; assuredly, the Social Democracy must act towards the peasants in such a way as to obtain their 'neutrality', but the party must not entertain or foster any illusion that such a goal could be achieved by revitalizing an archaic form of production; no social force could realize that task. At the beginning of the 80's Kautsky had written a series of important articles, the most significant of which appeared in the

---

[8] *Protokoll über die Verhandlungen des Parteitages der SPD. Abgehalten in Breslau vom 6. bis 12. Oktober 1895*, Berlin, 1895, p. 212.

[9] Ibid., p. 124.

Jahrbuch für Sozialwissenschaft und Sozialpolitik, dealing directly with the theme of Social Democratic agitation among the peasantry. Although he started from the premise that the socio-economic relations which enveloped the peasants made them individualists *par excellence* who could never become mainstays of Social Democracy, Kautsky nonetheless insisted that it was necessary for the SPD to win their 'neutrality'. How? On what basis? First of all, he said, by showing the peasants that the workers had no interest in exploiting them; indeed, the peasants could sell their produce profitably only if workers' wages were high. Kautsky insisted that Social Democrats should not abandon the peasants to their fate even though they were condemned to suffer economic ruin. 'I am not of this opinion,' he said. This did not mean, he continued, that the only road open to the peasants was proletarianization. A different road was conceivable, a different 'transitional stage' that would not 'conflict with the trends of present economic development'. It was necessary to create peasant leagues, which on the one hand would establish social institutions for the distribution of products, and on the other hand would channel the protests of the peasants towards political organization. The peasants would then come to understand that their backwardness could be overcome only by challenging the social system that was causing their ruin, and by adopting a non-antagonistic position towards the party and the proletariat which were struggling for a new form of society. Thus, on the one hand the Social Democrats must not appear to favour the expropriation of the peasantry, which was, on the contrary, the fruit of capitalist and bourgeois economic development; on the other hand, however, they could not act as the defenders of an archaic form of production. The task of the SPD was to ensure that the peasants' struggle against expropriation and proletarianization would lead them to develop forms of association compatible with the direction of historical development. These could first become a part of the general movement of emancipation of the toilers and later, in the framework of the socialist state, could be turned towards forms of modern socialization.

'We must not,' Kautsky wrote, 'burden ourselves with the odium of appearing to favour the expropriation of the peasants; we must make it clear that this expropriation is linked to specific conditions. . . . We must show the peasant that it is not we who are expropriating him, but rather the big landlord with his machines, the usurer with his interest rates, the big capitalist with his railroads which transport foreign grain, and the state with its taxes.'[10]

[10] 'Die Agitation unter den Bauern', in *Jahrbuch für Sozialwissenschaft und Sozialpolitik*, 1880, vol. II, pp. 16–25.

Kautsky, then, as is also apparent from other articles published in *Der Sozialdemokrat* during the same period, did not believe that a Social Democratic programme to defend the small farms in the framework of the existing order would be effective. But he did believe that it would be tactically useful for Social Democracy politically to mobilize the social dissatisfaction of the peasants against the ruling classes. It was the effects of capitalist development, the penetration of the market by American grain for example, that were turning the peasant 'from a defender of the established order into one of its fiercest opponents'.[11] It was on. this objective basis that Social Democrats could present themselves to the peasants as their 'best friends'.[12] In addition, Kautsky's desire to win the support of the peasants against the regime of the Emergency Laws, which still existed at this time, was evident. In a conference held in Vienna on 12 January 1881, Kautsky maintained that the Social Democrats would succeed in their efforts to mobilize the peasants against the established order to the extent that they were able to convince them that the party did not intend to expropriate them. If they felt secure on this point, the peasants would support the struggle for the expropriation of big industry and the large landed proprietors, for the cancellation of all state debts and mortgages, and for the end of military and fiscal burdens, and would incline favourably to cooperative organization of the small farms as a transitional stage to complete socialization.[13]

In 1894-5, when it appeared to Kautsky that the agrarian question was serving as the vehicle for an attempt to revise the Social Democratic programme in the direction of a capitulation to bourgeois-democratic reformism, he opened a frontal attack on the theses of Vollmar, Schönlank, David, and Quarck. The focus of that attack was opposition to any programme that would uphold the illusion that it was possible to revitalize the small farms in the context of the capitalist system by calling upon the bourgeois state as a source of support for them. This, Kautsky held, would threaten to place the party in the service of what was ultimately petty-bourgeois reformism. He insisted on the need to dissipate one fundamental error: Social Democracy struggled not to 'democratize' present society as a whole (which was not possible), but to broaden the possibilities of democratic action by the proletariat in the struggle for the conquest of power:

'*We demand institutions that allow more effective prosecution of the class*

---

[11] 'Die Revolutionäre Kraft des amerikanischen Kornes', in *Der Sozialdemokrat*, 24 October 1880.

[12] 'Die Sozialdemokratie und das Bauernthum', in *Der Sozialdemokrat*, 10 October 1880.

[13] 'Die österreiche Bauernbewegung', in *Der Sozialdemokrat*, 30 January 1881.

struggle and augment its revolutionary potential. This is the quintessence of the second part of our programme, through which we distinguish ourselves from the democrats and social reformers. . . . According to the agrarian commission, when we demand political freedoms and rights, it is not to lay the basis on which the proletariat can organize itself and conquer the state, but rather to "democratize all public institutions"; and when we demand social reforms, it is not to make the proletariat more capable of struggle, but rather "to improve existing conditions"!'[14]

Kautsky's polemic against the 'revisionists' on the agrarian question was thus an extension and specification of his polemic against *Staatssozialismus* and its attendant illusions. It expressed his fear that reformism was penetrating the ranks of Social Democracy, sowing the seeds of an ideological, if not an organizational, split in the party. Kautsky believed that the bourgeois press was correct when it described the slogan of 'democratization of all public institutions' 'within the existing state order' as a breach in the 'integral character of our movement that has been maintained up to now'.[15] The agrarian commission, Kautsky continued, wants the state to intervene in support of cooperatives 'for the sole purpose of increasing the value of landed property – a curious Social Democratic programme'!'[16] He countered that there must be no fetishism of state intervention, which was not progressive and anti-private *per se*; rather, the class character of the state itself must always be kept in mind. The advocates of the idea that Social Democracy should agitate for state intervention in support of peasant property had lost sight of the central point that it was absurd to expect the German state to furnish the means for putting an end to exploitation by the capitalists and Junkers and that it was 'equally absurd for us to increase the power of this state over the exploited'.[17] Even if agricultural cooperatives supported by state capital were created, in the present society these would remain isolated and could even create an agrarian labour aristocracy imbued with anti-socialist sentiments. Moreover, there would always be a danger (and here Kautsky was obviously thinking of the experiment of the *ateliers nationaux* in France in 1848) that the possible failure of such cooperatives could be held up by the ruling class as proof of the fiasco of socialist experiments In addition, these cooperatives would still remain farms producing for the market and would thus 'depend on the ups and downs of this

[14] 'Unser neuestes Programm', in NZ, XIII, 1894–5, vol. II, pp. 560–61.
[15] Ibid., p. 562.
[16] Ibid., p. 565.
[17] Ibid., p. 586.

market'.[18] To put the debts of the peasants in the hands of the state, as was also demanded by the supporters of a new Social Democratic agrarian programme, would only render them even more dependent on the ruling class and high finance, which would do good business out of them to boot.[19] We cannot, Kautsky emphasized, attribute to the present class state tasks which are the province of a new state during a period of transition to socialism.[20] It was unthinkable that the existing state could be forced to adopt a programme in defence of agriculture unless this programme also and primarily favoured large landed property: 'An agrarian programme, a programme that advances particular demands in defence of the interests of the population in the countryside, can only be a programme in defence of the *interests of the landed proprietors*. Reluctance to call for defence of the *small farms* in particular, so as not to provoke the reactionaries, necessarily leads to a programme that defends the interests of *landed property as a whole*, both *great* and *small*.'

That road, however, led to the notion of a 'harmony of interests'. Hence Kautsky's conclusion: 'a Social Democratic agrarian programme for the capitalist mode of production is an absurdity'.[21] Any reform that conflicted with the laws of capitalist development would remain without real effect. The question had to be posed on a different basis, namely in the light of the fact that 'for no class has the social revolution become so urgently necessary as for the peasants'.[22] Here Kautsky altered his position of 1880. Now, in 1894-5, he was no longer thinking in terms of a somewhat independent political mobilization of the peasants alongside the proletariat in the fight against reaction, but rather of a direct linkage of the agricultural proletariat of the great farms of the East and West to the struggle of Social Democracy. He called upon the authority of Engels, who intervened in the discussion with an article entitled 'Die Bauern-frage in Frankreich und Deutschland', published in *Die Neue Zeit* in 1895. Engels asserted that although Social Democracy had a duty to try to render the aches of the expropriation of the small peasants less humanly painful and to assure the peasants that once in power the socialists had no desire to expropriate small farms but rather intended to help them progress towards more socialized forms, the party could not avoid its responsibility to convince the peasants that it was 'absolutely impossible'

[18] Ibid., p. 591.
[19] Ibid., p. 610.
[20] Ibid., p. 612.
[21] Ibid., p. 617.
[22] Ibid., p. 618.

for them to survive 'so long as capitalism rules', given the 'inevitable direction of economic development'. In particular, the party must aim at directly winning over the agricultural proletariat in Eastern Prussia to combat the strength of the Junkers there. 'In the long run,' Engels wrote, securing the allegiance of this agricultural proletariat 'is more important than winning over the small peasants of Western Germany and even the southern middle peasants'. 'It is here, in Prussia east of the Elbe, that our decisive battlefield lies,' Engels concluded.[23] To Quarck, who had sought to transform Engels's admonition of the importance of the SPD's struggle against the brutality of capitalist exploitation into a 'reformist' approach, Kautsky replied that 'for Engels as well, the conquest of state power by the proletariat is the precondition for the nationalization of mortgage debts and the promotion of agricultural cooperatives by the state'.[24] It was necessary not to confuse this with the 'democratization of public institutions' as the 'precondition' for the rule of the proletariat.[25]

When Social Democracy defended the interests of the workers within the context of the existing order, Kautsky continued, it was defending the 'physical and spiritual personality of the worker' and augmenting his 'force of resistance' and 'capacity for struggle', thus favouring social development. Defence of the workers thus possessed a 'revolutionary' character. Defence of the peasants rested on a completely different basis. For any complete defence of the peasant meant in substance a preservation of his backward personality, marked by a retrograde spiritual tradition, by individualism and by social isolation, all consequences of a particular mode of production. It was thus impossible mechanically to extend the struggle to defend the proletariat to the struggle to defend the peasantry, precisely because of the different positions the two occupied in economic development.[26] Whoever in the ranks of Social Democracy struggled against the proletarianization of the peasants 'in the present society' could only deceive himself and others, falling into the arms of *Staatssozialismus* with the suggestion that socialist methods of real cooperation could be applied in the framework of capitalist society.[27] Polemicizing against David, Kautsky repeated that the only genuine defence of the peasantry lay in a task of clarification which would be hampered by anyone who suggested that 'it would be possible to improve

---

[23] Marx-Engels, *Werke*, vol. XXII, Berlin, 1963, pp. 501–2, 504–5.
[24] 'Noch einige Bemerkungen zum Agrarprogramm', in NZ, XIII, 1894–5, vol. II, p. 809.
[25] Ibid., p. 812.
[26] 'Arbeitschutz und Bauernschutz', in NZ, XIV, 1895–6, vol. I, pp. 19–21.
[27] 'Der Breslauer Parteitag und die Agrarfrage', op. cit., p. 112.

the conditions of the peasants in present society'.[28] As for the practical tactics of the SPD, Kautsky reaffirmed that Social Democrats were the bearers of the 'general interests of the proletariat' and that 'we can take the interests of the rest of the "masses" into consideration only to the extent that they are in accordance with those of the proletariat, or at least compatible with them'. He then concluded that of course the party must defend the interests of both the agricultural workers and the poor peasants compelled to sell their labour power in order to survive: 'The object of contention is simply the position of Social Democracy towards the small farmers, those who are in a position neither to hire themselves out as labourers nor to exploit the wage labour of others, who employ exclusively members of their own families and live exclusively from agriculture.' It was a real problem, but one whose political significance Kautsky immediately reduced, noting that 'in no modern civilized country do these peasants any longer represent a numerically decisive factor'.[29]

The crux of Kautsky's position on the agrarian question was not so much the soundness or otherwise of his prediction of the inevitable decay of small independent peasant property in the context of the general trends of capitalist development, as his claim that even at that time the social, political, and economic weight of this form of production was no longer important, and would decline rapidly henceforward. This conclusion not only did not convince men like Vollmar, who after the Breslau Congress and the victory of Kautsky's resolution found new reasons to pursue their own road with even greater determination, but also failed to persuade others, above all Bebel, who reacted negatively to both Engels's and Kautsky's positions, objecting that they revealed a doctrinaire abstraction that left entirely unanswered the question of how the agrarian problem, and in particular the plight of the small farmers, could and should be handled in the party's political agitation. In Bebel's view, the arguments of the Southern Social Democrats – and of other parties – about specific demands over mortgages or taxes could not be adequated scouted by counterposing an analysis of general historical trends to them. Bebel therefore considered the victory of Kautsky's resolution at the Breslau Congress a dangerous turn that would fuel new conflicts within the party.[30]

---

[28] 'Die Breslauer Resolution und ihre Kritik', in NZ, XIV, 1895–6, vol. I, p. 183.

[29] 'Ein neues Buch von Deville', in NZ, XIV, 1895–6, vol. II, pp. 805, 807–8.

[30] Bebel to Kautsky, letter of 27 September 1895, in *August Bebel Briefwechsel mit Karl Kautsky*, Assen, 1971, pp. 95–6; Bebel to Adler, letter of 20 October 1895, in V. Adler, *Briefwechsel mit August Bebel und Karl Kautsky*, Vienna, 1954, pp. 193–5.

Since some Social Democrats supported an 'agrarian charter' that would have entailed revision of the Erfurt Programme, and some leading revolutionaries like Bebel did not understand his positions, Kautsky decided to undertake systematic research on the agrarian question. The results were published in 1899, in the midst of the polemics between the revisionists, under the theoretical leadership of Bernstein, and the anti-revisionists within the SPD. In his *Agrarian Question*, which Lenin described on several occasions as 'the most noteworthy contribution to recent economic literature' since the publication of the third volume of *Capital*,[31] Kautsky systematized his positions on the basis of copious documentary material. Against the thesis of the Bavarian Social Democrats, who maintained that small and middle-sized farms had preserved their vitality, Kautsky reiterated the superiority of large estates in terms of costs, yields, economy of labour, and efficiency of the division of labour. He maintained that cooperatives, such as credit associations, were a factor of real progress because they favoured small peasants. But while it was clear that they represented an 'instrument of economic progress, it was certainly not progress towards socialism, as was often believed, but progress towards capitalism'.[32] The relation between large and small farms had to be understood in the dynamic of its development, not in the sense of a constant advance of the former at the expense of the latter through physical absorption, but rather in the sense that the increasing subordination of less developed to more developed agrarian techniques (linked to modern industry) created ever greater difficulties for the weaker and more backward sector of rural production, causing its ruin or its survival in merely barbarous forms. The alternative was an attempt at survival through cooperatives, which was precisely a path to capitalist progress.

Given the conditions of Germany, where there was a decline in the numerical importance of the peasants, 'who no longer represent the majority of the population in the countryside', and where the large estates were tilled by a 'major stratum of agricultural workers' who were as numerous as the peasants 'and whose interests in all essential points are identical to those of the wage workers in industry', the organizational and strategic task of the SPD was the formation of an irresistible revolutionary 'bloc' constructed essentially on a proletarian base. This was Kautsky's response to the advocates of revision of the party's programme: 'Once

---

[31] See the preface to *The Development of Capitalism in Russia*, in Lenin, *Collected Works*, vol. 3, p. 27.

[32] *Die Agrarfrage*, Stuttgart, 1899, p. 181.

Social Democracy has united into a "bloc" the entire mass of the proletariat and all those apparently independent agricultural and industrial
workers who are in fact only wage workers for capital, no force will be
able to offer any resistance to it. The principal task of Social Democracy
is and will remain to win over this mass, to organize it politically and
economically, to raise its intellectual and moral level, and to bring it to
the point at which it will inherit the legacy of the capitalist mode of
production.'[33]

Kautsky repeated what he had already clearly affirmed in his article
Unser neuestes Programm, that 'a Social Democratic agrarian programme
based on the defence of the small peasant would thus not only be futile,
but worse yet would endanger the Social Democracy in the most serious
fashion'.[34] He then traced out guidelines for the struggle to achieve 'the
neutralization of the peasants'. The SPD, discarding any contradictory,
reactionary and utopian defence of small farms, needed a programme of
defence of the human and civil conditions of the agricultural population
designed to favour their rapid integration into modern society, the
protection of their working conditions, the elimination of remaining
privileges of feudal origin, and the modernization of the social and civil
fabric of the countryside to accelerate its general economic development.
Social Democracy must avoid appearing either as a defender of the
particular interests of the small farmers or as an advocate of their expropriation, 'a shameful act' whose completion 'is one of the historic tasks
of the bourgeoisie'.[35]

2 Defensor Fidei: Against Bernstein and 'Ministerialism'

Kautsky published *The Agrarian Question* in the midst of the polemic
against revisionism, which had found coherent theoretical expression in
the celebrated work of Eduard Bernstein, *Die Voraussetzungen des
Sozialismus und die Aufgaben der Sozialdemokratie* (1899). Bernstein's
work was in turn a systematization of various particular theses he had
advanced in *Die Neue Zeit* in late October 1896 under the significant title
Probleme des Sozialismus. As we have seen, Bernstein's theories did not
come as a thunderbolt in a clear sky. They had behind them the practical

[33] Ibid., pp. 311–313.
[34] Ibid., p. 321.
[35] Ibid., p. 323.

revisionism of the Vollmars during preceding years. So much so that August Bebel, the party's prestigious and charismatic leader, commenting on the 'state of the party' after the Frankfurt Congress of 1894, sounded the alarm against the penetration of reformism and opportunism into the ranks of the party, crystallizing around the Southern Social Democrats:

'I do not want to deny,' Bebel had said in a speech to a Berlin party organization on 14 November 1894, 'that I have the impression that a process of dilution is occurring within the party, that it is opportunist water which is being added, that the class struggle is being muted, and that this current is flirting with all sorts of bourgeois reformist ideas. If the facts correspond to my impression, then this current must be combated with maximum determination.'[36]

The revisionists themselves were not afraid of being considered ideologically 'deviant'. They regarded themselves as the 'young blood' in a party dominated by a formal orthodoxy incapable of dealing with the problems of historic development posed for the workers' movement; they felt that they were in harmony with this history. Had not Marxism claimed to be the science of objective historic development? In their view, the terrain of contention was social reality; discussion of this reality could not be conjured into a 'struggle over principles'. In Germany – in fact, not only in Germany, but throughout the world – capitalist development was clearly taking a path different from that predicted by Marx in *Capital*, or so they claimed. The revisionists rejected the thesis that capitalist concentration was leading to growing proletarianization, excluding the working class from the benefits of the development of the forces of production, drastically reducing the viability of small and middle-sized companies, and consequently sharpening the class struggle in a revolutionary direction. The period of prosperity which opened around 1895, during which the bargaining-strength of the trade unions greatly increased as the demand for labour-power grew, confirmed the revisionists in their view that it was a mistake to expect a 'crisis' of capitalism and that the class struggle should instead be used as an instrument for a consciously reformist course. As Bernstein put it, 'the movement' became 'everything' and the goal 'nothing'. Socialism, the 'heretics' claimed, would result not from a cataclysmic revolutionary crisis but from the capacity of the workers' movement to intervene on specific problems with its own organized strength, progressively shifting the relationship of forces between political parties and social classes. The 'democratization' of the existing order was not the precondition, but the very substance, of

[36] In *Vorwärts*, 16 November 1894.

a socialism to be achieved through a consciously directed evolutionary process gradually assuring the predominance of social over private institutions.

Revisionism and evolutionary reformism found its manifesto in Bernstein's *Die Voraussetzungen*. In his book Bernstein argued that historical materialism was a mechanistic philosophy which deadened will and consciousness. The Hegelian dialectic was the Achilles heel of Marxism, since it rendered its theory of revolution more dependent on a logical schema than on real historical development. Social Democracy must consequently free itself from the ambiguity of a Marxism that was partly reformist and partly Blanquist. Bernstein concluded by challenging the central tenet of Marxism: its claim to be a valid science of social development. It was not true, he asserted, that a growing concentration of property was occurring. Not only was the number of owners actually rising, but they were also becoming more stratified, creating an intricate and multiform texture of continuous interests between them. The working class itself was likewise becoming stratified. Meanwhile, contradicting Marx's prediction that society would polarize into two enemy camps, a middle class of complex composition was expanding as property became diffused. Nor was the prospect of a 'collapse of capitalism' confirmed by either the present or the probable future dynamic of economic development. Although temporary crises could not be ruled out, capitalist society had acquired new instruments, primarily in the sphere of credit and market control, which excluded the prospect of disaster. Bernstein drew the consequence that: 'The prospects for socialism depend not on the regression but on the increase of social wealth.'[37] The tasks of socialism had thus to be redefined. Social Democracy must discard the idea that if capitalism continued to develop socialism lost all prospect. According to Bernstein, such a conception was a direct consequence of materialist monism. On the contrary, because subjective factors and spiritual forces were becoming ever more important in history, socialism should be seen as an ideal whose realization was one possibility among others in society. The SPD should have the courage to accept the terms of a confrontation with capitalism on the terrain of economic development, promoting a programme of reforms founded on full adherence to political democracy, abandoning any velleity of class dictatorship. It should seek to augment trade-union control by workers over the productive machinery of capitalism, popular participation in local power, and expansion of a strong

[37] E. Bernstein, *Die Voraussetzungen des Sozialismus und die Aufgaben der Sozialdemokratie*, Stuttgart, 1899, p. 51.

cooperative movement. This sort of socio-economic strategy in turn required a different political strategy – not the road of isolation of the proletariat, not a conception of class struggle culminating in the objective of the dictatorship of the proletariat, but a policy of agreements with the reformist tendencies of the liberal bourgeoisie and with popular and petty-bourgeois layers (peasants, employees), on the basis of their common interest in greater political and social democracy in opposition to the bureaucratic-militarist state, the Junkers, and the forces of big monopoly capital. In sum, the vocation of Social Democracy was to become the key force in a democratic and reformist process taking every tactical advantage from alliances with other oppressed layers, or any layers under attack by the existing regime. For Bernstein, all this constituted the road to socialism. He concluded: 'the influence of Social Democracy would be rather greater than it actually is if it had found the courage to free itself from a phraseology that is in fact outmoded and to present itself as what it really is today: a democratic-socialist reformist party'.[38] Finally, in keeping with his exhortation to accept social reality as it was, Bernstein invited the German proletariat and the SPD to approach national responsibilities and patriotic defence in a new spirit, and to reject a schematic and prejudiced anti-colonialism.

As we know, Bernstein's theses incited a wave of criticism from theoreticians like Kautsky, Plekhanov, Luxemburg, and Parvus, to mention only the major names. He was not handled with kid gloves. There was talk of 'apostasy'. For had not Bernstein been one of the best-known international socialists, the favourite of Engels, the close friend of Kautsky, the respected editor of *Der Sozialdemokrat*, the clandestine organ of German Social Democracy under the regime of the Anti-Socialist Laws? For Kautsky the polemic with Bernstein was the occasion for extreme embarrassment because of the strong ties of friendship that had linked the two men. Because of this bond, Kautsky hesitated somewhat before taking the field against Bernstein; but when he did the result was a response to revisionist theory that was synthesized, after publication of many articles in *Die Neue Zeit* and *Vorwärts*, into a book entitled *Bernstein und das Sozialdemokratische Programm, Eine Antikritik* (1899). Because of its systematic character and because of Kautsky's position as an eminent theoretician of international Social Democracy, this response assumed an official stature. In the course of the Bernstein–Kautsky polemic Marxism was put to its first great verification since the death of its founders – and in terms that fully justify the judgment of Schumpeter,

[38] Ibid., p. 165.

who commented that 'both sides deserve our esteem for the moral and intellectual level of their champions'.[39] Kautsky's attitude toward his old friend was similar to Bebel's. It was inspired sometimes by the conviction that Bernstein was completely lost to Marxism (in a letter to Victor Adler in October 1898 Bebel had written that he and Kautsky were then of the opinion that Bernstein was 'no longer recuperable'[40]), sometimes by the opinion that it was unthinkable to drive Bernstein from the party. Fear of the effects of a split in the SPD, which they knew could not be reduced to a minor episode, weighed against any expulsion of Bernstein. Behind the theorist Bernstein stood the practitioner Vollmar, with his many followers. The aim of Bebel and Kautsky was to reforge the practical unity of the party through an ideological defeat of the revisionists, in the illusion that if this was achieved, the revisionists would be isolated and cease to be very dangerous.

In his book Kautsky replied that, firstly, Bernstein had concocted a Marxism all of his own for the purposes of his polemic. Secondly, he wrote, economic development did not at all contradict the main lines of the analysis of Marx. Thirdly, Bernstein's proposal to transform the party of the social revolution into a reformist party would undermine the efficacy of the struggle for reforms themselves, for it would deprive Social Democracy of the power to wring concessions out of the ruling class. Bernstein's attack on the dialectic, in turn, was a misunderstanding of the method of Marx, who had never conceived the historical process in a speculative manner, but had simply analyzed the socio-economic forces that composed modern society and shown that these forces had irreconcilable interests whose conflict constituted the law of development of capitalism. The theory of the collapse of capitalism against which Bernstein expended so much ammunition was a theoretical extrapolation alien to Marxism. Likewise the theory of absolute impoverishment; it was no accident that the Erfurt Programme contained 'not a single word on the theory of collapse'.[41] When speaking of a capitalist collapse, Marxists were not referring to a mechanical economic process, but to the maturation of the proletariat, as a revolutionary class possessed of organizational and political-ideological independence, and as the essential determinant of the end of bourgeois society. What was essential in Marxist theory, Kautsky argued, was the demonstration that economic development not

---

[39] J. A. Schumpeter, *Capitalism, Socialism, and Democracy*, London, 1943, p. 347.

[40] Bebel to Adler, letter of 26 October 1898, in *Briefwechsel mit August Bebel und Karl Kautsky*, op. cit., p. 254.

[41] *Bernstein und das sozialdemokratisches Programme. Eine Antikritik*, Stuttgart, 1899, p. 43.

only maintained the proletariat in a subordinate position, but accorded it a declining relative share in the total production of social wealth. From this flowed the inevitability of the class struggle and its intensification. Bernstein's analysis of capitalist concentration, Kautsky argued, was superficially quantitative, missing the major point – the type of nexus between the various sectors of production in capitalist society, which assure the ever greater dominion of big industrial and finance capital. The dependence of small on large enterprises was increasing, as was the dependence of agriculture on industry. 'From its very origin,' Kautsky wrote, 'high finance has held governments in a position of dependence, by virtue of public debt. But the modern kings of finance dominate nations directly through cartels and trusts and subject all production to their power. In particular, it is they who create the very preconditions for production in all big industry, in coal and iron, the union of which increasingly determines the domestic and foreign policies of economic life as a whole.'[42]

The development of joint stock companies was no more than an expression of the concentration of capital, in the form of an ingathering of small capitals dominated by big stockholders. In this context, the worker suffered an increase, not in absolute poverty, but in social misery – in other words, a reduction in his share of the enormous wealth that was globally produced and which swelled the privileges of the upper classes. Hence the consequence on which Social Democracy based its rationale and its future as the party of the industrial working-class: 'The intensification of social conflict, the intensification of the proletarian struggle against the capitalist yoke.'[43] The evolution of the middle classes was merely a by-product of an overall development dominated by big capital and did not modify the laws of that development. Even those layers which, rightly or wrongly, considered themselves more privileged than the proletariat, were still essentially wage-earners and would have no alternative but to choose between the two fundamental classes in any social struggle.

As for the prospects of capitalism, Kautsky denied that a constant expansion of the market could overcome the limits determined by the contradiction between the tendency towards an ever greater increase in production and the restricted capacity of consumption of the popular masses. This insufficiency of demand was a rigorous consequence of the class structure of capitalist society. Because it was impossible to achieve

[42] Ibid., p. 79.
[43] Ibid., p. 127.

an equilibrium between production and consumption, capitalism was fated to suffer 'chronic over-production',[44] in other words, a situation of escalating generalized crises into which the socialist movement must intervene. In effect, Kautsky asserted, Bernstein had shed no new light on the problematic of socialism, for his objections to Marx's analysis of capitalism were simply repetitions of those that had long since 'been raised against socialism by liberal economics'.[45]

Moving on to the strategic implications of Bernstein's theories, Kautsky dwelt on the decisive importance of the connection between the proletariat's economic and political position in the existing society. Kautsky based his certainty that the victory of socialism was inevitable precisely on the significance of that connection. The rise 'of the economic power of the proletariat is continuing everywhere'; it was the inevitable product of capitalist development itself. The task of Social Democracy was to lend unity and independence to the class struggle, stamping it with the character of 'political struggle'.[46] Bernstein's decisive queries were these: 'Should the proletariat organize itself into an independent class party or should it form a broad democratic party together with other classes?' Or, to put it in terms of the programme: 'Should we elaborate a programme and tactics for Social Democracy to include all democratic classes or strata?'[47]

Kautsky's response was firm: the SPD struggled for democracy, but it was not a democratic-reformist party, since its objectives went beyond democracy or reforms. Democracy *per se* in no way meant the end of class rule; indeed, it was merely a 'form of rule by majority' and could therefore express either a class society subject to the rule of capital or another form of society. In sum, democracy was necessary for the proletariat, because it allowed the real relationship of social forces to emerge most clearly; but it was in no way sufficient, since it was fully compatible with bourgeois rule and capitalist relations of production. On the other hand, it was the most suitable instrument for the proletariat both to come to power and to exercise power.

'Undoubtedly,' Kautsky wrote, 'democracy constitutes the indispensable precondition for the elimination of class rule, but precisely because it is the only political form through which the proletariat can accede to class rule. The proletariat, as a subordinate class, must necessarily use

[44] Ibid., p. 145.
[45] Ibid., p. 158.
[46] Ibid., pp. 162-3.
[47] Ibid., p. 167.

democracy to put an end to all class differences. Without the class rule of the proletariat there can be no end to classes.'[48]

But to pose the question of the necessity of the class rule of the proletariat meant to pose the question of the dictatorship of the proletariat. In this connection Kautsky emphasized that Social Democracy had never counterposed the class rule of the proletariat to democratic rights; but democracy alone was unable to render that class rule superfluous. He thought that in the case of 'bandits' like certain Junkers, bankers, and generals it might not be possible to proceed 'with the fullest respect for their individuality'.[49] According to Kautsky, the dictatorship of the proletariat would take the form of the exercise of the class power of the proletariat, in the framework of democratic rights, to transform social relations and to repress, with the force and authority deriving from the consensus of the majority, the actions of those counter-revolutionaries not inclined to accept the acts of a socialist government. In substance, Kautsky replied to Bernstein, democracy is much, but it is not everything. Significantly, however, when Kautsky attempted to spell out the relationship between democracy and proletarian rule in the new state, his formulations were vague and ambiguous. 'I would not want to swear that the class rule of the proletariat will have to assume the forms of a class dictatorship,' he wrote. 'But neither present practice nor future prospects have yet proven in any way that democratic forms in themselves are sufficient to render the class rule of the proletariat superfluous for its emancipation.' His conclusion was that in any event 'the decision on the problem of the dictatorship of the proletariat' could be 'tranquilly left to the future'.[50]

In effect, Kautsky hinted that a political regime of 'class dictatorship' might prove to be an emergency necessity in combating a violent reaction, if democratic forms proved inadequate to assure the socio-economic domination of the proletariat gained perforce by democratic means. Moreover, he disputed Bernstein's description of democracy as a 'neutral' conquest of modern society, since the bourgeoisie, out of fear of revolution, was tending to abandon it. Hence, 'a progressive democracy in a modern industrial state is henceforth possible only in the form of *proletarian democracy*', that is, on the basis of a new social order.[51] If the Social Democratic Party renounced its independent character and its

[48] Ibid., pp. 170–71.
[49] Ibid., p. 172.
[50] Ibid., p. 172.
[51] Ibid., p. 193.

struggle for power, if it were to be converted into a 'people's party' as recommended by Bernstein, 'in which the class interests of the peasants and the petty bourgeoisie would have a decisive influence', it would inevitably wind up 'on the terrain of the established social order, of private property in the means of production, of the freedom of private production'.[52] Hence the historical and social necessity that the SPD remain more than ever 'the party of the social revolution' instead of turning itself into a democratic-socialist party.[53] For socio-economic development was indisputably creating the essential precondition for socialism itself: an increasing number of wage workers. Of course, if this trend faltered, if it could be shown that on the contrary the number of proprietors was rising, then the historic necessity of socialism would be negated by reality itself. Kautsky summed the problem up like this: 'The number of wage workers is rising. That is the basic starting point. . . . This is not a matter of statistical games but a question of the utmost seriousness, of the very reason for being of socialism. In itself the decline in the number of owners, which is acknowledged even in some bourgeois studies, does not demonstrate the necessity of socialism; but an increase in the number of owners would certainly demonstrate the impossibility and futility of socialism.'[54]

Kautsky's polemic against revisionism thus contained the following series of propositions, linking a general social theory to a specific view of the organization of the workers' movement. The inevitable decay of the dominant socio-economic system led to a growing aggravation of class contradictions. Only an ideologically and organizationally independent party of the industrial proletariat could be equal to the exigencies of the social conflict these unleashed. As the ruling class grew steadily weaker and the working class stronger, only a united leadership of the major components of the labour movement (trade unions, party) was capable of confronting the tasks on the political agenda. Favoured by the whole course of history, Social Democracy must henceforth struggle directly for power, seeking to win a majority among the masses. Strong in their consensus, it had no interest in provoking premature crises: it would harvest the ripe fruit of power when the ruling class lost subjective vigour and confidence.

Pursuing his attack on Bernstein, Kautsky wrote that the party must: 'Seize upon any legal possibility to develop our organization, win new

[52] Ibid., p. 179.
[53] Ibid., p. 181.
[54] 'Herunterreissen oder Kritisieren', in *Vorwärts*, 10 October 1899.

positions, accumulate experience and heighten the enthusiasm of the popular masses for our ideas. Our task is not to provoke catastrophes, but to avoid offering any pretext for such catastrophes and to act so as to win over the majority of the politically active masses in order that the ruling classes lose confidence in themselves and their ruin becomes inevitable.'[55]

According to Kautsky, however, the fact that Social Democracy was not striving to provoke 'catastrophes', that the party intended to respect the law, and that it regarded the struggle for democracy as indissolubly linked to the struggle for socialism, did not mean that it would definitely be able to avert a general political crisis, a 'catastrophe', in the process of coming to power. At the Stuttgart Congress of 1898, at which the 'Bernstein affair' first erupted after the publication in *Die Neue Zeit* of his *Probleme des Sozialismus* articles, which anticipated the themes of *Die Voraussetzungen*, Kautsky had asserted that while a peaceful road to socialism could be postulated above all in Britain, because of the strength of parliamentary democracy and the absence of militarism or a bureaucratic state in England, in those countries of continental Europe marked by a strong bureaucratic and militarist regime, or by a clear propensity of the bourgeoisie towards reaction – here he pointed to the political crises of the turn of the century in France, Spain, Italy, and Austria – the prospects were quite different. On the European continent today, he declared, 'there is only one democratic force, and that is the proletariat'. There socialists could not count on the further development of bourgeois democracy nor on decisive democratic conquests for the proletariat; the struggle for democracy therefore merged into the struggle for the victory of socialism. 'Is there anyone who believes that this victory is possible without catastrophes? I desire it,' he said, 'but I do not believe it.'[56] All this amounted to saying that Social Democracy was now the champion of democratic institutions against the reactionary inclinations of the bourgeoisie towards the sabres of militarism. But it also meant, precisely because of these leanings of the ruling classes, that the SPD had to consider the possibility of political 'catastrophes'.

But what was a political catastrophe in Kautsky's estimation? It would occur, he argued, if the balance of power between the two fundamental social classes shifted in such a way that conditions for the perpetuation of the previous order no longer existed, and the ruling classes inclined to reaction while the oppressed classes moved towards social revolution.

[55] 'Bernsteins Streitschrift', in *Vorwärts*, 16 March 1899.
[56] *Protokoll über die Verhandlungen des Parteitages der SPD. Abgehalten zu Stuttgart vom 3. bis 8. Oktober 1898*, Berlin, 1898, pp. 128–9.

How should the proletariat confront such a crisis of political equilibrium? What weapons should the workers use? Kautsky believed that an armed clash would draw them onto the terrain most favourable to the class enemy. Instead, they should direct the confrontation onto the ground where they were naturally strongest: the terrain of economic and social relations. The key initiatives of the proletariat would take the form of great mass social and political struggles – strikes and demonstrations. Once committed to a political-social confrontation of broad scope, the party and the workers' movement must make sure that they were capable of analyzing their prospects realistically. Here the criterion must always be to what extent their actions had won the consensus of the broad popular masses; they had an interest in intensifying conflict only when it was clear that this consensus was increasing. Kautsky assigned violence no active function of assault on the system of rule of the oppressor classes, but rather one of defence of the workers' movement once reaction itself had first resorted to violent methods. It is significant, however, that he never broached the question of what organizational techniques were necessary to prepare for the possible use of violence, even if purely defensively, by the working class. Nonetheless, Kautsky did clearly affirm that in his view the epoch was one of social revolution and not of conquest of democracy and reforms within the framework of the existing order. Polemicizing against the revisionist Paul Kampffmeyer, he wrote: 'We expect not the development of social peace, but the intensification of social war.' The object of the struggle was therefore 'complete state power'.[57] He went on to this description of the alternative political strategies that flowed from the two different socio-economic analyses: 'As long as we are convinced that the contradiction between the proletariat and the capitalist class is growing ever more acute and that the influence of the capitalist class over the state is constantly increasing, such that the conquest of state power becomes ever more necessary for the working class, so long as we hold firm to the conclusion that the essential preconditions for any important social change lie in the conquest of state power, the Social Democratic Party will remain in irreconcilable opposition to all bourgeois parties and will continue to constitute the central rallying point for the entire workers' movement, and to infuse its own spirit into the life of the trade unions and cooperatives, as well as into the activity of the representatives of the workers in the state and in the municipalities. . . . If, on the contrary, we are convinced that social

[57] Kautsky's answer to P. Kampffmeyer, 'Wohin steuert die ökonomische und staatliche Entwicklung?', in *Vorwärts*, 5 May 1901.

contradictions are becoming attenuated, that the proletariat is not facing a great, decisive, revolutionary struggle for possession of full state power, that it has already achieved sufficient basis for the development of a socialist society, and that all that is now needed is to build on this basis step by step, then we must expect that as the division of labour advances there will be a progressive fragmentation of the workers' movement into a sectoral force. The result would be to open the road to partial demands aimed at gaining a hearing from policy-makers in the state, and political subordination to those parties most capable of protecting particular interests at the state level'.[58]

Kampffmeyer answered Kautsky in the revisionist review *Sozialistische Monatshefte*. His response merits special attention, for it summarizes the points of view of the anti-orthodox current with particular clarity. Kautsky, Kampffmeyer asserted, maintained that economic contradictions were fated to increase in the course of capitalist development and that the problem of social control of production and consumption could therefore be posed only after the proletariat's victory over the bourgeoisie. If that was how things were, what could the task of the Social Democracy be prior to the conquest of power? Await the future in a substantially passive manner? Instead, Kautsky's critic argued, the SPD should develop the implications of the second section of the Erfurt Programme, which committed the party to the struggle for the growing democratization of state and society. If such a democratization turned out to be impossible, Kampffmeyer argued, that would mean that the ruling class was strong enough to assure an ever greater control over all society. In such an event the victory of the proletariat would anyway be a contradiction in terms. Kautsky, like all the orthodox party members, took comfort in a fetishistic notion of the historical 'necessity' of socialism and fostered illusions that increasing conflict between classes had to result, come what might, in the manner prescribed by revolutionary faith. All of which revealed a lack of critical spirit tantamount to pure dogmatism. A different road should be taken by the SPD. Abjuring passivity, the party must actively struggle for the democratization of the existing state and for partial reforms modifying the structures of capitalism. Instead of a religious faith in 'historical necessity' what was needed were specific analyses of particular situations and critical predictions.[59] Of course, it was possible that things might come to a frontal conflict, a 'struggle for

[58] 'Missverständnisse über Missverständnisse', in *Vorwärts*, 29 May 1901.

[59] P. Kampffmeyer, 'K. Kautsky und der "freie kritische Sozialismus"', in *Sozialistische Monatshefte*, no. 7, July 1901, pp. 494–8.

full state power between the bourgeoisie and the proletariat'; but such a possibility could arise only when the relationship between the two classes had reached a stage that by no means yet existed. The real question facing Social Democracy could be posed in this way: what was to be done to maximize its strength? Kampffmeyer's answer was that the labour movement should promote democratic-reformist action in every cell of social and productive life, thereby developing workers' consciousness – which was not an automatic product of historical development – in practice. He ended by stating that socialism must not be considered a necessity of history, but rather a possibility that could only be realized by renouncing the faith that it was guaranteed by historical necessity.[60]

Clashing with the revisionists over the general perspectives and forms of historical development, Kautsky likewise challenged them over the tactical and strategic line to be taken by the socialist parties towards bourgeois reformist governments (in fact, these were but two aspects of the same problem). Commenting on the 'Millerand case' in France, Kautsky reiterated that the proletarian party could develop only if it preserved full ideological and organizational independence, since the struggle for state power was now on the historical agenda. Against Bernstein, who had asserted that if Social Democracy was to adopt a politically active attitude, it would have to acknowledge that under certain circumstances 'partial participation in government by socialist workers' parties was not only admissible but even *an extraordinarily important duty*', Kautsky maintained that although 'under exceptional conditions and for a specific purpose' socialists could participate in a government alongside bourgeois democrats, this should be done only for the purpose of 'working together against a common enemy', while simultaneously safeguarding 'the principle of class struggle' and the independence of the socialist party 'in all circumstances'. Otherwise the road would be open to corruption, compromise and subordination. In any event, Kautsky argued, such a possibility was unthinkable in a country like Germany, which lacked an authentic democratic system.[61]

Kautsky considered Millerand's participation in the French government a twofold error: formally, it had occurred without 'the consensus of at least the great majority of the socialist organization'; and substantively Millerand had jettisoned the understandable need for the socialists to support the Waldeck-Rousseau government in order to shift the internal

[60] Ibid., pp. 503–4.
[61] 'Eine internationale Umfrage über sozialdemokratische Taktik', in *Vorwärts*, 5 October 1899.

balances within the ruling classes in their favour (which was what German Social Democracy had done in voting for a Caprivi Ministry), for the direct entry of a socialist into the government. The only result was that Millerand, in his position as 'socialist' Minister, found himself pledged to the major power structure of the bourgeoisie. Confronted with any bourgeois government, Kautsky concluded, socialists must always preserve their freedom of political judgment and full independence of behaviour, even if the government was marked by reformist or relatively progressive features.[62] Thus, Millerand's position in the Waldeck-Rousseau Cabinet was one of compromise and ultimately of political corruption, for this socialist was a Minister 'by the grace of the bourgeoisie and its *President du Conseil*' and could remain such only so long as his socialism did not conflict with 'the bourgeois goals of the government'.[63] Against those who maintained that the entry of individual socialists into governments could be an important step towards a gradual participation in power, Kautsky asserted that the conquest of power could only be the work of the proletariat as a class and could occur only when it was strong enough 'to undertake a victorious struggle against the entire bourgeois world'. This, he said, would take place 'not *through* a coalition but *against* a coalition' and would be the work of a politically united class.[64]

Kautsky defended his positions on these questions at the Congress of the Socialist International held in Paris in September 1900. In a resolution drafted by him and approved by the Congress several central theses were laid down. After asserting that 'in a modern democratic state, the conquest of political power as the task of the working class cannot be the product of a sudden blow, but on the contrary must result from long and painstaking work of proletarian organization in the economic and political field', it declared: 'in the countries in which governmental power is centralized', this power 'cannot be conquered gradually'. Kautsky's resolution did not rule out the possibility of participation by individual socialists in bourgeois governments. However, if an emergency situation of a 'transitory and exceptional character' arose which tactically warranted the participation of a socialist in a bourgeois government, then such participation would in all cases have to respect certain inflexible rules: 1) the great majority of the party must approve of the participation; 2) the

[62] 'Jaurès und Millerand', in *Vorwärts*, 1 August 1899.

[63] 'Burgermeister und Minister', in NZ, XIX, 1900–1901, vol. II, p. 796.

[64] 'Die sozialistischen Kongresse und der sozialistische Minister', in NZ, XIX, 1900–1901, vol. I, p. 44.

party representative would have to be 'mandated by his party'; 3) the socialist Minister would have to withdraw if the majority bourgeois government assumed a repressive attitude in conflicts between capital and labour.[65]

3   The Social Revolution: Lines for a Strategy

During the years between the debate over Bernstein's *Voraussetzungen* and the Dresden Congress of September 1903, at which the revisionists suffered complete defeat (although more apparent than real, as we shall see), Kautsky, in addition to his general theoretical polemics, strove to reemphasize the anti-reformist significance of the notion of the independent action of the proletarian party in three fundamental spheres: 1) the relationship between the party and the trade unions; 2) the role of intellectuals as agents of socialist science; 3) the necessity for discipline and unity in the practice of the party.

In the first years of the 20th century the relations between trade-union and party organization became a burning issue in German Social Democracy. The 'revolutionaries' maintained that it was the duty of Social Democrats to determine the line of march of the entire workers' movement and therefore also of the trade unions. The 'revisionists', on the other hand, supported the independence of the unions.

The 'free unions' in Germany, i.e. those linked to the SPD and led by Karl Legien, a party member, had developed a highly centralized structure, with a constantly expanding nucleus of paid functionaries. This apparatus had its base in a solid layer of skilled workers, who were relatively well paid and were increasing numerically amidst rapid industrial growth in the country. These workers were pressing for a politically 'neutral' trade-union policy with markedly economistic perspectives. Although the trade-union leaders officially proclaimed that relations with the SPD were excellent, in reality the theory of 'neutrality' – together with the tenets of revisionism – was sinking ever deeper roots in the union bureaucracy, whose conviction was that only wage struggles could guarantee constant organizational growth. It should be noted that union membership had indeed risen from 493,742 in 1898 to 887,698 in 1903.

Kautsky's response to this complex of problems was two-fold. On the

[65] *Cinquième Congrès International tenu à Paris du 23 au 27 septembre 1900. Compte rendu analytique officiel*, Paris, 1901, pp. 109–10.

one hand he evinced a fundamental optimism about the relations between the unions and the party; on the other hand, he continued to insist that only by bowing to the policies of the party could the trade unions steer clear of the shoals of purely empirical economism. If such an approach were adopted as the strategic line of the unions, he said, they would wind up serving the interests of the 'labour aristocracy' against those of the movement as a whole. Particularly in a series of articles entitled *Die Neutralisierung der Gewerkschaften* written in 1900, Kautsky demonstrated that despite his basic optimism, he had well understood the nub of the problem and the general shape of the dangers it contained. In his conclusions, however, he declared his conviction that 'perilous' tendencies would not prevail in Germany. 'Whenever the workers' organizations become strong,' he wrote, 'they always evince a tendency to place professional interests above class interests and to separate corporate agitation from the general class movement, which must ultimately be paralyzed by any sort of particularism.' The classic example of this phenomenon, to which periods of industrial prosperity were especially conducive, was England.[66]

For its part, the bourgeoisie sought to foster this process in every way, granting particular concessions 'to the labour aristocracy the more it tends to concern itself exclusively with its own corporate interests'. The bourgeoisie acted according to the principle of *divide and rule*.[67] The notion of 'neutrality' was not problematic in the sense that the unions were 'open to all workers regardless of religion or political affiliation', but rather in the sense that it posed the question of 'whether or not the trade-unions should engage in politics'.[68] In reality, if 'neutrality' resulted in the unions becoming the instrument of non-socialists, 'they would certainly not apply a neutral policy, but rather an anti-socialist one', thus causing a split in the workers' movement.[69] Kautsky's conclusion, as we have noted, was marked by optimism. He was convinced that 'these are no longer the times that gave rise to the sort of neutral labour aristocracy that exists in England', indeed that these times 'are gone for good'.[70] Shortly thereafter, emphasizing the indispensable need of the entire workers' movement for a scientific view of historical tendencies and social reality in their totality, Kautsky remarked that when the unions 'develop

---

[66] 'Die Neutralisierung der Gewerkscháften', in NZ, XVIII, 1899–1900, vol. II, p. 389.
[67] Ibid., p. 390.
[68] Ibid., p. 429.
[69] Ibid., p. 432.
[70] Ibid., p. 497.

among a proletariat lacking in revolutionary sentiments, they have a tendency to develop a spirit of corporative narrow-mindedness, the caste spirit of an aristocracy seeking to achieve a privileged position by comparison with their proletarian comrades and at their expense'.[71] While fully accepting the necessary division of tasks between trade union and party, Kautsky insisted that the two were nevertheless linked. For only their cooperation could assure the strength of both: a party not based on the unions rested on 'sand', while unions that did not reflect a socialist spirit were organizations subordinated to the ruling class. Hence his attack on 'union mandarins': 'Confinement within the horizons of trade-union life merely tends to make union functionaries limited and one-sided.' 'Only when the unions and the party stand shoulder to shoulder,' he concluded, 'are they up to the difficult tasks that arise from the mounting political and economic crisis of bourgeois society.'[72]

We have seen that Kautsky argued that when solid bonds between the party and the unions (that is, between the movement's united consciousness of its general goals and the struggle to defend the specific conditions of the workers) were lacking, trade unionism was inevitably debased to an empirical and opportunistic economism, not at all 'neutral' but of a politically conservative character. Kautsky saw such trade-union empiricism as one of the practical expressions of the broader and more general theoretical opportunism of the revisionists. When there were attempts to introduce a revisionist conception into the workers' movement, and especially into the party, he maintained, the question was not whether one scientific view should replace another (for him this was impossible, since he identified his own science as the only science of the historical process), but rather whether Marxism would be ousted by an un-scientific empiricism. In 1903 Kautsky wrote in this regard: 'Revisionism means neither the development of Marxism nor its replacement by another doctrine; in fact, it means the renunciation not only of Marxist theory, but also of any social theory.' For revisionism broke every necessary link between theory and practice within the workers' movement and plunged the proletariat into a blind alley: how could, in fact, the workers' movement set itself the task of changing society 'without developing a theory of society as a whole'? Revisionism's worst blow was to deprive the working class of its own science.[73]

Now, in his desire to reassert the unity of theory and practice and to

[71] 'Klassenkampf und Ethik', in NZ, XIX, 1900–1901, vol. I, p. 241.
[72] 'Zum Parteitag', in NZ, XXI, 1902–3, vol. II, p. 738.
[73] 'Drei Krisen des Marxismus', in NZ, XXI, 1902–3, vol. I, pp. 728–9.

combat equally theoretical revisionism and practical opportunism, particularly in the unions, Kautsky was led to lay heavy emphasis on the role of revolutionary science and of the intellectuals who were its bearers. In doing so, he exercised a deep influence on Lenin, who invoked the authority of Kautsky to justify essential aspects of his own theory of organization in *What Is To Be Done?* Kautsky, in effect, argued that the science produced by intellectuals provided the only crucible in which Social Democracy and proletarian struggle could be fused: 'The class struggle of the proletariat requires above all scientific depth; without the collaboration of "intellectuals" this class struggle cannot become a Social Democratic movement.'[74] But let us be clear; in no way did Kautsky suggest that the political-organizational leadership of the socialist movement belonged to intellectuals. They had the crucially important, but rigorously limited, task of contributing by their competence and knowledge to a scientific clarification of the relations between the socialist goal and the historic movement that necessarily tended towards it – a clarification without which the class struggle could not develop a revolutionary strategy. The role of intellectuals was thus highly important, but it stopped there: 'The task of the bourgeois elements endowed with scientific training, of the intellectuals or "academics" of our party,' Kautsky wrote, 'is to develop and diffuse an analysis of the major structures of the social order, and a broad socialist consciousness that rises above the interests of the moment – in other words, a revolutionary spirit in the best sense of the word. . . . What the workers ask of the academics is knowledge of the *goal*; on the other hand, they have no need of them for the leadership of their own class movement.'[75]

It was in this conceptual framework that Kautsky wrote his 'strongest' words on the dependence of the class movement on the science developed by intellectuals, words which Lenin recalled in *What Is To Be Done?*, describing them as 'profoundly true and important'.[76] (It should be noted, however, that Lenin introduced a significant variation in practice: in his account the scientific primacy of professional intellectual-revolutionaries was translated into natural leadership functions within the party and the movement.) Synthesizing his views in the article *Die Revision des Programms der Sozialdemokratie in Oesterreich*, Kautsky declared that 'it is completely false' that 'socialist consciousness' was the 'necessary and direct product of the class struggle of the proletariat', since although it

---

[74] 'Die Neue Bewegung in Russland', in NZ, XIX, 1900–1901, vol. II, p. 123.
[75] 'Akademiker und Proletarier', in NZ, XIX, 1900–1901, vol. II, p. 90.
[76] V. I. Lenin, *Collected Works*, vol. 5, p. 383.

was true that 'as a doctrine socialism obviously has its own roots in contemporary economic relations, as does the proletarian class struggle for that matter', it was also true that 'contemporary socialist consciousness can arise only on the basis of profound scientific knowledge'. But, 'the bearer of science is not the proletariat', which could not possess this science precisely because it was a subaltern class. Rather, it was *'bourgeois intellectuals'* who possessed it. Consequently, consciousness of the goal derived from science must be grafted onto the reality of the proletarian class struggle generated by exploitation: 'socialist consciousness is therefore an element imported into the class struggle of the proletariat from outside and is not something that takes shape spontaneously'.[77] In substance, then, the contribution the bourgeois intellectual become revolutionary could make to the workers' movement was rooted in the specific role the intellectual plays in the division of labour.

Kautsky's polemic against theoretical revisionism and the tendency towards opportunist neutralism in the unions, together with his energetic affirmation of the function of the revolutionary intellectual as an essential element in providing the workers' movement with its historical–critical knowledge, necessarily posed the problem of the internal discipline of party organization. How should dissent be dealt with? Writing to Victor Adler in April 1903 Kautsky maintained that there must be maximum tolerance in the case of workers, and that the party must be prepared to make 'the greatest concessions' to allow even elements lacking the necessary clarity to enter the Social Democracy. On the other hand, 'confused' intellectuals were 'harmful'. Intellectuals 'have only one task in our party: to defend clarity. Everything else is taken care of by the proletarians alone. When an intellectual, instead of defending clarity, does the opposite, he only causes damage'. The worker lacking in clarity would find his way by virtue of 'class instinct'; not so the intellectual.[78]

Hence the presence of a now avowedly revisionist current in the party must inevitably pose serious questions for the revolutionary nature of the party of the proletariat. Kautsky denounced revisionism precisely as a non-revolutionary theory aimed at altering the specific character of the party itself. His objective was to stem the revisionist current, to refute it theoretically and ideologically, and to defeat it politically. Concerned to maintain the theoretical and practical unity of the movement and to marginalize the revisionists, he also wanted to avoid a split in the party,

[77] 'Die Revision des Programms der Sozialdemokratie in Oesterreich', in NZ, XX, 1901–2, vol. I, p. 79.
[78] Kautsky to Adler, letter of 4 April 1903, in V. Adler, *Briefwechsel*, op. cit., pp. 415–16.

the effects of which he feared would cast doubt on the cohesion and unity of the proletariat. Revisionism thus had to be reduced to 'deadwood'.

'A party,' he wrote, posing the question of unity and dissent and emphasizing the difference between a party and a state, '. . . is an organization in which *individuals who share a common mode of thought and feeling, and engage in common actions unite* together to strengthen their own forces. The unity in thought and action of the members is the precondition for their effective action. It [a party] is an organization created to struggle against other parties. . . . To join such a party is a voluntary act.' Within a state forces might coexist with differing social perspectives, but such coexistence was contrary to the very purposes of a party.[79] The limits of dissent and discussion, particularly in a revolutionary party, were set by the need for substantial unity over its goals, without which paralysis would result: 'To discuss is a wonderful thing, but a fighting party is not a discussion club, and discussions that lead to no decision can only result in paralyzing and damaging the party.'

Of course, debates and differences of opinion were essential to the life of Social Democracy, but only if the necessary unity in the struggle against the common enemy was maintained.[80] Shortly before the Dresden Congress of September 1903, Kautsky, in pursuing his tactic of provoking the revisionists to make all their disagreements explicit so as to enable the revolutionaries to defeat them completely and thus acquire the authority needed to assert their own leadership fully, stated that the exponents of the Right were now putting an end to the ambiguity created by the combination of their great stir about the 'novelty' of their positions and their claim that 'no one wants any change' and that 'we are all united'.[81] His secret objective appears clearly in the letter to Adler quoted above: to isolate the revisionist intellectuals and, if it could be done without risking a split, to precipitate their departure from the party: 'If I could act to get the Göhres, Davids, and company to leave the party without causing a split, I would do so. But unfortunately I have to recognize them as party comrades, since any attempt to drive them out would involve evils even worse than those created by their presence. But if an opportunity of this sort ever arose, I would do my part.'[82]

In substance, this was a confession of weakness, which acknowledged the deep roots revisionism had sunk in the party. As for Bernstein, who

[79] 'Der Rückzug der Zehntausend', in NZ, XX, 1901–2, vol. I, p. 777.
[80] 'Zum Parteitage', op. cit., p. 730.
[81] 'Alte und Neue Taktik', in *Leipziger Volkszeitung*, 2 September 1903; and also 'Noch Ein Wort zum Parteitage', in NZ, XXI, 1902–3, vol. II, p. 750.
[82] Letter cit. of 4 April 1903 in V. Adler, *Briefwechsel*, op. cit., p. 416.

was not mentioned in this letter, Kautsky admitted that Engels would have treated him without ceremony. In a letter to Bebel written in January 1903 he wrote: 'If Bernstein had written his *Voraussetzungen* when Engels was still alive, the General would not have treated him as delicately as we have, but would have dispatched him with a kick and a cry of "Out, scoundrel!".'[83]

In 1902, in the midst of his campaign against revisionism prior to the Dresden Congress, Kautsky published another of the key works of his political-ideological career, which was to exert an enormous influence on international socialism. Its very title, *Die soziale Revolution*, spoke volumes. In this book the theoretician summed up all the themes explored in his many writings of the preceding years. He maintained that as 'state power gained in strength' so grew the resistance of the ruling classes to concessions in the countries of continental Europe.[84] He linked this increasing rigidity to the growing influence of finance capital, which was inclined towards militarism and a policy of violence 'at home and abroad'.[85] He reasserted the full value of democratic forms as an 'indispensable' instrument in rendering the proletariat 'mature' enough for the revolution. But he also declared that these forms were incapable of 'preventing this revolution', since in themselves they could not halt the development of capital and of social conflicts.[86] At this point he formulated a very clear and central conclusion; that contemporary politico-social development intensified the struggle between the two fundamental classes of society, whose power increased simultaneously, finally unleashing the social revolution as the proletariat's struggle for the conquest of state power was put on the agenda: 'Thus, the instruments of the power of capital are developing side by side with those of the proletariat, and the outcome of this development can only be a great decisive battle between the two, a definitive struggle that can end only when the proletariat has achieved victory.'[87]

Politically, the most revealing part of the work was the section devoted to the problem of the 'forms' and 'weapons' of the social revolution. After stressing that neither the 'forms' nor the 'moments' of revolutionary development could be predicted precisely (this was one of the *leitmotifs* of his analysis), Kautsky maintained that in the age of extensive indus-

[83] Kautsky to Bebel, letter of 5 January 1903, in *August Bebel Briefwechsel mit Karl Kautsky*, op. cit., p. 149.
[84] *Die soziale Revolution*, Berlin, 1907, p. 20.
[85] Ibid., p. 38.
[86] Ibid., p. 50.
[87] Ibid., p. 51.

trialization the social revolution, unlike 'previous revolutions', would no longer pit 'the vast majority of the people against a handful of exploiters', but rather 'a single class, the proletariat', against 'not only all the exploiting classes, but also the majority of the petty bourgeoisie and the peasants and a considerable portion of the intellectuals'.[88] Further, given the nature of the two great classes in struggle and their socio-economic bases, it was not to be expected, at least in Western Europe, that *'armed insurrections* with street fighting and similar warlike events' would again play the role they had in the past. Instead, the strike was destined to become an instrument of increasing importance, even on the strictly political terrain, 'the more the capitalist mode of production develops and the more capital becomes concentrated'. The strike 'will surely play a role of great importance in the revolutionary struggles of the future'.[89]

In effect, in this work as in all his previous writings devoted to the strategy of the revolution, Kautsky, after theorizing the inevitability of a frontal clash between the proletariat and the ruling classes, halted on the threshold of the problem of how the revolutionary class should act – to what extent it should even prepare itself ideologically – in the event, whose possibility he did not exclude, of the ruling class bringing its full repressive power to bear at the climax of the revolutionary struggle, by a resort to the bureaucratic militarism to whose extreme importance Kautsky himself was constantly drawing attention, in Germany above all. In this regard Kautsky became exceedingly vague, probably because he believed that in the final analysis a ruling class in decline would find itself increasingly paralyzed by the ascendant class, whose actions would essentially take the form of a politico-economic struggle culminating in strikes, propagandistic agitation, and the power of a massive consensus. Thus the Kautskyist road to the conquest of state power was a relatively 'peaceful' process marked by great mass social and political struggles backed up by the parliamentary action of Social Democracy.

The conflict with the revisionists culminated at the Dresden Congress (13–20 September 1903), held shortly after the great SPD advance in the elections of June 1903, when the party's vote rose from 2,107,000 in 1898 to 3,011,000, an increase from 27.2% to 31.7%. The revolutionaries and the revisionists read these results, to which some two years of economic recession had contributed, in opposite ways. To Kautsky in particular they seemed to confirm that during a period of serious domestic and international tensions, with the acceleration of German imperialist

[88] Ibid., pp. 52–3.
[89] Ibid., p. 55.

expansion, the construction of the large fleet desired by Von Tirpitz, and the reinforcement of the bloc between industrialists and Junkers, a growing portion of the population was turning to the Social Democratic Party as the rallying point for 'all those who want further progress of society'.[90] To the revisionists, on the other hand, the election results confirmed the correctness of their positions, particularly since their supporters had won large votes and had gained strength within the party's parliamentary caucus. In either case, revolutionaries and revisionists alike considered the success a confirmation of the organizational strength of the party machine, which neither side intended to endanger with a split.

The terms of the debate at the Dresden Congress were thus those of an ideological polemic: even Kautsky and Bebel had no intention of provoking a political and organizational break with those whom they nevertheless denounced as the Trojan horse through which bourgeois reformism was trying to penetrate the ranks of revolutionary Social Democracy. The tone of the exchanges was acerbic, but they remained confined to theoretical and ideological questions.

'Don't speak of unity and unanimity in the party,' Bebel told the Congress. 'They do not exist, I contest them most decisively; never, at no time, have the differences been as great as today'. 'For twelve years now,' he concluded, 'ever since the disagreements with Vollmar over the Erfurt Programme, we have been waiting to be able to overcome these differences. That is not the way forward! Now is the time to settle everything.'[91] Vollmar replied that the real tactics of the SPD were 'concrete', and therefore 'revisionist'. He accused Bebel of being a dictator who let Kautsky put words in his mouth: 'Now I have to turn against Bebel, although in my view it is not he but Kautsky who is calling the tune in all this, particularly since Kautsky has the merit of consistency. Kautsky is the fanatic of theory, the man who has become the German professor of the party, the man who would let the world, not to mention the party, be ruined rather than renounce a syllable of his fine doctrinaire system.'[92]

Kolb charged that Kautsky was nothing but an advocate of 'catastrophism', while 'revisionism is nothing but the tactic which we have practised up to now'.[93] Bernstein, for his part, repeated all the essential

---

[90] 'Klasseninteresse-Sonderinteresse-Gemeininteresse', in NZ, XXI, 1902–3, vol. II, p. 273.
[91] *Protokoll über die Verhandlungen des Parteitages der SPD. Abgehalten zu Dresden vom 13. bis 20. September 1903*, Berlin, 1903, p. 309.
[92] Ibid., p. 339.
[93] Ibid., pp. 348–9.

theses of his revisionism, in constant polemic against Kautsky. The attitude Kautsky took at the Congress was one of flexibility in practice and intransigence in theory. On the one hand he appealed for greater 'unity' around practical goals and affirmed that it was 'desirable' to lower the temperature of the debate. On the other hand, after expressing 'tolerance' for a current that he nevertheless accused of trying to alter both the tactics and strategy of the party, he threw down the gauntlet on theoretical questions. His final attitude was ambiguous, expressed in these significant words: 'When the revisionist comrades move closer to the bourgeois parties, when they try to march side by side with them, naturally they want to do so without sacrificing the interests of the proletariat; they are representatives of the interests of the working-class animated by the same zeal as ourselves. This is a fact which we have not the slightest intention of contesting. . . .'[94] Having thus salvaged, although not without contradiction, the common proletarian spirit of the two great contending currents in Social Democracy, Kautsky called upon the Congress to decide on its line and to choose between the two perspectives: 'Which of the tactics is correct depends on whether or not social contradictions are tending to sharpen.'[95]

The Congress approved an anti-revisionist resolution by a vote of 288 to 11. The resolution condemned 'in the firmest possible manner' revisionist attempts to replace the tactics 'we have employed victoriously up to now', based on class struggle and the objective of the conquest of state power, with a policy of compromise with the existing order. The content of this vote could scarcely have been more equivocal, however, insofar as such noted revisionists or revisionist sympathizers as Auer, Heine, Kolb, Legien, Quarck, Peus, Südekum, and even Vollmar himself voted with the majority. The victory of the Kautskys and Bebels on the theoretical terrain, won amidst the confusion of this kind of consensus, thus went hand in hand with a growth in the practical strength of revisionism within the movement. Bebel himself was forced to admit that in the last elections the revisionists had significantly increased their representation in the party's parliamentary fraction.[96]

Once the Congress was over, Kautsky, with a firm eye on appearances, issued a triumphant comment: 'the declarations and votes in Dresden signify the burial of theoretical revisionism *as a political factor*'.[97] But he

[94] Ibid., p. 389.
[95] Ibid., p. 382.
[96] Ibid., p. 320.
[97] 'Der Dresdener Parteitag', in NZ, XXI, 1902–3, vol. II, p. 814.

warned that things were not turning out exactly as could have been desired, that the advance of Social Democracy faced certain obstacles, the nature of which was not very clear. They were, however, related not so much to the party itself as to the general social context. 'Our party,' he observed, 'is growing numerically by leaps and bounds; but strangely, it is not growing in self-consciousness and audacity.' This was related to a disquieting 'change in the social and political atmosphere'. In sum, Kautsky perceived that the class enemy might yet be capable of conducting deceitful manoeuvres. 'Although it is true,' he continued, 'that we are in struggle with the entire bourgeois world, although our goal remains what it has always been, namely to overcome that world, the latter is still too strong not to exert powerful influences on our attitudes.'[98]

For their part, the revisionists emerged from the Congress more self-assured than ever. The *Münchener Post*, influential organ of Bavarian Social Democracy, protested vigorously against the ecclesiastical spirit of the radical majority, on the basis of which the positions of Bebel and Kautsky had allegedly to be accepted as 'the only gospel'.[99] Shortly before, while the Congress was still in session, the same daily had observed with irritation that ideological diatribes were threatening to cast doubt on the electoral victory of 16 June, during which radicals and revisionists had been united around a single concrete objective. It concluded that it was time to come to the point, to practical work, especially since the masses 'are exceedingly tired of useless theoretical squabbles and want to see some practical work, of the sort that equips them for the difficult road leading to their goal'.[100] But the most significant official position taken by the revisionists was set down by Von Elm in the pages of their theoretical review. Von Elm ridiculed Bebel for the fact that at the Congress he had been obliged on the one hand to rejoice in the great electoral victory won several months earlier and on the other to deplore that it was the revisionists, who 'would betray the masses', that had in large measure attracted the votes of the masses themselves. He denounced the poisonous weed of the 'cult' the radicals were erecting around Bebel; he emphasized the revisionist *leitmotif* that the majority of the party, which condemned reformism in words, had so far been effectively reformist in deed. He denounced the revolutionaries for the irresponsibility of their false claim that the workers' movement was already capable of administering state and society. 'Are our economic organizations,' he asked, 'already

[98] 'Zum 21. Oktober', in NZ, XXII, 1903–4, vol. I, p. 67.
[99] 'Der Parteitag', in *Münchener Post*, 25 September 1903.
[100] 'Dresden', in *Münchener Post*, 13–14 September 1903.

sufficiently powerful to be able to undertake the reorganization of society?' He replied: 'We who have conducted the painstaking labour in the unions and cooperatives from year to year, we who know the masses better, are also aware that major educational work is still needed before these organizations are capable of standing on their own two feet,' before it would be possible 'to transform bourgeois society into socialist society'.[101] Shortly thereafter, Kolb, another revisionist star, asserted in the same review: 'Revisionism is not dead; it is alive and on the march. . . . the number of undeclared revisionists is far greater than the number of noted spokesmen.' He attacked Kautsky's revolutionism as thoroughly contradictory. Kautsky, he said, wants a total revolution; but he does not want the only form which is characteristic of all revolutions, namely violence. He wants the masses to pour into the streets, but he toys with the illusion that mass action will remain well ordered within the limits of the political strike. 'But,' he observed caustically, 'does Kautsky believe that the bourgeoisie would submit to a mere political strike?' Kolb's conclusion was that people like Kautsky were working for the hangman.[102]

4   Towards the 'Final Phase' of Proletarian Class Struggle?

The critical year 1903 had witnessed a great electoral victory of the SPD and the ambiguous defeat of the reformist wing of the party by the left.

In an article entitled *What Next?* Kautsky surveyed the prospects facing Social Democracy in Germany after the 1903 elections. He maintained that in Germany it was impossible for the ruling class to apply successfully the policy of dividing the proletariat by granting concessions to certain layers of it, which had been employed for decades in England and the United States and which the bourgeoisie was now trying to imitate, with dubious effect, in France and Italy. In short, the bourgeois-reformist road would fail in Germany. But it would also be impossible for the bourgeoisie to take the opposite road, that of the ruling classes of the 'barbarous East': violent repression of the workers' movement. The proletariat in Germany, he said, was already too strong and irresistible a force for that, exactly because of the country's degree of economic

---

[101] A. von Elm, 'Der Parteitag des Sieges', in *Sozialistische Monatshefte*, no. 10, October 1903, pp. 729–35.

[102] W. Kolb, 'Theorie und Taktik', in *Sozialistische Monatshefte*, no. 12, December 1903, pp. 902–5.

development.[103] Two complementary factors made the German situation unique, Kautsky argued. On the one hand, a policy of concessions could not achieve success because the German proletariat had already attained political autonomy and a high level of ideological consciousness; on the other hand, in Germany, unlike England and the United States, there was no strong and conscious bourgeoisie to implement such a policy. In Germany – and here Kautsky developed a broad characterization of the German bourgeoisie with significant similarities to the analysis Parvus and Trotsky were to make of class relations in Tsarist Russia – the bourgeoisie had never become the leading political class in the country. By the time the bourgeoisie 'had risen politically and economically, the proletariat had already become a powerful force': its struggle for political power against the monarchy and the aristocracy was thus mitigated by fear of the threat from the working-class, which eventually led it to accept the overlordship of the princes and the Junkers. Kautsky argued that the German bourgeoisie remained more than ever under this protection, and he concluded that 'such a class has neither the strength nor the lucidity needed for a policy of concessions in the grand style'.[104] What course, then, should the SPD, fortified by its great electoral success of June 1903, now pursue?

Kautsky – and this was to be an element of great importance in the development of his positions – drew the party's attention to the growing weight of finance capital, a 'new bourgeois' stratum which was the embodiment at once of economic power and of brutal and unscrupulous use of violence as an instrument of political rule: 'In Germany, as in the other industrial countries, a layer of magnates of capitalism is arising out of the bourgeoisie itself. They are bringing the nation increasingly under their dependence. This stratum lacks neither strength nor audacity, also with respect to governments and those who hold power. . . . It everywhere represents the most brutal, provocative, and violent section of the bourgeoisie. The more it dominates governments, the less talk there will be of concessions to the workers and the more inclination there will be to use methods of violent repression. This goes for America and England, as well as Germany. In the latter country, the "liberal bourgeoisie" is too cowardly and weak, and high finance is too greedy and ruthless, for a policy of great social reforms.'

The weakness of the German bourgeoisie and the strength of high finance and reactionary large landlords were combined with an army

[103] 'Was Nun?', in NZ, XXI, 1902–3, vol. II, p. 390.
[104] Ibid., p. 391.

dominated by an officer corps of Junkers and a disciplined bureaucracy beholden to the wishes of the regime.[105] The only progressive force in Germany was thus Social Democracy, which, given this alignment of power, could not think of becoming a government party otherwise than as a ruling party – in other words after a social-political revolution. For the SPD to become a government party in the sense of a component in a coalition with bourgeois parties could lead only to bankruptcy.[106] Kautsky concluded that while 'a regime of major economic and political reforms' was excluded in Germany, a regime founded on the systematic repression of the workers' movement was also 'improbable', given the intrinsic strength of the position of the proletariat in the productive process and therefore in society as a whole. A swerve to reaction, while possible, would have no future, since 'the victory of Social Democracy is certain in any event in the foreseeable future'. This victory, he declared, was now a historical and social necessity.[107]

In an obvious continuation of the same themes, Kautsky wrote a preface to a new Polish edition of the *Communist Manifesto* which took up the question of whether the *Manifesto* was 'out of date'. He pointed to two intimately linked historical and social novelties of the contemporary situation: 1) the greater organized strength and political independence of the proletariat; 2) the impossibility of continuing to nurture any hope in an alliance between the proletariat and a progressive bourgeoisie, which no longer existed. The *Manifesto*, Kautsky observed, could still envisage alliances of the working-class with a bourgeoisie that waged a revolutionary struggle against the monarchy and the aristocracy. Today, however, 'one can no longer speak of a *revolutionary* bourgeoisie in any sense'. Industry was now dominated by high finance, which was anti-democratic and reactionary. As for the petty bourgeoisie, it had become 'the crack troop of reaction, in defence of palaces, altars, and thrones', whereby it sought salvation from the decadence to which it was condemned by economic development. The epoch in which the petty bourgeoisie outstripped all other social classes in its revolutionary ardour was irretrievably gone.[108] Marx and Engels had believed that a process of 'permanent revolution' would occur in the course of which bourgeois rule would pass over into proletarian revolution. Kautsky, explaining the

[105] Ibid., p. 392.
[106] Ibid., p. 398.
[107] Ibid., p. 398.
[108] 'Wie weit ist das kommunistische Manifest veraltet?', in *Leipziger Volkszeitung*, 23 July 1904.

specific role of the socialist parties in the epoch of the Second International and justifying their strategy, countered that the process of preparation, maturation, and fortification of the proletariat must be 'completed' '*apart from* the revolution, *before* the revolution', and 'not through methods of war, but rather those of peace'. The growth of the working class, in independence of all the other social classes and against them, was the road that would lead to the revolution. The tempo of revolutionary development, Kautsky observed, had been rather slower than Marx and Engels had expected in their *Manifesto*.[109] The only country in Europe in which an alliance with the progressive bourgeoisie was still possible was Russia. The revisionists were attempting to use the *Manifesto* to justify their policy of alliances with liberals in the West, but the political and social preconditions for such a strategy were lacking there. This was not the case in Russia, however, since in that country 'the bourgeoisie still has revolutionary tasks', although – and here Kautsky entered a qualification of great importance – even the Russian bourgeoisie 'has already acquired the reactionary outlook of the bourgeoisie in the West', because of its fear of the development of the proletariat.[110]

Kautsky's attention to the Russian situation during this period, shortly before the outbreak of the first Russian Revolution, is particularly evident in his polemic with Kelles-Krauz (who wrote under the pseudonym Lušnia). The latter had objected that in his book *Die soziale Revolution* Kautsky had not considered armed insurrection as a means of revolutionary struggle and had limited his argument to the role of the mass strike. Kautsky accused Lušnia of having failed to analyze the specific features of the German situation adequately and of erroneously expecting Germany to be the country in which a revolutionary upsurge would occur first, acting as a driving force for the rest of Europe. His subsequent remarks shed clear light on the nature of Kautsky's revolutionary perspectives for Germany and the rest of the continent. Kautsky did indeed think that there was no possibility that the German ruling class would apply a reformist strategy, and that Social Democracy must maintain positions of intransigence towards it. But he likewise held that social revolution, although it was the only historical possibility open to the proletariat, was not an imminent reality, and that in any event it would not begin in the Wilhelmine Empire, precisely because of the strength that the enemy's socio-political bloc to a large extent still preserved. He did expect, however, that if a revolutionary situation

---

[109] Same article, *Leipziger Volkszeitung*, 25 July 1904.
[110] Same article, *Leipziger Volkszeitung*, 27 July 1904.

matured in Europe, Germany would be drawn into it. In sum, the release of the revolutionary potential of the German proletariat required an overall situation that would weaken the grip of the ruling class. In spite of the constant growth of Social Democracy, he declared, Germany had an extremely stable government: 'Even today the German government is the strongest in the world.' It was for this reason that 'a whole series of states stand closer to the revolution than Germany'. First among these was Russia, which although its proletariat was 'much weaker and less mature' than that of Germany or England, on the other hand was also ruled by a moribund regime in full crisis. In Russia, given the relationship of political, social, and class forces – an autocracy with no future, an immature bourgeoisie, a revolutionary working class that 'is still at the stage at which it has nothing to lose but its chains and has a world to win' – the proletariat was more than ever the 'defender of the conditions of existence of the entire nation'. Kautsky believed that the war with Japan would 'hasten the victory of the revolution'.[111] But what would be the nature of this imminent Russian revolution? Kautsky excluded the possibility that it could result in a socialist regime: 'economic conditions in the country are still too immature for this goal'. The only possible outcome was a democratic government – not a regime upheld by the force of the bourgeoisie, but rather one behind which would stand a strong, forward-looking proletariat capable of winning great concessions. The working class would be the bulwark of Russian democracy. Sketching out a process of cause and effect on a continental scale, Kautsky asserted that a democratic Russia would give a powerful impetus to the struggle for democratic conquests in Germany, and especially in Prussia, where the 'three-class electoral system' could be overturned. In Eastern Europe it would unleash the national problem. Kautsky considered it possible that the German proletariat could succeed in obtaining a 'dominant position in the Reich' as a result of its struggles. This 'would ensure the rule of the proletariat in Western Europe and would make it possible for the proletariat in Eastern Europe to compress the stages of its own development and create socialist institutions artificially, through imitation of the German example'. It is 'society as a whole', Kautsky added, that 'cannot artificially skip over individual phases of development'; particular parts of society, however, could do so by availing themselves of the example and aid of others. The United States, for instance, had done this in a capitalist sense, furnishing 'the most splendid example' of the truth of the interdependence of the development of nations.[112] This was an important

---

[111] 'Allerhand Revolutionäres', in NZ, XXII, 1904–4, vol. I, pp. 623–4.
[112] Ibid., pp. 625–7.

analysis, not only because it contained a clear presentiment of the first Russian Revolution, but also because it gave full weight to the role the Russian proletariat would play in comparison to the other classes in the struggle for the conquest of democracy, and powerfully sketched a hypothesis of revolutionary chain reactions analogous to that which was to lie at the root of Bolshevik strategy during the years following 1917.

According to the Kautsky of 1904, hypotheses about the 'social revolution' were not mere abstractions. Indeed, the German theorist was plainly feeling the wind of a gathering revolutionary storm whose first signs he discerned in the great mass strikes that broke out in Holland, Sweden, and Italy between 1902 and 1904. Even in Germany, the number of workers involved in strikes or lockouts rose considerably in comparison to the preceding decade, reaching nearly half a million. 'We have entered a new phase in our struggle,' Kautsky wrote on the occasion of the Congress of the International in Amsterdam in August 1904, which was to debate the value and limits of the mass strike, 'perhaps already the final, definitive stage of the struggle for political power'. Kautsky interpreted the very attempt of the bourgeoisie to link certain fractions of 'ministerial' socialism to its own governments – accomplished in France and attempted in Italy – as a favourable sign. In Australia 'an entire ministry' had been formed of members of the Labour Party.[113]

Nevertheless, the danger of socialist ministerialism had to be averted, particularly at a time when the bourgeoisie was seeking to use it as a means of dividing the ranks of progressive socialism. Thus Kautsky defended at Amsterdam the resolution against 'ministerialism' adopted at the Paris Congress of the Second International in 1900 (and confirmed at the Dresden Congress of the SPD in 1903). Ministerialism could not be part of the 'rules of normal development of socialist action', Kautsky said. It could be considered, he continued, only 'in purely exceptional cases, for example, in the event of a war of invasion', i.e. in contingencies that required a temporary suspension of the conflict between the proletariat and the bourgeoisie to deal with a common danger. Kautsky also asserted that socialists could accept a 'reformist policy' only when such a policy was championed by a democratic bourgeoisie capable of renovating the social system; but even in this case acceptance should be limited to specific goals and there should be no perspective of general collaboration.[114]

[113] 'Zum internationalen Kongress', in NZ, XXII, 1903–4, vol. II, p. 584.
[114] Cf. the intervention of Kautsky, in *Sixième congrès socialiste internationale tenu à Amsterdam du 14 au 20 août 1904, Compte-rendu analytique par le Secrétariat Socialiste Internationale*, Brussels, 1904, pp. 135–6.

Thus, although Kautsky was optimistic about the strategic perspectives of international socialism and the revolutionary 'future' of Germany, he manifested great tactical prudence as far as immediate action in Germany in the present was concerned. He feared the repressive violence of what he called the most stable government in the world; he also feared the iron solidarity of the employers' front which had been organized to oppose the struggles of labour. (In 1903 the *Hauptstelle deutscher Arbeitgeberverbände* had been founded, an association which united the captains of heavy industry and the textile industry, while the *Verein deutscher Arbeitgeberverbände* grouped employers in light industry.) Hence his emphasis on the specificity of the German situation, even with respect to the use of the mass strike – that is, the general strike. 'The entire character of our system of government,' he wrote, 'makes it impossible to resort to the mass strike as a mere demonstration, as was just done so splendidly in Italy. If a mass strike occurred in our country, it would become a decisive struggle, a struggle for political power, for the destruction of the prevailing system of government.'

We have seen that a cautious conclusion was typical of Kautsky, who theorized the inevitability of escalating social conflict in general historical terms, yet constantly retreated to a passive *attentisme* when it came to the concrete conjuncture in Germany. He erected – and this was to remain a central feature of his writing – a sort of no-man's-land between strategy and tactics that could never be crossed in practice. On this occasion, he ended with the resounding finale: 'Until things mature in Germany a mass strike would be a useless provocation to our enemies.'[115] Kautsky wrote these words in October 1904. The party, he maintained, should however prepare itself to study and discuss the mass strike with a view towards the great changes that were in the air.

[115] 'Der Bremer Parteitag', in NZ, XXIII, 1904–5, vol. I, p. 9.

III

1905: The Radicalization of Kautsky

1 The Russian Revolution and the Congresses of Cologne and Jena

The year 1905, which saw the first Russian Revolution, marked a decisive stage in the development of German Social Democracy. The news from Russia, Kautsky was later to say, 'filled the entire world proletariat with unbounded enthusiasm for the mass strike'.[1] Saint Petersburg's 'bloody Sunday', 22 January 1905, was not a day of tranquillity in Germany either. Indeed, a gigantic strike of miners had broken out spontaneously on 7 January in the Ruhr. Workers of all currents, both organized and unorganized, joined in, creating serious difficulties for the trade-union leaders. The strike ended on 19 February; the powerful employers' organizations had made no substantial concessions, but neither had the Prussian government dared intervene with military force. The pitch of labour struggles was intense throughout 1905. There were 2,323 strikes and lockouts, involving a total of 507,964 participants. Demonstrations of sympathy and support for the Russian Revolution were held by workers and the SPD in many German cities. It was also the year of the first Moroccan crisis, during which German Social Democracy was confronted with a serious danger of war for the first time. In November and December there was agitation against the 'three-class electoral system' in Saxony. At the same time, the Imperial government was stepping up its rearmament programme. In autumn the regime hinted at the possibility of a German intervention against a victorious Russian revolution, and at the end of the year the Kaiser openly raised the question of repression against the SPD, which, he said, was threatening the internal cohesion and military capacity of the empire.

[1] *Der politische Massenstreik*, Berlin, 1914, p. 109.

This tense situation posed urgent questions for the party and the trade unions. What were the lessons of the Russian Revolution, in which great mass political strikes had played a role of prime importance? What was the relation between Russian and German conditions? How should the link between the party and the trade unions be consolidated? What was the impact of the role of the workers' movement on the other classes of German society? What should be done in the event of a danger of war?

The events of 1905 revealed an aspect of German politics that had hitherto lain largely concealed, namely the decisive weight of the trade-union leadership, which was now so great that it could exert a major and direct influence on the party leadership. The unions held their Fifth Congress in Cologne from 22 to 27 May 1905. The congress took place in the wake of the great Ruhr strike, which had demonstrated that the spontaneous combativity of workers, united beyond their organizations, could by-pass the union leadership. On the other hand, the strike had ended in failure, with a display of the determination of the employers' organizations. The lesson that was drawn by the leaders of the 'free unions' – and it should be recalled that these unions, linked to the SPD, had 1,429,303 members in 1905, compared with 191,690 in the Catholic unions and 117,097 in the Hirsch-Dunker unions – was that the mass strike was not feasible in Germany and therefore in practice had to be repudiated. The party, on the other hand, underwent an apparent radicalization, voting at its Jena Congress (17–22 September 1905) to adopt the weapon of the mass political strike in defence of electoral rights and the right of association against reactionary intrigues. The conflicting decisions of the two congresses posed the question of the relationship between the party and the unions. Which of the two organizations held supremacy in the workers' movement? The debate on this subject resulted in a victory for the 'radicals', but this victory, like that obtained in Dresden against the revisionists in 1903, proved to be more apparent than real. Indeed, the tension that very rapidly arose between the unions and the party demonstrated that the former could in effect dictate terms to the latter. In practice this resulted in the triumph of the theory that Germany belonged to the 'Western' and not 'Eastern' societies, like Russia, which meant that Germany would have to follow a legal, reform-ist, and non-revolutionary road. At its Mannheim Congress in 1906 (23–29 September), the SPD, after bitter internal conflicts, capitulated to the unions on the basis of a formula that allowed it to 'save face' officially. The result was a political and ideological cleavage within Social Democracy between those who wanted to apply the Russian 'lessons' to

Germany (Rosa Luxemburg in the first place) and those who opposed such a strategy, although for varying reasons.

Under the influence of the Russian events, the great strike in the Ruhr, and the sharpening of international conflicts (especially the Moroccan crisis), Kautsky underwent a process of considerable radicalization. As we shall see, he went so far as to propose that the strategy of the party be 'updated'. This 'updating' centred primarily on the question of the 'forms' of revolutionary conflict, in other words, the sort of actions the proletariat would have to consider in the course of its own struggle. In no way, however, did it put in question either Kautsky's faith in parliament as an instrument of proletarian power or his conviction that there was no future for a revolution by a minority.

At the end of 1904, in his continuing polemic against 'ministerialism', Kautsky wrote, paraphrasing Marx but without in any way repeating his critique of parliamentarism, that 'the conquest of state power by the proletariat' could not occur without the 'dissolution' of the 'instruments of power' of the old state (among which he cited, significantly, 'the state church, the bureaucracy, the corps of officials'). He further stated that the accomplishment of this task could not be 'the product of a putsch by a small minority of the working class' but would have to be 'the result of a prior economic, moral, and intellectual development of the mass of the proletariat' and of its organizations.[2] In 1905, reviewing the 'teachings' of the miners' strike in the Ruhr and the incapacity of the institution of parliament to deal with social problems, Kautsky repeated his conviction that what was at issue was a crisis not of the institution of parliament itself, but of its use in the context of the political crisis of the classes that held the majority in it.

'Parliamentarism,' he wrote, 'is the form in which the bourgeoisie rules over the state today. . . . What appears as the decline of parliamentarism is nothing but the political decline of the bourgeoisie, which no longer has any great political purpose. . . . But let the proletariat conquer political power and you will see how parliamentarism will gain a new lease of life and will produce fruitful effects! Even today, the proletarian elements in parliaments are the only deputies who still lend these institutions some meaning.'[3]

Committed to a strategy based on the theoretical and organizational unity of the German proletariat, subordinating the union movement

---

[2] 'Republik und Sozialdemokratie in Frankreich', in NZ, XXIII, 1904–5, vol. I, pp. 303, 307.

[3] 'Die Lehren des Bergarbeiterstreiks', in NZ, XXIII, 1904–5, vol. I, p. 778.

to the party, Kautsky launched a vigorous polemic against what could have been called the new, trade-union 'revisionism'. He fought this current ideologically, but he vastly underestimated its practical significance and real influence. Optimistically, Kautsky considered trade-union revisionism merely an instance of the ideological influence of theoretical revisionism on a few 'intellectual' spokesmen of the union leaders. Revisionists like Richard Calwer had, in effect, gone so far as to endorse the rhetoric of 'national' interest, even claiming that the German workers should not weaken the competitive strength of national capitalism through their wage demands. In practice this amounted to a call for a limitation on strikes. Kautsky vigorously opposed such proposals and held that only the struggle for wage increases could save the workers from the effects of the policy of the great cartels, which were pressing for domestic price increases so as to be able to lower their prices on foreign markets, thus driving down the living standards of the oppressed masses.[4] He trenchantly criticized the conclusions of the trade-union congress of May 1905. What completely eluded him, however, was: 1) that trade-union revisionism was a reflection of the attractive force of the ruling classes; 2) that this revisionism was the expression not at all of an ideological 'deviation' due to the influence of 'intellectuals', but of an organically reformist practice.

At the Cologne Congress the trade-union leaders had fully revealed a strategy that was resolutely hostile to any revolutionary perspective. Bömelburg, rapporteur on the item entitled 'the position of the unions on the general strike', flatly opposed the mass strike. We Germans, he said, have nothing to learn from the propaganda for the general strike now being waged in France, Belgium, and Holland. If the defeated miners of the Ruhr had any lesson to learn, he said, it was that 'without a strong organization, with a solid financial base, they cannot wage a struggle against the employers'.[5] He denounced the idea of using the general strike to resolve the social question as utopian and anarchistic, presenting the mass political strike as a variant of the general strike. True, he did not exclude possible recourse to the mass political strike in the indefinite future, to defend political and trade-union rights, but he stated unequivocally that any project that saw 'the mass political strike as a new instrument against reaction' was to be rejected decisively.[6] Bömelburg

[4] 'Eine revision der gewerkschaftlichen Taktik', in NZ, XXIII, 1904–5, vol. II, pp. 243–7.
[5] Protokoll der Verhandlungen des fünften Kongresses der Gewerkschaften Deutschlands, abgehalten zu Köln a. Rh. von 22. bis 27. Mai 1905, Berlin n.d. (1905), p. 216.
[6] Ibid., p. 219.

argued that any protracted halt in production was exceedingly dangerous for both party and trade-unions: it was the duty of the unions to see to it that discussion of the whole question 'ceased'. He even accused revisionists like Bernstein, who maintained that the mass political strike could be useful in defending democracy, of being mere 'literati', as were all other ideologues of the mass strike. 'Those who now talk so freely about the mass political strike haven't the slightest idea of the practical problems of the workers' movement,' he said scornfully.[7] He added: 'The reinforcement and expansion of our organization is, on the contrary, the best weapon against reaction.'[8] A resolution condemning the mass strike, presented by Bömelburg in the name of the General Commission of the unions, was adopted by a vote of 208 to 7. It denounced 'all attempts to establish a tactic defined by propaganda for the mass political strike', dismissed the general strike as anarchistic and admonished the workers not to allow themselves to be diverted by adventurist projects from 'the painstaking day-to-day work of building up their organization'.[9]

The resolution of the trade-union congress was so intransigent in its commitment to the legalistic-reformist road that it even went beyond the perspectives of a Bernstein, against whom Bömelburg directed some polemical barbs. In fact, the 'father of revisionism' did firmly reject any strategy that viewed the mass political strike as the 'prelude to the social revolution, in the sense of the overthrow of the present society' with the aim of instituting the 'dictatorship of the proletariat' or even of 'the proletariat's appropriation of the means of production, circulation, etc'. But he was not prepared to renounce the political strike as a 'means of exerting greater pressure on the government and on public opinion', either defensively against 'specific repressive measures' or for 'the conquest of specific demands'. For instance, Bernstein concluded, there would be no reason to hesitate in resorting to a mass political strike, even with all its dangers, against a restriction of electoral rights.[10] Yet another influential revisionist, writing what may be considered the official comment of *Sozialistische Monatshefte*, expressed concern at the narrowness with which the trade-union congress had approached the question and at its underestimation of the importance of taking adequate measures to defend political freedoms. 'The unions,' he wrote, 'have an even

[7] Ibid., p. 221.
[8] Ibid., p. 221.
[9] Ibid., p. 30.
[10] E. Bernstein, 'Ist der politische Streik in Deutschland möglich?', in *Sozialistische Monatshefte*, no. 1, January 1905, pp. 32-3, 36-7.

greater interest than the political parties in the maintenance of equal, direct, and secret universal suffrage.'[11] Finally, even the *Münchener Post*, while declaring that all was well between the unions and the party, expressed perplexity at the results of the congress and noted that it could not agree with the demand that any discussion of the use of the mass strike be prevented.[12]

For his part, Kautsky considered Bömelburg's point of view a manifestation of a minimalist trade-union spirit, committed to defending what had already been won but incapable of raising the masses' will to struggle, and paralyzed by fear of the strength of the employers' organizations. He repeated that the times were revolutionary: 'It is a strange irony of fate that the trade-union congress proclaimed the unions' need for tranquillity precisely in a year that has been the most revolutionary of the past generation.' In Russia there was revolt against the absolutism of the Tsar, while in America revolt had broken out against 'the absolutism of the trusts'. Now, Kautsky continued, Germany was the European nation closest to Russia in its political regime and closest to the United States in the strength of its employers' organizations. It thus represented a 'mixture' of these two countries.[13] It was true that because of the specific conditions of Germany a mass political strike would be possible only in a revolutionary situation; but what the Bömelburgs failed to understand is that 'we expect revolutionary situations in Germany too' and that exactly for this reason the German workers' movement must discuss the use of the mass political strike.[14]

Kautsky also exchanged sharply polemical thrusts on the mass political strike with *Vorwärts*, the central organ of the party. Under the direction of Kurt Eisner, the newspaper had taken an attitude favourable to the position of the unions and had attacked Kautsky. *Vorwärts* claimed that the mass strike would not be on the agenda until the unions had concluded their work of organization and that although its supporters did not formally pose the mass strike as an alternative to the parliamentary road, in practice they considered it 'the essential and decisive means of struggle of the proletariat'. The central organ of the party accused Kautsky, and with him Roland Holst, of replacing the anarchist utopia of the conquest of control of production through the general strike with another utopia

[11] A. von Elm, 'Rückblick auf den fünften Deutschen Gewerkschafskongress', in *Sozialistische Monatshefte*, no. 7, July 1905, p. 572.

[12] 'Der Kölner Gewerkschaftskongress', in *Münchener Post*, 10 June 1905.

[13] 'Der Kongress von Köln', in NZ, XXIII, 1904–5, vol. II, pp. 314–15.

[14] 'Die Folgen des japanischen Krieges und die Sozialdemokratie', in NZ, XXIII, 1904–5, vol. II, p. 493.

based on the project of 'attempting to conquer and consolidate political power through the mass political strike'. Kautsky in particular was attacked as an abstract and doctrinaire ideologue. Kautsky reacted harshly. He maintained that the situation of social conflict in Germany was such that if the trade-unions refused to accept the mass strike, it would break out 'without any trade-union organization at all and without any preliminary discussion'. It was unthinkable, he said, to base the strategy and organization of the party solely on the 'revolutionization of thought', since it was already necessary, given the prevailing tensions, to consider measures of action like the mass strike. Finally, he said that the party had to choose between two lines, the revolutionary one of *Die Neue Zeit* and the revisionist one of *Vorwärts*, the line based on the 'dictatorship of the proletariat', i.e. on the government of the proletariat alone, and the line of a government of conciliation with bourgeois democracy.[15] In October 1905, after the radical 'turn' of the party (which we will examine further on), five editors of *Vorwärts* were dismissed, Eisner among them.

Given the practical and theoretical problems on the agenda, the party as such was now called upon to take a position on the mass strike, under the pressure of the outcome of the trade-union congress. The Jena Congress of the SPD (17–23 September 1905) did just that. On the occasion of this Congress, Kautsky wrote an article in *Die Neue Zeit* focusing on the significance of the Russian Revolution, which he asserted had opened a new era in the history of revolutions. The revolution in Russia, he declared, was an imposing upheaval which had mobilized the proletariat of every city in the Tsarist Empire: it was a revolution 'in which the industrial proletariat constituted the most powerful motor force from the very outset'. He went on to compare the Russian 1905 to the Paris Commune. The Commune, 'despite the occasional forceful emergence of a socialist proletariat, constituted the *conclusion* of the era of bourgeois revolutions in Europe. The Russian Revolution, despite its bourgeois character, constitutes the *beginning* of the era of *proletarian revolutions* into which we are now heading.' Whereas 1871 ushered in an

---

[15] On the entire affair see the articles in *Vorwärts*: 'Zur Diskussion über den Gewerkschaftskongress', 18 June 1905: 'Unmögliche Diskussion', 19 July 1905: 'Ein Haufften Unrichtigkeiten', 20 July 1905; 'Debatten über Wenn und Aber', 2 and 5 September 1905; 'Die Fortsetzung einer unmöglichen Diskussion', by K. K., 6 September 1905; 'Debatten über Wenn und Aber', 8–9–10–13 September 1905. In addition, the articles of Kautsky: 'Die Fortsetzung einer unmöglichen Diskussion', NZ, XXIII, 1904–5, vol. II, pp. 684–6; 'Noch einmal die unmögliche Diskussion', in NZ, XXIII, 1904–5, vol. II, p. 785; 'Eine Nachlese zum Vorwärtskonflikt', in NZ, XXIV, 1905–6, vol. I, p. 315.

era of peace and development in bourgeois Europe, 1905 would open an era of crises and would create 'revolutionary situations of all sorts'.[16] Here Kautsky began to trace out the theory, later amply developed (we have already examined some of its premises), that the East was opening the revolutionary road for the West.

Bebel addressed the Jena Congress in a long speech that fully reflected Kautsky's analyses of the intensification of social contradictions in Germany, and his positions on the mass political strike. After asserting that the electoral victory of 1903 had induced reactionary circles to begin to question voting rights, and after expressing full satisfaction that the Dresden Congress of 1903 had united the great majority of the party behind revolutionary positions, Bebel noted the failure of the revisionist project of forging a great reformist bloc ranging from the right-wing of Social Democracy to the National-Liberals. He repeated that the SPD was an opposition party and was destined to remain isolated until the seizure of power. Then he expressed his conviction that the party should prepare itself for a period of great struggles and tensions. This period would be dangerous, because of the increased strength of the employers' organizations, the presence of 'scab' organizations of Catholic unions, the constant increase in the number of lockouts, and the reactionary plots against universal suffrage.

'It is only to our advantage,' he affirmed, 'if contradictions are driven to an extreme pitch, because that would create a clear situation in which there would no longer be any room for deviation, hedging, or compromise. . . . We must realize that we are heading into a situation out of which catastrophes will necessarily emerge unless the working class, by virtue of its numbers, education, and strength, is powerful enough to deprive the enemy of its inclination to precipitate catastrophe once and for all.'[17]

Having said this, he added that the workers could not favour such a cataclysm, because they would be its first victims, and that Social Democracy did not fabricate revolutions. He also reiterated, in significant tones, the reassuring guarantee to Social Democracy – one of the *leitmotifs* of Kautsky – represented by the automatic effects of capitalist development: 'We Social Democrats thus find ourselves in the favourable situation that we shall continue to grow no matter what our enemies do against us. We must grow, because capitalist society is growing and is thus increasingly generating the conditions that create new socialists.'[18] On

---

[16] 'Zum Parteitag', in NZ, XXIII, 1904–5, vol. II, p. 758.

[17] *Protokoll über die Verhandlungen des Parteitages der SPD. Abgehalten zu Jena vom 17. bis 23. September 1905*, pp. 291–2.

[18] Ibid., p. 292.

the practical attitude of the party, however, Bebel exhibited notable moderation, once again propounding the parliamentary road to socialism and the traditional legalist strategy: 'It is possible to maintain development on a peaceful terrain. This does not depend on us. . . . The course of development depends more on the attitude of our enemies than on us. Their method of action will prescribe our tactics; whether things proceed peacefully, so to speak naturally, or whether catastrophe will occur depends on them and them alone.'[19]

On the mass strike, Bebel criticized the conclusions of the Cologne trade-union congress and denied that the history of mass strikes demonstrated that they always end in failure. This was not merely 'a theoretical question, but an eminently practical one'; the mass strike was a 'means of struggle that must be used in certain conditions'.[20] Of course, he said, there could be no parallel between Russia and Germany: '. . . the conditions in Russia are so abnormal that these strikes cannot be posited as examples for us'.[21] Finally, taking a position against the 'neutrality' of the trade unions, Bebel asserted that although the unions were not political associations, they nevertheless had the duty to direct the workers toward Social Democracy.

After the opposition speeches of Schmidt, Legien, Peus, David, and others, a vote was taken on a resolution presented by Bebel which declared that the mass political strike had to be considered 'one of the most effective means' by which to defend universal suffrage and the right of association or (and here he introduced a use of the mass strike that was not entirely defensive) 'to win an important fundamental right' for the 'liberation' of the proletariat. Consequently, the resolution continued, adequate propaganda on the possible use of the mass political strike must be conducted.[22] The victory of the 'radicals' at Jena in 1905, as at Dresden in 1903, was overwhelming: their resolution was adopted by a vote of 287 in favour and only 14 against (among them the trade-union leader Legien), with two abstentions (among them Bömelburg, the very person who had led the attack on the use of the mass strike during the Cologne Congress).

Kautsky expressed full satisfaction with the results of the discussion and vote on the mass strike at Jena, drawing a connection between the congresses of Dresden and Jena. The former, he said, had marked the defeat of theoretical revisionism in the party, the latter of trade-union

[19] Ibid., p. 297.
[20] Ibid., p. 305.
[21] Ibid., p. 306
[22] Ibid., p. 143.

revisionism. The debate had 'clearly showed that those tendencies which have been characterized as trade-union revisionism have no support in the party, as had already been shown in the case of theoretical revisionism'. Completely underestimating the real weight of the leaders of the trade-union bureaucracy, not only in the unions but potentially in the party itself, he claimed that in the final analysis both varieties of revisionism remained 'limited to only a few persons'.[23] Shortly thereafter he restated this optimism, claiming that 'the mass of the party is united' and that 'revisionism is a general staff without an army', confined almost exclusively to intellectuals who would never be able to cause 'a split in the party'. Kautsky held that revisionism was not a real danger, but 'merely a phenomenon that is an inevitable accompaniment of the growth in our strength'.[24]

2   The Dynamics of the Russian Revolution – the 'Lessons of Moscow'

Kautsky's analysis of the first Russian Revolution revealed a radicalism influenced not only by the events in Russia but also by the rise of political struggles in Western Europe and Germany during preceding years (mass strikes in Belgium, Holland, Sweden, and Italy, the miners' strike in the Ruhr, the electoral victory of the Social Democracy in 1903, etc.). As we have seen, this radicalism culminated politically and theoretically in his proposal to reconsider the 'forms' of the revolutionary process, even in Germany.

In a polemic with Werner Sombart, who had claimed, in a study published in the *Archiv für Sozialwissenschaft und Sozialpolitik*, that the United States now represented a model of development for Europe similar to the model England had represented in Marx's analysis of 1867, Kautsky argued that there were no longer any universally valid models of social development. Marx, he observed, had studied England when that country was the scene of the highest development of both the capitalist class and the proletariat. Now, on the contrary, political and social relations were tending to create an increasing dichotomy between the major centres of development of the two fundamental classes. This divergence appeared most graphically in America and Russia, the former country being the seat of the greatest power of capital, the latter that of

[23] 'Der Parteitag von Jena,' in NZ, XXIV, 1905–6, vol. I, pp. 5 and 7.
[24] 'Eine Nachlese zum Vorwärtskonflikt', op. cit., p. 326.

the greatest strength of the working class. 'In America,' Kautsky wrote, 'more than in any other country, one can speak of the dictatorship of capital; on the other hand, nowhere has proletarian struggle attained such heights as in Russia.' Where did Germany stand? 'The *economy* of Germany,' Kautsky asserted, 'is closest to the American; German *politics* are closest to the Russian.' Hence, 'both these countries show us our future, which will be half American and half Russian in character'. He went on: 'It is in truth a singular phenomenon that precisely the Russian proletariat should now show us our future, for this future will express not the organization of capital but the revolt of the working class.' It was the proletariat of a country that was 'the most backward of all the great states of the capitalist world' which represented the future. Having said this, however, Kautsky placed a precise limit on the value of the Russian example, observing that Russian, like American, experience had to be understood critically. In other words, although it was necessary to draw the lessons of the Russian Revolution, it was equally necessary to grasp its specificity.[25]

Kautsky held that the 'extraordinary strength of the Russian proletariat' was rooted in two factors: 1) the lack of a strong indigenous capitalist class in Russia; 2) the historic necessity for a political revolution in that country.[26] Because of the social backwardness of Russia, but also because of the weakness of the local bourgeoisie, 'the effects' of a revolution in the Tsarist Empire 'could only be bourgeois', even though it could be guided only by a non-bourgeois class, namely the proletariat, which was the sole force capable of waging the struggle for the conquest of democracy and for modern capitalist development. Hence: 'despite its bourgeois objectives, the Russian Revolution finds its principal motor force in the proletariat'.[27] Because of this contradiction between the bourgeois economic character of the revolution and the 'socialist' character of its principal motor force, it was not possible, according to Kautsky, to expect the establishment of a normal bourgeois-democratic political régime in Russia. The country would inevitably enter a 'permanent' revolutionary process over a long period. In this manner, the 'historic mission' of Tsarism would ultimately have been to open the door to the 'permanent revolution' in Russia.[28] During this period Kautsky, fully wedded to the prospect that the Russian Revolution could unleash

[25] 'Der amerikanische Arbeiter', in NZ, XXIV, 1905–6, vol. I, pp. 676–7.
[26] Ibid., p. 677.
[27] 'Die zivilisierte Welt und der Zar', in NZ, XXIII, 1904–5, vol. I, p. 615.
[28] 'Die Folgen des japanischen Sieges und die Sozialdemokratie', op. cit., p. 493.

a series of great upheavals on the European continent, hailed the political rise of the Russian working-class more enthusiastically than he ever had before or was ever to do again.

'The [Russian] liberals,' he wrote, 'can scream all they want about the need for a strong government and regard the growing chaos in Russia with anguished concern; but the revolutionary proletariat has every reason to greet it with the most fervent hopes. This "chaos" is nothing other than *permanent revolution*. In the present circumstances it is under revolutionary conditions that the proletariat completes its own maturation most rapidly, develops its intellectual, moral, and economic strength most completely, imprints its own stamp on state and society most profoundly, and obtains the greatest concessions from them. Even though this dominance of the proletariat can only be transitory in a country as economically backward as Russia, it leaves effects that cannot be reversed, and the greater the dominance, the longer they will last. . . . Permanent revolution is thus exactly what the proletariat in Russia needs.'[29]

Kautsky was fully aware that Russian industrial development, due above all to the intervention of the state and to the penetration of foreign capital, had resulted in the creation of a weak indigenous bourgeoisie and a strong proletariat concentrated in large factories in the great urban centres. But he also realized that the general social and economic backwardness of the Tsarist Empire, with its immense agrarian question still unresolved, meant that socialists and workers had urgently to develop a programme for the broad masses of peasants, aimed at a bourgeois-democratic agrarian revolution. Because of the retardation of capitalist development in Russia, Kautsky adopted a bold attitude toward the Russian peasantry, unlike his attitude toward the German peasants, who were already trailing in the wake of capitalist economic forces. 'The peasant revolt,' he wrote, 'far from endangering the cause of the revolution, should favour it. . . . What the peasants are demanding – land, grain, livestock – cannot be found in the cities. It must be taken from the large landlords.' Now the Tsar was the greatest of the large landlords;[30] a good number of Liberals were also landlords and therefore opposed any policy that would accord with the interests of the peasants.[31] Thus, 'the revolutionary workers of the cities greet the peasants as their best comrades'.[32]

In Kautsky's view the political alliance between a socialist proletariat,

[29] Ibid., p. 462.
[30] 'Die Bauern und die Revolution in Russland', in NZ, XXIII, 1904–5, vol. I, pp. 674–5.
[31] 'Die Agrarfrage in Russland', in NZ, XXIV, 1905–6, vol. I, p. 414.
[32] 'Die Bauern und die Revolution in Russland', op. cit., p. 677.

leading the revolutionary process but unable to accomplish socialist tasks because of industrial backwardness, and a class of peasants, demanding land in struggle against the large landlords, inherently posed democratic political objectives, which the bourgeoisie could not support, and capitalist economic objectives. 'What is at stake in Russia in the first instance is not a *social* revolution, not the conquest of political power by one of the oppressed classes in order to initiate a *new* mode of production, but a *political* revolution to sweep away the political obstacles that prevent the full functioning of the mode of production that *already exists*. The historic role of the socialist industrial proletariat in this revolution is therefore not to lay the basis for a socialist society but to fight in the most intransigent and "radical" ways for what none of the other classes can support: the interests of *democracy*, initially still on the basis of the present society.' The proletariat must teach the peasants that a better existence is possible.[33]

This perspective had another consequence: in the event of the Russian proletariat 'achieving victory',[34] i.e. becoming the dominant class in the political framework of a democratic régime (and in this regard Kautsky clearly accepted the possibility of the Social Democrats in Russia participating in a coalition régime with parties of radical bourgeois democracy, an option he sharply excluded in Germany and the other developed countries), it would have to resist temptations to introduce agricultural measures of a socialist character, since such a policy would 'involve only disappointment and even dangers to the revolution'. The hour of socialist transformation had not yet sounded in Russia, not in industry and still less in agriculture.[35]

In November 1906 Kautsky began publication in *Die Neue Zeit* of what was to be his most complete work on the Russian Revolution of 1905. By an irony of history this essay, devoted to enumerating the motor forces and perspectives of the Russian Revolution, was published after Tsarism had regained control of the situation, dissolving the First Duma (in July 1906) and entrusting power to Stolypin, who subjected the country to a reign of terrorist repression and initiated an 'agrarian reform' that was aimed exclusively at the acceleration of capitalist development, the rapid proletarianization of significant layers of poor peasants, and the formation of a strong kulak class. Kautsky's article appeared just when Stolypin, who by then felt secure enough, had begun

[33] Ibid., p. 675.
[34] Ibid., p. 675.
[35] 'Die Agrarfrage in Russland', op. cit., p. 414.

to take repressive measures even against the Constitutional Democrats, the liberal opposition. The elections to the Second Duma in January–February 1907 still saw a strong shift to the left and a great increase in the strength of the Social Democrats, whose Duma delegation rose from 18 to 64. But the revolution was clearly on the ebb, as was shown by the dissolution of the Second Duma in July 1907 and the election of a Third on the basis of a highly restrictive electoral law, accompanied by intensified repression against the labour movement.

In his essay, *Triebkräfte und Aussichten der russischen Revolution* (Motor Forces and Perspectives of the Russian Revolution), Kautsky evinced a more radical approach than in his preceding articles of 1905–6 to the question of the social content of the alliance between the proletariat and peasantry in Russia, and in particular to the attitude the workers should take to the peasants and the struggle that should be waged against the large landlords. (It ought to be noted that when this essay was published Lenin referred to its author as 'the leader of the German revolutionary Social Democrats', commenting that Kautsky had vindicated with his own theoretical authority the correctness of the strategic slogan of the 'democratic dictatorship of the workers and peasants' and thereby the truth of the 'old premise underlying the whole tactics of the revolutionary Social Democrats' in Russia.'[36]) In his article of 1905 *Die Bauern und die Revolution in Russland*, Kautsky had exhorted the Russian socialists to maintain an attitude of 'neutrality' in the class struggle that pitted the peasants against the large landlords. While urging the urban proletariat to express full 'sympathy' for the peasants, he concluded that it was nonetheless not the task of the workers 'to incite the peasantry's hatred for the large landlords'.[37] His position at this time was inspired by his concern not to foster the consolidation of the sort of small landed property that would represent an obstacle to a future socialist transformation of agriculture. In his essay of November 1906, however, Kautsky altered his point of view, outlining a programme of avowedly subversive and revolutionary measures to lend substance to the alliance of urban workers and peasants. The peasants, Kautsky wrote, want land, technical assistance and investments, an infrastructure, schools, and so on. Absolutism could give the peasants no relief, while advanced liberals were willing to grant them land but insisted that any transfer of ownership must involve legal compensation for the landlords. But neither the peasants nor a state directed by the proletariat could afford the burden

---

[36] V. I. Lenin, *Collected Works*, vol. 11, p. 374.
[37] 'Die Bauern und die Revolution in Russland', op. cit., p. 675.

compensation would imply. It would amount to a new form of taxation. 'Only the *confiscation* of the large estates can allow a significant expansion of peasant-owned land without imposing new burdens on them.' Such a measure could be taken only by one class: the proletariat, directed by socialist parties, 'the only parties that would not shrink at this prospect'. Even this, however, would not be sufficient to lift Russian agriculture out of its backwardness. 'Without the abolition of the standing army, without a halt to naval rearmament, without the confiscation of the entire patrimony of the imperial family and the monasteries, without the liquidation of state debts, without the confiscation of the great monopolies that remain in private hands – the railroads, the oil wells, the mines, the steel factories, and so on – the enormous sums needed to rescue Russian agriculture from its terrible plight will never be found.'[38] Russia, Kautsky asserted, thus lacked the economic basis for a bourgeois-democratic struggle in the political-institutional sense. The bourgeoisie could no longer appeal, as it did in the bourgeois-democratic revolutions of Western Europe, to common economic interests shared by the popular masses, which had once enabled it to lead them in a struggle against autocracy. The proletariat in Russia had 'entered the political scene not as part of a merely democratic party, but as Social Democracy.'[39] The Russian situation therefore presented a number of new specific characteristics: 1) the Russian Revolution could not be properly defined as a 'bourgeois' revolution, since 'the bourgeoisie is not among its motor forces' in terms of political and ideological leadership; 2) at the same time, 'it cannot, of course, be said that it is a socialist revolution'; 3) consequently, 'in no case' would it be possible for the proletariat to set itself the objective of 'an exclusive rule, dictatorship', an objective for which 'the Russian proletariat is too weak and undeveloped'[40]; 4) the victory of Social Democracy, for which the party must of course strive, imbuing its members with confidence in its possibility, could be achieved only 'with the aid of another class', the peasantry, whose presence in the revolutionary bloc would necessarily limit the action of Social Democracy, which could not allow its own action to overstep the bounds of the economic interests of the peasants.[41] In outlining the future relations between the industrial working-class and the peasantry, Kautsky empha-

[38] 'Triebkräfte und Aussichten der russischen Revolution', in NZ, XXV, 1906–7, vol. I, pp. 324–7.
[39] Ibid., p. 329.
[40] Ibid., p. 331.
[41] Ibid., p. 332.

sized that 'it cannot be expected that the peasants will become socialists' yet at the same time that 'socialism can be constructed only on the basis of large-scale enterprises'. Recalling the relations that had marked the end of the alliance between the bourgeoisie and the proletariat during the bourgeois-democratic revolutions, he remarked that it was to be expected that after the 'present revolution' had created 'a numerous stratum of peasant proprietors', the 'same cleavage between the proletariat and the property-owning portion of the rural population' that 'already exists in Western Europe' would emerge in Russia. The historic mission of a Russian revolution culminating in the political victory of Social Democracy would be the creation of the material basis for an economic modernization which alone could lay the ulterior basis for a dictatorship of the proletariat and of a socialist mode of production. Thus, although the political initiative of the proletariat must from the very outset replace the failing impulses of the Russian bourgeoisie, it nonetheless 'appears unthinkable that the present Russian revolution could lead to the introduction of a socialist mode of production, even if the revolution should temporarily put Social Democracy at the helm'.[42]

The Russian Revolution not only inspired Kautsky to develop an important analysis of the class relations and internal forces in Russia, but also had some surprising effects on his conception of the forms the revolutionary process might assume in the western countries themselves. As we have seen, Kautsky had never excluded the possibility that the proletariat might have to resort to violence in responding to the violence of reaction, even in developed Europe. But this hypothesis remained very remote and abstract for Kautsky by comparison with the concrete project of a peaceful road, at the end of which the ruling classes would so lose confidence that they would eventually yield to the 'lessons of history' without a head-on struggle. The moment of evolution in Kautsky's outlook had clearly taken precedence over that of rupture. Confronted with the great mass struggles of the Russian working-class, however, and under the immediate influence of the armed insurrection in Moscow in December 1905, Kautsky wrote an article in *Vorwärts* (whose rightist editorial board had been ousted in October) in which he openly posed the question of the 'Lessons of Moscow'. In this article, dated 28 January 1906, he declared that it was now necessary to re-examine Engels's famous preface to Marx's *Class Struggles in France*, the text that German Social Democracy had so often used to justify its own legalism. Kautsky wrote: 'We must re-examine the opinion expressed by Engels in his preface to Marx's

[42] Ibid., p. 333.

Class Struggles in France, that the epoch of barricades is definitively over. What has ended is only the epoch of the old tactics of barricade fighting. This is what is proven by the battle of Moscow, where a small group of insurgents managed to hold out for two weeks against superior forces armed with all the means of modern artillery.' How was this possible? To answer this question Kautsky linked the victorious armed resistance of the insurgents to the favourable conditions created by the mass strike (about which, he observed, 'too little was known' during Engels's time). It was precisely the mass strike that had 'undermined the discipline of the army' and had intervened with full effect 'at the moment of the military action'. 'These are the lessons of Moscow,' he concluded.[43]

That Kautsky was well aware that such 'lessons' involved a change not only in the SPD's theory of revolution, but more particularly in the conception he personally had previously expounded is shown by the preface he affixed in October 1906 (i.e. at a time when he still held the ideas expressed in the article on 'Motor Forces') to the second edition of *Die soziale Revolution*. In this he explicitly broached, although in a significantly hesitant form, the question of the validity of the experiences and forms of struggle of the Russian proletariat for the West. He wrote: 'Today I can no longer affirm with certainty, as I did then [in 1902, at the time of the first edition], that armed insurrection at the barricades will no longer play a decisive role in the future revolution. The experiences of the Moscow street battles speak too loudly against this. . . . Of course, the relative success of barricade fighting in Moscow was possible only because the population of the city energetically supported the revolutionaries and the troops were totally demoralized. But who can say with certainty that something similar is not possible in Western Europe?' Kautsky then made an observation which is of great importance in understanding the limits within which he envisaged any repetition of the Russian experience. He said that the transformation of the Russian soldier from a 'shooting machine lacking any will of his own' into a soldier within whom the reflex of 'blind obedience' had been broken, was a result of the demoralizing and disorganizing impact of the 'unhappy war' conducted by Russia against Japan.[44] Thus his argument that the Russian 'lessons' might prove applicable outside the Tsarist Empire was linked to the premise that a similar weakening of the repressive forces of the ruling class was on the cards in Western Europe as well. In Germany in particular, where the 'strongest government in the world' ruled, it would

[43] 'Die Aussichten der russischen Revolution', in *Vorwärts*, 28 January 1906.
[44] 'Vorwort zur zweiten Auflage', in *Die soziale Revolution*, op. cit., pp. 5–6.

be necessary for the formidable military machine it commanded to enter
into crisis before the lessons of Russia could be applied.

3 The 'Mass Strike' Debate – the Party and the Unions

The resolution on the mass political strike that had been adopted at the
Cologne Congress of the trade-unions in May stimulated numerous
protests from organizations of the party, and even of the unions, between
June and August 1905. The Jena congress of the SPD in September then
officially sanctioned the radicalization of the Social Democratic movement by accepting, with a large majority, Bebel's resolution stipulating
the possible application of the mass political strike in Germany. (The
Russian Revolution provided the backdrop to this question and all the
discussions related to it.) But what was not clarified in these discussions
was the degree to which and the times when such a weapon could actually
be used in Germany. The problem was removed from the realm of
speculation by a real movement of protest that broke out in Saxony in
November 1905 and later spread to Hamburg, Alsace, and other regions,
finally sweeping Prussia itself. The target of this mobilization was the
restrictive laws regulating elections to the *Länder*. A decision on whether
or not to resort to the mass political strike now became necessary. In
practice, however, to raise such a question was also to pose the problem
of the relation between the party and the unions, which had taken profoundly different positions on this question at their respective congresses
of 1905. On 16 February 1906 a secret conference of executives of the
party and the unions was held. This gathering promptly revealed the real
balance of forces between the two organizations. The party capitulated
to the unions, committing itself to trying to prevent a mass strike with all its
might and, in the event that such a strike erupted anyway, to assuming
responsibility for leading it, with the unions playing a purely supporting
role. Immediately thereafter, a conference of trade-union leaders, held in
Berlin 19–23 February, displayed the truculence of the union leaders, their
dissatisfaction with the party and their claim to lead the workers' movement without any subordination to it. Legien put it clearly: 'What counts
for us is not the resolution of the Jena party congress but the Cologne
resolution.'[45] Müller affirmed that it was time to put an end to the

[45] *Partei und Gewerkschaften. Wortwörtlichabdruck des Punktes: 'Partei und Gewerkschaften' aus dem Protokoll der Konferenz der Gewerkschaftsvorstände vom 19. bis 23. Februar
1906*, Berlin, n.d., p. 6.

subordination of the unions, that the influence of the Russian events on the party and on the Social Democratic press had been deleterious, that the trade-union movement had to be guided not by a 'romantic spirit' but by a 'healthy realism', and that Kautsky, Rosa Luxemburg, and Franz Mehring must cease pontificating against the unions from the heights of their lofty ivory towers.[46] Another unionist, Bringmann, bluntly declared that the SPD was following the theories of Marx, Engels and Kautsky on the unions, but that these theories, formulated during a period of weakness of the trade-union movement, were no longer applicable and should forthwith be rejected. He launched a special attack on Rosa Luxemburg, the 'literary guide of the radicals', claiming that anyone who held radical positions 'cannot recognize any trade-union theory and knows only a theory of class struggle'. Finally, he concluded that it was high time to develop a formulation of trade-union theory that would no longer be subordinated to the political struggle.[47]

It was obvious that the rising tension between the party and the unions would have to be resolved one way or the other at the next congress of the party, which was to be held in Mannheim on 23–29 September 1906. In August Kautsky took up his position in an article entitled *Partei und Gewerkschaften* in which he asserted that the political dependence of the unions on the party was a historic necessity of the workers' movement. 'Not every trade-union movement' means 'class struggle' in itself, he wrote. The struggle generated by the conflict between capital and labour becomes 'a real class struggle' only when it is imbued with 'class consciousness'. 'The unions,' he continued, in terms that could only deeply irritate the supporters of the 'independence' and 'equality' of the unions, 'can be a means of class struggle, but can also become an obstacle to it.'[48] Pursuing his critique of the alleged need for an 'emancipation' of the unions, he maintained: 1) that a union 'represents in the first place only the interests of its members', whereas the party represents 'those of the entire proletariat';[49] 2) that in the final analysis 'the trade-union movement in itself is a movement with no final goal';[50] 3) that the imperative now sounded for every good unionist: 'struggle *for* the party in the unions'.[51]

While he was attacking the right, Kautsky found himself exposed on

[46] Ibid., pp. 1–3.
[47] Ibid., pp. 12–14.
[48] 'Partei und Gewerkschaften', in NZ, XXIV, 1905–6, vol. II, pp. 718–19.
[49] Ibid., p. 749.
[50] Ibid., p. 750.
[51] Ibid., p. 754.

the opposite flank. Friedrich Stampfer, writing in openly polemical tones in *Die Neue Zeit*, advanced the thesis that whilst a solution to the electoral question in Prussia was of paramount importance, in practice the party was demonstrating that it did not know what it wanted to do with the mass strike. His own view was that 'so far as the electoral movement' was concerned the mass strike had become a matter not of 'if' but of 'when and how'. Moreover – in a patent allusion to Kautsky – he observed that an opportunist position on the actual use of the mass strike was emerging, designed to embrace both 'revisionists' and 'radicals', exactly when it was necessary to move into action against the dominant system.[52] Kautsky responded to Stampfer with a 'methodological' lesson on the dangers for a politician of Stampfer's procedure. Incapable of evaluating the total balance of political and social forces, Stampfer had called for an activism based on a merely partial and one-sided assessment of them. In this, Kautsky was clearly evincing an apprehension that would increasingly preoccupy him in the future, indeed which he had already expressed in the past: fear of a clash with the full might of the Prussian state. Terming as 'infantile' Stampfer's confidence in 'a political change of such colossal proportions as the destruction of the *Junkertum*', he accused him of having fallen victim to 'voluntarism'.[53] Stampfer's reply was sharp. What was at stake, he said, was not an abstract methodological argument but the assumption of a concrete political responsibility; to renounce the struggle against the three-class electoral system in Prussia would mean 'betrayal of the cause of the proletariat' and even betrayal '*of the Russian Revolution*, the advance of which depends on its effects abroad, just as the advance of the electoral movement [in Germany] depends on the effects of the gigantic struggle now under way in Russia'.[54] In his subsequent rejoinder, Kautsky anticipated a position whose implications were later to lead him into an even more bitter polemic with Rosa Luxemburg and Anton Pannekoek. He repeated that it was impossible to play with fire in Germany; that when the mass strike occurred in the Reich it would assume 'such dimensions' as to become 'a life and death struggle', 'a struggle over the entire system of government';[55] that the SPD had always adhered to the position that 'revolutions cannot be fabricated';[56] that revolutions were not born voluntaristically but through the objective

[52] F. Stampfer, 'Wahlrechtsbewegung und Massenstreik', in NZ, XXIV, 1905–6, vol. II, pp. 755–8.
[53] 'Grundsätze oder Pläne?', in NZ, XXIV, 1905–6, vol. II, p. 782.
[54] F. Stampfer, 'Grundsätze und Pläne', in NZ, XXIV, 1905–6, vol. II, p. 853.
[55] 'Mein Verrat an der russischen Revolution', in NZ, XXIV, 1905–6, vol. II, p. 856.
[56] Ibid., p. 857.

maturation of historical circumstances;[57] that – and here Kautsky deployed his usual method of refuting what he considered an impulsive revolutionary acceleration towards the great struggles of the future, whose ultimate advent should be evenly awaited – 'only those who do not believe that there will soon be a turn in the world', who doubted that the coming years would bring a change in 'our political situation', could manifest an impatience that would lead to hasty and premature actions.[58]

The polemic with Stampfer ended only a few days before the Mannheim Party Congress assembled (23–29 September 1906). This Congress sanctioned a new unity between the party and the unions on the basis of common theoretical acceptance of the possibility of recourse to the mass strike in the indeterminate future, an agreement devoid of concrete significance in the present. The two reports on the mass political strike were given by Bebel, the head of the party, and Legien, the head of the unions. In his report Bebel indicated the full import of the victory won by the unionists in the secret conference of 16 February, the results of which he fully endorsed. After protesting against those who maintained that the mass strike should be risked even without the certainty of victory, he addressed the crux of the matter: without 'the adherence of the leaders and members of the unions', he said, 'the feasibility of a mass strike is unthinkable'. He then undercut any grounds for comparison between Russian and German conditions, between Russian methods of struggle and German procedures (in tacit polemic against the 'lessons' Kautsky drew from Russia). Since, he observed, in Russia the workers were fighting for a series of conquests which had already been won in Germany, 'there can be no comparison between the situation in Germany and the situation in Russia'.[59] It was true, he repeated, that in the event of attacks on the right to vote or on freedom of association, it would be necessary to resort to the mass strike in Germany. In practice, however, he echoed the view of the trade-union leaders that 'in the present situation of our organization' the 'risk' could not be taken.[60] Even more strongly did he reject the possibility of staging a mass strike in the event of a general mobilization for war, for that would mean putting the movement at the mercy of military tribunals.[61] Legien, fully satisfied with Bebel's speech, concluded that the differences between the party and the unions on the

[57] Ibid., p. 858.

[58] Ibid., p. 860.

[59] *Protokoll über die Verhandlungen des Parteitages der SPD. Abgehalten zu Mannheim vom 23. bis 29. September 1906*, Berlin, 1906, pp. 231–2.

[60] Ibid., p. 238.

[61] Ibid., p. 241.

mass strike (the use of which even he did not contest when 'the time' came)[62] were now 'of scant importance'.[63]

Kautsky intervened in this discussion to support an amendment, which he had drafted, to the resolution proposed by Bebel. It opposed the principle of equality between the party and the unions and codified the theses advanced in his article *Partei und Gewerkschaften*. Kautsky objected to Bebel's speech that it was not enough merely to affirm the unity in action of the two organizations, which was supported by everyone. The decisive problem, he argued, was this: what would happen in the event that agreement was not reached, if party-union parity was to be upheld at all costs? 'The answer,' he said, 'is rather simple. If no agreement is reached, then neither will we proceed to any action.'[64] At this point Kautsky openly posed the question of the rising bureaucratization of the party itself. The party, he said, was developing a 'weighty apparatus' into which it was not 'so easy to introduce new ideas equipping the party for new actions'. As for the unions, it was necessary to make sure that they had 'a content that would make it impossible for them to act as a brake'.[65] In this fashion Kautsky drew attention to the danger of the formation of a conservative bloc between increasingly bureaucratized party and union apparatuses. His solution was the supremacy of the 'Social Democratic spirit' with which the activities of the unions should be imbued and which should create the preconditions for common action by the entire movement. His amendment to Bebel's resolution declared that 'Social Democracy is the highest and most comprehensive form of the class struggle of the proletariat' and that 'no proletarian organization, no proletarian movement, can be fully up to its task unless it is imbued with the spirit of Social Democracy'.[66] The amendment was rejected.

The Congress discussions showed that the revisionists and the union leaders were quite satisfied with the position of Bebel. Polemics against Kautsky were a constant theme in all their interventions. David attacked Kautskyist 'radicalism' as expressed in the article of 28 January in *Vorwärts*. Kolb accused Kautsky of dogmatism, inconsistency, and lack of courage (anyone, he said, who is convinced that contradictions are sharpening 'should also have the courage to draw the logical conclusions and to say that we must prepare for this final, decisive struggle').[67] Quarck

[62] Ibid., p. 247.
[63] Ibid., p. 254.
[64] Ibid., p. 257.
[65] Ibid., p. 257.
[66] Ibid., p. 143.
[67] Ibid., p. 263.

and Gradnauer hailed the new course of relations between the party and the unions. Bömelburg retorted to Kautsky that the unions had no need of socialist lessons, since they were faithful to socialism by their very nature. For his part, Bebel told Kautsky that no question of principle divided them, but that it was necessary to avoid any resolution, 'correct or incorrect', that could sound like party abuse of the unions or union abuse of the party. Bebel's resolution declared that 'the deliberations of the Cologne Trade-Union Congress are not in conflict with the deliberations of the Jena [Party] Congress' and that 'any controversy over the significance of the Cologne deliberations' was 'outmoded'. It also maintained that in the event of a mass strike, the party and the unions would have to proceed in mutual agreement, that the unions were equal to the party, and that (and here there was a compromise with Kautsky's position, a portion of his amendment being accepted in softened form) the trade-union movement ought to be inspired by the 'Social Democratic spirit'. This resolution was adopted by an enormous majority, 386 in favour and 5 against. Among those voting in favour were Kautsky, Rosa Luxemburg, and Karl Liebknecht.

Kautsky's commentary in *Die Neue Zeit* on the significance of the Mannheim Congress is testimony to his incomprehension and self-delusion about it. He clung to the superficial fact that both the party and the unions had acknowledged the value of the mass strike, remarking with satisfaction: that the unions had accepted 'the point of view of the party' on the mass strike; that 'a powerful step forward on the road to fruitful collaboration between party and unions' had been taken; that just as the Dresden Congress had signalled the end of theoretical revisionism, the Mannheim Congress put an end to the hopes the enemy had placed in 'practical revisionism'; and that 'the mark of Mannheim' was 'above all a decisive left turn within the trade unions'.[68]

The historic victory of the trade-union bureaucracy and the retreat of the party before its show of force were thus hailed by the most prominent theoretician of the SPD as a great affirmation of the revolutionary spirit of the German workers' movement. 'It has been years,' Kautsky concluded, 'since there has been any party congress at which resistance to the revolutionary spirit was so weak as on this occasion.'[69]

The real significance of the congress, however, did not escape the revisionists, who cried victory in exuberant tones. Their comments were lucid and realistic. The *Münchener Post*, organ of Bavarian Social

[68] 'Der Parteitag von Mannheim', in NZ, XXV, 1906–7, vol. I, pp. 7–8, 10.
[69] Ibid., p. 10.

Democracy, observed that the congress had achieved full agreement between the party and the unions; that the conflict which had arisen in Dresden was now a thing of the past; that there could be no doubt whatever that the Mannheim deliberations on the mass strike had mirrored the 'growing influence of the unions in the party'; that Kautsky in particular had suffered a defeat; and finally, that the congress 'augured well' for the future of the German labour movement.[70] Von Elm, writing in the columns of the *Sozialistische Monatshefte*, spoke of a 'new era' in the history of the SPD, the conditions for which had been created by the repudiation of any anarcho-syndicalist temptations in the party.[71] David likewise applauded the great defeat suffered by the 'radicals'.[72] Kolb expressed confidence that the results of the congress had put the party back on the right road after so much controversy.[73]

[70] M. A., 'Der Parteitag von Mannheim', in *Münchener Post*, 3 October 1906.

[71] A. von Elm, 'Die Gewerkschaftsdebatte auf dem mannheimer Parteitag', in *Sozialistische Monatshefte*, no. 10, October 1906, pp. 834, 839.

[72] 'Die Bedeutung von Mannheim', in *Sozialistische Monatshefte*, no. 11, November 1906, p. 907.

[73] W. Kolb, 'Das badische Blochexperiment und seine Lehre für die Sozialdemokratie', in *Sozialistische Monatshefte*, no. 12, December 1906, p. 1020.

IV
'The Road to Power'

1 The Electoral Defeat of 1907: Imperialism, Patriotism and Social Democracy

In spite of all internal conflicts, the SPD had experienced an uninterrupted rise in strength ever since the end of the Emergency Laws. The great electoral victory of 1903 had particularly fortified the party's sense of security, which Kautsky ceaselessly interpreted in terms of social and ideological destiny. The election results of January 1907 thus came as the proverbial bolt out of the blue. The SPD obtained 3,259,000 votes; its percentage of the total vote fell from 31.7% in 1903 to 29% in 1907 and its number of seats in parliament dropped from 81 to 43. It was a stinging defeat.

One of the reasons for this reverse was the swing of a large section of petty-bourgeois public opinion towards acceptance of the imperialist policy of the ruling classes. Germany's isolation after the Moroccan crisis of 1905 and the heated domestic controversy over what attitude to take towards the native revolts in the German colonies in Africa had caused a violent division in the country. Nationalist currents, cleverly manipulated by Chancellor von Bülow, denounced Social Democracy as an antinational and anti-patriotic force. The 1907 elections thus became a plebiscite on the future of Germany as a great power and its role in world affairs. This was the first real encounter of the SPD with the integrating force of contemporary imperialism. Indeed, as Kautsky himself documented in his book *Sozialismus und Kolonialpolitik*, the party harboured decidedly pro-imperialist and pro-colonialist currents within its own ranks. The SPD, which had gone into the electoral battle fully confident and generally defending positions of clear opposition to the imperialist policy of the ruling class, received a jolt that had in no way been foreseen, or even deemed possible.

The programme the party had presented to the electors, in addition to advocating a series of democratic rights and reforms (universal suffrage, reduction of the working week, opposition to the bureaucratic régime, anti-protectionism, etc.), also focused on colonial policy, which it denounced as useless for the national interest and liable to stimulate internal corruption.[1] *Vorwärts* had intimated to its readers that Germany's role in world politics was a central issue in the elections, calling upon them to vote for the SPD in order to prevent 'the conflict of the cartels and trusts on the world market from triggering a devastating world war'.[2] After the defeat, the central organ of the party acknowledged that the election results left the door open to a 'world imperialist policy in the grand style' on the part of Germany.[3]

Who was to blame for the defeat? What were its causes? The party leadership believed that, as well as the general atmosphere of intensified social and political struggle and the ability of the bourgeoisie to forge a bloc with the peasantry and broad sectors of the middle classes, the main factors responsible were the fear the Russian Revolution had generated among wide strata and the wave of nationalism set off by colonialism and imperialism.[4] The revisionists claimed as one man, although with varying emphases, that the radicals were to blame for the defeat. They also maintained that if Social Democracy was to make further progress, it would have to insert itself more deeply into 'national reality'. The starkest and most violently polemical tones were sounded by Richard Calwer, an openly pro-imperialist Social Democrat, who called upon the party to break with liberalism and anti-colonialism (he considered colonialism a vital necessity of capitalist development) and to accept the prospect of the formation of a Central European zone under German hegemony (the main axis of German expansionist strategy). The SPD, Calwer said, should not play into the hands of foreign capitalists by adopting a policy of opposition to the government and should dispose once and for all of the doctrinaire notion of the radical wing, which was leading the party to isolation.[5] Bernstein, although without going to the lengths of Calwer's apologia for colonialism, also emphasized that he

---

[1] Cf. the text of the programme, 'Unser Wahlprogramm', in *Vorwärts*, 4 January 1907.

[2] 'Deutsche Wirtschafts- und Weltpolitik', in *Vorwärts*, 19 January, 1907.

[3] 'Der neue Reichstag', in *Vorwärts*, 8 February 1907.

[4] Cf. the text of the communiqué of the party leadership in *Münchener Post*, 12 February 1907.

[5] R. Calwer, 'Der 25. Januar', in *Sozialistische Monatshefte*, no. 2, February 1907, pp. 103–7.

thought the party's approach to the struggle against colonial expansion was mistaken and stressed the negative effect on public opinion of the anti-revisionist campaign conducted by the radicals.[6] In one interview, in particular, he deplored the deleterious influence of Kautsky, 'the repository of orthodox Marxism'.[7] On the opposite side, Rosa Luxemburg argued optimistically: the elections, she said, could be considered a defeat only if assessments were restricted exclusively to the electoral level; the isolation of Social Democracy in an atmosphere of imperialist nationalism and reaction indicated that the party was on the correct road leading to the revolution. 'The election results show,' she said in a lecture, 'that bourgeois society is rapidly approaching its end.'[8]

For his part, Kautsky acknowledged the blow represented by the defeat of 25 January. 'In the nearly forty year history of German Social Democracy,' he wrote, 'there has been no surprise like that of the recent elections.' He traced the general reasons for the defeat to the very repercussions of the strength of Social Democracy. The bourgeoisie, frightened not only by the electoral success of 1903 but also by the Russian Revolution, had succeeded in dragging considerable forces in its wake. Kautsky did introduce a new element into his analysis, however, which pointed in a direction opposite to his traditional conviction that the bourgeoisie was steadily declining in self-confidence and hence was chronically incapable of instilling a conservative ideology into the broad masses of the population. He admitted that the SPD had 'underestimated the attractive power of the colonial idea in bourgeois circles' and also acknowledged 'the spellbinding effect' that 'the colonial state of the future' had exercised even on those who 'have no economic interests in the colonies'.[9] To this factor he added another: the rancour of layers of the petty bourgeoisie against the party and the trade unions for having allegedly caused, through wage increases and consumer cooperatives, a decline in the standard of living of the middle classes and a rise in prices.[10] Now that the government could proceed freely with its projects, Kautsky held that only a reinforcement of the proletarian character of the party and of its organizational strength could provide the correct way towards a future recovery.[11] In an article published in *Vorwärts* he discussed the dis-

---

[6] E. Bernstein, 'Was folgt aus dem Ergebnis der Reichstagwahlen?', in *Sozialistische Monatshefte*, no. 2, February 1907, pp. 111–13.

[7] 'Ein Interview Bernsteins in "Temps"', in *Vorwärts*, 15 February 1907.

[8] Cf. the text in *Vorwärts*, 9 March 1907.

[9] 'Der 25. Januar', in NZ, XXV, 1906–7, vol. I, pp. 588–9.

[10] Ibid., p. 592.

[11] Ibid., pp. 594–5.

appointment that had arisen because 'for two decades' the SPD had become 'accustomed to expect only victories'. He also declared that the elections marked the end of any hope in the Progressive Liberals as an opposition party, since they had blatantly jumped on to the government bandwagon. He concluded that Social Democracy could and should count only on its own forces, confident of its own indestructibility.[12]

The electoral defeat of 1907 had almost immediate repercussions on the SPD's official attitude toward national debates on military issues and foreign affairs. Its traditional slogan of a people's militia as the alternative to a Prussian-type army, and its aversion to autocratic Russia, both legacies of the past, no longer sufficed to define a strategy in the epoch of the armaments race and of a confident imperialism. The chauvinist and colonialist wave that had played so large a part in its electoral defeat now made the SPD leadership very concerned to present an image to the country that would shield the party from the charge that it was an anti-national force.

In fact, this concern pre-dated the events of 1907. It is significant that even Bebel, not to mention the right of the SPD, had taken a lukewarm attitude toward the anti-militarist agitation conducted by Karl Liebknecht with particular vigour after 1904. Liebknecht maintained that this agitation was necessary if the authority of the officer corps over the mass of soldiers was to be weakened. It was plain that Bebel feared that the pursuit of anti-militarist propaganda by Liebknecht, which had culminated in February 1907 with the publication of his book *Militarismus und Antimilitarismus*, could lead to a direct conflict with the authorities and thus endanger the peaceful work of the party. A symptomatic hint of his prudence had occurred at the Mannheim Congress, during the discussion of whether the mass strike should be used in the event of the threat of a German military intervention in support of the Tsar in Russia. Bebel opposed this, claiming that the strike would in practice be not merely useless but also extremely dangerous for the future of the party – a statement that excited protests from Rosa Luxemburg.

The lessons that the leadership of the party and of the parliamentary caucus intended to draw from the January electoral defeat were eloquently revealed during the Reichstag debate on the military budget in April 1907. Bebel attacked Prussian discipline and the mistreatment of soldiers, protested against the financial burdens of military spending which fell on the shoulders of the masses, and maintained that a militia could assure national defence more effectively than the army. Noske then rose to make

[12] 'Das Ergebnis der Wahlschlacht', in *Vorwärts*, 27 January 1907.

a speech (on 24 April) that was to become the object of bitter controversy in the party, and to spur Kautsky to take up the question of the relationship between patriotism and Social Democracy. Noske contested the accusation that Social Democracy was an anti-national and anti-patriotic force. He said that there was no accusation 'more unjustified' than the claim that the SPD wanted to undermine the discipline of the army. 'Where in Germany,' he asked, 'except in the army, is there greater discipline than in the Social Democratic Party and the modern trade unions?' He continued, sliding faster and faster down the slope: 'As a Social Democrat I agree with the honourable Minister of War when he declares that German soldiers must have the best arms.'[13] Finally, he proclaimed that the Social Democrats would repel any aggression against their country 'with greater determination' than any bourgeois party, that the SPD wanted Germany to be 'armed as well as possible', and that 'the entire German people' had an 'interest in the military institutions necessary for the defence' of the 'fatherland'.[14] There could have been no more public funeral for the anti-militarist propaganda preached by Liebknecht.

Anxiety at the effects of anti-militarism, exhibited by some Social Democrats in the Reichstag debate in April, was also displayed by the German delegation to the Congress of the Socialist International held in Stuttgart in August 1907. Bebel declared the Germans' opposition to any recourse to the general strike in time of war, claiming that this was inapplicable under German conditions, thus attracting explicit criticism from Jaurès. The resolution that was finally adopted unanimously (proposed by Lenin, Rosa Luxemburg, and Martov) stated that when confronted with the threat of war the parties of the International pledged themselves to employ the most effective means (which were not defined) to prevent the outbreak of hostilities and, in the event of war, to do their utmost to bring it to a halt as rapidly as possible, seizing upon the crisis thus created to hasten the end of capitalist rule. This resolution, however, certainly failed to induce German Social Democracy to abandon its own moderate attitude. The SPD emerged from the International Congress as the party most afraid of appearing an anti-national force.

In 1905, the year of the Moroccan crisis and the intensification of German rearmament, Kautsky had written several articles dealing with Social Democracy's attitude toward war. In an initial essay, *Patriotismus, Krieg, und Sozialdemokratie*, he stressed the importance of proletarian

[13] 'Verhandlungen des Reichstags', XII, I Sess., 38. Sitz. vol. 228, Berlin, 1907, p. 1100.
[14] Ibid., p. 1101.

internationalism as the antidote to bourgeois nationalism and went on to discuss precisely those crucial points that were to be debated at Stuttgart two years later. He argued that 'the difference between offensive war and defensive war' was 'highly dubious in the majority of cases'.[15] As for the attitude of the proletariat in the event of war, Kautsky, expressing a viewpoint that was shared by Bebel, called 'the idea of a military strike' 'heroic folly' devoid of all practical value. 'As long as we do not have the strength to prevent the policy that leads to war,' he explained, 'we will also be unable to muster the strength to prevent the war.' All attempts to oppose war once it was a reality 'are condemned to failure'.[16] What, then, should be the line of Social Democracy in the event of war, after the failure of all attempts to prevent hostilities? Kautsky maintained that the proletariat was not yet strong enough to respond to war with revolution (since that would mean a military strike). 'But,' he continued, 'it [the working class] is sufficiently strong in all the capitalist states [and here the line that would later be expressed in the Lenin–Luxemburg–Martov resolution approved at Stuttgart is discernible] to make sure that any damaging and useless war becomes the point of departure for a revolution that would establish a proletarian régime and thus open the road to a lasting peace.'[17]

This article by Kautsky was expressly cited during the 1907 Reichstag debate by Chancellor von Bülow, who accused Kautsky, 'interpreter of Marxist dogmatism', of giving voice to an anti-national point of view. The chancellor also expressed the conviction that 'the great mass of German workers' would 'do their duty' in the event of war.[18] Kautsky answered von Bülow by saying that the proletariat could consider a war 'just' only if it constituted the 'continuation of its own domestic policy, directed against any exploitation or oppression'. Such a war, however, exceptional enough by nature, was no longer a realistic contingency. As for the difference between offensive and defensive war, it was 'too formalistic'. What was important was 'not the form' but 'the content'.[19]

In a series of articles published in the *Leipziger Volkszeitung* in May 1907, just after the April Reichstag debate and the 'Noske case', Kautsky dealt more systematically with the relationship between patriotism and Social Democracy. He maintained that bourgeois patriotism was a product of inter-imperialist conflicts and constituted the prelude to the

[15] 'Patriotismus, Krieg, und Sozialdemokratie', in NZ, XXIII, 1904–5, vol. II, p. 366.
[16] Ibid., p. 370.
[17] Ibid., p. 371.
[18] Quoted in *Vorwärts*, 15 December 1905.
[19] 'Patriotismus und Sozialdemokratie', in *Vorwärts*, 16 December 1905.

'ruin' of the nation.[20] From the practical standpoint, the contemporary situation was determined by the fact that 'in no country' was Social Democracy 'yet strong enough to force a limit to armaments', although 'in all cases it is already strong enough to make governments fear war, behind which they see the threat of revolution'.[21] What was to be done in the event of war? In the preface to a pamphlet published in June 1907 collecting all these articles Kautsky indicated the line the SPD should take in such an eventuality: 1) combat any chauvinist wave, appearing before the masses as an intransigent opponent of the war; 2) prepare, step by step, to harvest the fruits of popular opposition as the inevitable disillusionment with the war developed; 3) thus, 'at the end of the war' prepare to achieve 'great successes'; 4) oppose proposals of the type advanced by the French anti-militarist Hervé, to 'provoke a catastrophe at the beginning of the war that would break the back of the masses for a long period'.[22] This time (unlike in his 1905 articles) Kautsky did not speak explicitly of revolution as a consequence of war but limited himself to predicting the certainty of 'great successes'. In addition, it was significant that he indicated a road of opposition to the war based on ideological agitation, without any sort of action that could be construed as extra-legal (strikes, demonstrations, etc.). Kautsky's approach remained essentially legalistic, fearful of any action that might endanger the official existence of the party. His rapprochement with the positions of Bebel was quite evident. So too was his turn away from the views expressed in the January 1906 article in *Vorwärts* and the October 1906 preface to the second edition of *Die soziale Revolution*, towards more moderate positions.

Meanwhile, the attitude taken by Noske during the Reichstag debate on the military budget had incited a violent dispute throughout the party.[23] A particularly sharp attack was launched against Noske by the *Leipziger Volkszeitung*, which accused him of having capitulated to the pressures of nationalism in order to draw applause from the bourgeois and government press.[24] Bernstein, on the other hand, had taken up the defence of Noske in the name of the revisionists, maintaining that on the questions of both 'militarism in general' and 'defence of the fatherland in

[20] *Patriotismus und Sozialdemokratie*, Leipzig, 1907, p. 12. The articles cited above are collected in this pamphlet.
[21] Ibid., p. 24.
[22] Ibid., p. 5.
[23] Cf. the summary of the debate on the party press presented by *Vorwärts*, 8 and 16 May 1907, under the title 'Militarismus und Sozialdemokratie'.
[24] 'Kehrt Marsch nach Damaskus?', in *Leipziger Volkszeitung*, 29 April 1907.

particular' the SPD deputy had merely expressed the proper Social Democratic point of view. If anything was damaging to the party, Bernstein said, it was anti-militarist propaganda.[25]

The 'Noske case' exploded resoundingly at the Party Congress held at Essen in 1907 (15–21 September), revealing the full extent of the internal conflicts within the party, if revelation was indeed necessary. Noske declared that his parliamentary speech was 'a natural consequence of the position on war maintained by Social Democracy up to now' and that the criticism directed against him from the left would lead 'straight into the anarchist camp'. To defend himself against these criticisms he stated that he subscribed 'word for word' to what Kautsky had written in the introduction to *Patriotismus und Sozialdemokratie*.[26] Bebel also defended Noske and identified his own position with the latter's. In addition, he declared himself prepared to 'shoulder arms' in the event of a defensive war against Russia, rampart of reaction in Europe, 'on which reaction in Germany relies in the first instance'.[27] Bebel thus sanctioned a patriotic war against Russia conducted by the army and government of the Kaiser, on the grounds that Russia was the bulwark of reaction, even in Germany. The resolutely anti-militarist positions of Liebknecht and Zetkin were singled out for attack by revisionists like Vollmar and David, who declared their complete satisfaction with the positions of Noske and Bebel.

Kautsky intervened in the debate in a direct polemic against Bebel over the possibility of the SPD's allowing itself to be lured into a war of defence, the reality of which was exceedingly ambiguous in any event and was likely to draw the party and the proletariat into the propagandistic falsifications of the government. After emphasizing the ambiguity of the concepts of 'aggression' and 'defence', Kautsky said, in words that were to be prophetic: 'I could not guarantee that in all events we would be able to grasp such a difference with any certainty, that we would always be in position to know whether the government was leading us by the nose or whether it was representing the national interests against a war of aggression.' He continued: 'We must not allow ourselves to determine our policy on the basis of whether the war is one of aggression or defence. Instead, this must be our criterion: Are the interests of the proletariat and democracy in danger or not?'. Finally, he enumerated the perils of the present situation: 'The outbreak of war would, in effect, be

[25] E. Bernstein, 'Patriotismus, Militarismus, und Sozialdemokratie', in *Sozialistische Monatshefte*, no. 6, June 1907, pp. 435, 439.

[26] *Protokoll über die Verhandlungen des Parteitages der SPD. Abgehalten zu Essen vom 15. bis 21. September 1907*, Berlin, 1907, pp. 229, 230, 231.

[27] Ibid., p. 255.

an international question and not a national question for us, since a war between great states would become a world war, would engulf all Europe, and not merely two countries. One fine day the German government could convince the workers that they were under attack, the French government could likewise convince the French workers, and we would then find ourselves confronted with a war in which the German and French proletariats would march with equal enthusiasm behind their own governments and massacre and slaughter each other. This must be averted, and it will be averted if we reject the criterion of a war of aggression and instead adopt the criterion of the interests of the proletariat, which are international interests. . . . The German workers are in solidarity with the French workers and certainly not with the Prussian reactionaries and junkers.'[28]

At the end of the discussion a resolution was presented stipulating that in parliamentary debates on the military question the floor should be taken only by those deputies capable of offering a 'complete guarantee that they would take a determined position against militarism, along the lines of the resolution of the International Congress' (of Stuttgart).[29] It was rejected by a large majority.

2   On the Sharpening of Class Conflict: 'The Road to Power'

The period 1907–9 was of decisive importance in the history of German Social Democracy and the trade-union movement. The solutions adopted on a series of problems showed that in the conflict between party and trade unions which had erupted at the Mannheim Congress the balance was now swinging decisively to the side of the union leadership. Under the impetus of the effects of the economic crisis that broke out in 1907, which caused a decline in the number of union members in 1908 and 1909, along with a slackening of economic struggles and a hardening of the resistance of the employers, the union leaders questioned the party's call for the traditional strike on 1 May, denouncing it as a dangerous opportunity for reprisals by the employers. The strike was in fact sustained, after much negotiation between the unions and the party about financial aid to those victimized by reprisals. But the incident demonstrated how far the union leaders had drifted from any revolutionary attitude or

[28] Ibid., pp. 261–2.
[29] Ibid., pl 174.

spirit. They likewise resolutely opposed – finding a considerable response within the party – the expansion of the Social Democratic youth movement, which had been founded in 1904, grew under the influence of the events of 1905–6, and was distinguished by its anti-militarist orientation. It was now clear that the SPD was increasingly subject to the initiative and influence of the moderate unions, whose determination and strength had first been unequivocally demonstrated in the turn they had imposed on the party in 1906, after the conflict over the mass strike that had erupted in 1905.

For its part, the SPD was itself witnessing the constant consolidation of a bureaucratic apparatus which, precisely in the period 1906–9, was transformed into a close-knit and carefully selected body of full-time functionaries, primarily concerned to extend the influence of the party by greater administrative and organizational efficiency in the pursuit of fundamentally electoralist objectives. These men were naturally legalist, conservative, traditionalist, little inclined to welcome new ferments or ideological turmoil.

Another eloquent manifestation of the rising strength of the right in the German workers' movement was the violation by the Social Democratic representatives of Baden, Bavaria, and Württemberg of the express prohibition against voting in favour of the state budgets in the *Länder*, which had been laid down at the Congresses of Lübeck (1901) and Dresden (1903).

This substantial consolidation of the positions of the right-wing of the German labour movement occurred during a period that was itself far from tranquil. The economic crisis of 1907–9, which saw about a million unemployed in Germany, a stagnation of production, a rise in the prices of mass consumer goods and industrial products, and a further increase in the prices of raw materials, precipitated widespread unrest among the masses. The most spectacular expressions of revolt were the huge demonstrations in Prussia and Saxony against the class voting system for the *Länder*, which followed one after the other from the last months of 1907 through the spring of 1909. The international situation was now also overshadowed by conflicts between the imperialist states that visibly threatened world peace.

Kautsky's reaction to the changes within the German labour movement and German society on the one hand, and to the deterioration in the international situation on the other, was to advance an analysis that was in many respects quite lucid, as we shall see. But there were two important limits to this lucidity to be noted immediately. Firstly, failing to appreciate the full force of attraction of the imperialist system on the organizations of the workers' movement, he did not realistically assess the influence of theoretical and trade-union 'revisionism'. Secondly, even while correctly evaluating the aggravation of internal and international social conflicts, he preserved an illusory confidence that Social Democracy as a whole remained substantially united. Assuming that the growth of the proletariat as an economically productive class would be automatically reflected in a growing political independence, he did not consider it really possible that the politics and ideology of the bourgeoisie could penetrate into the ranks of the proletarian army. Although he examined the difficulties and dangers ahead seriously, his analysis led him to fundamentally optimistic strategic perspectives. As he saw it, the march of the workers' movement could be interrupted by temporary halts and even setbacks, but it would nevertheless register an irresistible progress, just as the decline of the bourgeois economy and bourgeois politics were equally ineluctable. Kautsky conceived of the reactionary bent of the bourgeoisie and of imperialism solely as symptoms of the decadence of their exponents, and not as signs of the ascent of a new and unscrupulous force capable of victoriously mobilizing the whole society for its designs. For him, the rise of the 'social revolution' remained the dominant tendency of the historical epoch.

In May 1909 Kautsky published *Der Weg zur Macht* (*The Road to Power*), which, as he pointed out in its preface, constituted 'a complement' to his 1902 essay *Die soziale Revolution*.[30] As we shall see, the articles and essays he had written during the period immediately prior to May 1909 generally reflected the central lines of the analysis he put into systematic form in *Der Weg zur Macht*. In his new book he evinced firm confidence in the inevitable exacerbation of internal and international conflicts which would open the door to a revolutionary era, even if, as he was later to say in his autobiography, *Das Werden eines Marxisten*, this work already shows traces of disappointment, in that he had previously overestimated the effects of the Russian Revolution, 'its intensity and duration and therefore the repercussions it could have in the West'.[31]

Kautsky formulated the significance of the economic crisis in the general thesis that it was a 'ridiculous hope' to assume that the cartels and trusts could 'regulate production and thus deal with the crisis'. 'The struggle against the crisis,' he maintained, 'must therefore henceforth be waged only as a struggle against the totality of the capitalist mode of

[30] *Der Weg zur Macht*, Vorrede zur ersten Auflag, Berlin, 1920, p. 3.
[31] *Das Werden eines Marxisten*, op. cit., p. 138.

production and not simply against its parts.'[32] Polemicizing against the conclusions of Tugan-Baranovski's book *Der moderne Sozialismus in seiner geschichtlichen Entwicklung*, Kautsky claimed that the period of rising real wages which had begun in the 1850s in England and the 1870s in Germany was 'at an end'. The new century had ushered in a period of stagnation or even outright decline in wages; workers could not defend themselves through sectoral struggles or partial conquests in parliament.[33] The condition of the workers was the resultant of a series of contradictions: while the productivity of labour was rising, on the one hand the employers' organizations were gaining in strength and on the other hand there was a growth of the proletariat, whose 'struggle for existence' was becoming 'ever more acute'. This proletariat possessed two major weapons: 'theoretical clarity' and 'discipline', the two great forces that had made the development of Social Democracy possible.[34]

In this context Kautsky renewed his attack on the reformists, whose major theoretical and practical sin was their failure to understand that the revolution was an inevitable historical reality. The specific feature of the contemporary situation, Kautsky wrote, was the simultaneous rise in the strength of the two social armies in struggle. This meant that the proletariat had to struggle for the conquest and defence of power: 'What appears to the "reformists" as the peaceful transition to socialism is in fact only the increase in the strength of both contending classes, which face each other in irreconcilable enmity. . . . The transition to socialism thus means the transition to great struggles that will shake the entire structure of the state and are destined to become ever more violent; they can end only through the overthrow and expropriation of the capitalist class.' The possibility and legitimacy of this lay in the fact that the capitalists were no longer indispensable to economic and social development, whereas the proletariat was precisely essential to it. 'The transition to socialism,' wrote Kautsky, ' is only another expression of the constant aggravation of class conflicts, the transition to an epoch of great and decisive class struggles, which we may sum up under the name social revolution.'[35]

The vote of the Southern Social Democratic delegations in favour of the state budgets in their respective *Länder* moved Kautsky to repeat a condemnation he had already expressed in the past. 'So long as the class

[32] 'Zum 1. Mai', in NZ, XXVI, 1907–8, vol. II, p. 114.
[33] 'Verelendung und Zusammenbruch', in NZ, XXVI, 1907–8, vol. II, p. 549.
[34] 'Zum Parteitag', in NZ, XXVI, 1907–8, vol. II, pp. 854, 856.
[35] 'Reform und Revolution', in NZ, XXVII, 1908–9, vol. I, p. 222.

contradiction between the bourgeoisie and proletariat remains irreconcilable,' he wrote, 'there can be no state power' capable of attracting the
confidence of both classes and for which both classes can simultaneously
vote the 'means of existence'.[36] The dangerous path of the Southerners
was a road that led to sectoral interests and parliamentary illusions,
dividing and weakening the proletariat, 'as is demonstrated clearly
enough by party history outside Germany'.[37]

Condemning the Southern Social Democrats' vote for the regional
budgets in violation of the party resolutions, Kautsky took a position at
the SPD Congress in Nuremberg (13–19 September 1908) that clarifies
his attitude toward the struggle between currents within the party – an
attitude that might be termed in a contemporary expression 'democratic
centralism'. He demanded that the minority accept unity in action and
discipline, thus showing that he had not understood that unity and
discipline could be demanded only if strategic and tactical differences had
not gone beyond a certain threshold. After Bebel had censured the
particularism of the Southern Social Democrats and their petty reformism,
Kautsky declared: 'In theory we can certainly be, and are, of differing
opinions, but in tactics we must be united; the minority must yield to the
majority, otherwise we wholly cease to be a party. One can be a good
comrade without believing in the materialist conception of history, but
one is in no sense a good comrade if one does not submit to the congresses
of the party.'[38]

Nevertheless, Kautsky knew very well that behind this practical
behaviour lay an entirely different political strategy and analysis of social
reality. The vigour of the opposition to any reaffirmation of the Lübeck
and Dresden resolutions forbidding Social Democratic parliamentary
delegates to vote for the budgets in the *Länder* was demonstrated not only
by the fact that the resolution to that effect passed by no more than 258
to 119, but also by the fact that 66 delegates from Bavaria, Baden,
Württemberg, and Hesse openly declared that 'in all particular questions
regarding policy in the *Länder*' they recognized the authority only of the
Social Democratic organization of the appropriate *Land*.[39]

In the realm of international relations and imperialist rivalry, Kautsky,
commenting on the rising tension between Austria and Serbia (and

[36] 'Der Parteitag über die Budgetbewilligung', in NZ, XXVI, 1907–8, vol. II, p. 934.
[37] 'Maurenbrecher und das Budget', in NZ, XXVII, 1908–9, vol. I, p. 46.
[38] *Protokoll über die Verhandlungen des Parteitages der SPD. Abgehalten zu Nürnberg vom 13. bis 19. September 1908*, Berlin, 1908, p. 387.
[39] Ibid., p. 426.

thereby among the great powers) over Bosnia-Herzogovina, warned that it was no longer possible to view such events as localized conflicts. Such regional conflicts, he said, threatened to 'provoke a world war'. They must be considered in connection with imperialism, 'which is the policy of capital as a whole in all the great modern states' and caused 'bitter conflicts' that provide the incendiary material that could ignite any partial conflict into a world war.[40] Imperialist rivalry, which corresponded to the political rise of finance capital, had the fundamental effect of rendering the policies of the bourgeoisie within the various states increasingly inflexible. The capitalist class became increasingly reactionary and strove to force the proletariat into a position of isolation. The middle strata would either be proletarianized or become satellites of capital. The danger of the situation for the proletariat was that its numerical growth was not yet matched by sufficient political influence. Hence the necessity of unity and the greatest possible organizational strength. 'The isolation of the proletariat,' Kautsky wrote, 'is growing ever more pronounced: its political influence at this stage is not rising commensurately with its numbers, organization, and economic importance; while as the intermediary attitude of the strata that formerly stood between capital and labour passes away, the predilection of the ruling classes for methods of violent repression against the proletariat is increasing. Simultaneous with this turn in the internal policy of the capitalist states, there has also been a turn in their foreign policy.'[41]

While up to the 1870s European wars had been waged 'in the name of the national idea', in other words, for the unification of divided nations, since the 1880s the trend had been towards the subjugation of foreign nationalities within single states.[42] Surveying the prospects ahead, Kautsky predicted that an Austrian attack on Serbia would certainly lead to world war, with Russia, Italy, England, and France aligned on one side and Germany and Austria on the other.[43]

The pamphlet *Der Weg zur Macht* was directly born of this approach and represented its systematization. Certain chapters and sections of chapters were in fact excerpted from some of these articles we have cited. Kautsky was concerned to reassert the inevitability of the socialist future. 'The proletarian revolution,' he said, 'cannot be halted, since it is inevitable that the working class in its development will oppose capitalist exploitation.'[44] He likewise declared that in the event of a crisis of the

[40] 'Oesterreich und Serbien', in NZ, XXVII, 1908–9, vol. I, p. 863.
[41] 'Oesterreich und die Mächte', in NZ, XXVII, 1908–9, vol. I, pp. 941–2.
[42] Ibid., p. 943.
[43] Ibid., p. 948.
[44] *Der Weg zur Macht*, op. cit., p. 24.

dominant system, 'the only possible revolution is henceforth a *proletarian revolution*'.[45] Given the relationship of classes and the nature of the state, there could be no illusion 'that the proletariat can ever dominate the state together with the property-owning class'. Hence, if a coalition government was formed, it would necessarily be the destiny of the workers' party not merely to be prevented from taking any action in favour of the proletariat, but to become an 'accomplice in repressive actions against the proletariat'. The only practical result would be defeat, 'compromising the party of the proletariat and disorienting and splitting the working-class'.[46]

Kautsky reiterated that the dictatorship of the proletariat was the 'only form' in which the proletariat could exercise 'political power' and its own 'exclusive rule' (*Alleinherrschaft*).[47] On the question of legality and violence, he reproduced to the letter his old point of view as expressed in 'A Social Democratic Catechism': the question of violence would be decided by the reaction of the ruling class to the political rise of a proletariat strong in the consensus of the majority. 'We are neither supporters of legality at any price, nor revolutionaries at any price. We know that we cannot create historical situations at will and that our tactics must conform to these situations,'[48] Kautsky concluded on this point. As for perspectives, he hazarded the prediction (and this was one reason why his work was entitled *The Road to Power*) that it was 'highly probable' that in the rather near future there would be 'significant shifts in the relationship of forces in favour of the proletariat in Western Europe', if not situations of the 'exclusive rule' of the working class.[49]

Of crucial importance in this famous text were the 'conditions' Kautsky described as necessary for arriving at that great shift in the relationship of class forces capable of rendering an anti-popular régime 'untenable': 1) the existing régime must 'counterpose itself to the mass of the people in a decisively hostile manner'; 2) there 'must be a great party that organizes the masses and stands in irreconcilable opposition'; 3) 'this party must represent the interests of the great majority of the nation and enjoy their confidence'; 4) 'confidence in the established régime, in its strength and stability, must be shaken even within its own instruments, the bureaucracy and the army'.[50] But how could one tell whether these conditions existed? The essential test in Germany was the capacity of the proletariat and the party to struggle decisively for the transformation of the semi-

45 Ibid., p. 26.
46 Ibid., p. 28.
47 Ibid., p. 28.
48 Ibid., p. 65.
49 Ibid., p. 65.
50 Ibid., pp. 66–7.

parliamentary régime into a completely parliamentary régime, thereby opening the way for the full deployment of the strength of the party, whose potential was objectively guaranteed by the fact that the majority of voters were now proletarians who had only to be brought to the necessary political consciousness. The road to power lay precisely through this struggle, to be pursued through a combination of methods such as the development of party organization, greater electoral consensus, and the mass strike (which he again recommended should be used with caution).

Kautsky argued that the struggle for democracy could be identified with the struggle for socialism, because of the very nature of the historical situation. Given the isolation of the proletariat, the 'expression "reactionary mass"'[51] had been transformed into a reality, the reactionary mass being composed of all social and political forces other than the proletariat. Under these conditions, there could be 'no more talk of *premature* revolution'. Moreover, in the event of war, the proletariat was the only class that could look forward to its conclusion 'with great calm'.[52]

Kautsky considered any economistic struggle of the traditional type superseded by the existing economic and social crisis and by the reactionary inclinations of the ruling class. What he expected was an inevitable counterposition of two great social armies on the field of battle. 'The decisive weight of proletarian action is once again being thrown into the scales of *politics*, more decisively than at any time in the past two decades. Naturally, the concerns of the workers are still directed in the first instance towards social reforms and the protection of labour. But here there is a general stagnation, which cannot be overcome within the current relationship of forces or present foundations of the state.'[53]

The alternative was now clear: either the strategy of the bourgeoisie, the unleashing of imperialism, or that of Social Democracy, the struggle for socialism: 'Imperialism, as we have seen, is the only hope, the only idea, that still attracts the bourgeoisie. Aside from that there is but one alternative: socialism. The madness of imperialism will thus take hold more and more, until the proletariat acquires sufficient strength to determine the policy of the state, to overcome imperialism, and in this way to replace it with socialism.'[54]

The lucidity of this analysis was incontestable. At the same time,

[51] Ibid., p. 111.
[52] Ibid., p. 105.
[53] Ibid., p. 89.
[54] Ibid., p. 151.

however, it plainly left unanswered key questions which the entire analysis by its very nature posed. There was a serious lack of balance between the image Kautsky presented of domestic reaction and imperialism on the march and the strategic perspective he offered the workers' movement. He saw the social conflict looming, but he predicted it would occur in conditions substantially favourable to an ever stronger proletariat. What was to be done if imperialism fell upon the toiling masses before socialism had reached maturity? What roads would be open then? What choices? It is indicative that Kautsky, while he saw violence as a trap of reaction, was highly cautious in advising the masses to respond to reactionary violence with a general strike. His approach was the consequence of a constant overestimation of the factors that would render the march of Social Democracy to political and social power irresistible and a correlative underestimation of the organized violence of the bourgeoisie as an instrument for the maintenance of capitalist social domination.

In any event, Kautsky's work appeared too radical to the leadership of the party, which requested that it appear as the opinion of the author, without any official character. For their part, the revisionists threatened a scission if *Der Weg zur Macht* appeared under the imprint of the party. They accused Kautsky of leading Social Democracy down the road to isolation and reiterated their own policy of alliance with the petty bourgeoisie and democratization of existing society. The trade-union leaders also rejected Kautsky's theory as completely unacceptable.

Bernstein's analyses during the same period could not have been more different from Kautsky's. In an essay entitled *Die internationale Politik der Sozialdemokratie*, published in *Sozialistische Monatshefte* in May 1909, he presented the danger of war as a distortion of the natural and objective tendencies of the world economy, which pointed precisely in the direction of agreements among states. He wrote: 'The economic development of nations will intensify their enmity: what nonsense! As if nations were petty shopkeepers competing for a limited clientele such that a gain for one necessarily represented a loss for the others. A mere glance at the development of the commercial relations among the advanced countries demonstrates the fallacious character of these ideas. The most industrially developed countries are simultaneously *competitors* and *customers* of one another; likewise, their trade relations expand simultaneously with their mutual competition.' Thus, the most authentic thrust of the epoch was not towards conflict, but towards international concord: 'The era in which peoples attempted to subjugate one another is finished in Europe, and the same will more and more tend to be true in

Asia. We have entered a new epoch, an epoch in which international law will prevail.'[55] The task of Social Democracy in Germany in the new epoch was to develop its parliamentary activity and its campaign for reforms, against a ruling class whose bourgeois-democratic standards were immature.[56]

[55] E. Bernstein, 'Die internationale Politik der Sozialdemokratie', in *Sozialistische Monatshefte*, no. 10, May 1909, pp. 620–21, 623.
[56] Cf. E. Bernstein, 'Revisionismus und Programmrevision', and 'Der Stil des Reformismus', in *Sozialistische Monatshefte*, no. 7, April 1909 and nos. 19–20, October 1909.

V

The Genesis of Kautsky's 'Centrism'

1 Two Strategies for Prussia in 1910

Der Weg zur Macht was published just at a moment when hope was rekindling in the revisionist wing of the SPD of a pact with the Progressive Liberals for a programme of reforms. The Conservative–Liberal bloc had foundered on the need for a financial reform to raise funds for the armed forces. The coalition of agrarian conservatives and commercial-industrial liberals had broken up over the proposals of Chancellor von Bülow, who sought to combine an intensification of indirect taxes, the burden of which fell essentially on the popular masses, with an inauguration of direct taxes at the expense of agrarian interests. In addition to these fiscal programmes, there were projects to reform the electoral system in Prussia, favoured by a spectrum ranging from the National-Liberals and Progressives to the Social Democrats. In the end, the Conservatives succeeded in rejecting Von Bülow's proposed fiscal reform. This led, on 14 July 1909, to the Chancellor's resignation and his replacement by Bethmann-Hollweg, who had hitherto been Prussian Minister of the Interior. The ensuing reorganization of progressive-liberal forces, who in March 1910 founded the Fortschrittliche Volkspartei (Progressive People's Party), and the simultaneous formation of the Hansabund, assembling those business interests opposed to the conservative-agrarian bloc, appeared to the revisionists in the SPD to create the possibility of a new reformist era in Germany.

A major debate erupted in the party. Should the party support the fiscal reform, on the grounds that it struck directly at conservative interests, or should it reject that reform because of its ultimate goals? Should the party adopt a position that would leave the door open to an alliance with the liberals, or should it maintain its position of intransigent opposition? While the reformists waged a battle, beginning at the

133

Magdeburg Congress of 1910, for a reformist course, the radical wing assumed an attitude of intransigence. The SPD, the radicals maintained, could not vote for taxes that were aimed at strengthening imperialism just because some of the taxes were direct and therefore fell on the shoulders of the privileged classes. Kautsky expressed his opposition by affirming that 'if 500 million in new *direct* taxes are requested in the Reichstag in order to continue rearmament over the next several years', Social Democracy could certainly not vote in favour 'simply because the taxes are direct', 'without taking account of how they will be used'.[1] In Kautsky's view, the only proper Social Democratic response to the divisions that had broken out within the bourgeois camp was – as he wrote in September 1910 on the occasion of the Leipzig Congress – not only, or not so much, to exploit 'the contradictions among the bourgeois parties' for legislative purposes, but rather (which was 'much more effective') to launch a propaganda campaign aimed at 'wresting the proletarian masses from the bourgeois parties'. These parties, despite their contradictions, were generally oriented in an increasingly conservative direction. The choice before the SPD, he said, was between the struggle against 'bourgeois society as a whole' and the clumsy attempt of certain SPD deputies to conduct isolated manoeuvres against partial sectors of the conservative front, 'in Prussia only the Junkers, in Baden only the *Ultramontanen*'. Optimistic that 'theoretical revisionism' had been 'buried' definitively, Kautsky was now concerned about '*practical* revisionism', the expression of a particularistic activism.[2]

But what was the concrete road to preservation of the unity of the party and the workers' movement? In effect, the events of 1909 and 1910 were a patent demonstration that the party was highly disunited, and that nothing divided it so acutely as the problem of its guidance of any mass movements.

The promise of electoral reform, like that of fiscal reform, first advanced by Von Bülow in 1908 and later repeated by Bethmann-Hollweg, was not kept. The revisionists had hoped to be able to establish an alliance between Social Democracy and bourgeois and petty-bourgeois sectors of progressive-liberal orientation on the question of the suffrage. But the bloc of Conservatives, Catholics, and National Liberals was more than strong enough to thwart reform, above all in Prussia. The result was that in March 1910 Bethmann-Hollweg withdrew his project, which was in any event a timid scheme that in no way amounted to a genuine democrat-

[1] 'Der Leipziger Parteitag', in NZ, XXVII, 1908–9, vol. II, p. 912.
[2] 'Zum Parteitag', in NZ, XXVII, 1908–9, vol. II, pp. 841–2.

ization of the electoral system. Meanwhile, however, the resistance to reform during the Reichstag debates and the defeat of the Chancellor's proposal were punctuated by mass mobilizations of great intensity in Germany, especially in Prussia. These mobilizations were endorsed by the positions adopted at the Congress of Prussian Social Democracy in January 1910, which declared that extra-parliamentary mass action was the primary way to put an end to the Prussian electoral system and achieve full democratization of municipal elections. The radicalism of the SPD in Prussia, which found a powerful exponent in Heinrich Ströbel, threatened any prospect of alliance between Social Democrats and Progressive Liberals, and therewith the main strategy of revisionism.

The scale of mass agitation in Germany was due not only to the electoral question but also to the material pressures of the economic crisis, which had still not been overcome. These difficulties led to many strikes and lockouts. In February 1910 there were demonstrations in large parts of the Empire, with a mass mobilization that culminated in a gigantic procession in Berlin on 6 March. Broad sectors of the conservative and Catholic press began talking of revolutionary plots. In subsequent months, turmoil steadily increased. In September and October, tension flared up in the Berlin suburb of Moabit, where a strike led to bloody clashes between police and demonstrators. Predictably, these events revived debate over the mass political general strike, which now became a burning issue within the SPD. Was Germany heading for its own 1905? The spread of demonstrations and the struggle against the reactionary electoral system inclined the most radical of the Social Democrats to think so. But the political determination of the conservative forces, who yielded nothing, the resolute resistance of the employers, who were highly organized and prepared for the firmest intransigence, and the strength of the Prussian and Imperial governments, whose police and military reserves remained stable, convinced the SPD leadership, and still more the declared revisionists, that any frontal clash between the mass movement and the state apparatus, backed by the assembled forces of social and political reaction, would infallibly lead to a defeat of the workers' movement, and a general political retrogression in Germany. At the same time, differing assessments of the conjuncture also precipitated a division in the radical wing of the SPD, which had hitherto embraced Luxemburg and Kautsky despite their divergences of outlook. A dispute now broke out between the two which marked the end of the old alignments within the party, and gave rise to the genesis of a 'centre' ranging itself between neo-radicalism and revisionism. Kautsky was to become the principal theoretician of this centre.

Analysing the Russian Revolution of 1905, Rosa Luxemburg had concluded that the Russian working class had set new horizons for proletarian struggle throughout Europe – in its use of the mass strike, in its combination of economic and political actions, and in its dialectic between popular spontaneity and party organization. The most comprehensive fruit of these reflections was her celebrated essay of September 1906, *Massenstreik, Partei und Gewerkschaften* (*The Mass Strike, the Party, and the Unions*). The Russian Revolution, she wrote, had been 'the first historic experience on a very large scale' of the mass strike.[3] It represented for 'the first time in the history of the class struggle' a 'grandiose realization of the idea of the mass strike' and had 'thereby opened a new epoch in the development of the labour movement'.[4] Luxemburg explicitly posed the urgency of applying the 'lessons' of Russia to Europe, and to Germany in particular. This application, she argued, was possible because of the objective 'sharpening of class antagonisms in western Europe'.[5] She pointed to mass struggles and the political general strike as 'the method of motion of the proletarian mass' and the 'phenomenal form of the proletarian struggle in the revolution'.[6] The task of the 'leadership', i.e. the party, was to guide and discipline the spontaneous struggle of the proletariat, which was the expression of objective social conflicts.[7] Elucidating the relationship between masses and party, Luxemburg attacked the mechanistic-bureaucratic conception that it was necessary first to organize the proletariat and then engage the struggle. Rather there was a dialectical unity of the two moments, in which organization was a formal crystallization of the exercise of struggle: 'The rigid, mechanical-bureaucratic conception cannot conceive of the struggle save as the product of organization at a certain stage of its strength. On the contrary, the living dialectical explanation makes the organization arise as a product of the struggle.'[8] Luxemburg also criticized the theory and practice of the SPD towards unorganized workers. She maintained that in a revolutionary period it was not so much formal adherence to an organization that was important, as the revolutionizing value of social struggles and class conflicts. She therefore fought against

[3] 'The Mass Strike, the Political Party and the Trade Unions', in *Rosa Luxemburg Speaks*, New York, 1970, p. 155.
[4] Ibid., p. 156.
[5] Ibid., p. 162.
[6] Ibid., p. 182.
[7] Ibid., p. 190.
[8] Ibid., p. 196.

any 'underestimation of the unorganized proletarian mass and of their political maturity'.[9] Luxemburg continued by saying that there could be no greater error than to fail to understand the significance of the Russian Revolution, which expressed, 'in the particular conditions of Absolutist Russia, the general results of international capitalist development'. The Russian Revolution was thus 'the forerunner of the new series of proletarian revolutions in the West'.[10] The German workers should therefore 'learn to look upon the Russian revolution *as their own affair*, not merely as a matter of international solidarity with the Russian proletariat, but first and foremost *as a chapter in their own social and political history*'.[11] In sum, the German workers' movement had to learn from the Russian.

When the great mass mobilizations erupted in Germany in 1910, Rosa Luxemburg judged that the situation was finally ripe to apply the 'lessons of Russia' in practice. Kautsky, on the other hand, who in *Der Weg zur Macht* had already remarked self-critically that he had not foreseen the 'temporary defeat of the Russian Revolution',[12] drew the opposite 'lesson' from the Russian events. If the great popular upheaval had not succeeded in attaining its objectives in Russia, a country in which the ruling class was much weaker than in Germany, it was unthinkable that the German workers' movement in 1910, in a country with the world's strongest government and an especially powerful army, should throw itself into mass political strikes that would inevitably turn into an open confrontation with the entire state apparatus and the ruling bloc. The inevitable result, as Kautsky was later to say in writing about Rosa Luxemburg after her death, would be 'an annihilating defeat'.[13]

In March 1910, Luxemburg turned to the problem of the type of mass action and party leadership necessary to lend a coherent thrust to the struggle for electoral reform, in an article whose title itself was significant of her approach: *Was weiter?* She declared that the party must 'have a clearly defined plan' for the mass movement.[14] Taking up her theses of 1906 and applying them to the German conjuncture, Luxemburg assigned the party and the trade unions functions which the leaders of these bodies considered thoroughly alien to them. Recalling the assertion of the *Communist Manifesto* that 'the emancipation of the working class must be

[9] Ibid., p. 198.
[10] Ibid., p. 203.
[11] Ibid., p. 204.
[12] *Der Weg zur Macht*, op. cit., p. 33.
[13] *Rosa Luxemburg, Karl Liebknecht, Leo Jogisches*, Berlin, 1921, p. 15.
[14] Rosa Luxemburg, *Gesammelte Werke*, Dietz Verlag, Berlin, 1972, vol. II, p. 289.

the work of the working class itself',[15] she emphasized the internal dynamic of mass mobilizations, which had a dialectical logic of growth of their own: on the one hand they could not be abstractly planned in advance; on the other hand, they would result in demoralization and defeat if they were not supported and guided by the party. 'The manifestations of the will of the masses in political struggle cannot be artificially maintained at a given and constantly equal pitch over time; they cannot be limited to a single form. They must grow, attain their own peaks, find new and more effective forms.'[16] Luxemburg also maintained that a political strike in Germany would revitalize the international socialist movement.[17] In a further article published several days later, with another highly eloquent title, *Zeit der Aussaat*, Luxemburg maintained that it had been decades since a situation so favourable to 'the spread of Social Democratic doctrine' had existed in Germany, and particularly in Prussia. The 'doctrine of the class struggle' would find fertile ground not in the 'grey theory of books' but in the action of the masses and in their street demonstrations.[18] The choice facing the SPD, she said, was between a strategy founded on struggle against mere effects of the capitalist system (militarism, monarchy, etc.) and a strategy of struggle against the capitalist system as a whole.[19] To be sure, demands for democratic reforms were steps forward for the proletariat, but these struggles must be conceived as stages in the march to 'the conquest of political power, for the realization of socialism'.[20] Finally, Luxemburg concluded that victory or defeat could 'not be calculated or decided in advance by anyone'.[21]

The position argued by Rosa Luxemburg, which shifted the decisive terrain of the struggle from parliament to extra-parliamentary action (although she did not counterpose the two), which assigned the workers' organizations the task of directing the spontaneous movement of the masses, and which postulated that the times and forms of proletarian action could not be prescribed in advance, struck at the ABC of conventional Social Democratic practice. In the eyes of the party and trade-union leaders, she had sinned above all by tending to divest these organizations of their right to control popular struggles, in other words, of the very

[15] Ibid., p. 299.
[16] Ibid., p. 290.
[17] Ibid., pp. 298–9.
[18] Ibid., pp. 300–1.
[19] Ibid., p. 302.
[20] Ibid., p. 303.
[21] Ibid., p. 303.

possibility of subordinating them to a strategy conceived within the framework of preestablished legality. In addition, by insisting on the inevitable and intrinsic element of risk involved in any great class conflict, she threatened the sense of security that accompanied their practices of control.

Kautsky declared openly against Luxemburg's theses, on the fundamental grounds that any appeal to the Russian Revolution henceforward obscured the contrast of specific conditions in Russia and Western Europe. The prevailing class relations were different and so, therefore, were their consequences for socialist strategy. So far as the German situation was concerned, Kautsky was persuaded – as was Franz Mehring, who expressed the view in *Die Neue Zeit* that the SPD had 'every reason' not to ignite the powderkeg before the coming elections to the Reichstag, on which it should concentrate all its reserves[22] – that the strategy of Social Democracy had to be contained fundamentally within the limits of the parliamentary struggle. In that manner the fruits of extra-parliamentary agitation could be harvested in the form of electoral gains. To Luxemburg, who maintained that the Russia of 1905 had something to teach the Germany of 1910, and that any mass movement tended by nature to unite economic and political struggles closely and dialectically, Kautsky objected: 1) that the reference to Russia in 1905 was not valid; 2) that in Germany, where political and civil rights had already been won, economic demands could not be immediately connected to political demands in the course of struggle. It was the lack of any political rights for the Russian proletariat that turned any major movement in the Tsarist Empire into a political struggle. Hence the dialectic cited by Rosa Luxemburg was merely an aspect of the specificity of Russian conditions. In addition, it was natural that wherever a revolution broke out mass struggle would combine both dimensions; in Germany, however, the revolution was yet to come. To try to lend a revolutionary form to a content that was not revolutionary would be to sow defeat. Moreover, Luxemburg had not taken account of another glaring difference between Russian and German conditions, which, once introduced into the argument, demonstrated the divergences between the 1905 process in Russia and the 1910 process in Germany: 'So far as the Russian example is concerned . . . the first successful mass strike was waged there under conditions that do not exist in Prussia today: a war ignominiously lost, an army disorganized, all classes of the population full of hatred and contempt for the government. [In Russia] the mass strike represented the

[22] F. Mehring, 'Die sicherste Politik', in NZ, XXVIII, 1909–10, vol. I, p. 914.

final blow that brought down a tottering regime. We today cannot take any initiatives on the basis of such an example.'[23]

Taking up the military analogy introduced by Luxemburg, who had asserted that 'street demonstrations, like military manoeuvres, are usually only the prelude to the struggle',[24] Kautsky wrote that 'modern military science distinguishes two types of strategy, the *strategy of annihilation* and the *strategy of attrition*',[25] which corresponded to two different phases of a relationship of forces and could not be abstractly counterposed. In the past, before the conquest of political freedoms and the right to organize, the workers' and people's movement lacked the conditions in which to wage struggles of attrition and was therefore compelled to undertake decisive sorties. (Russia, according to Kautsky, was still in just this phase.) 'The strategy of attrition [*Ermattungsstrategie*] was impossible for the revolutionary class at first. To arrive at it the ground had first to be prepared through the right to vote, the right of assembly, freedom of the press, freedom of association.' To be sure, the strategy of attrition did not exclude battles, but it entered them under proper conditions: 'The strategy of attrition differs from the strategy of annihilation [*Niederwerfungsstrategie*] only in the fact that it does not aim at the decisive battle directly, but prepares it long in advance and is only inclined to engage such a battle when it considers the enemy to have been sufficiently weakened.'[26]

Kautsky – and here the origin of his 'centrism' can be seen – was also concerned to distinguish his own position from that of the revisionists. He claimed that a strategy of attrition had nothing in common with the tactic of revisionism, since the former 'begins from the irreconcilability and constant aggravation of the class conflict between the proletariat and the possessing classes, whereas the latter expects an attenuation of class conflicts'.[27] Given these premises, Kautsky branded the positions of Luxemburg as a misunderstanding of the conjuncture and her theories of the dynamic of the mass struggle as general psychological considerations that would remain valid 'for any mass action'.[28] He wrote sarcastically: 'Once a mass action begins, it is necessary to rush forward rapidly, from street demonstrations to the demonstrative strike, from the demonstrative strike to the strike that drives the enemy to the wall, and then

[23] 'Was nun?', in NZ, XXVIII, 1909–10, vol. II, p. 36.
[24] Luxemburg, *Gesammelte Werke*, op. cit., p. 289.
[25] 'Was nun?', op. cit., p. 37.
[26] Ibid., p. 38.
[27] Ibid., p. 39.
[28] Ibid., p. 69.

what? What "intensification" yet remains?'[29] Kautsky maintained that such a line, proper in the Russian situation Luxemburg was examining, was contradicted not only by the prevailing conditions in Germany but also by the 'experiences on which the strategy of attrition of our party is based'.[30] 'It would have been quite frivolous,' he wrote, 'for our party to have pledged itself to settle accounts with a powerful enemy like the caste of Junkers and the Prussian government in the space of several months. But we have never done this. German Social Democracy has never raised the slogan: annihilation of the present régime through ever more intensive actions in the space of several months, but only the slogan: *no truce in Prussia until the right to direct, secret, equal suffrage is won.*'[31]

Luxemburg's advocacy of a forward march punctuated by 'hurrahs' would place the proletariat before a stark alternative: 'either annihilate [the enemy] or be annihilated'.[32] Kautsky did not absolutely exclude the use of a strategy of annihilation, i.e. a frontal conflict; it was appropriate, he said, in two specific cases: either if the enemy became extremely weak or if it threatened the freedom of action already won by the proletariat and therewith its possibilities of political and organizational development. Both such cases, however, would require the necessary prior accumulation of forces.

It was now time for Rosa Luxemburg and Kautsky to draw the final balance of their divergent analyses of the German situation and of their different conceptions of the revolutionary process. In doing so, they suddenly revealed the depth of the cleavage that had arisen between two comrades who had previously been the ideological leaders of the long struggle of the radicals against revisionism.

In her article *Ermattung oder Kampf?* Rosa Luxemburg accused Kautsky of separating the phases of the mass movement with formal and scholastic distinctions that were wholly unrelated to reality. She repeated that analogies with Russia were all the more valid if Germany itself was also heading into 'times of tempestuous conflict between the proletariat and ruling reaction', as was presently the case.[33] The real alternative facing the SPD in Prussia, she said, was between a line directed at containing the electoral movement within the limits of bourgeois liberalism, in alliance with the Liberals, and a line designed to fortify the class independence of the proletariat and to prosecute a 'comprehensive

[29] Ibid., p. 69.
[30] Ibid., p. 69.
[31] Ibid., p. 71.
[32] Ibid., pp. 71–2.
[33] Luxemburg, *Gesammelte Werke*, op. cit., p. 353.

critique of the general economic and political class relations'.[34] Kautsky, she wrote, confined himself to proposing 'nothing other than a strictly parliamentary line'. He refused to understand that the use of the mass strike under German conditions now constituted a necessary complement to parliamentary action.[35] Having said all this, Luxemburg delivered her harshest blow: Kautsky was giving theoretical cover to the positions of moderates within the party and trade unions who aspired to nothing more than a return 'as quickly as possible to the old comfort of the daily parliamentary and trade-union routine'.[36]

Kautsky in turn charged that 'Luxemburgism' represented a new strategy. He insisted that this strategy was founded on a fundamental methodological error, namely inability to grasp specific conjunctures and produce specific analyses. It was an accusation Kautsky had already levelled against Luxemburg at the beginning of the polemic. But now, in response to her article *Ermattung oder Kampf?*, Kautsky developed his argument more systematically. The problem, he maintained in his essay *Eine neue Strategie*, was not to establish analogies between the mass mobilizations in Russia in 1905 and those in Prussia in 1910 and then, on that basis, to uphold similar tactics and strategy. Instead, these mobilizations had to be situated in the differing class, social, political, and state relations prevailing in the two countries. Kautsky's view of the context of the Russian experience was as follows: 1) in 1905 the Russian government was the weakest in the world; 2) this government was no longer receiving consistent support from any social class, since even the capitalists and big landlords considered its weakness and incapacity the cause of the crisis in the country; 3) the military defeats inflicted by the Japanese had completely disorganized and demoralized the army, which deprived Tsarism of its customary capacity for repression; 4) the peasants had begun a massive social agitation. In these circumstances, he said, the industrial proletariat was able to stamp the strike movement with a revolutionary character: 'this was the situation in which the mass strike movement grew and eventually acquired irresistable force'.[37] In addition, the fact that proletarian action in Russia was identical to the mass strike arose from the conditions of the working-class itself, which in the absence of 'any possibility of legal organization' was able to manifest its protest in no other way than through 'a *single* method: the *strike*'. Hence,

[34] Ibid., p. 356.
[35] Ibid., p. 361.
[36] Ibid., p. 371.
[37] 'Eine neue Strategie', in NZ, XXVIII, 1909-10, vol. II, pp. 366-7.

'the strike became a vital necessity for the Russian workers'.[38] To attempt mechanically to transpose this situation into a different context, Kautsky told Luxemburg, was merely an abstract exercise. 'Even Cervantes knew that what is heroism in one set of conditions becomes Don Quixotism in another.'[39] If the conditions of Prussia were examined concretely – not on the basis of the single element of the presence of mass mobilizations and the necessity for the proletariat to rebuff the policies of reaction, but rather in the light of the whole balance of class forces – it should be obvious that they needed a strategy that took full account of their specificity. 'In present-day Prussia the situation is completely different from that in Russia five years ago,' Kautsky argued. 'Here we have to deal with the strongest government that exists anywhere. In no other country are the army and bureaucracy so highly disciplined,' in no other country was the cult of power so strongly rooted among broad layers of the masses themselves. Behind the state stood, 'in solid manner', a class of exploiters 'of unequalled strength and brutality'. Hence the analogy with Russia so dear to Rosa Luxemburg, when considered properly, turned out to be quite false: 'In Russia in 1905 the government was completely isolated. In Prussia today it is the proletariat that is isolated in any action.'[40] But the relationship of class forces was not the only factor that distinguished the Germany of 1910 from the Russia of 1905. Also different – and this, Kautsky said, was what Luxemburg did not understand – was the proletariat's relationship to the instruments of its own action. Whereas in Russia the strike was a victory in and of itself, in Germany, where the proletariat could apply its tactics and strategy through its associations, press, elections, etc., the strike had a quite different meaning.[41] It was thus not, as Luxemburg had claimed, the principal form of the revolutionary process. Turning to polemicize against Anton Pannekoek, who had emerged as another exponent of neo-radicalism, Kautsky revealed how far he stood from any position that lent essential weight to extra-parliamentary action as opposed to legal-parliamentary action. It was the entire logic of social development, he observed, that was substantially different in Russia and in Germany. 'The notion,' Kautsky wrote, 'of a period of mass strikes that produce no initial practical result but nevertheless erupt continually, with brief respites for the purpose of gathering new forces, until the enemy is brought down, finds its proper justification

[38] Ibid., p. 367.
[39] Ibid., p. 368.
[40] Ibid., p. 368.
[41] Ibid., pp. 368–9.

in the *economic* backwardness of Russia. Such an approach is in complete contradiction with the conditions under which the struggle unfolds in a highly developed industrial country with an advanced concentration of capital and centralized organizations of both the proletariat and the employers and their government.'[42]

Precisely this specificity meant that from the outset a mass political strike in Germany would have to be conducted according to a plan and a precise goal, that it would have to 'take on the entire state', that it would not have the character of a local demonstration. Indeed, such a strike would face a terrible defeat unless it could count on 'a political result'. In Germany it could not be assumed that a strike would alter its character from an economic struggle into a battle for the streets through spontaneous development.[43] Kautsky reiterated his traditional view that the mass political strike was a weapon that could be used only once in Germany; since it was likely to provoke a class confrontation between the proletariat and the state, it would represent an active preparation of the revolutionary climax and not a particular moment of the revolutionary training of the masses. Whereas Luxemburg and those who supported her positions expected '*a period of mass strikes*', he considered the mass political strike, under German conditions, 'a unique event' 'in which the entire proletariat of the Reich brings all its forces to bear' in a 'life and death struggle, a struggle that either brings down our enemies or destroys, or at least paralyzes, all our organizations and all our strength for years'.[44] There followed the most comprehensive definition of the 'strategy of attrition' yet given by Kautsky. It showed that with the ebb of the Russian Revolution and the consequent victory of Tsarist reaction, without the international repercussions he had once expected, the preservation and reinforcement by tried and true methods of the organizational apparatus of the SPD had become the fundamental guarantee of any future proletarian progress for Kautsky. It is striking that he, who had constantly warned against practical and theoretical revisionism and against the danger of bureaucratism, seemed not to perceive what Rosa Luxemburg had so acutely grasped: that a cleavage was arising between a 'goal' that was socialist and a 'means' that was ever more thoroughly administered by a conservative and moderate bureaucracy, which was now concerned to fortify the organization solely within the dominant system.

[42] Ibid., p. 372.
[43] Ibid., p. 373.
[44] Ibid., p. 374.

'By a strategy of attrition,' Kautsky wrote, 'I mean the entirety of the practice pursued by the Social Democratic proletariat since the 1860s. . . . This practice begins with the assumption that the war against the present state and the present society must be waged in such a way as to constantly strengthen the proletariat and weaken its enemies, without allowing the decisive battle to be provoked so long as we are the weaker. We are served by anything that disorganizes our enemies and undermines their authority and combativity, just as anything that contributes to organizing the proletariat, that widens its horizons and combativity, increases the confidence of the popular masses in their organizations. This applies not only to parliamentarism, but also to the movement for wage increases and to street demonstrations that are conducted success-fully.'[45]

In Luxemburg's view these positions represented a major retreat from the positions Kautsky himself had upheld in the past. But the essential point of her reply to Kautsky was a fundamental dissent from his assess-ment of the strength of both the Imperial government and the Prussian government, which motivated her special emphasis on the value of the Russian example for Germany. She considered the judgment that the Bethmann-Hollweg government was the strongest in the world to be a matter of convenience for Kautsky. In her view, the Imperial government was in reality a pure expression of reaction, 'without plan, without political direction', composed of 'flunkeys and bureaucrats instead of statesmen'. It was: 'in domestic policy the plaything of a vulgar clique of junkers and of the shameless intrigues of the court rabble, in foreign policy the plaything of an irresponsible personal régime that only a few years ago was the despicable bootlicker of the "weakest government in the world", Russian Tsarism; it is based on an army composed of Social Democrats to an enormous extent, with the most stupid training and the most infamous mistreatment of soldiers anywhere in the world.'[46]

Kautsky's entire procedure, Luxemburg insisted, amounted in effect to a 'general tendency' to 'construct a sharp opposition between revolu-tionary Russia and parliamentary "Western Europe" and to present the important role the mass strike had played in the Russian Revolution as the product of the economic and political *backwardness* of Russia'.[47] It is interesting to note that precisely those of Kautsky's positions which

[45] Ibid., p. 418–19.
[46] Luxemburg, *Gesammelte Werke*, op. cit., p. 391.
[47] Ibid., p. 395.

Luxemburg regarded as instances of 'marshiness' were considered by Lenin the expression of a realistic assessment of the prevailing relationship of forces in Germany.[48]

2 The 1912 Elections and the 'New Liberalism'

The exhaustion of the mass movement for electoral reform in Prussia emboldened the revisionists to revive their campaign for the formation of a bloc between liberals and Social Democrats in support of reform. The credibility of this project was strengthened by the division that had now erupted in the anti-revisionist camp between the moderates who had adopted more parliamentarist positions and intransigent radicals who advocated essentially anti-parliamentary action. In the meantime, in July 1910, in express violation of the directives of the party leadership and party congresses, the Social Democratic parliamentary caucus in Baden voted in favour of the *Landtag* budget. This deliberate infraction of discipline foreshadowed a general recrudescence of the revisionist line on a national scale. The Party Congress at Magdeburg (18–24 September 1910) revealed the full complexity of the situation and the contradictions that existed within the party. On the question of the reform of the electoral system in Prussia, the revisionists and centrists lined up against the new radicalism, but on the question of the action of the Baden Social Democrats the centrists and new radicals united in condemning the latter's breach of discipline and 'violation of principle'. Luxemburg denounced the position of the revisionists on the Baden issue (and more generally their attempt to restrict the struggle to the parliamentary arena), declaring that 'these deputies attribute no value to a demonstration of opposition to the class state',[49] i.e. to the principle of voting against the budget. On the other major question, that of the mass strike, she maintained that it was illusory to believe that the mass movement could be directed mechanically; the alternative, she said, was either to lend the movement a conscious leadership or to abandon it 'to chaotic confusion'.[50] The opposition of the trade-union leaders to this line was to be expected.

[48] Cf. in this regard R. J. Geary, *Difesa e deformazione del marxismo in Kautsky*, in *Storia del marxismo contemporaneo*, '*Annali*', Feltrinelli, Milan, 1974, p. 91.

[49] *Protokoll über die Verhandlungen des Parteitages der SPD. Abgehalten in Magdeburg vom 18. bis 24. September 1910*, Berlin, 1910, pp. 306–7.

[50] Ibid., pp. 429–30.

The Congress accepted a resolution presented by Luxemburg which repeated that the use of the mass strike to settle the electoral problem in Prussia would be taken into consideration; but significantly the section of the resolution that demanded that the necessary propaganda be conducted for it was deleted. Moving to the Baden incident, the Congress approved a resolution that raised the possibility of expulsion of anyone who further violated congress decisions in this matter. But the proposal of the radicals that such expulsion be automatic was rejected.

In July 1911, just as the SPD was approaching the general elections of 1912, the second Moroccan crisis broke out. Huysmans, the secretary of the International Socialist Bureau, called the attention of the parties of the Second International to the dangers of the crisis and to the necessity of taking a common attitude towards it. The position taken by the leadership of the German Social Democratic Party was very revealing. Primarily concerned with the effects any stance against German foreign policy might have on the party's electoral prospects, it minimized the danger of any major war, showing small inclination towards any international mass action. Luxemburg bitterly denounced the SPD leaders' inability to understand the imperatives of the situation, and accused them of sacrificing the anti-imperialist struggle to the exigencies of parliamentary tranquility. Imperialism was again becoming a question of burning actuality, as was the question of the position Social Democracy should take toward it. How should the danger of war be combated? Wherein did this danger consist? Should Social Democracy fight it alone, or should it seek alliances? Was war inevitable or could it be averted in the end? What was the connection between capitalism and imperialism? Did imperialist capitalism inherently mean war or were there pacific countertendencies among the capitalist forces?

At the Jena Congress of 1911 the radicals, prominent among whom, in addition to Luxemburg, were Lensch, Zetkin, and Liebknecht, launched a fundamental attack on the party leadership, which had taken a substantially passive attitude on the Moroccan question. Luxemburg charged the leadership with inertia in face of the imperialist threat and concluded that it was necessary to develop action among the masses 'against militarism and against colonial policy in general'.[51] She then found herself drawn into a direct and violent polemic with Bebel, behind whom the revisionists rallied. Bernstein's perspectives were the exact opposite of the fears of an aggravation of imperialist conflicts manifested

---

[51] *Protokoll über die Verhandlungen des Parteitages der SPD. Abgehalten zu Jena vom 10. bis 16. September 1911*, Berlin, 1911, p. 349.

by Luxemburg. He declared: 'The war will not occur so rapidly, if indeed it ever does occur.' The danger, he said, was not so much of war as of the negative effects of the warlike spirit 'on the internal politics of various countries'.[52]

In effect, the target date the party was impatiently awaiting was the election of January 1912. It was no accident that the SPD, to which the defeat of 1907 was still a scalding memory, now played down the issue of foreign policy and the danger represented by imperialism, assuming a highly cautious attitude on these questions. The party's aim was to create the most favourable conditions in the electoral contest for good relations with the less conservative liberals, in other words, with those sectors which, although not opposed to the massive German arms programme in principle, were concerned about its domestic economic consequences and attendant fiscal burdens. To facilitate this alliance the SPD abruptly abandoned opposition to the armaments programme, concentrating its election campaign on a common denominator that could appeal to all the party's potential allies: opposition to indirect taxes affecting consumers. The electoral results produced by agreements with the Progressive Liberals confirmed all revisionist expectations: the parties of the Liberal and Social Democratic opposition won the majority of votes (61.4%) and of seats (206 out of 397). The Social Democrats alone obtained 4,250,000 votes (34.8%) and won 110 seats, surging to the fore as the strongest party in the Reichstag. Would this victory usher in a new reformist era in domestic politics? The revisionists were at the height of their optimism. Bernstein wrote that the task of the party was to form a left bloc in the country to struggle for the extension of reforms.[53] But precisely on the question of military spending the National Liberals abandoned the Progressive Liberals and Social Democrats to isolation. The disappointment could not have been more bitter. The electoral victory proved ineffective in altering the relationship of forces between the fundamental classes, and Social Democracy found itself in a situation of practical impasse that was to last to the outbreak of the war. Any possibility of the SPD transforming its position within the framework of the institutions of the Empire had collapsed.

The reformists, full of enthusiasm at the electoral victory, went so far as to hope that German foreign policy might now be 'democratized' as well. If such an objective could be attained, they argued, the precondi-

---

[52] Ibid., p. 239.

[53] E. Bernstein, 'Bedeutung und Aufgaben des Sieges', in *Sozialistische Monatshefte*, no. 3, February 1912, pp. 146–7.

tions for a great national reconciliation would be created. The *Münchener Post* expressed these viewpoints with disconcerting candour: 'A parliament which, in conformity with the Social Democratic programme, assumes the *responsibility for war and peace* would be much less inclined toward a policy of armaments in time of peace than would an adventurist diplomacy conducted behind closed doors. But if a war should come to pass despite everything, at least the danger of this war being waged against the will of the people would be excluded. The "unity of the nation" which is demanded by nationalists in times of serious danger of war cannot be achieved otherwise than through the parliamentarization of foreign policy.'[54]

Declarations like these made it very clear that the revisionists were willing to extend a hand, albeit under specified conditions, even to nationalist circles in Germany.

After his 1910 polemic against Luxemburg, Kautsky was increasingly to characterize his own positions as 'centrist'. His 'centrism' was rooted in a theory that differed from both revisionism and the 'new radicalism', although from now onwards he was to direct his attacks more and more against the 'rebels' of the far left. The theoretical nucleus of Kautskyist centrism became a compact combination of two related hypotheses: that it was possible to break up the bloc of non-socialist forces in domestic politics and that the capitalist forces linked to militarism would not necessarily prevail and provoke a world war. A certain rapprochement with the positions of Bernstein was evident in both cases.

On the question of the electoral agreement between Liberals and Social Democrats, Kautsky revealed how far he had drifted from his previous theses, according to which all non-socialist forces constituted a 'reactionary mass'. His conviction that it was more than ever necessary to rely on increasing the party's influence in parliament led him to look on the prospect of establishing relations with non-socialist sectors with a new interest. On questions of both domestic and foreign policy, he was objectively drawing closer, although with caution and qualification, to arguments he had once combated bitterly during his polemic against the revisionists. He now maintained that capitalist development had generated a 'new' middle class that stood in contradiction to both big capital and the proletariat. The SPD, he argued, should seek to exploit this contradiction, together with its political-ideological expression: the 'new liberalism'.

[54] 'Die Sozialdemokratie und die auswärtige Politik', in *Münchener Post*, 23 January 1912.

'Social Democracy is not alone in the world,' he wrote in an article dealing with the themes of the 1912 election campaign. 'So long as we do not command an absolute majority, it will always be one of our important tasks to exploit the contradictions among the bourgeois parties and to direct the brunt of our attack against those who are most dangerous and damaging to the proletariat at any given moment.'[55]

In September 1911, in an attempt to provide a socio-economic foundation for the policy of electoral pacts with the liberals, Kautsky launched a theme that was to culminate in a famous article, written in February 1912, after the elections. Aside from the big capitalists and the junkers, he said, it was necessary to take account of the strata of the new middle bourgeoisie (small industrialists, artisans, shopkeepers, peasants, the army of white-collar workers, intellectuals, and professionals), who felt threatened by the large industrialists and landlords as much as by the proletariat. These petty-bourgeois strata, incapable of a consistent policy of their own, wanted imperialism but not war; an increase in the exploitation of the proletariat but not the deprivation of its rights or its prostration; the subjugation of the working class through corruption but not through violence; a great fleet and a strong army, but no new taxes. In sum, they wanted capitalism 'but not its consequences'. It was thus in the interest of the proletariat to utilize the contradictions of this 'new middle class', while nonetheless keeping in mind that it was incapable of 'energetic opposition'.[56] It is obvious that in this analysis Kautsky had abandoned his previous point of view that all that could be expected from the petty bourgeoisie was subordination to the most reactionary sectors of capital.

After the elections which had yielded the SPD 110 Reichstag seats and more than 4 million votes, Kautsky let out a cry of triumph: 'Things can't go on much longer, and the great majority is behind us.'[57] It was in this context that he rounded out his argument on the new role of the intermediary strata in an article called *Der neue Liberalismus und der neue Mittelstand*, published in *Vorwärts*. After posing the question of whether there was a renaissance of liberalism in Germany, and if so in what way this could modify the Marxist analysis, Kautsky outlined the terms of the problem in this way:

'If one agrees with Marx that the development of the capitalist mode of production sharpens class conflicts, then the contraction of the bourgeois world into a single reactionary mass must also intensify, and

---

[55] 'Praktische Wahlagitation', in NZ, XXIX, 1910–11, vol. II, p. 34.
[56] 'Zum Parteitage', in NZ, XXIX, 1910–11, vol. II, pp. 798–9.
[57] 'Die Wurzeln des Sieges', in NZ, XXX, 1911–12, vol. I, p. 581.

liberalism must become ever more reactionary. If, on the other hand, this is not the case, if liberalism were again to become a decisive party in the struggle for democracy, then this would inevitably lead to one conclusion: that the Marxist prognosis was false; that class conflicts are not sharpening, but declining in intensity'.

Kautsky, who in the past had tenaciously upheld the former of these hypotheses, now advanced another possibility, which he claimed was the correct position: 'A third response is nevertheless possible. The course of capitalist development does in truth produce tendencies toward the concentration of the bourgeois world into a single reactionary mass. At the same time, however, such development also produces ever new fissures in this mass, which are capable of dividing it very deeply'.

According to Kautsky, the proletariat should intervene in this process as an autonomous force, exploiting the contradictions of the enemy camp. To seize those opportunities meant to seek a more favourable terrain of conflict – through reforms, which were the 'only weapons for new conquests'. Statistics in hand, Kautsky maintained that no stratum of the population had expanded in recent years more rapidly than these 'new middle classes', i.e. the layer composed of intellectuals and employees. Their great electoral importance meant that Social Democracy could not afford to ignore them. More concretely, however, what could the SPD expect from this new middle class? By their very nature, some intellectuals and employees would be co-opted by the ruling class, while others, indeed the majority, constituted a restless and exploited mass, oscillating between conflicting positions. A generally urban stratum, these 'new middle classes' welcomed imperialist policies, since they provided jobs; at the same time, they had no common interests with the agrarian Conservatives and the Catholics of the Centre. Their attitude toward Social Democracy was determined by their fundamental lack of confidence in the action of the masses, in whose political force and future this layer did not believe. They could be drawn closer to the SPD, Kautsky wrote, only to the extent that the party demonstrated its strength to them. The contradictory character of the attitude of these strata found its own expression in the 'new liberalism', hostile to Social Democracy but even more hostile to the agrarian Conservatives and the Catholic Centre. For its part, Kautsky affirmed, the SPD could certainly not expect the 'new liberalism' to become a consistently democratic force capable of struggling for profound political and social changes. What could be expected was that the Progressive Liberals would contribute to bringing the plans of reaction to grief. Kautsky said that he did not believe in the independent future of the 'new liberalism'; he even held that in the long run it was destined to undergo a decisive internal crisis that would lead either to its reabsorption into the conservative camp or to its ultimate alignment with Social Democracy (a process that could occur either through actual unification or through a number of partial choices by different components of liberalism). In stark opposition to the proposals and analyses of Luxemburg, Kautsky announced that without falling into 'parliamentary cretinism' or 'overestimating the power of the Reichstag and the significance of the new liberalism', it was necessary to understand 'that the central focus of our political development once again lies in the Reichstag and that parliamentary struggles can help us take a significant step forward in the present situation', naturally while relying essentially on the masses, 'who remain the solid base of our strength'.[58]

Kautsky's emphasis on the parliamentary struggle was the product not only of enthusiasm for the 1912 election results but also of a particular assessment of the significance of the Reichstag. In the preface to the second edition of his 1903 essay on parliamentarism and direct legislation, re-issued under the title *Parlamentarismus und Demokratie*, Kautsky maintained that some elements in the SPD equated the crisis of the policies of the bourgeois parties in parliament with a crisis of parliament itself. Such an identification, he argued, was incorrect. In reality, the crisis of parliamentarism was the product of the crisis of the ruling parties. He criticized the errors of those who questioned the possibility that parliament could be an effective instrument of political and social change: 'Instead of speaking of the decay of the bourgeois *parties*, which is finding expression everywhere and therefore also in parliament, there has been talk of the decay of parliamentarism as if the institution of parliament and the participation of the proletariat in struggles in parliament and for parliament were increasingly useless in the workers' fight for emancipation'.[59]

3 The Defence of the Parliamentary Road – Against Pannekoek

In 1912 Kautsky was drawn into yet another great polemic, this time against Anton Pannekoek. The issues that triggered the dispute were

[58] 'Der neue Liberalismus und der neue Mittelstand', in *Vorwärts*, 25 February 1912.
[59] 'Vorwort zur zweiten Auflage', op. cit., p. 6.

several: Kautsky's energetic insistence on the centrality of progress toward the conquest of a parliamentary majority and his correlative insistence on the significance of parliament as an instrument of social transformation; the fact that he systematically linked this strategic perspective to a conception of organization that rejected spontaneous mass actions and subordinated proletarian consciousness to the planned designs of the party centre; above all, the fact that he harboured hopes that the coming social transformation would be substantially peaceful, even in an epoch of imperialist violence at home and abroad. Pannekoek's positions significantly repeated some of the themes and arguments of Luxemburg, but also displayed some conceptions that had hitherto been foreign to her, especially in his attitude toward the state and to parliamentary institutions.

In 1910 Pannekoek had decisively supported Luxemburg, convinced that the key issue determining the internal life of the worker's movement was the contradiction between the will to struggle of the masses, including the unorganized masses, and the inability of the leadership to give expression to that will. He charged that Kautsky had an oversimplified and unrealistic conception of the general strike. A general strike, Pannekoek said, could not be understood in Kautskyist fashion, as a single act. Rather, the mobilization of the masses had to be seen as a historic process punctuated by mass strikes, guided by organizations (party and unions).[60] Responding to Kautsky's article against Luxemburg, *Eine neue Strategie*, Pannekoek argued that Kautsky's positions were based on an unjust oversimplification of the theses of his opponent and that in fact no one thought the Russian experience could be repeated mechanically, any more than anyone conceived the revolution as the product of a collapse of capitalism: the revolution had to be understood as an historical process.[61]

By now Kautsky had decisively shifted the weight of his criticism from the revisionists to the radicals. He even went so far as to assert that the new radical current was moving towards an isolation that would put it outside the ranks of Social Democracy.[62] To this isolated minority, grouped around the *Leipziger Volkszeitung* and the *Bremer Bürgerzeitung*, he counterposed the solid unity of the majority of the party forged at the Jena Congress of 1911, a unity 'that had not been seen in quite some

[60] A. Pannekoek, 'Zur Diskussion über die Taktik', in *Leipziger Volkszeitung*, 23 April 1910.

[61] A. Pannekoek, 'Das Ziel des Massenstreiks', in *Leipziger Volkszeitung*, 2 July 1910.

[62] 'Der zweite Parteitag von Jena', in NZ, XXIX, 1910–11, vol. II, p. 876.

time', over the questions of both war and elections.⁶³ The polemic
with Pannekoek revealed what political outposts Kautsky was now
prepared to take up.

The dispute started with an article by Kautsky, *Die Aktion der Masse*,
whose central thesis was that a spontaneist conception of mass action,
which failed to distinguish between organized and unorganized masses,
could only lead to blind and hazardous activism. So far as the parliamentary road to power was concerned, Kautsky maintained that there
was 'nothing more comical' than to transform the problem of the forms
in which the party could assume power into a theoretical question.
Whether it would attain its goal 'through universal suffrage, through
parliament, or through mass actions' was a matter not of will but purely
of concrete analysis of specific conjunctures.⁶⁴ Such analysis clearly
showed that the right way forward was not a 'new tactic' as desired by
the new radicals, but the traditional tactic founded on 'building the
organization', the 'conquest of all positions of power' possible, the 'study
of the state and of society', and 'the education of the masses'. This, he
said, was the path that 'has brought our party victory after victory for
more than four decades'.⁶⁵ But the most significant theme in Kautsky's
essay – which was to become the centre of the polemic – was his assessment of the relationship between unorganized and organized masses in
political action. Kautsky displayed a complete distrust of any 'fusion'
of these two components, precisely because the unorganized masses
were vehicles of a spontaneism whose consequences were uncontrollable.
The essence of Social Democratic strategy, by contrast, was the conscious
planning of the struggles waged by the organized masses, who could
be guided and disciplined. The more spontaneous mass actions spread,
however, the more a 'wholly unpredictable element' would be introduced 'into our political life'.⁶⁶

Pannekoek, in an essay entitled *Massenaktion und Revolution*, published in *Die Neue Zeit* in July 1912, vehemently asserted that only a total
failure to understand the main features of the present epoch could lead
socialists to repeat unaltered the tactics and strategy of the past. To some
extent Pannekoek reiterated elements of the analysis Kautsky himself
had once adopted, for example in *Der Weg zur Macht*, but he proceeded
to conclusions that Kautsky had never drawn, of a clearly anti-parlia-

⁶³ Ibid., p. 873.
⁶⁴ 'Die Aktion des Masse', in NZ, XXX, 1911–12, vol. I, p. 84.
⁶⁵ Ibid., pp. 116–17.
⁶⁶ Ibid., p. 116.

mentary and revolutionary character. The hallmarks of the epoch, Pannekoek wrote, were on the one hand the 'growing strength of the working class' and on the other imperialism; on the one hand the proletariat's 'rising consciousness' of its own strength and on the other 'the impotence of parliament' and of the 'parliamentary actions' of Social Democracy. These, then, were the components determining new forms of popular struggle, 'since mass actions are a natural consequence of the imperialist development of modern capitalism and increasingly constitute the necessary form of the struggle against it'. The mass struggles of 1905 in Russia and their sequels in Prussia, he argued, were not 'accidental'. Given the solid battle-readiness of imperialism, the epoch of slow and steady political and industrial ascent by the workers' movement was over. To preserve its positions and prevent itself being rolled back, the proletariat now had to go over to the attack: 'its defence now lies primarily in assault'. Henceforth, Pannekoek continued, developing a thesis that was to become a permanent element of his future political thought, if the proletariat did not exercise power it was not because of any lack of objective conditions, which on the contrary were fully at hand, but because of an ideological and cultural subordination to the ruling class, which had become the prime weapon of bourgeois rule. Mass actions, on the other hand, were the prime crucible for the ideological revolutionization of the masses. The problem of a 'new ideological orientation' formed the real terrain of conflict between 'radicalism and revisionism', between the revolutionary line and the parliamentarist line, between those who understood the new reality and those who, failing to do so, remained wedded to the old strategy. There were, he said, two essential factors in the rule of the bourgeoisie: 1) 'the ideological supremacy of the ruling minority'; 2) the state power whose superior organization allowed it to rule. The more the first declined in importance because of the development of the proletariat, the more the second became the decisive front-line of the forces in struggle.[67] At this point Pannekoek drew a conclusion about the attitude of the revolutionary proletariat toward the state which was to be of great importance in the history of socialist thought, for it represented a bridge between the reflections of Marx on the Paris Commune and the theses of Lenin in *State and Revolution*. In complete opposition to the position Kautsky had defended ever since the final decade of the 19th century, Pannekoek expressly declared that the proletariat in Germany must

[67] A. Pannekoek, 'Massenaktion und Revolution', in NZ, XXX, 1911–12, vol. II, pp. 541–3.

struggle not for the conquest of the state, but for the destruction of the bourgeois state machine. He wrote: 'The struggle of the working class is not simply a struggle against the bourgeoisie for state power as a prize; it is a struggle *against* state power. The main problem of the social revolution is to increase the power of the proletariat to such a pitch that it exceeds the power of the state. *The content of this revolution is the annihilation and dissolution of the instruments of state power by the instruments of power of the proletariat*'.[68]

Pannekoek too referred to economic weight, consciousness, and organization as the three pillars of proletarian strength. But in his analysis consciousness and organization acquired a meaning wholly different from that attributed to them by Kautsky, for whom they were always to be applied and tested, in Germany at least, exclusively on the parliamentary terrain. Pannekoek did not deny that in principle the conquest of power through the parliamentary road was a possibility; but he asserted that such a conquest could be posited only in those countries in which the principles of parliamentarism and democracy were fully observed. The error of German Social Democracy, he said, was to attempt to apply a parliamentary strategy in a country with an emasculated parliament. The defining characteristic of Germany was that the strength of the workers' movement was circumscribed by an anti-democratic constitutional context; hence the workers had no choice but to break the power of the enemy. 'These conditions', Pannekoek wrote, 'naturally do not exist by accident. The lack of constitutional foundations for popular rule in a country with a highly developed workers' movement is precisely the necessary form of capitalist rule. This demonstrates that real power lies in the hands of the possessing classes. So long as this power remains intact, the bourgeoisie is capable of denying us even the formal means that could serve to oust it peacefully. The bourgeoisie must be beaten; *its power must be smashed*'. The conflict between the power of the two contending classes would continue until 'one of the two opposing sides in struggle lies vanquished, its power annihilated, and political rule falls into the hands of the victor'. Pannekoek maintained that the working class was permitted to advance peacefully only so long as it was weak. Once the proletariat acquired real strength, as in the present epoch, this very strength determined an objective change in its relations with the ruling class. He then sketched out the scenario of the future: 'The ruling class will seek to demolish the workers' movement with physical force. The proletariat

[68] Ibid., pp. 543–4.

will resort to mass actions, from the most simple forms of assemblies to street demonstrations and ever onward to the most powerful form of the mass strike'.[69]

In a phase of accelerating workers' power, organization and consciousness became two internal moments of the same dynamic of the movement in struggle, dialectically interrelated in an ascending spiral. Struggle made the workers more conscious and better organized; rising consciousness and organization made possible a higher level of struggle. These ideas, already adumbrated by Luxemburg, acquired more solidity and coherence in Pannekoek's account, partly because they were better integrated into a more specific examination of German conditions themselves. Because of the rising strength of the mass of the proletariat and the systematic resistance of the ruling class in the imperialist epoch, which made it impossible to continue along the road of partial conquests, the essential terrain of organization now lay where maximum revolutionary pressure by the proletariat could be achieved. 'The organization of the proletariat, which we emphasize is the most important instrument of strength of the working class, must not be confused with the particular form of its present organizations and unions. . . . *The essence of proletarian organization is a complete ideological change in the character of the proletariat*'.[70] Pannekoek's solution of the problem of how to confront the repressive forces of the state was rather optimistic. Here again he followed Rosa Luxemburg. He maintained that the demonstrations of 1910 had shown that coercion was 'powerless' against 'a united popular mass'. In addition, he insisted, the army was not at all a secure instrument for the ruling class, since 'it is composed of sons of the people, and to a growing extent of young workers who have already absorbed the rudiments of class consciousness in their family homes'.[71] Thus, the process of social revolution would take shape as 'the progressive disintegration of all the instruments of power of the ruling class, especially the state, and constant elevation of proletarian power to its highest peak'.[72]

Pannekoek charged that Kautsky's essay *Die Aktion der Masse* had presented a wholly erroneous account of the relationship between organized and unorganized masses. The unorganized, he argued, were not the petty-bourgeois or sub-proletarian crowds of the past, but masses of proletarians integrated into the process of large-scale capitalist

[69] Ibid., pp. 545–6.
[70] Ibid., p. 548.
[71] Ibid., p. 549.
[72] Ibid., p. 550.

production. They were workers who, because of the omnipotence of capital, had lost confidence in all organizations. The task of the organized was therefore to place themselves at the head of all the masses in struggle. Only then could organization become a real factor in the internal dynamic of the struggle, and not merely a formal structure. 'Labour in the service of capital', Pannekoek wrote, has given the masses 'an instinctive discipline'. Relying on this objective fact, Social Democracy should intervene to take advantage of the general rebellion against exploitation. The formal aspect of the difference between organized and unorganized masses had 'lost' its real significance.[73] In this situation, the essence of mass struggle and extra-parliamentary action was to exert an influence on the political scene directly rather than through the mediation of representatives in a powerless parliament.[74] Kautsky's perspective was 'a theory of passive expectancy', 'in the sense that it would let the great actions of the masses mature in a fundamentally passive manner, as if they were natural events, instead of preparing and leading them forward actively at the right time'.[75] This was the conception of a 'passive radicalism' that converged with revisionism in its belief that 'conscious activity is exhausted in the parliamentary and trade-union struggle'. Kautsky's only divergence from revisionism, Pannekoek held, lay in his assumption that 'catastrophes' were necessary to put an end to capitalism; but these would occur independent of 'our will and intervention'.[76]

On the question of the attitude of the proletariat in the event of war, Pannekoek accused Kautsky of opportunistic pessimism, since he not only posited the possibility that conflict might not be prevented, but that the proletariat would be drawn into a general wave of chauvinism. Pannekoek countered that the struggle against the war was an aspect of the revolutionary process, that a war would signify economic catastrophe for modern capitalism, and that the proletariat would do its revolutionary duty. His note of optimism here exhibited an underestimation of the organizational resilience of imperialist capitalism and at the same time of the risks of ideological conditioning of the masses by the ruling class. 'Confronted with the machinations of international big capital', he wrote, 'the German proletariat, whose organizations are the strongest in the world, cannot rest with folded arms or place its trust

[73] Ibid., pp. 590–91.
[74] Ibid., p. 586.
[75] Ibid., p. 591.
[76] Ibid., pp. 591–2.

in any presumed pacifist tendencies in the bourgeois world. It can only enter into action, from the very onset of any threat of war, and pit its strength against the instruments of power of the government'.[77] The struggle against the war would unleash precisely that revolutionary process which Kautsky was incapable of understanding.

The polemic with Pannekoek now led Kautsky to systematize his 'centrist' position fully. In substance, Kautsky retorted to Pannekoek: 1) that his conception of the masses was a mere idealized abstraction which passed over all the problems of the relationship between organization and masses, falsifying the very notion of organization with a veritable 'cretinism of mass action'; 2) that his conception of the 'destruction' of the state evinced a comparable simplism, which ignored the technical problems of social management and ended in semi-anarchism; 3) finally, that his faith that the masses would do their full revolutionary duty in the event of war revealed an equal naïveté, which was incapable of situating the masses realistically in their overall historical context.

In his article *Die Neue Taktik* Kautsky declared that the theories of Luxemburg and Pannekoek had indeed given rise to a new tactic, but one which should certainly not supplant the old. The masses of whom the new radicals spoke, Kautsky maintained, were figures of their imagination. It was necessary to have the greatest 'respect for the proletarian masses' of the real world, who were intellectually and morally superior to any other, but there must be no blind adoration of them. 'Their conceptions' should be respected, although 'only to the extent that they are imbued with class consciousness': their 'blind instincts' should not.[78] This argument signified total opposition to the type of relationship between organized and unorganized masses proposed by Pannekoek, and resolute defence of the traditional basis of Social Democratic organization. When Pannekoek, Kautsky wrote, extolled the dynamic of mass struggles as a constant process of growth that improvised its own structures en route, he failed to understand that the essential goal of the workers' movement was not struggle in and of itself but specific results of struggle. The indiscriminate use of struggle led not to ever greater strength but to exhaustion and decomposition. Nothing was more dangerous than to throw oneself into struggles 'with a perilous underestimation of the strength of the adversary and an enormous overestimation of one's own forces'. No error could more seriously jeopardize organizations from which the working class expected

[77] Ibid., p. 615.
[78] 'Die neue Taktik', in NZ, XXX, 1911–12, vol. II, p. 659.

realistic assessments, undermining any trust of the class in the party. Pannekoek's undifferentiated appeal to the 'revolutionary spirit' of the masses was pure idealism.[79] His pessimism about the prospects of proletarian struggle if it did not manage to deal a decisive defeat to the existing order derived from his failure to understand the role of working-class organization in contemporary society. Here Kautsky revealed the basis of his own 'strategic optimism', his confidence in the slow but sure advance of proletarian organization and its inevitable fruition in the form of a growing consensus and ultimate conquest of a majority in parliament. He declared it impossible for the ruling class to succeed in breaking the connection between the proletariat's role in economic production and its independent political expression. Reaction, according to Kautsky, could be only transitory: it was doomed to failure in the end. 'The attempt, the effort', he wrote, 'to destroy the organizations of the working-class certainly increases as these organizations become stronger and more dangerous to the established order. But the ability of these organizations to resist also increases to the same extent, and yet more so their irreplaceability. To deprive the proletariat of any possibility of organization has become impossible in the developed capitalist states today. . . . Any destruction of working-class organizations today could only be a passing episode'.[80]

For Kautsky, proletarian organization meant the party and the trade unions: these were the structures to be defended and strengthened; idealist bluster about the need to create new forms of organization was mere verbiage.[81] To the charge that his was a 'passive radicalism' Kautsky replied, using the same arguments he had advanced against Luxemburg, that active radicalism of the type proposed by the theoreticians of the 'new tactic' was based on a total lack of comprehension of the specific conditions of the developed capitalist countries – including the implications of capitalist development for state institutions themselves – and a simplistic transference to the West of forms of struggle proper to backward states like Russia.[82] 'Up to now', Kautsky wrote, 'the conflict between Social Democrats and anarchists consisted in the fact that the former wanted to conquer the state, the latter to destroy it. Pannekoek wants to do both'.[83] At this point Kautsky developed a wide-

[79] Ibid., pp. 690–91.
[80] Ibid., p. 691.
[81] Ibid., pp. 691–2.
[82] Ibid., p. 695.
[83] Ibid., p. 724.

ranging argument about the attitude of Social Democracy, not toward the potential shape of the 'state of the future' after the victory of the working class, but towards the 'present state' which it opposed, in diametrical contrast with the views of Pannekoek. In his articles, Pannekoek had maintained not only that to struggle against the ruling class the SPD had to struggle against the state, but that the precondition for the victory of Social Democracy was the outright destruction of the bourgeois state. Kautsky, on the other hand, had written as far back as the 90's, in *The Agrarian Question*, that 'public affairs today are too complex, too manifold, and too extensive to be expedited by dilettantes working in their spare time': they required 'expert and trained people, paid functionaries who dedicate themselves to such tasks completely'. The idea of a 'government of the people and through the people in the sense that public affairs should be administered not by functionaries but by popular masses working without pay during their spare time' was 'a utopia, even a reactionary and anti-democratic utopia, no matter how many democrats and revolutionaries may champion it'. The problem of 'modern democracy' could not be solved by an irrational and utopian revolt, but demanded a 'more just distribution' of functionaries 'throughout the country' and 'their submission to the will of the people and, at least in part, a change in the manner in which these functionaries are selected and promoted'.[84] Now he asserted that if the party and the trade unions themselves could not do without a bureaucratic apparatus, this should teach socialists something about the role of functionaries in the state and about the technical division of labour within the state apparatus. How could the state be destroyed? The fact was that 'none of the present ministries will be eliminated by our political struggle against the existing government'. The programme of the party did not call for the destruction of the bureaucratic apparatus of the state, but for its control and for the election of high functionaries alone. What the SPD demanded and was entitled to demand was a different governmental policy.[85] Thus, the perspective of the fight against the semi-parliamentary state was not a struggle for the destruction of the state, but a struggle to obtain a genuine parliamentary-democratic state. For all these reasons, the paralysis of the state in the course of working-class struggle must be a purely temporary phenomenon. Mass strikes could constitute only 'episodes of the class struggle of the proletariat'. The objective of a mass strike 'cannot be to destroy state power, but only to

[84] Op cit., p. 473.
[85] 'Die neue Taktik', op. cit., p. 725.

compel the government to yield on a particular question, or to replace a government hostile to the proletariat with a government favourable to the proletariat'.[86] This formulation substantially modified Kautsky's previous conception of the mass political strike, for in the past he had maintained that this was the 'ultimate' weapon of the proletariat, to be used only with the onset of a revolutionary crisis; it was not an instrument for the resolution of particular questions, even issues of great importance. A mass action, Kautsky continued, emphasizing its subordination to parliamentary action, cannot aim at 'the *destruction* of state power, but always only at a *shift* in the relationship of forces *within state power*'.[87]

According to Pannekoek, parliament was powerless. Kautsky had no objection to discussing a crisis of parliamentarism, but he traced this crisis back to a crisis of political leadership of the ruling classes, which feared the strength of the proletariat in parliament. If parliament has lost its importance, Kautsky said, this is due to the bourgeoisie: 'Parliament is only an image of the present interests and relationship of forces of modern society. It is not parliament as a mechanism that is in decay, but the bourgeois majority which puts ever new obstacles in the path of parliament. If the majority changes, the mechanism will start to function again'.[88]

In this sense, even the crisis of parliamentary action of the SPD was merely an aspect of the general relationship of forces in Germany, which also circumscribed mass actions themselves and their possibilities of success. 'One can speak of the impotence of the Socialist parliamentary delegations only there where the mass actions of the proletariat are also impotent', wrote Kautsky.[89] Under such conditions, the goal of Social Democracy remained what it had always been, and the 'new tactics' were of no use. 'The objective of our political struggle', Kautsky wrote, 'remains what it has been up to now: the conquest of state power through the conquest of a majority in parliament and the elevation of parliament to a commanding position within the state. Certainly not the destruction of state power'.[90] His conclusion was highly polemical, branding the 'new tactics' as 'cretinism of mass action': 'In a period of extraordinary tensions, mass political strikes and street disorders can unleash significant forces in favour of some of our demands. The greater class conflict and

[86] Ibid., p. 726.
[87] Ibid., p. 727.
[88] Ibid., p. 728.
[89] Ibid., p. 730.
[90] Ibid., p. 732.

mass anger are, the more quickly and frequently we must expect such explosions to erupt. But they remain an unpredictable phenomenon and cannot be considered permanent and normal methods of proletarian struggle. To direct the entire workers' movement toward mass actions is merely to replace the old one-sidedness for which Marx coined the expression parliamentary cretinism with a new cretinism, which we may define, continuing the metaphor, as a cretinism of mass actions'.[91]

So far as the attitude of the proletariat in the event of war was concerned, Kautsky charged Pannekoek with falling into ethical revolutionism. It was useless to assert verbally that the mass strike was a 'categorical imperative' for the proletariat. Instead it was necessary to take account of the concrete conditions in which a war could break out, as well as of the recent lessons of history. The conditions for the success of a strike against a war were identical to those of a struggle against the danger of a war. If the proletariat failed in the latter, if a wave of general chauvinism took hold, 'the mass strike will not be feasible'. When Pannekoek spoke of mass actions he overlooked the fact that the SPD received only about a third of the vote in Germany, that broad strata were still under the influence of the ruling classes, and that in the event of war even a portion of those who voted for Social Democracy would prove susceptible to chauvinism. The lessons of the Boer War in England, as well as of the war against Japan in Russia, where there was no strike against the outbreak of hostilities in 1904, and the conquest of Libya by Italy, where there was no strike in 1911 at the onset of the war, clearly demonstrated the power of the ruling classes and their governments to condition the masses ideologically in a military conflict.[92] By this time Kautsky had also adopted the positions of Bebel on war of defence as opposed to war of aggression (a distinction he had previously deemed highly dangerous for the proletariat). He maintained against Pannekoek that it was inadmissible to attempt to prevent military mobilization at any cost even 'when the state itself is the attacked party and not the aggressor'. In such an event the masses would certainly feel that the danger of invasion was real, a reaction of which Pannekoek did not take account. Recourse to the mass strike if war threatened should not be excluded, Kautsky said, although it would not be 'probable' if the government felt it had general support.[93] Its applicability and success depended on the concrete situation and on the assessment the party

[91] Ibid., p. 733.
[92] Ibid., pp. 660–63.
[93] Ibid., p. 662–3.

made of it; they were not the proper object of a 'categorical imperative'.

Although Kautsky's polemic against Pannekoek, like his earlier affray with Luxemburg, involved general differences of method, the real nub of the dispute was their opposite assessments of the political prospects for the SPD. Whereas Kautsky held that any head-on confrontation with the apparatus of capitalist power in Germany would lead to failure all along the line, given the coercive strength of the German state and ruling classes, and would drive the workers' movement into retreat, Luxemburg and Pannekoek held that never before had there been such a favourable opportunity for a strategic victory of the movement, which had never been so strong and combative, if only the leaders of the party and the trade unions would understand the possibilities of the conjuncture. The new radical tendencies now started to ancitipate the accusation of capitulation by the SPD leadership, a charge that was to become increasingly widespread within the revolutionary wing of Social Democracy, until it would finally be taken up by the future Communist Parties during and after the First World War.

These antithetical perspectives were further polarized and clarified by the subsequent development of the polemic between Kautsky and Pannekoek, which not only tended to 'go beyond' the traditional strategic horizons of German Social Democracy, but also introduced important themes that would later be assimilated and extended in Communist literature at the end of the War and during the early twenties. Pannekoek, responding to Kautsky once again, argued explicitly that Kautsky's conceptions of organization reflected a cult of 'formal structures'; that the traditional tactics of the party had been thrown into crisis not by mere theory but by the new combativity of the masses; that 'the destruction of the instruments of state power is not an artificially predetermined goal but an inevitable result of the struggle'; and that – a claim of great importance in the history of revolutionary socialism, anticipating later conceptions – the destruction of the bourgeois state meant not the end of state organization as such but the genesis of a different type of social power, that of the proletariat. When the bourgeois state apparatus 'fell to pieces' and its power 'was abolished', there would simultaneously 'emerge a new organization of society – the structures of democratic struggle created by the proletariat itself', representing the ascendent social power of the proletariat and assuming 'those functions that are necessary to the general organization of production'. Pannekoek declared that Kautsky no longer had any confidence in the revolutionary will of the proletariat. Hence his fear that in the event of war the workers would fall victim to the prevailing chauvinism, and his inclination 'to place all his hopes in presumptive tendencies towards disarmament at work in the bourgeois world'.[94]

The immediate context in which these disputes over the tactics and strategy of the workers' movement occurred was not encouraging for any of the currents within German Social Democracy and posed difficult problems for all of them. The great miners' strike that erupted in the Ruhr between 11 and 19 March 1912, openly sabotaged by Catholic organizations, had met fierce resistance not only from the employers but also from the repressive agencies of the state. There were violent clashes, with workers killed and wounded. The strike ended in a heavy defeat and prison sentences. Another important strike broke out on the docks between mid-July and mid-August 1913, beginning in Hamburg and then spreading to other cities. It too met extremely strong resistance from the employers and was repudiated by the union leaders, which provoked great resentment among the workers. It also ended in a severe defeat, with harsh reprisals and layoffs. Meanwhile, the situation was little more favourable in other sectors. The Social Democrats had achieved nothing in the Reichstag. In the Prussian elections of June 1913 the party registered only a slight advance, increasing its delegation from 7 to 10, a result of the rigged election laws which the party had not been strong enough to modify. In Baden the SPD suffered a severe defeat in the regional elections. Even the rise in party membership between 1912 and 1913 was modest: a 1.3% increase, from 970,112 to 982,850. The growth in trade union membership was only 0.73%, from 2,530,390 to 2,548,763. Support for the party press also left something to be desired. An atmosphere of crisis was slowly condensing in the SPD. There was a generalized feeling of 'stagnation'. The radicals blamed it on a political line which curbed the militancy of the masses. The revisionists and centrists gazed with concern at the formidable barriers erected by the conservative resolve of the ruling classes, and condemned the radicals as exponents of an adventurist line.

The result was an inflammation of the ideological tensions within the party, reflected in the violence of Kautsky's prosecution of the quarrel with Pannekoek and Luxemburg. Realizing that the mass actions and strikes of the time, ill-tolerated or even opposed by the official leaderships, expressed an objective dissociation from the traditional organizations of the labour movement, Kautsky reacted by accentuating his

[94] A. Pannekoek, 'Kautsky über "die neue Taktik"', in *Leipziger Volkszeitung*, 9, 10, 11 September 1912.

attacks on the radicals. Organization, Kautsky wrote in December 1912, was not an instrument of struggle 'in general' but an instrument of 'victorious' struggle.[95] In July 1913 he assailed the 'new radicals' for their praise of the combativity of the unorganized workers. Who were these unorganized workers? Kautsky asked. They were merely unreliable and unconscious elements, lacking any sense of solidarity and seeking 'their own advantage at the expense of their brothers'. How could these people be the 'most solid foundation' of proletarian struggle?[96] The inability of the advocates of mass action to found a coherent strategy, Kautsky argued, was due to their oscillation between blind faith in the autonomous virtues of the masses and blame of the leaders of their organizations for their practical defeats. They were cats chasing their own tails: 'The supporters of mass action spin round and round in a strange circle. On the one hand they say that the masses are infallible, that they always successfully drag the recalcitrant leaders behind them. But when the masses do fail in spite of all this, the leaders suddenly become guilty of not urging the masses forward'.[97] Pursuing this argument, and significantly referring to the supporters of the Russian model as 'Our Russians', he accused his neo-radical opponents of failing to provide the means necessary for their own ends, and thereby of falling into an intolerable revolutionary moralism that blamed others for their own lack of success: 'Our "Russians" acknowledge that spontaneous agitation constitutes the precondition for a spontaneous mass strike. They do not see any powerful agitation of this type among the German masses; but they find it too tedious to wait for historic events similar to those in Russia to stimulate the masses. They claim that this spontaneous agitation must come first, and then, when it does not come, they categorically demand that the party artificially create this spontaneity through an immediate "bold initiative"'.[98] (The allusion to Luxemburg was clear.)

Kautsky's main concern was obvious from his anxious query: if we in Germany follow a strategy of head-on confrontation, and in the course of it 'we are annihilated and our organizations go to the devil', then 'what would remain'?[99] The 'lessons' of Russia, he maintained, had to be learned in their entirety. 'The movement of chronic strikes' in a

[95] 'Der jüngste Radikalismus', in NZ, XXXI, 1912–13, vol. I, pp. 438–9.

[96] 'Nachgedanken zu den Nachdenklichen Betrachtungen', in NZ, XXXI, 1912–13, vol. II, p. 539.

[97] Ibid., p. 536.

[98] Ibid., p. 560.

[99] Ibid., p. 559.

country like Russia, whose labour movement lacked any articulated structure and any means of struggle other than frontal clashes, had succeeded in 'winning liberty' but had not succeeded in 'defending it'. 'The endless succession of strikes so exhausted the proletariat that the workers were no longer capable of offering sufficient resistance to counter-revolution'. He concluded that in a country like Germany, with a high development not only of proletarian organization but also of defensive weaponry in the hands of the ruling classes, and in 'non-revolutionary times' to boot, 'the idea of chronic mass strikes is simply absurd'.[100] Given the predictable aggravation of class conflicts, the use of the mass strike would indeed have to be considered, but in a manner exactly opposite to that recommended by the new radicals, one which respected 'German conditions': 'the mass strike today is not the precondition for our further progress; on the contrary, our present consolidation is the precondition for a future mass strike'. Only with the advent of a situation that naturally 'drives the working class to such a state of agitation' as to draw into struggle Social Democrats and trade unionists, unorganized workers, and even large numbers of adherents of enemy organizations, would the preconditions for the success of a mass strike exist.[101] Kautsky pointed out that internal differences within 'Marxist' tendencies, which had not emerged during the period of unity in the polemic against revisionism, were now a reality for all to see.[102]

While Kautsky was advancing these arguments, Rosa Luxemburg was developing her own opposite perspectives for stimulating a mass strike to achieve the abolition of the restricted suffrage in Prussia. Within the SPD, debate on the mass strike was in practice once again on the agenda, rekindled by the mass political strike of 14–24 April 1913 in Belgium, directed precisely at altering the electoral law, and the elections of 16 May 1913 in Prussia, which dramatized yet again the monstrous inequity of the franchise for Social Democracy. The results of the Prussian elections were as follows. The SPD, with 775,171 votes (28.38%) of the total, won only 10 seats in the Prussian parliament. The Fortschrittliche Volkspartei, with 183,452 votes (6.72%), won 38 seats; the Freikonservative Partei, with 54,583 votes (2.00%), won 54 seats; the Nationalliberale Partei, with 370,575 votes (13.56%), 73 seats; the Zentrum Catholics, with 451,511 votes (16.53%), 103 seats; and the Deutschkonservative Partei, with 402,988 votes (14.75%), 147 seats.

[100] Ibid., p. 560
[101] Ibid., p. 567.
[102] Ibid., p. 533.

Luxemburg closely linked her account of the mass strike in Belgium to the situation that had emerged in Prussia, attacking not only the party's tactics, but its entire strategy. She denounced the policy of alliance with the liberals and the use of the strike purely as a means of exerting parliamentary pressure. In a speech in Berlin on 22 July 1913 she maintained that the mass strike was an expression of the autonomous growth of the self-organization of the proletariat, in a context of offensive struggle. 'The history of the party and the trade unions shows us that our organizations flourish only when they are on the attack. It is then that even the unorganized rally to our banners'.[103] Shortly before, she had denounced as pure opportunism the fact that even though the mass strike had been used successfully in Sweden, Holland, Belgium, Italy, Spain, Russia, France, Austria, Switzerland, and Hungary, the pro-letariat was considered 'not yet mature enough for the mass strike' in Germany, the country of 'exemplary organization, discipline, and electoral success'. Her conclusion was diametrically opposed to those who argued that the organization had to be strengthened before a mass strike could occur. 'It is too often forgotten in our ranks', she asserted, 'that the class struggle is not the product of Social Democracy; on the contrary, Social Democracy itself is only a product of the class struggle, its most recent product'.[104] The example of Belgium, she said, demon-strated how combative the unorganized masses were once they were immersed in the reality of struggle.[105]

Luxemburg responded to Kautsky's accusation of 'Russianism' with ironic scorn. In past times, she said, he himself had been judged 'a Russian' and a 'romantic revolutionary'. Now, however, the alpha and omega of his alphabet were 'nothing but parliamentarism'. 'Electoral victories and more seats in parliament' was the sum total of all he could find to propose. The simple teachings of practice, Luxemburg held, were sufficient to refute Kautsky's negative assessment of the unorganized workers: 'To this question of theory ... respond the simple facts of the *practice* of both the political and trade-union struggle. Every great trade-union struggle has always relied on the support of the unorganized, and important advances in organization have always been the result of great struggles in which the unorganized have participated'.[106]

The debate on the general strike at the Jena Congress of 1913 (14–20

[103] Luxemburg, *Gesammelte Werke*, op. cit., vol. III, p. 263.
[104] Ibid., pp. 251–2.
[105] Ibid., p. 254.
[106] Ibid.

September), the last congress of the SPD before the First World War, demonstrated the balance of forces in the party between the advocates of the various strategies. In her speech to the congress Luxemburg summarized all her major arguments and concluded with the following words, which in her view represented the real will of the masses in Germany: 'We respond to all the attacks of reaction by saying clearly and openly at our congress: let us sharpen our weapons and be prepared!'[107] Of all the interventions against Rosa Luxemburg, the most explicit and revealing was that of Gustav Bauer, vice-president of the general commission of the trade unions, who accused her virulently of adventurism. The Congress, after rejecting an amendment proposed by Luxemburg and others, approved a resolution on the general strike which substantially repeated the decision of the Mannheim Congress of 1906, to the effect that a general strike would be used, when it proved necessary, 'only with the most complete agreement among all the organs of the workers' movement'.[108] Abstract acknowledgment of the significance of the mass strike had now been transformed into a ritual, while strategic disagreements remained deeper than ever. In practice, use of the 'dangerous weapon' of the mass strike was once again consigned to the indefinite future.

4   The Debate on Imperialism in the SPD

Concurrent with the conflicts over internal questions during the years 1911 to 1914, disputes also developed in the SPD over the practical attitude the proletariat should take to the danger of war and the theoretical assessment the party should make of the nature of imperialism. In effect, it was clear that the tactics and strategy of Social Democracy would have to be altered if the escalation of inter-imperialist conflicts into an international conflagration had to be regarded as inevitable. In the domestic arena the radicals were convinced that all non-proletarian groups and classes were in large measure politically homogeneous; they therefore combated any hopes, which they regarded as futile and disorienting, in hypothetical reformist tendencies among the 'new liberals'. Similarly, in foreign policy they were convinced that the hopes of some Social Democrats that anti-imperialist tendencies among certain sectors of the

---

[107] *Protokoll über die Verhandlungen des Parteitages der SPD. Abgehalten in Jena vom 14. bis 20. September 1913*, Berlin, 1913, p. 293.

[108] Ibid., pp. 192–3.

bourgeoisie would make an effective struggle for disarmament and international concord possible, were equally misleading and erroneous. Radicals like Pannekoek, Lensch, and Luxemburg maintained that armaments were an irremediable economic necessity for the bourgeoisie in the era of imperialism. In their view the proletariat should base its own policy on this objective and immutable fact, without weakening its action by seeking fruitless agreements with bourgeois pacifists, however sincere their illusions in the nature of contemporary imperialism.

Kautsky constantly sparred against these positions. During these years he developed an analysis of imperialism that complemented his analysis of the domestic situation. Had he embraced the radicals' theses on imperialism, he would have been unable to avoid re-thinking his internal strategy, which was now largely based on the prospect of a progressive democratization of existing institutions (precisely the thesis for which he had attacked Bernstein in the past) and on growth of Social Democracy within them. While Rosa Luxemburg bitterly assailed him for having evolved from a 'romantic revolutionary' into a pure and simple parliamentarist, Lensch accused him of having abandoned any consistent struggle against imperialism to become a propagandist of international pacifism.

In reality, Kautsky had indeed relinquished his past hopes in a progressive and rapid bankruptcy of the bourgeoisie both internally and internationally. He now felt that the ruling system commanded rather greater reserves than had been suspected. He no longer believed in the prospect of rapid change; and above all, he was convinced that the outbreak of violence either in Germany or abroad would mean disaster for the workers' movement. In his view the only available road was the struggle of the proletariat and Social Democracy to maintain an internal situation permitting a 'normal' growth of the labour movement, and to prevent the outbreak of an imperialist war, which would hand unchallenged power to the most brutal, reactionary, and imperialistic forces. Moreover, he did not believe that the proletariat could construct a new state organization in the heat of struggle. He thus advocated a 'peaceful revolution', or at least the most peaceful one possible, as the only way to maintain the necessary 'technical continuity' of institutions.

In 1910, commenting on the inconclusive debate at the Copenhagen Congress of the Second International on the attitude to be adopted to the danger of war, Kautsky had written: 'It is utopian to believe that bourgeois pacifist conferences or visits by friends of peace to foreign governments can abolish the danger of war and introduce disarmament and submission to international courts'. For, he continued, 'national conflicts, like social conflicts, cannot be overcome in the bourgeois world of competition'. The only road forward was that of the 'international solidarity' of the proletariat, 'the sole important force capable of guaranteeing international peace today'.[109]

This attitude, which denounced belief in the possibility of bourgeois pacifism as utopian, soon underwent a profound change. Between 1911 and 1913 Kautsky undertook a study that was to culminate in his celebrated work of September 1914, *Der Imperialismus*, against which Lenin directed his polemic in *Imperialism, Highest Stage of Capitalism*. Kautsky outlined an analysis based essentially on the following theses. In the past several years, finance capitalism had come to the forefront of the internal and international scene. The finance capitalists, who drew their profits from the export of capital, represented the most reactionary and militarist force in domestic politics, since they had a direct interest in transforming each national state into an apparatus of support for their own expansion. Imperialism was therefore directly linked to finance capitalism. But the interests of finance capital were not identical to those of industrial capital, which could expand only by broadening its markets through free trade. It was from the industrial sector that impulses towards international concord arose in the bourgeois camp; and it was with this sector that Social Democracy should link up to safeguard peace. Imperialism, the expression of one phase in capitalist development and the cause of armed conflicts, was not the only possible form of development of capitalism as a system of production. It was not predetermined that imperialism necessarily constituted the highest stage of capitalism. In fact, it could be conjectured that the imperialist phase would give way to a subsequent phase of 'ultra-imperialism', founded on agreement among the great industrial concentrations and consequently among the capitalist states.

Within less than a year of his comments on the Copenhagen Congress rejecting the illusions of bourgeois pacifism, Kautsky began writing in a completely different tone. He now asserted that it was necessary 'to support and strengthen the movements of the petty bourgeoisie and bourgeoisie against war and the world arms race'. He declared his opposition to the thesis that 'war is strictly linked to the essence of capitalism and is therefore inevitable',[110] and from now on sought to sustain it with an economic analysis of modern capitalism. Kautsky

[109] 'Der Kongress von Kopenhagen', in NZ, XXVIII, 1909–10, vol. II, pp. 775–6.
[110] 'Krieg und Frieden', in NZ, XXIX, 1910–11, vol. II, p. 101.

laid the foundations of his new interpretation in a review of Rudolf Hilferding's book *Das Finanzkapital*, published in 1910. After characterizing the significance of finance capital in no uncertain terms ('the capitalist future belongs to finance capital', which represents 'the most brutal and violent form of capital, both in the struggle of international competition and in the internal class struggle'), and explaining that henceforth 'not England but the United States constitutes the country that shows us our social future under capitalism',[111] Kautsky maintained that the economic costs of rearmament, while they favoured the development of some sectors of industry, were detrimental to others, either because they imposed financial burdens, or because they reduced the consumption of the broad masses, or because they diminished the rate of accumulation and therewith capacity for competition. 'The rapid rise of the United States' he observed, 'is surely due not least to the lack of a standing army in America'[112] – demonstrating that rearmament was certainly not an economic necessity of capitalist development, but was rather the result of a specific economic policy due to the weight commanded by particular forces within the state.

Kautsky was henceforward to develop these ideas into an increasingly integrated theory. He now argued that it was not so much colonial policy that produced the trend towards violence in relations among states, but rather the international efforts of finance capital to stake out zones of profitable penetration, where the work force could not defend itself. This violence was now manifested constantly in the relations between the strongest and weakest European states. The source of the political power of finance capital, which aimed at subjugating all society, could be traced back to its union with militarism and the bureaucracy.[113] Kautsky maintained that imperialism was indeed a product of capitalism, but not the essence of capitalism. He wrote: 'Those factors which constitute vital elements in the process of capitalist production, without which it could not exist, can naturally be overcome only when capitalist production itself is eliminated. But it is a crude misconception to consider every phenomenon generated by the process of capitalist production as one of its vital or indispensable elements'.

Kautsky continued by drawing a parallel between imperialism and the tendency toward the lengthening of the work day. Neither, he said,

---

[111] 'Finanzkapital und Krisen', in NZ, XXIX, 1910–11, vol. I, p. 769.
[112] Ibid., pp. 803–4.
[113] 'Banditenpolitik', in NZ, XXX, 1911–12, vol. I, pp. 2–3; 'Nochmals die Abrüstung', in NZ, XXX, 1911–12, vol. II, p. 850.

was a vital component of the process of capitalist production. Both were merely techniques that could be replaced by others to assure what was the real vital necessity of capitalism: the realization of profit. 'The extraction of surplus-value is a vital element of the capitalist mode of production. It generates the tendency towards the lengthening of the work day. The latter, however, is not at all a vital element of capitalism. Capitalism can prosper, even more effectively, with a shorter work day. The pressure to increase surplus-value is still exerted, even when the working day is shortened, but it takes other forms. The shorter the work day, the greater – for example – is the effort to replace human labour with machinery. Similarly, the constant expansion of the market is also a vital necessity for capitalism. At a certain level of capitalist development the most convenient means to achieve this aim appears to be the conquest of colonies or spheres of influence, which leads to the arms race. If this method were proscribed, the result would not be the collapse of capitalism, but only the necessity of using other methods to achieve its expansion'. Kautsky's political deductions from this economic logic were as follows: 'The arms race rests on economic *causes* but not on economic *necessity*. Its suspension is in no way an *economic impossibility*. That in itself, however, tells us nothing about the *probability* of the advent of disarmament. Powerful classes have an interest in the arms race. Whether or not their resistance will be overcome is a question of *political power*, a question that cannot be decided in advance but can be answered only by the success, or failure, of the struggle against the arms race. The first precondition for success is therefore energetic agitation in support of our demand'.[114]

In principle, Kautsky observed, one could conceive of the transition to a stage of ultra-imperialism. Whether or not this would become a historical reality in the near, medium, or far future would depend on the dynamic of socio-political development. The goal of capitalists was to arrive, through a victorious competitive struggle, at monopoly. But since this struggle became unduly dangerous and fruitless once it exceeded certain limits, it might be that 'in this stage of the struggle the contestants are mature enough for a mutual agreement. The apparent necessity of competition would then be laid aside, and the cartel, the trust, would be born. Under it the participants would prosper rather more than under the arms race of free competition'. This economic process could also find reflection in agreements between states: 'What

[114] 'Der erste Mai und der Kampf gegen den Militarismus', in NZ, XXX, 1911–12, vol. II, pp. 106–7.

has been happening in growing measure for the past two decades in the realm of mutual relations among companies is now beginning to occur in mutual relations among capitalist states. They all aim at expansion, all increasingly disturb the others, and all meet mutual obstacles. Because of this they increase their armed forces and augment the costs of expansion to such an extent that all profits are squandered. Nevertheless, these methods continue so long as some states believe that they can acquire sufficient strength through armaments to be able to annihilate their competitors and monopolize the world market. The further this prospect recedes, however, and the clearer it becomes that the prosecution of the struggle based on competition ruins all those who take part in it, the closer draws the stage at which the competitive struggle among states will be eliminated by their cartelization. This does not at all mean the renunciation of expansion by national capital, but only the transition to a less costly and dangerous method of pursuing it'.[115]

The political purpose of Kautsky's analysis was to vindicate the possibility of Social Democracy pursuing its forward march along tried and true paths. The real import of his account of imperialism was to assure the proletariat the necessary time to assert its growing weight against the forces of finance capital and their militarist-bureaucratic allies. A different pattern of capitalist development could check these elements, which would otherwise render world war inevitable. In Kautsky's view the new phase of capitalism which he postulated would not signify 'a victory of internationalism or of eternal peace'; nor, of course, could it lead to 'complete disarmament'. What could and should be done, he said, was to reverse a course of development which, if it continued, would 'make world war *inevitable*, and soon'. Nevertheless, Kautsky went much further in his hopes for the possibility of a new international course, soon claiming that it was conceivable that wars between great European states could be averted 'forever'. But he thought that in order to transform what was merely a possibility into reality it would be necessary for the proletariat, whose strength was rising 'year by year', to succeed in bringing its own weight to bear against the danger of world war.[116] Now, just as Kautsky identified high finance as the motor force of reaction and imperialism within each nation, on the international scene he viewed Germany as the most advanced example of imperialist expansion. This, in turn, was the result of the particular predominance of militarism and bureaucratism in Germany and the

[115] Ibid., pp. 107–8.
[116] Ibid., p. 108.

relative lack of developed bourgeois-democratic institutions. England and France, he observed, did not want rearmament. The arms race was provoked essentially by Germany; England and France were seeking an agreement to limit arms. War constituted the 'necessary alternative' if an agreement was not reached.[117] The charges to be made against Germany were clear: 'It is not only the condition of existence of the capitalist world, but also the lust for power of leading circles in Germany that is preventing an agreement on disarmament among the great powers, to which the other powers would subscribe'.[118] These accusations against leading circles in Germany were later to constitute the favourite themes of the 'crusade' waged by 'democrats', once the War began, against the authoritarianism of the Central Powers and German imperialism in particular. At the time they were intended by Kautsky to foster the struggle of the SPD to isolate the narrow but powerful circles that had an interest in unbridled power politics aimed at a victorious war.[119] Commenting on the inter-parliamentary socialist conference held in Berne in May 1913, Kautsky repeated that only the proletariat could be considered a consistent champion of peace; that the bourgeois camp was dominated by a constant oscillation between warmongering and attempts at agreements. Hence, he said, 'the near future is becoming ever more unpredictable. . . . Tomorrow may easily bring us either world war or general agreement and disarmament'. Exactly because of the duplicity inherent in the bourgeois camp, proletarian action would assume maximum importance: 'precisely because the bourgeois world is so divided internally, we can act all the more effectively and should not miss any opportunity to do so'.[120] Should the alternative of peace be lost, then not only world war, but also one of its necessary consequences would become inevitable: a revolution in Russia. Said Kautsky: 'The Russian revolution cannot be stopped; it will become an accomplished fact if there is any profound change in world politics. A revolution born of war, however, is the most violent sort of revolution'.[121] In fact, the triumph of a bellicose spirit would be a 'mistake' for European capitalism itself, since rearmament would only limit the capital available for investment in the undeveloped countries outside Europe.[122]

According to Kautsky, to assume that there would be war, to consider

[117] 'Nochmals die Abrüstung', op. cit., p. 848.
[118] Ibid., p. 853.
[119] Ibid., p. 854.
[120] 'Der Berner Konferenz', in NZ, XXXI, 1912–13, vol. II, pp. 267–8.
[121] Ibid., p. 269.
[122] 'Nochmals die Abrüstung', op. cit., p. 848.

it an inevitable necessity of capitalist development, as the 'new radicals' did, aided the plans of German imperialism, just as the insensate revolutionism of the radicals aroused the ire of internal reaction. Imperialists and extremist revolutionaries agreed that war was necessary; the former considered it the basis for the further development of national power, the latter the basis for the proletarian revolution. Social Democratic agitation for the preservation of peace would be gravely damaged if there were comrades who considered the 'idea of disarmament' an 'unrealizable utopia' and regarded 'the arms race not as a particular method of pursuing capitalist interests but as a vital necessity of economic development for the present order'. In sum, Kautsky charged, 'the comrades who attack our agitation in this manner can present themselves as very revolutionary. It is not for the revolution that they are working, however, but for the German government and the warmongers'.[123]

Discussing the practical attitude of Social Democracy in the event of war, Kautsky clung to the general position that if the proletariat was not strong enough to destroy a warmongering government before the war, still less would it be able to do so through actions like strikes once the war had broken out. This was his traditional position. But now he no longer started from the assumption that the SPD could not make any distinction between a war of aggression and a war of defence. In 1912, invoking the position of the General Council of the First International of September 1870, which called upon the French workers to do their duty as citizens and defend their country, Kautsky wrote that no proletariat could remain indifferent to the fate of the nation in the event of invasion.[124] Two years before he had said that if the danger of invasion loomed, 'everyone would be transformed into patriots, even those who are imbued with internationalist sentiments' and that an inflamed mob would crucify anyone who had the 'super-human courage' to oppose the patriotic-nationalist wave.[125] A mass strike against a war, he asserted, could only be successful if it was clear that the state was not 'threatened by an enemy invasion'.[126] The greatest danger for Social Democracy, he now emphasized in an article dated November 1912, was the systematic deceit employed by nationalist circles to inflame the masses through the means of popular communication.[127] The task of Social Democracy

[123] Ibid., p. 854.
[124] 'Der Kreig und die Internationale', in NZ, XXXI, 1912–13, vol. I, p. 192.
[125] 'Krieg und Frieden', in NZ, XXIX, 1910–11, vol. II, p. 104.
[126] Ibid., p. 103.
[127] 'Der Kreig und die Internationale', op. cit., p. 192.

was thus to mount effective counter-propaganda.[128] Kautsky then dealt with what to do if war did break out. To begin with, he made a distinction between the sort of action to pursue when 'the mass of people want war most passionately' and when the masses 'condemn it most passionately'. 'In the former case', he wrote, 'we will not be able to do much more than protest, in the party press and from the tribunes of popular assemblies and parliament, against the war and in favour of peace. In the latter case it will be our duty and responsibility to do our utmost to direct popular passion towards paths and goals that appear most advantageous'. The question could not be decided *a priori*; it was necessary to follow the development of the situation consequent on the attitudes taken by respective governments.[129]

What clearly emerges from Kautsky's analysis is that he did not consider revolutionary opposition to the war possible within a single nation, and still less any united international opposition. Since a strike against the war by a proletariat that had not been strong enough to prevent the outbreak of the war was a lost cause from the outset, his advice was to safeguard the SPD organization, avoiding any clash that could destroy it, and in the course of the war to press for a peace that would recreate the conditions for resuming action in the traditional ways, while denouncing the responsibilities of the ruling classes. The question of how to take practical advantage of the war was one that had to be left to the further development of the situation.

The influence of Kautsky's analysis of imperialism on the SPD was strikingly demonstrated at the Chemnitz Congress of 1912. In his opening address, Haase, the president of the party, pronounced the slogan that was supposed to animate the party in its struggle against the danger of war: 'Concord among civilized nations, peace among peoples, freedom for all peoples!'[130] This trinity corresponded perfectly to the content of Haase's introductory report to the discussion on imperialism, in which he reproduced the essence of Kautsky's recent analysis, sometimes almost literally on central points. He said that it was certainly true that 'imperialism is not peaceful and has *tendencies* toward *armed* conflicts'; but there were also 'other tendencies'.[131] *Economic inter-dependence is a factor that works against the warmongers.*[132] Haase also regarded

[128] Ibid., pp. 191–2.
[129] 'Der zweite Parteitag von Jena', in NZ, XXIX, 1910–11, vol. II, p. 874.
[130] *Protokoll über die Verhandlungen des Parteitages der SPD. Abgehalten in Chemnitz vom 15. bis 21. September 1912*, Berlin, 1912, p. 192.
[131] Ibid., pp. 410–11.
[132] Ibid., p. 412.

British attempts to arrive at an agreement on disarmament as significant,[133] counterposing these to the fact that in Germany '*all the bourgeois parties have lined up behind the banner of imperialism*'.[134] In his speech Bernstein emphasized the importance of the anti-imperialist struggle and the dangerous character of imperialism, but he also stressed the 'counter-tendencies' inherent in capitalist development itself, which favoured international concord. In sum, Bernstein's positions on this issue now stood quite close to Kautsky's. (Neither Kautsky nor Luxemburg were present at this congress; both were ill.) Denunciation of the 'utopian' character of the positions upheld by Haase and Kautsky came from Lensch and Pannekoek. Lensch declared that Social Democracy could not rely on the 'possibility' of a non-imperialist evolution of capitalism, since imperialism was the reality of capitalist development. The 'counter-tendencies working against imperialism', he said, were 'none other than those tendencies working against capitalism as a whole, namely socialism'. Appeals to the English disarmament proposals were valueless, for these proposals merely expressed the desire of one sector of the imperialist camp to maintain a status quo favourable to it; they were no indication of any possibility of peace.[135] Pannekoek linked a similar theoretical analysis to the need to prepare mass action. Parliamentary opposition to militarism, he said, while necessary, was not sufficient; 'at given moments' opposition had to be conducted 'through the action of the masses themselves'. He concluded by reiterating his opposition to any policy that counted on the existence of bourgeois anti-imperialist 'counter-tendencies': 'We therefore emphasize that in the struggle against imperialism the workers must not rely primarily on any sort of tendency opposed to imperialism within the bourgeois world, but only on themselves. In themselves they will find the strength to defeat imperialism'.[136] Liebknecht associated himself with the positions of Haase and Kautsky. The Congress also heard the loud and significant voices of those revisionists who were already backing imperialism. Quessel, like the radicals, believed that the reality of imperialism was an objective fact (he had to express his 'agreement with the viewpoints of comrades Lensch and Pannekoek' on this). But he argued that it was the duty of the SPD to sustain the German government when the government acted effectively to protect 'the equal rights of German industry',

[133] Ibid., pp. 409–10.
[134] Ibid., p. 412.
[135] Ibid., pp. 415–16.
[136] Ibid., p. 423.

since this corresponded to 'the interests of the proletariat'.[137] The resolution on imperialism, which committed the party to struggle against imperialism and for peace, 'concord among nations', disarmament, and free trade,[138] was adopted with only two opposing votes and two abstentions.[139] Once again, the vote on the resolution suggested a unity that did not correspond to reality.

Just how deeply the mentality that viewed reforms within established institutions as the strategic axis of the party had penetrated the SPD, was demonstrated by the attitude taken by its parliamentary delegation to a project presented by the government in March 1913 to finance new military spending. The programme was put forward in the atmosphere of tension generated by the First Balkan war and the introduction of three-year military service in France. The government proposed direct taxation, which, in 1913 as in 1909, was opposed by the conservatives. Should the party vote in favour – and the SPD vote would be decisive – so as to impose the financial burden on the wealthiest classes and defend the living standards of the masses, or should it vote against, in the name of a consistent struggle against militarism? It was obvious that a vote in favour would in no way foster the 'disarmament' the Chemnitz Congress had cited as one of the vital aims of Social Democracy. Support for the government project, upheld by David and the revisionist leaders against the opposition even of Bernstein, who allied with 'centrists' like Ledebour, triumphed within the Social Democratic parliamentary group. At the Jena Congress of 1913 Rosa Luxemburg played the role of a Cassandra, speaking words that would be confirmed less than one year later. The question of the vote, she said, must be approached as a choice between two evils: either take a position against a measure that was just in and of itself, namely direct taxation, since it was to be used for a purpose that must be rejected, or abandon the struggle against militarism. 'I believe', she affirmed, 'that the second choice is the greater evil for the Social Democrats from any angle'. 'If', she told the congress, 'you place yourselves on the terrain of the decisions of the majority of our fraction [in parliament], then you put yourselves in a position when war breaks out and we can no longer stop it, where you will face the question of whether to cover military expenses through direct or indirect taxes, and you will find yourselves voting for

[137] Ibid., pp. 429–30.
[138] Ibid., pp. 529–30.
[139] Ibid., p. 434.

war credits'.[140] A resolution that upheld the general principle of direct taxation in defence of the living standards of the masses, without referring to the specific case at hand,[141] was approved by a vote of 336 to 140. Among those voting in favour was Karl Liebknecht.

In late 1913 Kautsky published an article in the *Leipziger Volkszeitung* summing up the events of the year. He drew one major conclusion, imposed, he said, by the lessons of reality. So far as opposition to rearmament was concerned, the hopes that had been invested in progressive bourgeois currents in Germany had proved wholly illusory. 'Nothing more can be expected from bourgeois democracy in the struggle against militarism', he wrote. He maintained the general terms of his contrast between 'the industrial employers' who 'prosper the more, the less is the burden of military expenditure' and 'surely need peace', and finance capital with its warlike tendencies. In practice, however, it was necessary to note that the latter, which had an interest in 'public borrowing and the growing indebtedness of states', was gaining the upper hand and that industry linked to armaments constituted a greater and greater sector of the economy as a whole. There was no change, however, in Kautsky's inclination to view the overall situation in terms that were still favourable to Social Democracy. By way of consolation, he was able to affirm that 'fear of a confrontation with us has already resulted, in at least one case, in the costs of rearmament being born exclusively by the possessing classes'. Nevertheless, he did see the dangers of the moment and, reasoning in essentially parliamentary terms, expressed the conviction that 'with 2 million more votes' the SPD would have won 'the majority of the German people' and would be able to approach 'the direct struggle for power' as a 'highly current problem'. The principal task of the party was thus to prevent chauvinism from spreading among the masses, since 'in the epoch of general military service, no great war can be waged without chauvinist agitation'.[142] Kautsky closed with a warning against the 'adventurism' of the 'new radicals' and their strategy of mass action, pointing to the strength of the ruling classes and their spirit of violence. Only a further electoral 'breakthrough' could redress present prospects.

---

[140] *Protokoll über die Verhandlungen des Parteitages der SPD. Abgehalten zu Jena*, op. cit., p. 487.

[141] Ibid., p. 187.

[142] 'Das Jahr 1913 und Erbschaft', in *Leipziger Volkszeitung*, 31 December 1913.

VI

World War, Imperialism, the Russian Revolution

1 The Hypothesis of 'Ultra-Imperialism'

At the outbreak of the First World War, Kautsky played a significant role in the special session of the SPD parliamentary caucus held on 3 August 1914 to decide what attitude party deputies should adopt in the Reichstag vote on the war credits, scheduled for the following day. The session decided, by 78 to 14, that the SPD should vote in favour of them. The most energetic leader of the majority was David, who was later to be prominent among those Social Democrats prepared to give full support to German imperialism.

Kautsky's approach to the crisis was fully consistent with the positions he had developed during previous years. The idea of a frontal clash with the ruling class was wholly alien to him; he was determined that the party not appear anti-patriotic; and he wanted it to preserve maximum room for political manoeuvre, without being victimized by systematic repression. At the same time, however, he held that it was of prime importance for the political future of Social Democracy that the party refuse to compromise itself by unconditional adherence to the policy of the Imperial government. On 27 July 1914 he had written to Viktor Adler that he had been 'very surprised' by the Austrian ultimatum to Serbia and that he saw the rush to war as an 'act of desperation' on the part of people incapable of any far-sighted policy. If a world war should break out, Kautsky continued, 'then our policy would be exceedingly difficult, since one cannot work simultaneously for the destruction of Austria and of Tsarism'. On the other hand, he added, 'to limit oneself to wringing one's hands over the horrors of war is not a policy'.[1] This was a very revealing letter, for it showed unmistakably that Kautsky had abandoned the positions formerly expressed in *Patriotismus und Sozial-*

[1] V. Adler, *Briefwechsel mit August Bebel und Karl Kautsky*, op. cit., pp. 596–597.

demokratie, when he had argued that the fundamental duty of Social Democracy was to struggle against the militarism of its own country, and had denied that it was possible to support a war on the basis of a counter-position between liberal-democratic and authoritarian powers. He now viewed the international conflict precisely through the prism of that counterposition, implicitly assigning Social Democracy a particular role within it. For Kautsky, in effect, the difficulty for the SPD now lay in the fact that Germany might find itself in a struggle against Tsarism, in alliance with Austria, 'the prison house of peoples'. It is indicative that the letter contained not one word about the role of Germany as the spearhead of imperialist expansionism in Europe, or its primary responsibility for the deterioration of international relations – which Kautsky had energetically asserted and denounced in the very recent past.

Kautsky was invited to attend the session because of his reputation as a theoretician, even though he was not a member of parliament. According to his own, oft repeated account, he went to the meeting intending to recommend abstention on the vote over war credits. This line, however, was rejected by the caucus, which divided between those who advocated voting for the credits and those who advocated voting against. Then, 'only because this [abstention] had been rejected by everyone', he proposed that the Social Democrats make their 'approval of the credits conditional on assurances as to the objectives of the war'. In other words, the government should commit itself not to pursue aims of conquest but only those of defence. He did not feel he could recommend an outright vote against the credits, 'in view of the lack of clarity' about the exact responsibility for the war.[2] Later, in his 1937 work *Sozialisten und Krieg*, Kautsky maintained that the spirit of his position was that if the government refused to make such a commitment about the objectives of the war, war credits should be denied it.[3] When his line was rejected and the parliamentary group divided into a majority that opposed asking for commitments from the government and a minority that opposed voting for the war credits under any circumstances, Kautsky argued, successfully, that the SPD statement to the Reichstag explaining the party's affirmative vote should contain a sentence declaring that if the war assumed a character of conquest on Germany's part, Social Democracy would decisively oppose it. This sentence, however, was deleted from the text at the specific request of Chancellor Bethmann-Hollweg.

[2] 'Die Wahrheit über den 3. August', in *Vorwärts*, 1 January 1916; see also Ein Schlusswort, in NZ, XXXIII, 1914–1915, vol. II, p. 567.

[3] *Sozialisten und Krieg*, Prague, 1937, pp. 446–455.

(How close the 'intimacy' of the Imperial government and German Social Democracy had now become!)[4] Kautsky henceforward found himself thoroughly enmeshed in those distinctions between defensive and offensive war which he had previously branded a source of confusion.

Kautsky's attempted mediation came to nothing. As is well known, party discipline compelled even Liebknecht to accept the decision of the majority on 4 August. But the session of 3 August saw the onset of a process of political division within the SPD that was to become ever deeper. It was also the beginning of the isolation of Kautsky, who occupied an 'intermediary position' in which, as he later pointed out, he stood 'virtually alone'.[5] Kautsky's analysis of the war and its perspectives make it evident that his major objective was the re-establishment of conditions that would allow the party to resume the path that had been interrupted by the outbreak of hostilities. This attitude was closely linked to his assessment of imperialism. Since he did not believe that imperialism was the highest stage of capitalism and simultaneously maintained that the war would create grave difficulties for the European governments and ruling classes, and an economic decline of the continent, he held that the correct perspective was to direct the discontent of the masses towards the immediate attainment of democratic conquests, and to renew the forward march of a strong working class towards power. In all his analyses Kautsky constantly underscored four concomitant effects of the war: 1) the decline of Europe; 2) the rise of anti-imperialist struggles in the colonies; 3) the ascent of the United States, destined to assume the leadership of the capitalist world; 4) the end of Tsarist Russia. This was a global prospect of profound changes, but certainly not ones which would culminate in the international socialist revolution.

On 21 August 1914 Kautsky published an article in *Die Neue Zeit* that drew all these essential elements together. He spoke of unprecedented geopolitical changes after the war, the decisive aspect of which would lie precisely outside Europe. The real victor in the war, he said, would inevitably be the United States, which would reap the greatest benefits: 'The reconstruction of the economic ruins of Europe after the war will be impossible without American aid. The defeated states, at least, will fall into a position of dependence on American finance capital'. The economic decline and financial ruin of Europe might well render it impossible to amass the great amounts of capital necessary for a new

[4] Ibid., pp. 459–460.
[5] *Das Werden eines Marxisten*, op. cit., p. 142.

arms programme, and so 'deprive imperialism' of its foundations, thus compelling by the force of circumstance that policy of international concord which had not been born of political choice.[6] Turning to the situation in which the SPD found itself, Kautsky at least partially accepted the position of David, who insisted on the mission of the struggle against Tsarist despotism (as if this mission could be executed by the soldiers of the Kaiser). Kautsky wrote that the positive side of the conflict, namely that it was a 'war against the Russian Tsar', was contradicted by the negative side, that it was a war 'also against the democracies of England and France'. Whatever these contradictions, however, in practice he spoke of the 'necessity of defending one's own homeland', while nevertheless noting that this task created a 'fatal dilemma' between national loyalty and 'international solidarity'.[7] But such a dilemma, he argued – here Kautsky's fundamental preoccupation becomes evident – should not precipitate a division within the party. Hence his call for unity above and beyond all differences, since a split would be 'fatal'. 'In war', he wrote, 'discipline is the first requisite not only in the army but also in the party'. 'Not *criticism* but *loyalty* is the most important condition for our success today' – only thus could the most urgent task of the hour be accomplished: 'to preserve the organizations and organs of the party and the trade unions intact'.[8] The summons to the left of the SPD, led by Liebknecht, Luxemburg, and Mehring, to accept party discipline was patent.

In all the major articles he wrote during the second half of 1914, Kautsky developed these themes, attempting to moderate conflict within the party as much as possible and to concentrate on the resumption of its work once the war was over. He declared that discussion of the significance of the vote of 4 August 1914 could be fruitfully pursued as 'valid historical research' only *'after the war'*.[9] Cancelling any force to what he had called the 'dilemma' between national defence and internationalist solidarity, he wrote in September 1914 that in reality there was no contradiction between the two terms. Indeed, the German Social Democrats and French Socialists, 'without the slightest enmity towards their brothers across the border', had each voted for war credits in order to provide the means for the defence of their respective nations.[10] Shortly thereafter he wrote that once the war had actually begun only

[6] 'Der Krieg', in NZ, XXXII, 1913–1914, vol. II, p. 845.
[7] Ibid., p. 846.
[8] Ibid., p. 846.
[9] 'Die Vorbereitung des Friedens', in NZ, XXXII, 1913–1914, vol. II, p. 881.
[10] 'Wirkungen des Krieges', in NZ, XXXII, 1913–1914, vol. II, p. 982.

one question remained: 'victory or defeat?' The possibility of working for 'the defeat of one's own land', he said, should be ruled out completely.[11] The main problem was to ensure that defence was understood in terms of the democratic principles of the 'independence and territorial integrity of the nation'. Since the war was an accomplished fact, the various socialist parties should prepare a 'democratic peace', making sure that their own respective governments would not practice an imperialist and annexationist policy. Kautsky therefore recommended not Germany's 'isolation' but its 'concord' with the other world powers.[12]

This approach can be characterized as a fundamental conciliationism. Kautsky strove above all to combat any talk of the 'failure' of the Second International. In a polemic against Mehring, who had declared that the 'collapse' of the International was a 'devastating fact' of reality,[13] Kautsky maintained that on the contrary 'unity around principles' remained; there was merely 'a diversity of conceptions', which could and should end as soon as the 'transitory situation that had generated it' ended.[14] Indeed, he continued, in an essay entitled *Die Internationalität und der Krieg* expressly devoted to defending the thesis that the International was not bankrupt, the facts demonstrated the correctness of its analyses. 'The outbreak of the war', he wrote, 'signifies not the *bankruptcy* but on the contrary the *confirmation* of our theoretical conceptions. . . . We have no regrets, nothing to revise. We feel decisively strengthened in the conceptions we upheld prior to the war'. Kautsky argued that those who spoke of bankruptcy had expected something of the International it never could have produced. 'There are people' he said, referring to Luxemburg, Mehring, and Liebknecht, 'who claim that the International is bankrupt, since it did not succeed in preventing the war' – but in doing so, they 'demand from the International something that has never been seen in world history: that a party which is still too weak to conquer political power and determine the policies of states should be strong enough to prevent the inevitable consequences of these policies under all conditions'.[15] It should be noted that Kautsky was falsifying the positions of his opponents to some extent, since although it was true that the current of 'new radicals' tended to underestimate the hold of

---

[11] 'Die Sozialdemokratie im Kriege', in NZ, XXXIII, 1914–1915, vol. I, p. 1.

[12] 'Rohrbach über den Krieg', in NZ, XXXIII, 1914–1915, vol. I, p. 323.

[13] F. Mehring, 'Erinnerung aus dem Kriegsjahre 1870', in NZ, XXXIII, 1914–1915, vol. I, p. 9.

[14] 'Die Internationale und der Burgfrieden', in NZ, XXXIII, 1914–1915, vol. I, p. 18.

[15] 'Die Internationalität und der Kriege', in NZ, XXXIII, 1914–1915, vol. I, pp. 225–226.

chauvinism among broad layers of the masses, they had denounced the International and German Social Democracy not for failing to prevent the war but for not having struggled against it, and primarily for having voted to grant the Imperial government the credits with which to prosecute it. Kautsky, for his part, spoke not of bankruptcy but merely of discovery of the objective limits of the International. What had disappeared was the expectation of 'a common position of the entire socialist proletariat'; what the war had provoked was the division of socialists into 'different camps'. The International, Kautsky concluded, 'is unable to prevent' this division. Hence his assessment of the International as an instrument operative essentially during time of peace: 'it is not an effective instrument in war, but is essentially an instrument of peace'; 'it can bring its full force to bear only in peace-time', and in war can act only 'to reconquer peace'. Hence also the fact that 'the victory of the nation in war never constitutes an end in itself but only a means by which to achieve a lasting peace'. Thus, the task of each party during the war was to 'struggle for peace'.[16] Peace would breathe new life into the International.[17] Social Democracy, Kautsky would say in March 1915, must struggle so that the end of the war would signify the opening of an era of international peace founded on mutual respect for the independence of nations.[18] If international peace turned out to be impossible, if imperialism prevailed, then a second world war would be inevitable, as would the 'ruin of Europe for an entire historical period, during which capitalism will continue to be viable', with the United States advancing from a position of leadership already consecrated by the First World War to an even more complete dominance.[19]

Luxemburg issued a stinging and contemptuous reply to Kautsky, whom she called the 'theoretician of the swamp': 'The world-historical call of the *Communist Manifesto* needs an essential amendment and now, after the Kautskyist correction, reads like this: workers of all countries, unite in time of peace and cut one another's throats in time of war!' According to Luxemburg, Kautsky's theory that the International was essentially an instrument of peace and 'not an effective instrument in war-time' would inaugurate 'a wholly new "revision" of historical materialism, compared to which all the past attempts of a Bernstein

---

[16] Ibid., pp. 248–250.
[17] Ibid., p. 243.
[18] 'Eine Erörterung des Rechts auf Erörterungen', in NZ, XXXIII, 1914–1915, vol. I, p. 740.
[19] 'Wirkungen des Krieges', op. cit., pp. 970–971; see also 'Die Vorbereitung des Friedens', op. cit., p. 878.

appear as innocent child's play', a revision that would culminate in petty-bourgeois utopianism. Instead, it was necessary to demand the reconstruction of the International on the basis of a militantly anti-imperialist programme, so that it would struggle against the present war from the revolutionary standpoint of the proletariat.[20]

Their differing interpretations of the function of the International now constituted the major front of conflict between the Kautskyist and Luxemburgist conceptions. Luxemburg urged a strategy based on the action of the proletariat, whose task, she said, must be to intervene in the crisis opened by the war to promote a revolutionary and international break with capitalism. Kautsky's strategy, on the other hand, aimed at a democratic peace, seen as the precondition for a recovery of the International on the basis that had been shattered by the war. The Kautskyist perspective was closely linked to a particular assessment of the nature of the war and the imperialism that had generated it. In September 1914 Kautsky published in *Die Neue Zeit* an article, *Der Imperialismus*, which presented the conclusions of the positions he had expressed during the years immediately prior to the war. In an introductory note, Kautsky explained that the essay had been completed before the outbreak of hostilities but had been brought up to date since. Behind its formally theoretical guise, his analysis led to a series of concrete tactical and strategic consequences. He wrote: 'Does it [imperialism] therefore constitute the ultimate possible expression of the world policy of capitalism, or is another possibility conceivable? In other words, does imperialism constitute the only remaining possible form of the expansion of exchange between industry and agriculture under capitalism?'[21] In responding to this question, Kautsky maintained that imperialism was only one specific way in which the capitalist countries resolved what was indeed a permanent necessity of capitalist development itself: to guarantee industry the agrarian hinterland from which to extract raw materials and foodstuffs. He supplied this definition of imperialism: 'Imperialism is a product of highly developed industrial capitalism. It consists in the tendency of every capitalist industrial nation to subjugate and annex an ever larger *agrarian* area, without regard to the nations inhabiting this area'.[22] One of the consequences of ever greater industrial development was that capitalism constantly modified the relationship

[20] R. Luxemburg, *Ausgewählte Reden und Schriften*, vol. II, Berlin, 1951, pp. 518–519, 522–523.
[21] 'Der Imperialismus', in NZ, XXXII, 1913–1914, vol. II, pp. 919–920.
[22] Ibid., p. 909.

between agriculture and industry, to the detriment of the former and the advantage of the latter. This was why capitalism found it necessary to control an ever larger agrarian zone subject to intensified exploitation. The impossibility of assuring this relationship within national boundaries led the capitalist countries to a systematic policy of subjugation of external zones. This, Kautsky emphasized, constituted an ineradicable economic exigency of capitalist development itself. But the proof that such a tendency was a vital prerequisite for capitalism did not at all demonstrate that any of the particular and specific forms it might assume constituted 'an irreplaceable necessity for the capitalist mode of production'.[23] Imperialism was just one of these specific forms. In the past, however, free trade had been another. Modern imperialism was born of the need for general control of industrial expansion. The export of capital, technology and skilled labour, combined with the development of an infrastructure (railways, etc.) in the subject territories themselves, had generated imperialist policies aimed at the creation of either colonies or of spheres of influence. 'These', Kautsky affirmed, 'are the more important roots of imperialism, which has put an end to free trade'.[24] Kautsky held that the economic tendency of imperialism to subjugate territories that furnished raw materials was ineliminable. The only force that could block it was the political victory either of the proletariat in the developed countries or of the colonial peoples: 'The domination of the subjugated nations will come to an end only when these peoples, or the proletariat of the industrialized capitalist countries, become strong enough to throw off the capitalist yoke. This aspect of imperialism can be overcome only by socialism'.[25] But, Kautsky observed, 'imperialism also has another aspect',[26] the political means by which it sought to respond to the indispensable economic exigency of expansionism. The World War was the inevitable consequence of a specific type of response by particular large capitalist countries: anarchic and unbridled military competition, burdening the entire economy, except those sectors profiting from arms production, with escalating and eventually unendurable costs. The irrationality of this imperialism could give rise to a bourgeois effort supported by 'every capitalist able to look beyond the immediate moment', to resolve problems of output and market not through mutually destructive conflicts but through an appeal to general class interests.

[23] Ibid., p. 917.
[24] Ibid., pp. 919–920.
[25] Ibid., p. 920.
[26] Ibid.

Kautsky imagined that the call of labour for international solidarity might in the future be matched by a call of capital: 'Capitalists of all countries, unite!'[27] If capitalism persisted in the policy that had led to war, its end would become inevitable in an era of strife-ridden imperialism, since the system would then have proved incapable of expressing common international interests in a beneficial form. If, on the other hand – and this, Kautsky said, was still possible, since economically capitalism was viable so long as the extension of zones furnishing raw materials under conditions of exploitation was not halted (in other words, provided that this process was not interrupted by the 'rising political opposition of the proletariat') – capitalism were to renounce destructive conflicts and anarchic competition for raw materials, regulating the latter by a higher phase of international monopolism, then a new phase of capitalism was conceivable, beyond the imperialist phase that had culminated in the World War. This would be the phase of 'ultra-imperialism'. 'From the purely economic standpoint', Kautsky wrote, 'it is therefore not excluded that capitalism may yet experience a new phase, namely the *transposition of the policy of the cartels to the realm of foreign policy* – in other words, a phase of ultra-imperialism, which naturally we would have to combat as energetically as we combated imperialism, but the danger of which would take a different form, not a world arms race and threat to world peace'.[28]

During the first months of the war Kautsky listed the following transformations of the world political scene that would inevitably result from the conflict: 1) the rise of the United States to the position of the world colossus of capital, as a necessary consequence of the illusory struggle between England and Germany for domination of the world market;[29] 2) the initiation of an anti-colonial struggle of vast and historic proportions;[30] 3) the transformation of Tsarist Russia.[31] But however great these changes, Kautsky was now convinced that the alternative 'imperialism or socialism' (an alternative in which he had firmly believed in the past) constituted a great over-simplification of the complexity of the real historical situation. In his view the reduction of capitalism to the policy of imperialism and the concomitant thesis that the workers' movement was facing either a revolution in the near future or an irre-

[27] Ibid.
[28] Ibid., p. 921.
[29] 'Wirkungen des Krieges', op. cit., p. 970.
[30] 'Der Krieg', op. cit., p. 845; 'Wirkungen des Krieges', op. cit., p. 973.
[31] 'Wirkungen des Krieges', op. cit., p. 974.

mediable fall into nihilistic opportunism, were equally false. Against such positions, he held that the proletariat should consider the possibility that the capitalist system might survive and undergo a transition to a higher form. The workers therefore had every reason to continue their progress towards ever greater maturity without falling into the embrace of either revolutionism or opportunism, options as radical as they were simplistic and politically destructive. On the other hand, while he denied that imperialism and the war would necessarily signify the objective and definitive ruin of capitalism in the short run and therefore the necessity for a resolute revolutionary intervention, he was not prepared to conclude that the proletariat should renounce the struggle for socialism merely because it was possible that capitalism might have an ultra-imperialist future. On the contrary, Kautsky held that the objective basis for socialism coexisted with the possibilities of capitalist development and that the question of the timeliness of socialism would be decided when the workers recovered democratic rights, when peace was re-established, and when the International was reconstructed – in other words, under the conditions which had existed prior to the war, which alone could allow the proletariat to judge whether the subjective maturity of the socialist forces was sufficiently great for the exercise of power.

In this regard the polemic between Kautsky and Heinrich Cunow in the spring of 1915 is illuminating. Cunow maintained not only that imperialism constituted a necessary phase of capitalist development, but also that the very aggressivity of the imperialist powers demonstrated that the capitalist system was far from having exhausted its historic possibilities – indeed that it was still in its 'youth'. According to Cunow, the imperialist phase could not be considered as other than a historically progressive experience and an indispensable precondition for socialism. From this perspective he concluded that in both form and substance imperialism was identical to capitalism itself – thereby rejecting Kautsky's thesis that imperialism was only one possible expression of capitalism. Cunow maintained positions from the right that coincided with the positions of the radicals on the left, except that he held that imperialist capitalism was on the rise, whereas the radicals maintained that it was nearing its end. They agreed, however, in their common identification of capitalism and imperialism. Kautsky further developed his theses on imperialism in the course of his reply to Cunow, distinguishing between 'type of policy' and 'economic phase'. Imperialism, Kautsky argued, was precisely the former rather than the latter. He then applied this distinction to the determination of the political attitude of the proletariat.

Cunow had declared that to seek to eliminate imperialism in a period when the rule of capitalism was still unchallenged was to attempt abstractly to conjure away a necessary phase of economic development. Kautsky retorted that precisely because imperialism constituted a contingent and not a necessary form of capitalist development, the proletariat could and should oppose it. Did the proletariat, Kautsky asked, 'have a specific policy of its own to counterpose to that of finance capital, and therefore also to imperialism?' He replied that the question of the necessity of imperialism could in no case be posed merely speculatively, but only in the light of whether it was also necessary for the proletariat, in the sense that the latter's 'conditions of existence' were inevitably linked to the development of imperialism.[32] That, he said, could be excluded, because the antithesis between capital and labour was rooted in the permanence of exploitation and not in the particular political context of the exploitation itself.

Kautsky charged that Cunow's analysis was a mechanistic one. Cunow still believed that the objective basis for socialism was the collapse of capitalism – he merely postponed the time of the advent of socialism, claiming that capitalism still had a long historical epoch in front of it. In reality, Kautsky said, it was impossible to attempt through scientific methods to ascertain the exact moment of 'maturity' and exhaustion of capitalism. But 'has it ever happened in history, even once, that a mode of production fell into such ruin that it could no longer move forward?' The proof of the maturity of socialism did not lie purely on the level of objective economic processes. It was determined by the subjective political movement unleashed by class conflicts. Of course, if economic development was insufficient, then Social Democracy could not implement its political programme. Socialism could triumph only on the basis of a sufficient development of the forces of production, combined with an adequate level of maturity of the proletariat as a subjective agent: 'The precondition for the accomplishment of such a task is surely the availability of adequate productive forces. If these are lacking, Social Democracy will fail in the execution of its programme'.[33] But the objective conditions for socialism existed in the capitalist countries. Modern technology could assure workers a sufficient wage while simultaneously reducing the working week. The necessary concentration of industry had been attained. 'In this respect', Kautsky wrote, 'I maintain that we have already reached the historically necessary stage. . . . I therefore

[32] 'Zwei Schriften zum Umlernen', in NZ, XXXIII, 1914–1915, vol. II, pp. 107–111, 114.
[33] Ibid., p. 141.

maintain that the objective preconditions for socialism are present in the capitalist countries'. This, however, was only one aspect of the question. The other was that of the 'subjective preconditions', which was more 'complicated',[34] since it concerned not only objective economic forces but also relations among social classes. It was the capacity of the proletariat to determine the shape of these relations to a greater or lesser degree that was the decisive index of whether or not a society was 'ripe' for socialism. 'There are two trends', Kautsky wrote, 'that become especially important: that of the *sharpening of class contradictions* and that of the *moral bankruptcy of capitalism*. The moral bankruptcy of capitalism is something different from its economic bankruptcy. I doubt whether the proletariat will ever allow the latter sort of bankruptcy to occur; the moral bankruptcy must occur rather earlier'.[35]

Elsewhere Kautsky asserted that Marx himself 'counted on growing crises, but not on a permanent difficulty in pursuing production at all'. Indeed, according to Marx, 'the capitalist mode of production was inevitably headed toward ruin not because of its economic impotence but because it produced "its own gravedigger", the working class'. Economic crises and depressions were powerful revolutionizing forces, not because of their mechanical effects, but because they stimulated dissatisfaction and an awakening of consciousness that led to the formation of a revolutionary will. Hence Kautsky's conclusion: 'what we expect, on the basis of the *Communist Manifesto*, is that the transition from capitalism to socialism will always be the *political* result of the *conquest of political power by the proletariat* and not of the automatic collapse of the capitalist mode of production'.[36]

During his polemic with Cunow, Kautsky explained in what way 'ultra-imperialism' could check the rise in the strength of the proletariat. Having posited that imperialism did not represent the objective end of capitalist development and that the latter, from the purely economic standpoint, could continue its course, Kautsky insisted that in order to remain in the saddle capitalism would have to acquire new credibility in the eyes of the masses. This it could do only if it managed to put an end to the predominance of the sort of policy represented by imperialism. However, if finance capital succeeded in adopting a new course that eliminated imperialist conflicts and inaugurated an epoch of international bourgeois co-ordination, then it would be possible for capitalism to

[34] Ibid., p. 142.
[35] Ibid., p. 143.
[36] 'Nochmals unsere Illusionen', in NZ, XXXIII, 1914–1915, vol. II, p. 268.

recover a certain prestige. 'If such an era of ultra-imperialism should come to pass', Kautsky wrote, 'then it is possible that at least the trend toward the moral bankruptcy of capitalism could be temporarily mitigated'.[37] If, on the contrary, the imperialist trend prevailed, 'a second world war' would become 'inevitable'. Kautsky outlined the ultra-imperialist alternative like this: 'In the event that an accord of nations, disarmament, and lasting peace are achieved, then the worst of the causes which were increasingly leading to the moral bankruptcy of capitalism before the war would recede. Naturally, the new phase of capitalism would soon inherently give rise to new vices, perhaps even worse than their predecessors, under the weight of which not only the proletariat, which must feel oppressed and exploited in any phase of capitalism, but also more neutral classes and layers, would suffer. But at the same time, ultra-imperialism, like the Manchester capitalism of the 1850s and 1860s and the imperialism of the turn of the century, up to the international rise in prices, would initially usher in an era of new hopes and expectations within capitalism'. This, however, did not mean that the 'moral bankruptcy' of capitalism 'would be postponed for a long period'.[38]

It should be noted that Kautsky's analysis of the perspectives of the proletariat during a possible era of 'ultra-imperialism' contained certain persistent contradictions. For, on the one hand Kautsky described ultra-imperialism as a sort of international collective capitalist planning based on a general agreement to exploit 'peacefully' the backward zones furnishing raw materials and foodstuffs. This, he said, would permit a recovery of capitalist prestige and thereby weaken the struggle of the working class, precisely because the success of socialism presupposed the 'moral disarmament' of capitalism as a system. On the other hand, the triumph of ultra-imperialism presumed the defeat of the imperialist line and therefore of the bloc of national finance capital and militarism within the bourgeoisie. This would be possible only if bourgeois contradictions sharpened and the proletariat helped to defeat the imperialist tendencies; in other words, if the proletariat won great successes in its defence of democratic conquests within existing institutions and in the mobilization of its international organization. Thus, ultra-imperialism was depicted simultaneously as the maximum of capitalist power and the maximum of the proletariat's capacity to bend the bourgeoisie in a non-imperialist direction. This contradiction was never resolved.

[37] Ibid., p. 144.
[38] Ibid., p. 145.

In either case, Kautsky held that imperialism was the greatest enemy of the proletariat in the sense that the definitive consolidation of imperialism would signify ruin for all the social classes in struggle – in other words for society as a whole. Kautsky had now moved far from his past positions, when he had believed that the result of a world war would be socialism. His new sense of the resilience of capitalist development undermined his previous convictions and led him to believe that there was no future for any class on the basis of common social ruin. For him, imperialism meant such general ruin. The task of the proletariat was thus to struggle to break out of the imperialist tragedy, to foster an era of international peace, and to intervene in capitalist contradictions in a context of economic, social, and political normality. The price of this normality might be passage through an epoch of ultra-imperialism, whose general form would represent the conversion of free competitive capitalism into concord among states – betokening a new upswing in the productive forces in the framework of international disarmament, economic reorganization in various countries, and democracy as an internal method of regulating political and social relations.

Imperialism as general ruin and the absurdity of the notion that revolution could be 'grafted onto' a society in ruins – such were Kautsky's leitmotifs in 1917. 'Should we raise the slogan: prosecution of the war until the social revolution?' he asked. 'This would mean prosecution of the process of annihilation of both capital and labour until the complete ruin of capitalism'. Such a course would bankrupt the heirs of capitalism and nullify their inheritance: 'a sure method of annihilating capitalism but also of rendering socialism impossible'. What Social Democracy needed was peace, which would 'provide a terrain enabling the proletariat to intervene powerfully in future struggles, as it is doing in war and as it did before the war'.[39] It would be hard to find words in more explicit contradiction with the position of Engels, which even Kautsky had cited in the past, and which Lenin was now constantly recalling, that a great European war would mark the end of capitalism and the advent of socialism as a governing force. Kautsky's real appeal throughout the war was for a return to the road that had been interrupted in August 1914. His conviction that the resumption of the strategy of the past was not only possible, but inevitable, rested on the central theoretical premise that democracy, understood as the 'participation of the popular masses in state policy, in institutions', represented the necessary political reflection of the indispensable economic role of the proletariat in produc-

[39] *Serbien und Belgien in der Geschichte*, Stuttgart, 1917, p. 47.

tion, as an essential element of the modern capitalist system. 'This development', Kautsky wrote, 'that is, the expansion of modern democracy and of the strength of the proletariat, is as necessary a product of the capitalist mode of production as the effort of particular capitalist strata to extend the boundaries of their national state. Now, the tendency towards democracy expands among the popular masses within the modern state under all circumstances, while the tendency towards the extension of the state is of interest to capital only under specific historical conditions'.

Hence Kautsky rebuked those who 'see only imperialism in the modern state and not the necessity of democracy, taking this necessity in all the senses of the term, both as an *unrenouncable demand* of the proletariat and as the *inevitable product* of the "laws of motion" of capitalist production itself'.[40] Democracy, he continued, grew incessantly with these laws, 'despite all the obstacles that may arise temporarily'. The power of democracy as a contemporary reality was such that it could be felt even during the World War itself. This was not 'only a struggle among different imperialisms, but also between imperialism and democracy, between more or less democratic states and more or less imperialist and militarist ones'. Kautsky expected that the end of the war would bring the bankruptcy of imperialism and a 'powerful advance of democracy, even though not yet the complete victory of the proletariat'.[41]

Internally, Kautsky expected that the end of the war, with its 'lessons' of the disastrous results of imperialism, would see a strengthening of democracy. Internationally, he believed that a new spirit would lead to a Society of Nations, which he deemed the precondition for the establishment of freedom of commerce and trade, an expansion of the forces of production, and a renunciation of imperialist rivalry. There were strong similarities between Kautsky's perspectives and various features of the pre-war programme of Bernstein. In his 1915 work *Nationalstaat, Imperialistischer Staat, und Staatenbund* Kautsky declared that the far right and far left of the party were committing the same error, although from opposite points of view. They both believed that 'imperialism constitutes a necessity for the present mode of production'. This *'coincidentia oppositorum'* also made their positions interchangeable. The extremists of the right were prepared to support imperialism; those of the left sought to bring down imperialism, abandoning the task of

[40] Ibid., p. 93.
[41] Ibid., p. 94.

propaganda for socialism, by trying to introduce it immediately. But it was no accident that on the basis of the common thesis that imperialism was 'inevitable', those who lost faith in the 'immediate practical introduction of socialism' ended up in the ranks of the zealots of imperialism.[42] (One striking example of such a transformation was the case of Paul Lensch, who, after first supporting the radical positions on imperialism, became a pro-imperialist in the course of the war.)

Kautsky now sketched out a rapid analysis of the historical phases of capitalist development and their relation to imperialism. The latter, he observed, whose 'characteristic is the union of finance capital with industrial capital', superseded that period in which the modern economy received its vital dynamism from industrial capital, with its tendencies toward 'peace among peoples, limitation of the absolute power of the state through parliamentary and democratic institutions, and a policy of frugality in state budgets', and with its hostility 'toward tariffs on food products and raw materials' (except for a temporary inclination toward protective industrial tariffs during its infancy). Under the catalytic pressure of the trusts and the centralization of the big banks, the primacy of industrial capital had been replaced by that of finance capital, unifying the two forms of capital and directly subjugating the state. 'The state orientation of finance capital', Kautsky wrote, 'is now rising to the level of a general orientation of all the economically dominant classes of the advanced capitalist countries'.[43] The power bloc welded by finance capital and militarism was playing out its hand in the World War. If capitalism was unable to find a new direction once the conflict was over, it would fall into a 'chronic condition of warfare'. Having arrived at this point, Kautsky explained what he meant by a 'capitalism of a new age of reason'. He insisted that peace and democracy at home and abroad could serve capitalist economic development better than imperialism.[44] The road that capitalism could travel most effectively, he claimed, was not that of military conquest but of regulated, negotiated expansion based on free trade and the international division of labour.[45] But an industrious and pacific international exchange of wealth demanded the replacement of 'war of all against all' by agreement between states through international organizations and a spiritual reformation of nations. 'In the future, the best and most fruitful means for extending

---

[42] *Nationalstaat, imperialistischer Staat und Staatenbund*, Nuremberg, 1915, p. 17.
[43] Ibid., pp. 22–23.
[44] Ibid., p. 70.
[45] Ibid., p. 73.

the internal market lies not in the expansion of the national state in the direction of the formation of a multi-national state, but in the union of diverse national states, with equal rights, into a league of states. *The league of states and not the national state or the colonial state constitutes the shape of the great empires needed by capitalism to realize its ultimate, highest form, within which the proletariat can assume power*'.[46]

Kautsky thus identified the highest stage of capitalism not with imperialism, but with ultra-imperialism. Hence his programmatic reaffirmation of the value of the democratic method, understood as the parliamentary method. What would bring the proletariat to power, Kautsky maintained, was not revolutionary violence pitted against the violence of imperialism, but the peaceful increase in the strength of the proletariat within representative-democratic institutions. So long as economic and social development was dominated by capitalism, the task of Social Democracy could only be to struggle for its own organizational autonomy and to support those bourgeois and petty-bourgeois layers that resisted the 'policy of imperialism'. Social Democracy could not act according to the precept 'the worse, the better'; it could not take the position that the working class had an interest in curbing economic development just because this development was occurring in the form of capitalism. It was the duty of Social Democracy, Kautsky wrote, 'to defend the interests of the proletariat against capitalism, to combat capitalism, but also and at the same time to favour economic development, even though this development will necessarily express itself as capitalist progress so long as society is not organized in a socialist manner'.[47] This progress, when it occurred in the political and institutional forms of democracy, constituted the best basis for the 'physical, spiritual, and political' strengthening of the proletariat.[48]

Kautsky's postulation of the alternative of a catastrophic continuation of imperialism or an 'ultra-imperialist' phase, either a new triumph of the bloc of finance capitalism and militarism or a reassertion of rationalizing and democratic tendencies within capitalism, led him to seek a strategy of alliances between the non-imperialist sectors of the bourgeoisie and petty-bourgeoisie and the proletariat. This amounted to a continuation of the policy he had advocated during the last years of peace before 1914. If imperialism was characterized by the subjugation of industrial capital by finance capital, he said, then it was necessary to

[46] Ibid., p. 75.
[47] Ibid., p. 78.
[48] Ibid., p. 80.

strive to end this subjugation and to break its reactionary and militaristic framework. In a 1914 essay, *Der imperialistische Krieg*, Kautsky dealt thoroughly with this aspect of proletarian strategy. Jettisoning the position expounded in *Der Weg zur Macht*, that imperialism was welding all non-socialist forces into a reactionary mass, he now maintained that the war and its 'lessons' would tend to create growing contradictions within the bourgeoisie and the other non-proletarian social strata. The capitalists 'do not at all form a compact mass. The interests of the capitalists in industry are in no way identical to those of the finance capitalists or even the landlords. There are differences and contradictions even among the industrial capitalists themselves, between heavy industry and the textile industry, for example'. In addition, there were the intellectuals, who possessed no class unity; and there were the 'older classes'.[49] Given this multiplicity of interests and their political implications, 'the proletariat cannot be indifferent to the question of which enemies it must confront, or to the manner in which the mutual struggles of the other classes are resolved. The proletariat must study their contradictions and must intervene in these struggles consciously and deliberately. Otherwise Social Democracy will remain, so long as it does not command a majority, "a powerless minority", exactly as Engels said'.[50] Kautsky claimed that only a perspective of this sort would allow the proletariat to intervene 'in all contemporary struggles' and that this was the tactical and strategic substance of the 'centrism' of Marx and Engels.[51] Since imperialism 'is not a necessity for the development of industrial production in the context of the rule of capitalism, but only one of the means by which super-profits are obtained', and since the prosecution of imperialist goals was a 'question related to the *strength* of the classes that have no direct interest in imperialism',[52] the common problem of these classes was to prevent the pursuit of imperialist policies.

The future, Kautsky observed, might see a juxtaposition of the international unification of imperialism against the proletarian international. 'It is not at all out of the question', he wrote, 'that the present war could end in such a way that the imperialists of the leading great powers of both camps arrive at an agreement to divide and exploit the world. Yes, we must even consider the possibility that the world may see the spectacle, shameful for us, of the realization of the International of the imperialists

[49] 'Der imperialistiche Krieg', in NZ, XXXV, 1916–1917, vol. I, p. 452.
[50] Ibid., p. 453.
[51] Ibid., p. 454.
[52] Ibid., pp. 477–478.

before that of the International of the socialist parties. Naturally, an imperialist understanding is not what we strive for. What we need is understanding among peoples, above all the proletariat, under the leadership of the Socialist International. The imperialist international can bring peace, even a secure peace under certain conditions, but in that event the exploitation of peoples by unified international finance capital would become more gigantic and better planned. Nevertheless, the resistance of the proletariat should then emerge ever more powerfully, for the international class struggle of the proletariat would no longer be obfuscated and hampered by national differences of any sort. It is not our intention to prophesy. Today it is absolutely impossible to predict what the outcome of the war will be. An international entente of the imperialists is only one of the many possible conclusions to the present conflict'.[53]

Developing his analysis of the relationship between social classes and imperialism, Kautsky asserted that while the growing dangers of imperialism provoked contradictions within classes other than the proletariat, so long as imperialism retained its power it tended to forge a general reactionary bloc that absorbed even sectors of the proletariat itself. If imperialism were really the 'last word of capitalism', Kautsky wrote, then 'we would be dealing with a reactionary mass as a durable, and not a transitory, phenomenon; it would remain until socialism came to power and put an end to class differences once and for all'. Kautsky evoked this possibility, but his own conviction was that 'the policy of imperialism will fall into bankruptcy even before capitalism'.[54] The prospect of a 'reactionary mass' becoming a reality as an anti-socialist front was linked, Kautsky argued, to the contingency of capitalism failing to supersede its imperialist phase. In that event, the various non-proletarian strata, for all their undeniable real or potential contradictions, would plunge into a decisive historic crisis, and the conflicts between the bourgeoisie and the socialist proletariat would become so sharp as to provoke a situation that would tend to forge a bloc of 'all the opponents of socialism'. 'An unexpected increase in the strength of socialism to a point where it is perceived as a threat by bourgeois society as a whole could lead to the formation of a reactionary mass'.[55]

It is well known, of course, that Kautsky's theory of imperialism and ultra-imperialism was subjected to a violent and disdainful critique by

[53] Ibid., p. 483.
[54] 'Imperialismus und reaktionäre Masse', in NZ, XXXV, 1916–1917, vol. II, p. 113.
[55] Ibid., p. 115.

Lenin in his work of 1916, *Imperialism, Highest Stage of Capitalism*. In the July 1920 preface to a new edition of this study, Lenin described Kautsky's theories as 'the complete renunciation of those same revolutionary principles of Marxism that writer has championed for decades'.[56] The political substance of this apostasy, was an opportunism designed to 'obscure the profundity of the contradictions of imperialism and the inevitable revolutionary crisis to which it gives rise'.[57] Conceiving of imperialism as the 'culminating historical phase' of capitalism and as its 'decay', Lenin argued that Kautsky's prediction of a stage subsequent to imperialism amounted to an outright political betrayal. Denying the equivalence between crisis of imperialism and socialist revolution, an inevitable result was to disarm the proletariat and deprive it of the necessary determination in the revolutionary struggle for the overthrow of capitalism and the conquest of political power.

In examining Lenin's riposte, it is noticeable that his polemical zeal led him to oversimplify Kautsky's theses seriously, robbing them of some of their essential features. First of all, in disputing Kautsky's definition of imperialism, Lenin denounced its falsity in terms so harsh that he claimed that Kautsky ignored the fact that 'imperialism is, in general, a striving towards violence and reaction', that 'the characteristic feature of imperialism is *not* industrial *but* finance capital'.[58] In reality, as we have amply seen, Kautsky was not at all unaware of the connection between imperialism on the one hand and violence and reaction on the other. On the contrary, he emphasized that violence was a product of the dangerous policies of imperialism, since the latter had the twofold tendency to consolidate reaction at home and to create zones of commercial influence and economic exploitation abroad, in contradiction with the principles of free trade. Likewise, Kautsky was scarcely unaware of the connection between finance capital and imperialism, for he attributed the triumph of imperialism precisely to the domination of finance capital over capitalist society as a whole. Thus, when Lenin cited Kautsky's definition of imperialism as 'a product of highly developed industrial capitalism'[59] as proof that Kautsky had failed to understand the role of finance capital, he was viewing the definition formalistically. In fact, Kautsky's reference to 'industrial capitalism' in this quotation was clearly intended to refer to capitalism in general in the epoch of

[56] V. I. Lenin, *Collected Works*, vol. XXII, Moscow 1964, p. 192.
[57] Ibid.
[58] Ibid., p. 268.
[59] Ibid., p. 268.

contemporary industrialism; so much so that when he drew a distinction between 'industrial capitalism' and 'finance capitalism' Kautsky assigned the former a position subordinate to the latter in the epoch of imperialism, and when he posited the hypothesis of a non-imperialist evolution, he did so by postulating a division between the two components. Similarly, it appears that when Lenin cited the passage in which Kautsky wrote that the imperialist industrial countries sought to resolve the problem of raw materials by annexing 'all large areas of *agrarian* territory',[60] in order to show that his opponent remained imprisoned in a conception of imperialism confined to the schemata of the old colonialism, he was misrepresenting Kautsky's positions. What Kautsky meant to assert (as is quite unequivocal in the very passages Lenin himself cites repeatedly and extensively on other points) was that the general tendency of the imperialist powers to seek reservoirs of raw materials and food in terri- tories outside Europe constituted the most striking manifestation of the conflict among the great powers competing for *general* economic domination. He indisputably related imperialism 1) to finance capital; and 2) to the attempts of finance capital to alter the relationship of forces and economic systems of the great states. Kautsky did not ignore the tendency of imperialist powers to annex even metropolitan territories wrenched away from their rivals. Here is what he wrote in *Serbien und Belgien in der Geschichte*, published in 1917: 'Imperialism furnishes a scientific explanation of the present war only when it is regarded as the phenomenological product of a specific type of capitalism, namely "finance capitalism". . . . In the preceding period of capitalism, during which industrial capital dominated in more simple forms, the bourgeoisie was oriented in a liberal direction and aspired to the national state. In the period of imperialism it abandons liberalism and seeks to expand beyond the confines of the national state, through the annexation of territories which are deprived of rights or held in conditions of inferiority: colonies or protectorates. When two highly developed capitalist states plunge into struggle over the annexation of the same territory, one may speak of a purely imperialist war'.[61]

The real substance of the theoretical and political conflict between Kautsky and Lenin must be sought primarily in their views of the future of capitalism as a social system. For Lenin, the historic necessity of the revolution and the duty to struggle to transform the imperialist war into a civil war, and therewith into a socialist seizure of power, flowed

[60] Ibid., p. 268.
[61] Op. cit., p. 5.

from his analysis not only of imperialism in general, but also of the First World War in particular, as the expression of a comprehensive crisis of capitalism, whose ultimate stage was now prey to parasitism. One of the key theses of this analysis was that only revolutionary violence could provide an effective response to the now systematic and permanent violence of the imperialist ruling classes. For Kautsky, on the other hand, the historical situation left open various possibilities. Capitalism had not necessarily reached its end. It is significant that his first comments on the imperialist war took the form of a prediction of the decadence of Europe and of a great future for the youthful capitalism of the United States. Kautsky's emphasis on the possibility of an 'ultra-imperialist' phase of capitalism, of the constitution of an International of capitalist countries united together to exploit the world, explained why he refused to view the outcome of the war in terms of the exclusive alternative: imperialism or socialism in the near future – an alternative which, by declaring imperialism to be the definitive crisis of capitalism, made the social revolution the sole task of the hour. Moreover, while Lenin called for civil war and revolutionary violence, Kautsky rejected such a call (he had always rejected it, even during the years when Lenin nevertheless called him a genuine Marxist), because he was persuaded that the only basis for the construction of socialism was the parliamentary conquest of the state machine. He was convinced that this machine was a technical instrument that could be submitted to democratic controls and oriented to new purposes (in this respect his position was radically different from that of Marx in his writings on the Paris Commune), but not replaced or shattered by the assault of the mass movements, as Pannekoek had maintained in the polemic of 1912. All this led Kautsky to a strategy of democratic-parliamentary struggle for a majority within existing representative institutions. In the last few years before the World War, Kautsky had begun to vacillate at the superior resistance demonstrated by capitalism, losing his confidence in any rapid or proximate victory over it. He reacted by increasingly retreating to respect for democratic-parliamentary rules, as the only permanently valid measure of the real relations among classes and of the maturity of the proletariat. Since the proletariat had been too weak to prevent the outbreak of the war, it was still less capable of opposing that war by semi-revolutionary or revolutionary methods once it had broken out. Similarly, he concluded that the sole basis for socialist victory was a demonstration of proven political will and maturity: a working class too weak to defend democracy should have no illusion that it could seize power by the short-cut of violence. Such an illusion would merely represent a sectarian political and social immaturity, whose price – if a violent road were actually attempted – would inevitably be an inability to administer society.

There is no doubt that Kautsky's delineation of an 'ultra-imperialist' future for capitalism, although based on a realistic awareness of the further possibilities of development of the reigning system, was politically incoherent and contradictory. For on the one hand he spoke of an internationally unified capitalism and a rejuvenation of capitalist prestige: in sum, a fortification of the capitalist mode of production. On the other hand, he seemed unable to draw the political conclusions from this prospect, and imagined that such a process would be fully compatible with a utopian degree of international peace, with the restoration of parliamentary democracy and the strengthening of the united energies of the socialist proletariat. The contradiction was rooted in his overestimation of the power of the nexus between the economic and political roles of the proletariat. Kautsky remained convinced that the economic importance of the working class was sufficient to guarantee political democracy in the state and allied institutions – that is, the regulation of relations between classes by the 'democratic method', apart from contingent episodes of reaction. Kautsky seemed to have no suspicion that an 'ultra-imperialist' phase might instead take the form of a general trend towards a bureaucratic accentuation of capitalist oppression and a progressive debilitation of the political representatives of the socialist parties in parliament.

2   The Birth of the USPD

Kautsky's attitude towards the 'domestic truce' between the SPD and the German government after 4 August 1914 and to the 'defence of the fatherland' was meanwhile progressively shifting towards active criticism of the party majority, which gave nearly complete support to the government. He did not, however, share the attitude of Liebknecht, who had initially bowed to party discipline (and thus voted for the war credits on 4 August 1914 against his will), but then, on 2 December 1914, was the only member of the Reichstag to vote against another grant of war credits, thus defying the instructions of the party. Kautsky supported the Centrist opposition of Haase and Ledebour, who changed their positions as the illusion of a war of defence collapsed, and on 20 March and 20 August 1915 abstained on war credit votes, while intensifying their criticism of the oppressive internal régime within Germany. The difference between the opposition of Liebknecht and that of the 'Centrists' was not merely quantitative, but qualitative. Liebknecht considered the demand for peace without annexations – the main slogan of the 'Centrists' – utopian. Liebknecht's line became increasingly radical, calling for agitation against the war as such, while the 'Centrists' opposed the 'domestic truce' in order to dissuade the government from its imperialist objectives. The Centrist strategy was designed to bring about a return to the pre-war situation.

The conflict between Liebknecht's positions and those of the more moderate 'Centrists' became evident in June 1915. On 9 June the radical oppositionists presented the party executive and parliamentary group with a document, drawn up on the basis of a draft by Liebknecht himself, which denounced both the imperialist character of the war and the complicity of the SPD deputies with the government. The policy initiated on 4 August 1914, it declared, represented the beginning of a line that meant 'not only the bankruptcy of the party' at a moment of historic crisis, but also 'an ever graver break with our previous principles'. Charging that it was becoming 'ever clearer' that the character of the war was one of 'imperialist conquest', it called for respect for the resolutions of the Stuttgart Congress of the International in 1907, which committed every party to exploit a war for purposes of class struggle and to work to 'bring the war to an end as quickly as possible'. Finally, the document denounced the fact that 'the Reichstag fraction, of which the majority of the leaders of the party are members, has abandoned opposition to the policy of imperialist conquest'.[62]

On 19 June 1915, just ten days after the 9 June manifesto, Bernstein (who had joined the 'Centrists' because of his disagreement with the majority's support of the war), Haase, and Kautsky published a manifesto of their own in which they denounced German plans, as set out in a document submitted by major consortia to Chancellor Bethmann-Hollweg on 20 May, for colonial expansion, war reparations, and the annexation of various European territories (inhabited by more than 7 million Belgians and 3 million French). More moderate than the signatories of the 9 June manifesto, who had called the vote of 4 August the beginning

[62] 'Protestschrieben oppositioneller Sozialdemokraten vom 9. Juni 1915 an den Vorstand der SPD und den Vorstand der sozialdemokratischen Reichstagsfraktion gegen die Burgfriedenspolitik', in *Dokumente und Materialien zur Geschichte der deutschen Arbeiterbewegung*, Band 1, Juli 1914–Oktober 1917, Berlin, 1958, pp. 169–171.

of a degeneration of German Social Democracy, Bernstein, Haase and Kautsky on the contrary recalled the declaration of the SPD Reichstag caucus on 4 August opposing any war of conquest or aggressive policy of imperialist circles. This document, *Das Gebot der Stunde*, counter-posed popular 'desire for peace' to the evils of war. It called upon Social Democracy to fulfil its duty to voice the general desire to put an end to the massacres and to oppose the policies of annexation and imperialism. The manifesto concluded by emphasizing the potential division between the majority and the opposition in the SPD: 'If our party does not have the strength to take the necessary decisions, then it is incumbent upon us to come forward as the advocates of the policy we have characterized as the correct one'.[63] It was significant that Bernstein, Haase and Kautsky not only referred positively to the spirit in which the SPD had voted for war credits in August 1914, but also that, unlike the signers of the 9 June manifesto, they avoided mention of any necessity to intensify the class struggle within the country because of the situation created by the prolongation of the war.

Kautsky in particular viewed the evolution of relations between the majority and the two oppositions (the 'Centrist' opposition and the opposition grouped around Karl Liebknecht and Rosa Luxemburg) in the light of his growing concern at the 'breakdown' of the unity of the party caused by the two extremes: the pro-government wing of the Davids and the trade-union leaders on the one hand and the intransigent revolutionary oppositionists on the other. In a letter to Viktor Adler dated 28 November 1914 Kautsky had once again defended his 3 August 1914 position on the war credits (i.e. a recommendation to vote in favour of the government if the latter declared itself against annexations and the infringement of the rights of other peoples, otherwise to abstain). Kautsky viewed Liebknecht's vote against the war credits as not only ineffective but even 'ridiculous'. Most of all, he feared it could become the 'point of departure for a split'. The other group – David, Heine, Südekum, and the union leaders – he continued, were also working, 'against their own will', for a split. He expressed concern for the difficult position in which the 'Centre' found itself: to the extent that it did not oppose the right, it facilitated the shift of a portion of the working class to the 'Luxemburg group', while to the extent that it did oppose the right, it appeared as composed of 'people who differ from Rosa Luxemburg only in their lack of courage'.[64] A few months later, on 11 February

[63] The text is in E. Prager, *Geschichte der U.S.P.D.*, Berlin, 1921, pp. 72–74.
[64] V. Adler, *Briefwechsel . . .*, op. cit., pp. 606–607.

1915, shortly before the attack by Haase and Ledebour on the government's policy in March, Kautsky wrote another letter to Adler in which he suggested that the greater share of the responsibility for a possible split now rested with the right. 'Our unity is not increasing', he wrote, 'but diminishing. Some months ago it still seemed that the greater danger to unity came from the left, from the "followers of Rosa". Today it is coming from the right. The people grouped around David and the trade-union leaders believe that the time has come to purge the party of any "Marxism". . . . Naturally, what they want is not a split but their domination over the entire apparatus of the party and our reduction to the position of mute figureheads. On the other hand, I am not working for a split either, but the conflicts are becoming more exasperating every day, and one fine day there might be an ultimatum that would make war inevitable. . . . We must be prepared for the harshest internal struggles. . . . Hitherto I have been counselling peace in the party, so far as I have been able. Now I can no longer do so'. In the same letter Kautsky spoke of the 'terrorism' the right was introducing into the party.[65]

It is clear from yet another letter to Adler that Kautsky, while apprehensive of the effects of a split in the party, was also eyeing the rising opposition to the line of the right that was developing in the party and in the parliamentary caucus.[66] Torn between fear of a split and awareness that internal opposition was growing because of the errors of the right, Kautsky strove to infuse the party with a conception of discipline that would not be so rigid as to prevent the expression of dissent.[67] The fact that 'grave conflicts' had arisen in the party was certainly not positive, he observed; but 'once such conflicts exist, confronting them freely is the only way to alleviate the evil'. If it was impossible to 'make propaganda' for what one considered just, then party membership became 'an intolerable constraint'.[68] 'What endangers the party is not the *expression* of the conflict but its *existence*'.[69]

In practice, this appeal for tolerance was doomed to complete failure by the progressive exacerbation of the internal conflicts within the SPD. On 1 January 1916 the 'International' group, i.e. the Spartacist wing of the party opposition grouped around Liebknecht, Luxemburg and

[65] Ibid., p. 611.
[66] Ibid., p. 625.
[67] 'Persönliche Ueberzeugungen und Parteidisziplin', in NZ, XXXIV, 1915–1916, vol. I, pp. 129–133.
[68] 'Freiheit der Meinungsässerung und Parteidisziplin', in NZ, XXXIV, 1915–1916, vol. I, p. 161.
[69] Ibid., p. 168.

Mehring (in other words, the far left), organized a national conference
in Berlin with a platform denouncing the official party line and criticizing
the weakness of the 'centrists'. The SPD leadership replied by expelling
Liebknecht from the parliamentary caucus on 12 January. Kautsky
spoke of the need for an agreement to salvage the unity of the party,
based on the abandonment of intolerance by the majority and the
acknowledgment of the right of the minority to express its opposition
publicly: 'We are in a situation in which every step the party takes is
fraught with dangers, the greatest of which', threatening the entire
party, was that 'the minority remains mute', while 'only the majority
continues to appear as the representative of the party'. 'Therefore', he
wrote, 'the existence of the party is at stake. To save it, the minority
must no longer allow itself to be excluded from the public scene even
though there is a danger that the majority may resort not only to the
sharpest protests, which is to be expected, but even to acts of intolerance'.
On the other hand, Kautsky exhorted the minority not to act 'rashly'.[70]

A further crucial development in the organizational scission within
the party occurred in the parliamentary caucus on 24 March. The
minority refused to vote in favour of the government. Haase motivated
its negative vote by denouncing both the internal repression in the
country and the government's imperialist objectives abroad. The majority
of the parliamentary caucus decided, by a vote of 58 to 33, to expel the
entire minority from the caucus. The minority then formed a caucus of
its own, the *Arbeitsgemeinschaft*. Its members were not yet expelled from
the party itself, but by now the internal temperature had risen steeply.
The background to the conflicts in the SPD was the constant deterioration in the living conditions of the masses, which had fallen precipitously.
The conflict between the 'Centrist' and Spartacist oppositions was also
acute. The former disagreed with the call for the formation of a new
International, and rejected the latter's inclination to constitute a separate
party, transforming political opposition into organizational secession.

Commenting on the division of the parliamentary caucus of the SPD,
Kautsky gave political support to the oppositional *Arbeitsgemeinschaft*.
In his view, the organizational unity of the party was now experiencing
its most dangerous crisis since the end of the Emergency Laws against
the Social Democrats. He asserted that the majority bore the political
responsibility for this, since it had turned the vote of 4 August 1914
into the beginning of a 'new epoch' that broke with the traditions and
principles of the party. The Kolbs, Davids, and Heines, exploiting votes

[70] 'Fraktion und Partei', in NZ, XXXIV, 1915–1916, vol. I, pp. 275–276.

in favour of the government and war-time emergency regulations, had increasingly forced through their own 'national-social policy', creating an impossible situation for those who did not follow them.[71] Nevertheless, Kautsky still sought to maintain a dialectical unity within the party. Although the responsibility for the events in the parliamentary caucus in March, he said, fell upon the majority which had adopted a mechanical conception of discipline which left no room for dissent, both sides had to work together in the party. 'The intentions of the minority in no way incline toward the division of the party, and the very logic of events does not impel them to do this', he commented – revealing how little he had understood the connection that now existed between political-ideological dissent and organizational questions. 'The conditions that caused the split of the parliamentary group', he wrote, 'are rooted in the nature of parliament; these conditions do not obtain in our organizations'. Within the SPD itself the contest between the majority and the opposition could unfold without provoking a scission, provided the necessary space for political disagreement was assured within the party.

'If both parliamentary caucuses', he continued, 'work side by side and not against each other, then the great organism of the party will not be shaken by the disputes of the two within the structure. . . . But let us take care that this remains a struggle of convictions. The struggle over great principles elevates us, strengthens us, and increases our power of attraction among independent minds. Only a struggle based on personal defamation degrades the party and undermines its recruiting ability'.[72]

In effect, even after the split of the parliamentary caucus, Kautsky still sought to insist that the traditional manner in which the party had regulated internal conflicts in the past remained valid. Such a line, possibly viable in peace-time, was wholly inadequate to a situation where the masses were becoming increasingly radicalized by the sufferings of the war, while those whom Kautsky called the 'national socialists' rallied fulsomely to the Imperial government. The tensions in the party could no longer be controlled by mere declarations of tolerance. From the spring of 1916 onwards, there was a sharp deterioration in the situation. On 1 May Liebknecht was arrested and later sentenced to imprisonment after a demonstration in Berlin. The movement of strikes and demonstrations, despite obstruction from collaborationist Social Democrats, intensified throughout the country. Luxemburg and Mehring were soon

[71] 'Die Spaltung der Fraktion', in NZ, XXXIV, 1915–1916, vol. II, pp. 33–34.
[72] Ibid., p. 36.

arrested as well. The government tightened police surveillance of the working class. In these conditions, Kautsky realized that the appeal of the opposition was spreading irresistably; his main concern was to prevent it being captured by the Spartacists. In a letter to Viktor Adler dated 7 August 1916 he wrote that the question was now sounding: 'Is the party to act as a government party or an opposition party?' Explaining his attitude toward Liebknecht, he noted that the sufferings of the popular masses 'are producing mounting irritation and exasperation, and what is called "radicalism" is spreading as a result. It is too early to tell whether the majority of the party now supports the opposition. What is certain is that a great number of symptoms show that it [the opposition] is growing. The question is not *if*, but what sort of opposition will win – the sort that wants to destroy the party or the sort that wants to become the majority within the party. The danger from the "Spartacus" group is great. Its radicalism corresponds to the immediate needs of the broad, undisciplined masses. Liebknecht is now the most popular man in the trenches. This is universally confirmed by all those returning from the front. The dissatisfied masses understand nothing of his policy, but they see him as the man who is working for an end to the war, and this is what counts for them. To the "Spartacists", however, the growth of the opposition within the party appears too slow. Patience has never been their strong point. They want to leave the party. This would be quite all right for a large portion of the right, especially the General Commission [of the trade unions] and its little appendage, the party leadership. They too would like to see the opposition leave the party before it becomes the majority. The General Commission is playing the decisive, leading role in this, while the party leadership is the indecisive sector, being dragged along, drawing back in face of the consequences of its own acts. Strange as it may seem, the *Arbeitsgemeinschaft* is the element still holding the party together in face of these two extremes. Had it not been formed, Berlin would have been conquered by the "Spartacists" and would be outside the party. On the other hand, if the left parliamentary group had been constituted in an independent position a year ago, as I desired, the "Spartacus" group would have acquired no weight at all'.[73]

This letter is of critical importance for the light it sheds on Kautsky's attitude toward the 'national socialists' and the 'Spartacists'. In it can be read the reasons for Kautsky's later support for the secession from the SPD in 1917: 1) his conviction that the opposition was on the way

[73] V. Adler, *Briefwechsel . . .*, op. cit., pp. 630–631.

to winning over the majority; 2) his desire to confiscate the political leadership of the opposition from the 'radicals'; 3) his effort to preserve the unity of the bulk of the party, confining dissent as far as possible to the realm of ideology.

Meanwhile, however, the political logic of the conflict within the SPD was moving unstoppably towards an organizational split. It was the majority that took the initiative – in keeping with the wishes of the Haase-Ledebour-Kautsky 'Centre', who shrank from the responsibility of a scission. On 7 January 1917 the 'Centre' and 'Spartacist' groups held a general conference in Berlin to respond to the creeping expulsions and discriminatory administrative measures being taken by the majority against both oppositions. The conference was attended by 157 delegates (19 of whom were members of parliament). About 30 of them belonged to the Spartacist wing. The central themes of debate were the attitude to be taken toward war and peace and the relations to be adopted towards the supporters of the majority. The oppositionists made no call for a split, but showed their resolve not to renounce their own political identity. Kautsky drafted the 'peace manifesto of the opposition', in which the conference formulated the following major goals: 1) a rapid end to the war; 2) peace not at any price but 'without victors and vanquished', 'agreement without infringement on the rights of others'; 3) not a peace of diplomats but of the peoples of the warring countries, who alone were capable of checking the belligerent ambitions of the great powers; 4) full identification of Social Democracy with the self-determination of peoples; 5) disarmament; 6) peace to be guaranteed in future by the proletariat.[74] The response of the trade-union leaders and the majority Social Democrats was swift; they decided to expel the opposition. On 16 January the General Commission of the trade unions announced its determination to remain fully loyal to the government in the hour of the country's struggle for existence. On 18 January the party leadership, by a vote of 29 to 10, expelled the *Arbeitsgemeinschaft* and the leftist groups linked to it, with the evident aim of preventing any chance of the opposition winning over a majority of the party.

Faced with this precipitation of events, Kautsky sought to ensure that the opposition, or at least the most consistent portion of it, should in the hour of its break with the majority invoke continuity with the traditions of the party. He strove to put the onus for the split on the 'majority faction'. In addition, he expressed doubt that the self-pro-

[74] 'Friedensmanifest der Opposition', in *Leipziger Volkszeitung*, 8 January 1917.

claimed majority really had the support of the majority of party members and insisted that it was not the opposition but the right that was abandoning the past principles of the SPD. In February 1917 he wrote that 'in forty-two years of activity in international Social Democracy' he had observed that all the splits that had occurred in Austria, England, France and Russia had seen minorities declare not only their political opposition but also their desire to found new organizations. In Germany things were different, he said. There it could be seriously doubted whether the opposition represented only a minority of the party and whether the forces that commanded a majority of the party leadership and parliamentary caucus still had the allegiance of the majority of the rank and file.[75] A verification of the real relationship of forces would be possible only at a regular party congress, which would reveal the changes in the orientation of the membership that had probably occurred. Under these conditions, the administrative and disciplinary measures taken by the leading bodies controlled by the majority were, according to Kautsky, wholly arbitrary and illegitimate. 'The Russian Tsar himself', he declared, 'no longer enjoys the luxury of being able to liquidate any opposition through simple administrative deportation, without any trace of judicial procedure or even having to listen to the accused'.[76] He concluded: 'The process of disintegration now under way in our ranks is caused primarily by the fact that a party congress is not possible, nor the free agitation a congress presupposes. The greater and more energetic number of comrades have been eliminated from party activity, and what remains of this activity is naturally contained within the narrowest limits. The conflict in the party is rooted not merely in the fact that there are two currents, which are indeed moving further and further apart, but also in the fact that the lack of a congress and the impossibility of deciding which current actually has the majority should make maximum tolerance necessary on the part of the leading bodies of the party'. But this tolerance was lacking among a leadership that had used war-time conditions to strengthen its own 'position of power'.[77] Kautsky, who had always upheld the necessity of party unity, did not view the situation with any vigorous resolve to forward the opposition. His attitude was pessimistic. *Vorwärts* had defended the decision of the party leadership as an amputation necessary 'to realize the unity of the workers' movement at a higher level'; Kautsky replied

[75] 'Parteispaltung?', in NZ, XXXV, 1916–1917, vol. I, p. 489.
[76] Ibid., p. 495.
[77] Ibid., p. 497.

that what was actually occurring was the 'disaggregation of the party'.[78]

Kautsky's resistance to accepting the reality of the split within the SPD was such that his main demand continued to be the right of the opposition to exist in the party. 'The opposition', he wrote, 'has . . . no reason to provoke a split before the next congress. What it must demand is only the necessary freedom of movement to be able to express itself as an opposition within the party'. Given the division of political lines, which inevitably found expression in differing attitudes in the Reichstag, the opposition 'should be guaranteed the use of the only free tribune still available today, namely parliament. The opposition must oppose with all its might the tendency to suffocate the entire opposition press or to transform it into the official agency of the leadership'.[79] Kautsky reminded both the 'majority faction' and the 'Spartacists' that if matters should come to the actual formation of two workers' parties, there should be no illusion that it would be easy to reunify the two parties after the war, given the conflicts and lacerations that would have occurred between them.[80] In a harsh attack on the majority which belied his later affirmation, when he returned to the SPD, that his contradictions with the majority had been secondary while his differences with the 'Spartacists' had been antagonistic,[81] he commented that a party built by majority supporters would be a 'national social' party 'to a large extent dependent on the good will of the bourgeois parties'.[82] Thus, if it came to the formation of two parties, one would be 'a democratically organized party' while the other would be a party 'subjected to a centralized bureaucracy'. One would be internationalist, the other prepared to subordinate internationalism to whatever could 'serve its own people'. One would be committed to promoting 'a struggle for the emancipation' of the working class, the other essentially to defending 'its most immediate material interests'. One would be determined to re-establish the tradition of the party, the other transformed into 'a genuine national social party'. One would be based on the most combative layers of the proletariat, the other on the less militant strata of the proletariat and petty-bourgeois white-collar workers, on those groups which led 'an intermediary existence between the proletariat and the capitalist class'.[83] The 'national social' party would end up competing with the Catholic Centre Party

[78] Ibid., p. 498.
[79] 'Zwei Arbeiterparteien', in NZ, XXXV, 1916–1917, vol. I, p. 585.
[80] Ibid., p. 586.
[81] 'Mein Verhältnis zur USPD', op. cit., p. 6.
[82] 'Zwei Arbeiterparteien', op. cit., p. 587.
[83] Ibid., p. 588.

and the Progressive Liberals for the allegiance of the same constituencies.[84]

Given his approach to the internal struggle in the SPD, it was predictable that Kautsky would not favour the transformation of the ideological and organizational fissure within it into the foundation of a new party. Hence his behaviour at the conference called by the opposition in Gotha, 6–8 April 1917, which was to become the founding congress of the Unabhängige Sozialdemokratische Partei Deutschlands (USPD – Independent Social Democratic Party of Germany). It voted to form a new party by 77 to 42: among those voting against were Kautsky, Bernstein and Kurt Eisner. The new party was born divided. Its common denominator was opposition to the pro-governmental line of the majority over the war. Beyond this, however, the potential for conflicts within the USPD can be seen merely by listing the most famous figures who joined it: Bernstein, Eisner, Kautsky, Haase, Ledebour, Hilferding, Mehring, Luxemburg, Leibknecht and Zetkin – a spectrum of opinion divided by the most profound ideological, political and organizational divergences. Right centrists, left centrists, and Spartacists had fought and would continue to fight ferociously with each other. What brought them together for the moment was a negation. It would soon be shown that the political prerequisites for transforming this negative unity into positive agreement were lacking.

Consistent with his opposition to the construction of a new party and his insistence on the importance of the Social Democratic tradition, Kautsky first voted against the foundation of an independent party and then, once the decision was made, sought – together with Bernstein and Eisner – to see to it that the old name of the party was maintained. For years now, the aged theoretician had been subjected to a crossfire of violent criticism from many of the major figures of the new party. Significantly, however, the manifesto in which the USPD justified the reasons for its own foundation was not only written by Kautsky but was approved with only one dissenting vote.

The content of this manifesto corresponded exactly to the analysis Kautsky had developed during the preceding period. It accused the 'government socialists', trade union leaders, and SPD parliamentary caucus of having adopted and consolidated during the war the tendencies of the pro-government right of the pre-war period; of having succumbed to national socialism and national liberalism; of having broken with the tradition of the party; of having failed to influence the policy of the government in any way; of having sacrificed the freedoms of the workers;

[84] Ibid., p. 589.

of having put themselves at the disposal of the government's war-time mobilization of industry. To the policy of the 'government socialists' the manifesto counterposed the need to launch 'a campaign against rising prices and unemployment', as the basis of workers' struggles in the post-war period. Declaring that 'the popular will must become the supreme law' (which suggested an appeal for a democratic republic), the manifesto demanded an immediate amnesty for political prisoners, full rights of association, freedom of the press and freedom of assembly, introduction of the eight-hour day, and equal and secret universal suffrage for both men and women to all elective bodies.

The manifesto also hailed the second Russian Revolution, which had brought down Tsarism. In Russia, Kautsky wrote, even the bourgeoisie had pronounced itself for the democratic republic, while the government socialists in Germany accepted the principle of the monarchy. This was a policy that provoked failure after failure; it led 'not to the reinforcement and rising enthusiasm of the proletariat, but to the weakening of its power and the diminution of its influence'. Against this sort of policy Kautsky held up the 'shining example' of the Russian workers, who had shown their ability to pursue a 'socialist and democratic policy' and whose action had overthrown Tsarism, 'the strongest bastion of reaction'. At this point, the manifesto drafted by Kautsky spoke of the objectives of peace, in terms that were characteristic of the position of the 'Centre': 'The workers of Russia have struggled to establish democracy and to open the road to socialism. But they have also struggled for peace, for the most rapid end to the most frightful of all wars by the conclusion of a peace based on the foundations of our common socialist principles. . . . We seek a peace through concord among peoples, without direct or disguised annexations, on the basis of the decision of peoples themselves, with international limitation of armaments and compulsory tribunals of arbitration. We see these institutions not as magic instruments to assure peace, but as the most effective aids to the proletarian struggle to preserve peace, our major task after the war. . . . Against the national solidarity of classes we stand for the international solidarity of the proletariat, the international struggle of the working class'.[85]

The USPD programme was essentially aimed at the recovery of the proletariat's freedom of action, within the framework of a democratic parliamentary republic. It is no accident that it contained not a word about any future shift of the class struggle in a revolutionary direction.

[85] 'Manifest des Gründungsparteitages der USPD vom 6. bis 8. April 1917', in *Dokumente und Materialien* . . ., op. cit., pp. 594–597.

Representative democracy, political liberty with civic rights of association, and a democratic peace, not the struggle for socialism or the onset of a revolutionary process – these were the slogans of the 'Centre' and of Kautsky himself. In sum, it was a programme for a reversion to the road that had been closed by the war, in the context of the crisis now generated by the war. Socialism was postponed until a majority was obtained in parliament, after the re-establishment of the mechanism of the parliamentary political struggle. Although Kautsky's draft was accepted by the 'Spartacists' for tactical reasons in the particular conjuncture of 1917, it made future ruptures within the new party inevitable. Meanwhile, Kautsky's adherence to the USPD led inevitably to his dismissal from the editorial board of *Die Neue Zeit*, the party's theoretical journal which he had founded in 1883.

3 For a 'Peace without Annexations'

We have seen that both the manifesto *Des Gebot der Stunde* and the programme Kautsky composed for the founding congress of the USPD emphasized the demand for a peace based on renunciation of all annexations – a notion closely linked to Kautsky's strategic concern to resume the road that had been interrupted in Germany on 4 August 1914. This was a conception equally distant from the positions of the 'government socialists' and of those who denied that a democratic peace was possible and held that the struggle against the war was the beginning of a revolutionary socialist process. The international socialist conference held in Zimmerwald in Switzerland, on 5–8 September 1915, at the initiative of the Italian Socialist Party, was the first international gathering of the socialist movement after the crisis of August 1914. The conference united, or rather witnessed a confrontation among, thirty-eight delegates from various countries. A resolution drafted by Lenin called for the transformation of the 'domestic truce' in the belligerent countries into civil war. It exhorted the Socialist Parties to break not only with 'social chauvinism' but also with the so-called Centre, which had yielded Marxist positions to the chauvinists. It warned socialists not to allow themselves to be infected by the 'hope that, without the revolutionary overthrow of the present-day governments, a possibility exists of a speedy democratic peace, which will be durable in some degree and will preclude any oppression of nations, a possibility of disarmament, etc.' It declared that 'only the social revolution of the proletariat opens the way to peace and freedom for the nations'. The only way out of the objective crisis was the 'conquest of political power by the proletariat'.[86] This resolution was rejected, as was Lenin's call for a break with the Second International and the construction of a new International. The manifesto that was adopted by the majority at Zimmerwald, drafted by Trotsky, typified the outlook of the international 'Centre'. It called for political struggle against the 'domestic truce' as well as struggle against the imperialist governments to achieve a peace without annexations – in other words, characteristically Kautskyist demands.

The conference of Kienthal (24–30 April 1916) once again rejected Lenin's positions and reiterated the need for a peace without annexations. At the same time, however, it marked a turn to the left. Although they did not endorse the call for the foundation of a new International or the slogan to turn the imperialist war into a civil war, the resolutions adopted at Kienthal criticised any form of support to the belligerent governments more drastically, denouncing any vote in favour of war credits and denying that the strategic or military position of any given country could modify this principle. The Kienthal Conference declared that the Executive Committee of the International had abandoned its duty to combat social chauvinism resolutely and that socialism alone could end imperialism and ensure peace. All this put a very different construction on the 'struggle for a peace without annexations' inherited from Zimmerwald – one that Lenin and the revolutionary left could view as a first step towards a new internationalism, while 'centrists' like Kautsky saw it as a drift towards radicalism.

Kautsky argued that 'defence of the fatherland', votes for war credits, and annexations (in other words, war aims) all had to be considered in the light of their concrete consequences in specific historical situations. From the end of 1916 to the first half of 1917 he maintained that it would be a mistake, for example, to adopt a position of abstract principle on the problem of national 'defence'. Above all, recalling the position taken by Marx in 1870 at the beginning of the Franco-Prussian war, as well as the attitude of Bebel, he maintained that Social Democracy was not opposed to national defence in and of itself.[87]

'Rejection of national defence as a matter of principle', Kautsky wrote, 'is in conflict with our programme. . . . To reject national defence would be to announce the impotence of a people before any armed

[86] V. I. Lenin, *Collected Works*, vol. XXI, Moscow 1964, pp. 347–348.

[87] 'Sozialdemokratische Anschauungen über den Krieg vor dem jetzigen Kriege', in NZ, XXXV, 1916–1917, vol. I, pp. 297–298.

foreign government. It would mean that until the social revolution breaks out, what happens to peoples is a matter of complete indifference to us. It would leave a clear path for any unscrupulous conqueror'.

But to say that Social Democrats accepted the principle of national defence did not mean that once a war broke out they had to support the foreign policy and military strategy of a bourgeois government and imperialism.[88] The conceptions of Marx, Engels, Bebel, and Wilhelm Liebknecht certainly had nothing to do with the policies of governments; they advocated the right to defence 'not in the name of the particular national interests of their own country, but in the name of international democracy'.[89] In practice the essential criterion for determining the attitude of the proletariat and of democrats was the political nature of the aims of the war. In this sense, the question of which side was the aggressor in the formal sense could never be decisive (since a country could initiate a war for reasons that were substantially defensive): 'The issue over which a war breaks out *is neither the only, nor the most important element,* in determining our attitude towards it. Much more important is our assessment of the *objectives of the war*', since it was these that defined the nature of the war and the real basis for a future peace.[90] It was war aims alone that were relevant to the international proletariat in fixing its policy. In the present World War, Kautsky said, Social Democracy must struggle for a peace without annexations, as the necessary foundation for an ulterior resumption of internationalism and of social struggle. 'The dispute in our ranks over national defence is now quite clear. It does not consist in the fact that some accept national defence while others reject it, but rather that for some their attitude toward the government is a function of national defence, while for others their attitude toward national defence is a function of their assessment of the policy of the government. In this regard we should never lose sight of the fact that the expression "national defence" is merely a euphemism for the conduct of the war'.[91] Hence Kautsky's appeal to the Zimmerwald Manifesto: 'Only those parties and minorities [of parties] that determine their attitude toward governments not on the basis of national defence but solely on their judgment of the policy of governments and which stand before these governments in full liberty, not only in form but also in substance, only these can re-establish the

[88] 'Die Landesverteidigung', in NZ, XXXV, 1916–1917, vol. II, pp. 121–122.
[89] 'Sozialdemokratische Anschauungen . . .', op. cit., p. 300.
[90] Ibid., p. 304.
[91] 'Die Landesverteidigung', op. cit., p. 123.

International and assume the leading role in bringing about concord among the nations at war. Zimmerwald has proven this'.[92]

4 Russia, 1917: 'Democracy First, Then Socialism'

In the manifesto he drafted for the Gotha Congress that ratified the birth of the USPD, Kautsky had hailed the February Revolution in Russia as a shining example of democratic and socialist politics, contrasting the struggle of the Russian workers to the degeneration of the German 'government socialists'. He then wrote a close analysis of Russian events in a fundamental article entitled *Die Aussichten der russischen Revolution*, which surveyed: 1) the relationship between democracy and socialism; 2) the relationship between the proletariat and the bourgeoisie; 3) the relationship between the proletariat and the peasantry; 4) the international effects of the revolution, both on the World War and on the internal political situation in Central Europe.

The consolidation of the Russian Revolution, Kautsky declared, would signal 'a new epoch for all Europe' and in particular would constitute 'a powerful advance of the political forces of the toiling classes throughout the capitalist world'. Commenting on the internal dynamic of the revolution, Kautsky noted that because of the leading role played by the working class, which possessed 'a strong class consciousness' and leaders armed with 'the science of the twentieth century', the revolution had a 'predominantly proletarian' character from the outset.[93] The fundamental question in Russia therefore revolved around the roles that would be played by the working class and the bourgeoisie. 'The consolidation of the conditions of the new state order', he wrote, 'strictly depends on this question: rule of the proletariat or rule of the bourgeoisie?'[94]

According to Kautsky (rehearsing many of the essential points of his analysis of the 1905 revolution in Russia), the historical peculiarity of the Russian Revolution was that the leading role of the socialist proletariat was combined with general social and economic backwardness and an insufficient numerical expansion of the working class as a social-productive force, which made it unthinkable that the Russian Revolution

---

[92] Ibid., p. 127.
[93] 'Die Aussichten der russischen Revolution', in NZ, XXXV, 1916–1917, vol. II, pp. 9–11.
[94] Ibid., p. 10.

would become a socialist revolution capable of initiating a new form of production superseding capitalism. This contradiction could be resolved only by understanding the function of democracy, not merely as a formal procedure but as a substantive means to assure economic and social development in a context defined by three critical factors: the political influence of the proletariat; the needs of the peasant masses, who had an interest in bourgeois-democratic ownership of land; and the weakness of the advanced productive sector, in other words of industry. 'The proletariat', Kautsky wrote, 'urgently needs two things: *democracy* and *socialism*. Democracy means the most extensive political freedoms and rights for the popular masses, the transformation of the institutions of the state and the local administrative bodies into pure instruments of the popular masses. Socialism means the transformation of private production for the market into social production, that is, state, communal, or co-operative production, for the needs of society. The proletariat needs both in equal measure'. After these assertions, Kautsky commented – a significant remark in the light of his future attitude toward the Bolshevik régime: 'Social production without democracy could become a most oppressive bond. Democracy without socialism would allow the persistence of the economic dependence of the proletariat'.[95]

Democracy was not an ideal exclusive to the proletariat. But it was the proletariat that now fought for it most energetically, since the bourgeoisie could live without democracy, while the proletariat lost all possibilities for action if there was no democracy. Moreover, democracy could be introduced 'wherever' there was proletarian struggle. Socialism, on the other hand, was an aim characteristic only of the proletariat. The introduction of socialism was impossible if modern forces of production were insufficiently developed, not only because of the consequent technological obstacles, but also and even more importantly because the proletariat would be too weak to direct economy and society.[96] The Russian Revolution should thus aim at the consolidation of a democratic republic, in which a progressive government could promote the rapid development of modern industry and so strengthen the working class numerically and mature it politically. This prospect was possible only in the context of a democratic system. Democracy, the exercise of civic freedoms, facilitated the formation of a proletariat capable of becoming a ruling class, and thereby provided the basis for socialism.

[95] Ibid., p. 11.
[96] Ibid., pp. 11–12.

'Democracy', Kautsky wrote, 'is now even more important than the economic elevation of the proletariat'; it alone constituted the 'foundation' on which 'a process of lasting growth of the popular masses is possible'. 'For this reason', he continued, the significance of democracy was not only that it made 'the conquest of political positions possible. It also had inestimable value in areas where it offers no immediate practical advantage from the standpoint of *Realpolitik*. In order to liberate themselves, the workers, in addition to growing in numbers and winning certain material advantages, must also become "new men", endowed with those capacities which are necessary for a new order of state and society. These abilities are acquired only through class struggle, which, as a process directed by its own participants, must not be guided by secret committees that issue orders to the proletarian masses, but requires democratic rights and freedoms'.[97]

The backwardness of Russia, Kautsky argued, was patent from the relationship between the city and the country. The urban industrial proletariat in Russia was too weak numerically. In 1913, only 24 million people lived in cities, 150 million in the countryside. Because of the low level of general economic development, this imbalance was aggravated by the lack of adequate communications and the intense social and political isolation of the rural population.

In this context, Kautsky held, socialization could not prevail in a democratic political system in the near future, for its necessary preconditions were lacking. 'There is no doubt', he observed, 'that Russian capitalism still furnishes too limited a base for development in a socialist direction'. This did not mean that there were no important sectors that should be subjected to measures of public control or should become social property. Indeed, it was necessary to proceed forthwith to the nationalization of the major industries, railroads, mines, and metallurgical complexes. In addition, Kautsky held that the property of the Tsar and the monasteries should be confiscated and the estates of the large landlords nationalized. These sectors, he said, should be managed by the democratic state, in a climate of full freedom for the proletariat. In private industry the proletariat should enjoy maximum opportunities to defend its own interests: protection of labour; the eight-hour day; unemployment insurance; distribution of food products to the working population at low prices. Finally, to cover growing state expenditure, progressive taxes would have to be introduced, falling exclusively on the shoulders of the possessing classes. These, he argued, were the

[97] Ibid., p. 13.

measures the new Russia needed if it was to establish a political democracy with an advanced social content.

For Kautsky political democracy was the necessary form of the class struggle in Russia and the proper gauge of the real relationship of class forces. 'This', he commented, 'may be defined as a bourgeois reformist programme and not a programme of proletarian revolution'. But it was the only programme which, because of its advanced reformist character, could take account of the strength of the proletariat and the peasantry on the one hand and the weakness of the bourgeoisie on the other, and yet, because of its non-socialist character, simultaneously accord with the overall backwardness of modern industry in Russia. The relationship between bourgeois reformism and social revolution depended on the dynamic evolution of social struggle and economic progress. Whether the programme leant 'this way or that', i.e. in a more bourgeois or more proletarian direction, 'depends on quantitative elements'. However, 'here again', Kautsky continued, 'quantity, when sufficiently increased, must yield a new quality. The proletariat, as soon as it finds its feet, will inevitably do its utmost to exploit the situation in the direction outlined above [i.e. in the direction of social revolution], and in so doing will clash with the resistance of the capitalists and large landlords. Exactly when this happens will depend on the relative strength of the proletariat'.[98]

As for the peasants and the attitude the proletariat should take toward them, Kautsky reiterated his analysis of 1905, declaring that the workers had every interest in aiding the peasants to gain land. Once this had been won, the peasants would feel linked to the cause of the revolution, and the counter-revolution would lose its strength, above all because the great majority of the army was composed of peasants. 'When the peasants are won over, the army will also be won to the young republic and will become a force for its defence'.[99] Kautsky's conclusion was that if Russian democracy succeeded in stabilizing itself, the East would be rejoined to the West, and a common road would be open to the conquest of political power by the proletariat: 'the mass movement and mass organizations would then be assured the most solid foundation for the conquest of political power in Eastern Europe, at least as firmly as in the West'.[100] It should be noted that the East was to be reunited with the West on the common basis of political democracy, as the 'general form' of the

[98] Ibid., pp. 11–12.
[99] Ibid., pp. 18–19.
[100] Ibid., p. 20.

conduct of the social struggle for socialism.

In August 1917 Kautsky singled out two urgent necessities for the Russian Revolution: 1) the attainment of peace; 2) the convocation of a Constituent Assembly. It was Kautsky's view that the movement for peace could unite the Russian working class and the progressive parties of the new republic with the action of the Western proletariat in a common framework of democracy. It also corresponded to the need to safeguard Russian democracy itself: 'War and democracy are two phenomena that are not easily compatible. . . . A rapid peace is indispensable for the success of the Russian Revolution'. Nevertheless, the peace Russia needed was not just any peace at any price. Peace could be real only if it was 'without annexations and reparations, based on the right of self-determination of peoples on both sides'. It was thus related to the problem of a more general peace.[101] The Russian Revolution must also integrate itself into the action of the International. 'Revolutionary Russia alone is not capable of concluding peace on the foundations it chooses. This is a task of the International; it is its duty, both to the Russian Revolution and to itself'. The international socialist movement should understand that a failure of the revolution in Russia would retard and hamper 'the process of democratization in Central Europe'.[102]

Kautsky's insistence on the need to convoke the Constituent Assembly in Russia was consistent with his analysis of the importance of democratic procedures for the future of that country. He observed that a radicalization was occurring in the internal struggle among those classes 'that took part in the destruction of the old government'. He viewed with concern the possibility that this struggle might burn itself out without the creation of any general representative institution. (Kautsky did not mention soviets, a form he would not have deemed suitable for the representation of all classes and therefore as the basis for a national government.) '*The election of the Constituent Assembly*', he wrote, 'is an urgent necessity. Not in order to neutralize the conflicts among classes and parties, but rather to permit a more accurate assessment of their strength and thus to lend their struggles a more rational foundation'.[103] Here there re-emerged again Kautsky's traditional theme of the need to endow any great state with a general technical-political instrument of leadership. For Kautsky this instrument could only be a Constituent

[101] 'Stockholm', in NZ, XXXV, 1916–1917, vol. II, p. 507.
[102] Ibid., p. 508.
[103] Ibid., p. 506.

Assembly and therefore a parliament.

When the Bolsheviks seized power in Russia Kautsky wrote a comment, *Die Erhebung der Bolschewiki*, in which he emphasized the dangers of a 'dictatorship of the proletariat' in such a backward country and examined the factors that had led to Lenin's victory. But there was no 'condemnation' of the insurrection. His condemnation came only later, when the Bolsheviks dissolved the Constituent Assembly, an act he viewed as a break with democracy. It is significant that he first hailed the advent of the Bolsheviks to power not in terms of a *'coup d'Etat'*, but as the accession of the proletariat to power: 'For the first time in world history, the proletariat has now conquered governmental power in an entire great state'. But he continued by asking: 'How will all this end?' Analysing the social and economic conditions of Russia, he highlighted the difficulties facing the new régime, particularly the fact that three-fourths of the Russian population lived in a backward countryside. But he did not overlook some positive features: the existence in the great cities, the centre of political life, of 'very modern large-scale industry'; the revolutionary spirit of a proletariat (note this) 'completely free of the bourgeois traditions that burden the workers of Western Europe'; the guidance of this proletariat by Marxist leaders. Thus everything would depend on the way in which the contradiction of an advanced revolutionary proletariat in a generally very backward country was handled. Discussing the contrasting policies of the Bolsheviks and Mensheviks towards the problem that had divided the two currents of Russian socialism, how to prevent the 'exclusive power' of the bourgeoisie, Kautsky underscored the factors that had favoured the triumph of the Bolshevik line. The Mensheviks had relied on a coalition government, the Bolsheviks on a dictatorship of the proletariat supported by the revolutionary section of the peasantry, and on immediate peace. The peasants' hunger for land and the masses' desire for peace, neither of which had been satisfied, had swung the balance decisively to the Bolsheviks, assuring their victory. But, Kautsky continued, the very factors that had given the Bolsheviks their victory posed a serious threat to them after the seizure of power, because of the internal contradictions of class relations in Russia. The advanced proletariat, a minority, had been able to seize power in the cities (and thus make itself master of the entire country, since only the cities had real weight in a decisive contest) by taking advantage of the democratic struggle of the peasants in the countryside. Now, however, the fact that the proletariat controlled only the cities would become a disadvantage; the workers would have to confront the anarchy in the countryside, and the danger of civil war would soar the moment the bourgeoisie was violently assaulted. 'The outlook of the Bolsheviks', Kautsky wrote, 'was the most straightforward and corresponded more than any other to the class situation of the proletariat; but it has also threatened to sharpen to the maximum the contradiction between the intense effort of the proletariat and the low level of development of the empire'. The Bolsheviks now had to take account of the threats arising primarily from the particularism of the peasantry. Kautsky concluded that the Russian working class was not capable of introducing socialism and that it should therefore refrain from installing a 'dictatorship of the proletariat', since 'in the conditions of Russia' this would open the road 'to the political and social disintegration of the country, to chaos, and thus also to the moral bankruptcy of the revolution, to the counter-revolution'.

The Russian Revolution had so far been dominated by the failure of coalition governments which could have completed 'their mission only if they had rapidly achieved peace and convened the Constituent Assembly'. The inability to satisfy these exigencies had led to the victory of the Bolsheviks. Given the unresolved problems in Russia, Kautsky did not take a position against the Bolsheviks in principle. He expected them to act as a decisive force for a social change which would not conflict with political democracy (which meant convocation of and respect for the Constituent Assembly). He had respect for the Bolsheviks, and something more as well. 'Now', he wrote, 'we will see whether the fears about their rise were justified. They do not lack energy. In their ranks are extremely intelligent comrades, rich in experience. But the inherent difficulties of the real conditions are enormous. If they succeed in overcoming them, it will be something extraordinary. A new epoch of world history is beginning'. Looking forward to the advent of parliamentarism in Russia (when they took power the Bolsheviks promised that they would do what none of the other governments since the February revolution had done, namely convoke the Constituent Assembly), Kautsky urged a parliament linked to the masses: 'The introduction of a parliament is one aspect of democratization, but it is not sufficient in itself. Important as the dependence of the government on parliament may be, it leads to democratization only when it is accompanied by the growing dependence of parliament on the popular masses. A parliament is deprived of strength when it cannot rely on the mass of the people'.[104] Kautsky, in other words, was reaffirming his classical point of view: defence of universal suffrage and political democracy on

[104] 'Die Erhebung der Bolschewiki', in *Leipziger Volkszeitung*, 15 November 1917.

the one hand, insistence on the role of socialists in bringing the social weight of the toiling masses to bear within political democracy and representative institutions on the other hand. The subsequent evolution of the Russian Revolution, especially the dissolution of the Constituent Assembly and the abolition of universal suffrage by the Bolsheviks, leading to what Kautsky was to call the 'dictatorship' of the Russian Communists, was to be denounced by him as a double betrayal, of democracy and of socialism. It was then that the 'insurrection of the Bolsheviks' assumed the character of a *coup d'Etat* in his eyes.

VII

The German Revolution and the Struggle against Spartacism

1 The Nature of Socialization and the Role of the Councils

According to his own testimony in 1924, Kautsky found himself 'almost completely alone' during the war in his 'intermediary position' between the government socialists and the Spartacist left.[1] In reality, as we have seen, he had played a significant role in the birth of the USPD. His claim, however, suggested his awareness of how difficult it had become for him to exert any political influence on the major trends of the German labour movement. In his 'intermediary position' he was again marching shoulder to shoulder with his old friend Bernstein. In this regard Kautsky later wrote: 'I then found myself closely linked to Bernstein. We came together again during the war. Each of us preserved his own political physiognomy, but in practical action we found ourselves almost always in agreement. So it has continued to the present day'.[2]

This convergence with Bernstein, against whose revisionism he had once polemicized so vehemently, had in fact a precise political explanation. Kautsky held that the major axes of political and ideological agitation during the war should be: peace without annexations; creation of a Society of Nations; international peace tribunals; democratization of the German state. All these were themes with which Bernstein not only agreed but regarded as the essence of his own democratic-reformist programme. After the October Revolution in Russia, the emergence of Bolshevism as an international current and its fusion with German Spartacism, and the clear intention of the revolutionary Social Democratic currents and later of the Communist Parties to create a new

[1] *Das Werden eines Marxisten*, op. cit., p. 142.
[2] Ibid., p. 142.

International, drove Kautsky to a theoretical position where opposition to Communism became the virtually exclusive, or in any case fundamental, purpose of all his work after 1917. In this domain as well his agreement with Bernstein was complete. To Kautsky – veteran theorist of the organizational unity of the proletariat, of the need for a parliamentary majority as the precondition for the assumption of power, of the technical indispensability of parliament and representative democracy in all great modern states, of civil and political liberties as the common patrimony of all society – Bolshevism appeared as a demon of scission in the ranks of the working class, a merciless and barbaric force destroying the political freedoms won by popular struggles over the course of decades, the champion of an implacable bureaucratic, police, and militarist dictatorship. It was as though the spectres of Weitling, Blanqui, Bakunin and Tkachev, rolled into one, were stalking the earth again, this time armed with all the force and violence of the ex-Tsarist empire, thanks to a *coup d'Etat* conducted against democracy and genuine socialism.

Throughout the German Revolution of 1918–1919, Kautsky called incessantly for the organizational unity of the proletariat and for the defence of the democratic republic, convinced that only the re-establishment of civil order and industrial production could permit an effective struggle for socialism. He condemned both the Noskes and the revolutionary attempts of the Spartacists. But his proposals for a 'third road' collided with the internal division of the labour movement and with the spontaneous forms the social crisis had assumed in Germany. As time went on Kautsky increasingly directed the brunt of his attacks against the revolutionary left, until he finally put the entire responsibility for the failure of socialism in Germany, and even for the success of Nazism, on the Communists, whose determination to rule unopposed and contempt for democratic methods had broken the back of the workers' movement, giving the fascist movements themselves lessons in political technique. Kautsky was to maintain that the dictatorship born of the action of the Bolsheviks in the East had been fatal in two respects. On the one hand, it could not be exported to the West, which rejected it as a model; but on the other hand, it exercised sufficient sway on the workers' movement outside Russia to prevent democratic socialism from achieving its full potential. In effect, according to Kautsky, Russian Communism was incapable of understanding the specific nature of Western society, so could never be effective as an example in itself, but it could and did condemn the whole Western labour movement to impotence for a historical epoch.

The essential strategic aims advanced by Kautsky during the German crisis of 1918–1919 were these: 1) democratization of state institutions; 2) convocation of a national Constituent Assembly; 3) revival of production and socialization of some industries; 4) political unity of the proletariat as a preliminary to its organizational reunification; 5) rejection of civil war, which would prepare the victory of reaction, and defence of democratic-parliamentary methods; 6) institutionalization of workers' councils as instruments of mass organization and not as an alternative 'state' counterposed to parliament as the representative organ of all social classes. Expounding his view of what was needed to provide a solid foundation for the democratic republic after the collapse of the empire, he wrote towards the end of 1918: 'The mass of the population must side with the democratic republic; the present corps of officials must be deprived of any power of command, except as necessary to facilitate demobilization; in place of a standing army, a militia must be constituted, insofar as an armed force is necessary. The rule of the functionaries, who are presently controlled by the councils of workers and soldiers, must in normal times be replaced by autonomous administrative bodies elected by universal and equal suffrage. Even today, all high functionaries who do not enjoy the confidence of the workers and soldiers and who can be replaced by elements who are competent and worthy of trust must be so replaced. The task of the national assembly is to provide a lasting foundation for the German democratic republic'.[3]

Kautsky thus considered that conditions now existed in Germany to create, through the democratic republic, the most favourable basis for the struggle of the socialists for power: 'Only ignorance and division among the workers can retard the advent of socialism under the democratic republic'.[4] Hence the urgency of the most rapid possible return to conditions of internal order. Hence also his opposition to violence: 'The method of violence, whoever may resort to it, endangers precisely what needs to be attained and prevents the inevitable social and political struggles from being fought out through methods of democracy, without disturbing tranquillity and order. Violence leads to civil war'.[5] Kautsky's opposition to civil war was inspired by a number of motives. He was convinced that the only justifiable recourse to violence by the proletariat would be to defend representative democracy; he was persuaded – as

---

[3] *Was will die deutsche sozialistiche Republik?*, n.d. and n.l. [1918], pp. 1–2.
[4] Ibid., p. 2.
[5] Ibid., p. 3.

he had been as far back as 1893, when he wrote *Der Parlamentarismus, die Volksgesetzgebung und die Sozialdemokratie* – 'that a real parliamentary régime can be an instrument of the dictatorship of the proletariat as much as an instrument of the dictatorship of the bourgeoisie'; and he was certain that the only valid content of a proletarian 'dictatorship' was socialist legislation, enacted by a parliament in which the working class had obtained a majority. Thus he held that recourse to civil war as a path to power was an open confession of an attempt to win by force what could not be obtained through consent, which in the absence of any popular consensus would inevitably provoke a reactionary regression. Even where apparently successful, as in Russia (in no case could it be successful in Germany), it ushered in at most not the dictatorship of the proletariat but the dictatorship of a section of the proletariat over the rest of the population, and in the final analysis the dictatorship of the party which represented only this part of the proletariat.

'Today', Kautsky wrote in 1918, in *Demokratie oder Diktatur*, 'we ourselves are living through a revolution. Today we find ourselves facing the question, dictatorship or democracy? not in Russia but in Germany'.[6] Illustrating the relationship between democracy and dictatorship, Kautsky set out a number of significant equations. Socio-economic development, he argued, equalled strength of the proletariat; strength of the proletariat equalled vigour of democracy; vigour of democracy equalled full opportunity for the training of the working class in struggle. Capitalist development, proletarian strength and democracy together constituted the preconditions for a new socialist régime. On the other hand, lack of socio-economic development equalled weakness of the proletariat as a class; absence of democracy equalled inexperience of the masses. In these circumstances, a revolutionary dictatorship could only be the work of a minority sect, counterposing democracy and dictatorship to justify and perpetuate its own power, and so laying the basis not for socialism but for a bonapartist régime. 'If one were to maintain, following the model of the bourgeois revolutions, that revolution equals civil war and dictatorship, then one would have to draw the conclusion that a revolution necessarily leads to the rule of a Cromwell or a Napoleon. But this is not at all the necessary outcome of a proletarian revolution, provided the working class constitutes the majority of the population and is organized democratically, thereby assuring the preconditions for socialist production. By dictatorship of the proletariat

---

[6] *Demokratie oder Diktatur*, Berlin, 1918, p. 8. This work will henceforth be cited as DoD.

we can mean nothing other than the rule of the proletariat on the basis of democracy'.[7]

Kautsky held that on the whole the preconditions for socialism existed in Germany but that they had to be consolidated through: 1) the revival of production in a democratic republic, enabling socialization to proceed on an effective foundation; 2) the unity in action of the working class. 'Socialism', he wrote, 'which means general prosperity within modern culture, is possible only through a powerful deployment of the productive forces that capitalism bears within itself. . . . A state apparatus which has squandered these riches through a foolish policy, such as an unsuccessful war, does not necessarily provide a favourable point of departure for the most rapid diffusion of prosperity throughout all strata'.[8] The initial priority for the German proletariat was therefore to exert its influence on the forms of economic recovery after the war within the framework of capitalism. Thereafter the working class could seek to assume direct management of industry, once its demonstrable maturity and power of attraction had rallied the majority of the population to its side. To pursue such a process the proletariat needed the general framework of a democratic republic, together with political and organizational unity in its own ranks. 'What is decisive', Kautsky wrote, 'is no longer the material but the subjective factor. Is the proletariat strong and intelligent enough to take this social planning into its own hands? In other words, does it possess the ability to extend democracy from the political to the economic system? . . . It can be said with certainty that a people is not ripe for socialism so long as the majority of the masses are hostile to socialism and do not want to hear about it'.[9] Hence, the proletariat in Germany must not shirk electoral tests and verdicts, contrary to the course taken by the Bolsheviks in the Russian Revolution.

Kautsky believed that the preconditions for socialism now existed in Germany; the problem was to be able to take advantage of them: 'In a number of industrial states the material and ideological preconditions for socialism appear to be present in sufficient measure. We are firmly convinced that this is the case in the German Reich. Here the question of the political rule of the proletariat now depends only on its strength, and above all its unity. At this point, only internal division can lead us astray'.[10] The following question then became decisive: should the

[7] Ibid., p. 47.
[8] Ibid., p. 50.
[9] Ibid., p. 23.
[10] Ibid., p. 53.

struggle of the proletariat be directed towards a democratic representative régime or towards a class régime, realizing the dictatorship of a section of the masses over all the rest of the population? 'The contradiction between democracy and dictatorship in Russia found its most evident expression in the question of the Constituent Assembly', Kautsky wrote: 'that is, whether it was correct to put all political power in the hands of a representative body elected through equal, direct, and secret universal suffrage, as Engels demanded in 1891, or whether in place of this national assembly, it was necessary to create an assembly elected on the basis of an indirect, unequal, class-based, and limited suffrage reserved for certain privileged strata of workers, soldiers, and peasants'.[11] The success of the Bolsheviks in Russia, Kautsky argued, was a product of the weakness of the roots of democracy in that country and of the forces opposing Bolshevism. Regardless of whether or not the methods of the Bolsheviks were correct, these favourable conditions did not exist in the West, especially in Germany: 'The outcome of any attempt to sweep aside or eliminate equal and direct universal suffrage, to replace a national assembly with a permanent centralized assembly of councils of workers, soldiers, and peasants, would be civil war, complete economic ruin, and ultimately the victory of counter-revolution'.[12]

In sum, Kautsky was persuaded that the strength of the proletariat lay wholly in its ability to put itself forward as the most democratic class in society. If, on the contrary, the workers opted for a violent confrontation with other social strata, they would inevitably prove weaker than the counter-revolution ranged against them, since they would be completely isolated, losing any possibility of rallying new social forces to them, and would be inferior to the enemy on the strictly military level. Kautsky also argued that democracy was a technical necessity for socialist management of the economy and the political system, to prevent nationalization of the means of production from leading to a bureaucratic despotism: 'As a means of liberation of the proletariat, socialism without democracy is unthinkable'. If democracy was lacking, 'a communist economy' could only become 'a basis for despotism'.[13] The essence of socialism was to create a 'social organization of production', but also a 'democratic organization of society'.[14]

Kautsky approached the question of socialization in strict relation to

[11] Ibid., p. 9.
[12] Ibid., pp. 56–57.
[13] Ibid., p. 10.
[14] Ibid., p. 11.

the degree of capitalist development and the role of the working class and the trade unions, in an essay published in February 1918, *Sozial-demokratische Bemerkungen zur Uebergangswirtschaft*, which discussed the problems of the 'transition' from capitalism to socialism. Reiterating his earlier criticisms of 'state socialism', Kautsky maintained that it was a mechanical 'theory of harmony between capital and labour' to believe that the extension of the economic functions of the capitalist state and the concentration of capital under the aegis of the banks and cartels constituted in themselves the premises of the 'objective organization' of socialism. 'This comfortable conception of an imperceptible transition to the state of the future, caused by the diligent activities of the capitalists themselves, leads merely to this: the main task of the proletariat would then be to support the class of capitalists, for to do so would be to foster the liberation of the proletariat itself'.[15] In reality, Kautsky said, the basis for socialism was not an increase in the role of the state and in the concentration of capital. The real hallmark of socialism was the democratic intervention of the proletariat and its organizations, on the foundations, of course, of prior capitalist development. Without this intervention, there would be no qualitative change in capitalism, whatever its degree of advance or modernity. The essence of a socialist economy was the regulation of production for social goals by democratic means.

After the collapse of the German Empire and the formation in Berlin, on 9–10 November 1918, of a government composed of representatives of the SPD and the USPD, Kautsky traced out the lines of a programme of socialist action. Its task, he said, was to lay the basis for the implementation of the Erfurt Programme, around which 'the great majority' of the proletariat had united, having conquered 'political power' on 9 November. How was this political power to be expressed? His reply was emphatic: through the establishment of a 'democratic republic', an institutional form fully adequate to accomplish the transformation of society, provided the majority of the population cast their ballots for a socialist government in free elections in the future. The perspectives the German proletariat, acting in the framework of the democratic republic, should present to the nation were: democratization and socialization.

The democratic republic, so Kautsky maintained, 'constitutes the indispensable political foundation of the new collective order'. Socialists must sustain the republic 'unshakably' and consistently. Democratiza-

[15] *Sozialdemokratische Bemerkungen zur Uebergangswirtschaft*, Leipzig, 1918, p. 160.

tion in Germany meant the breakup of the bureaucratic-military machine inherited from the Empire, and its replacement by full parliamentary democracy. Kautsky explained: 'This is . . . our task. Integral to it is first of all the most rapid dissolution of the standing army and the complete elimination of the commanding position the officer corps has hitherto occupied within the army and thereby within the state. The place of the army must be taken by a popular armed force with a training period of two or three months per soldier. The lower grade officers must not be professional soldiers but receive their training while continuing to work in their civilian professions. Only the instructors and high-ranking officers should remain professional soldiers. . . . The power of the centralized state bureaucracy must be broken by the submission of this bureaucracy to a national assembly elected by the freest universal suffrage, and the immediate transfer of the broadest rights of self-administration to the municipalities (in the context of the constitution), the districts, and the provinces. Police powers must also be devolved from the central state to the municipalities and districts, without exception. The supreme instance of this self-administration should everywhere be democratically elected assemblies of the municipalities, districts, and provinces. The central state can also confer a portion of its administrative tasks, the collection of taxes for example, on the administrative entities constituted and controlled by these assemblies. It goes without saying that those democratic rights which have already been won, such as freedom of the press, of assembly, and of association must be defended'.[16]

Such were the main lines of the democratization of the state advocated by Kautsky, in accordance with his traditional view that centralization should be tempered with controls exercized by autonomous local bodies. Kautsky then proceeded to outline a scenario for the 'socialization' of the economy. His first words were directed against any idea that a destructive class struggle should be unleashed within industry. 'The German republic must be a democratic republic. But it must become more: a socialist republic, a collectivity within which the exploitation of man by man will no longer have any rights of citizenship'. Having said this, however, Kautsky asserted that the revival of production after the war was in any event the necessary precondition for socialization: 'Nevertheless, the question of *production itself* is even more pressing than the question of the *form of production*. To revive it and set it in

[16] *Richtlinien für eine sozialistisches Aktionsprogramm*, [Berlin, 1919], pp. 3-4. The pamphlet dates from January 1919.

motion again is our most important task. This constitutes the prerequisite for any attempt to socialize production'.[17] This did not mean, however, that production should be left to continue in its old form. Kautsky predicted that a socialist government would immediately make its impact felt by 1) socializing those sectors of production that could technically be transferred from a capitalist to nationalized statute; 2) subjecting other branches of production to the control of 'unions' whose task would be to provide for the supply of raw materials, the sale of products, and the regulation of the conditions of production. The leadership of these unions, he said, should be composed of representatives of the employers, the workers' councils, the consumers, and the state (each component contributing one-fourth of the total). Workers' councils should also be established in non-unionized factories.[18] Kautsky warned against the danger of bureaucracy and counselled against the illusion that socialism required that industry be managed by a 'centralized bureaucracy'. Instead, what was needed was 'the broadest possible autonomy' for the management of companies.[19] One important form of democratic organization in the economy, he remarked, was the creation of consumers' associations. Finally, it was essential that the municipalities acquire the full right to administer those aspects of socio-economic life that fell within their own direct compass.[20] So far as the foreign policy of a socialist state was concerned, Kautsky declared that the abolition of 'any form of secret diplomacy' was a vital necessity for a new democracy.[21]

While Kautsky was advancing these proposals for socialization, the Provisional Government formed after the collapse of the Empire had no serious intention of introducing any real changes in the economic structure of the country. Kautsky himself had occasion to discover this through personal experience. On 24 November 1918 the government appointed a 'Commission for Socialization', chaired by Kautsky himself. Among the other members of the commission were Hilferding, Cunow, and representatives of non-socialist parties, like Rathenau. The task of this consultative body was to present proposals for socialization, which were later to be examined by the future National Assembly. Its work, however, remained without the smallest effect. The commission had been created because the governing Social Democrats, aware of the need

[17] Ibid., pp. 4–5.
[18] Ibid., pp. 5–6.
[19] Ibid., p. 8.
[20] Ibid., pp. 10–11.
[21] Ibid., p. 16.

to confront an issue urgently posed by the struggle of the workers themselves, were determined to keep it confined within a legal framework, and to thwart any direct initiative by the industrial proletariat in its work places. The moderate political purposes the SPD assigned the commission were indicated in the clearest possible manner by an article published in *Vorwärts*, official organ of the party, on 5 December 1918. This asserted that the 'task of the commission for socialization' would be 'to act from the outset with such prudence that no fear of irrational experiments need arise and no one [among the industrialists] could suffer for resuming activity that had been interrupted by the war'.[22] The commission recommended first of all the socialization of monopolistic sectors, particularly coal and iron mines, large landed estates and forests, insurance companies and mortgage banks, with compensation for their former owners. It stipulated that socialized enterprises should be governed by the application of the 'principles of Social Democracy', in keeping with which elected representatives of the workers would have 'a special and decisive influence in determining wages, working hours, and conditions of safety'. These representatives would also be guaranteed 'an adequate knowledge of the course of affairs'. Nevertheless, as is clear from the letter of resignation it sent to the government on 3 February 1919, the commission found no real desire on the part of the government to apply any of its recommendations.[23] In fact, the majority Social Democrats, who dominated the Provisional Government, had no intention of promoting any action that could prejudice the decisions of the future parliamentary government of the Reich that would emerge from national elections, or that could jeopardize the conservative coalition between the SPD, the trade-unions, the high state bureaucracy, and the General Staff, established immediately following the collapse of the Empire. The principal concern of the SPD was to restore internal order and to revive production. In practice, this was also the primary preoccupation of Kautsky. On this basis, he was increasingly mending his fences with the SPD, now that the disputes of 1917 over 'domestic truce' and 'annexations' were rendered irrelevant by the restoration of peace. In effect, hostility to the strategy of the Spartacists united Kautsky with the SPD rather more strongly than any disagreement over the modes and pace of 'socialization' could have divided him from it.

[22] 'Die Sozialisierungskommission', in *Dokumente und Materialien zur Geschichte der deutschen Arbeiterbewegung*, Band 2, Berlin, 1957, p. 538.
[23] Cf. the documents on the activity of the commission contained in *La rivoluzione tedesca 1918–1919*, edited by D. A. Ritter and S. Miller, Milan, 1969, pp. 282–302.

Kautsky, like the SPD majority, was fully committed to convocation of a National Assembly, which he expected to become the parliament of German democracy, oriented under the leadership of Social Democracy to the social renovation of the country. His hostility to all those who sought to counterpose the democracy of workers' and soldiers' councils, as the organs of a new type of state, to parliamentary democracy was therefore total.

From late 1918 onwards, Kautsky unequivocally expressed what would always remain his position on the relationship between institutions of the council type and parliamentary institutions. He believed that the network of councils did indeed have a role of great importance, constituting an indispensable instrument of proletarian struggle during the period of destruction of the old order, as effective organs of mass combat. Moreover, he stressed that the councils could be important even during the period of construction of the new order, as organs of control, defence, and organization at the point of production. But Kautsky denied that the councils could become the organs of a new state power, precisely because they were class institutions, whereas the democratic state must repose on an institution such as a national assembly or parliament that represented all social classes and strata. The strategy of the German Revolution should not be to pit the councils against a national assembly but to utilize the councils to shift the centre of gravity of the national assembly to the left. Kautsky formulated these positions quite lucidly in a pamphlet published at the end of 1918, *Nationalversammlung und Räterversammlung*: a significant analysis, which adapted the premises of his essay of 1893 on parliamentarism and direct legislation to the situation of Germany in 1918–1919. Kautsky completely rejected the Communist assessment that the national assembly was an institution for paralysing the class energy of the proletariat, which could be stimulated only by the councils. Kautsky replied that it was impossible to adduce any evidence that 'a national assembly must be against socialism by nature, while a council of soldiers must necessarily be in favour of it'.[24] To those who demanded a purely council form of representation on the grounds that this would eliminate conservative or reactionary forces from the process of political decision-making, Kautsky objected that a parliament could equally eliminate the political and social weight of such forces. The advocates of a 'dictatorship' of the councils were seeking to resort to formal and mechanical methods to combat conservative forces; the proponents of universal suffrage and a parliament, on the other hand,

[24] *Nationalversammlung und Räteversammlung*, Berlin, n.d. [1918], p. 2.

relied on substantive methods of more durable efficacy. The capitalists and privileged layers, Kautsky argued, could never acquire supremacy in a parliament by virtue of their numerical strength alone; they could do so only if they still commanded real influence and possessed the political ability to rally an electoral majority. But if these forces could exert such influence, then socialism certainly did not correspond to the will of the masses, who composed the great majority of the population. If they were converted to socialism, then the masses would be fully capable of transforming a parliament elected by universal suffrage into an instrument for social change. Hence, if a democratic system was unable to become the means for the realization of socialism, it was a pure illusion to believe that the councils could supply such an instrument. For Kautsky, the counterposition of councils to parliament masked the design of a dictatorship by a minority, disguised in the formula of a democracy distinct from parliamentary sovereignty, branded as bourgeois.

The councils, Kautsky argued, ought not to be chosen as the sole form of electoral representation even if they enjoyed the support of the majority of the population, for they were deficient both technically and politically. To opt exclusively for the council form would be to introduce a system based on work place and occupation, that would exalt particularist and corporatist tendencies, creating and consolidating divisively localist interests and loyalties. Such a system would be inherently fissiparous. In parliamentary elections to a national assembly, on the other hand, social interests were homogenized and great political parties came to the fore. In a period of social crisis and scarcity of resources, the council technique of representation by trades would unleash a struggle for wage and category privileges. In such circumstances, the contest between bourgeois parties and socialist parties at parliamentary elections would give way to the struggle 'of candidates of the various socialist factions competing against one another'. 'What is stimulated is not party solidarity but division into sects'.[25] The ungovernable chaos that would inevitably result could only be remedied by the introduction of terror, as in Russia.[26]

What Kautsky proposed was not an exclusive alternative: either national assembly or council assembly. Rather, he sought their integration, each fulfilling different and specific tasks. He even considered that the councils could perform an essential revolutionary function, albeit a limited one. The councils, he said, had proved to be 'indispensable and

[25] Ibid., pp. 2–5.
[26] Ibid., p. 6.

highly useful in the first phase of the revolution' for the purpose of achieving the 'overthrow of the old authorities'. Even in the second phase, their function did not disappear, but changed. When the hour arrived for the construction of socialism, for which a central representative body – parliament – was needed, the task of the councils would be to ensure that it constantly heard the voice of the workers in their class organization.[27]

In a highly industrialized country, Kautsky wrote, it was not possible to build a new social order unless two prerequisites were at hand: 1) a central political leadership to coordinate the economy; 2) an authority founded on a full democracy able to impose its decisions on all social groups, in a climate of order and civic peace. An industrialized nation like Germany could not survive in a climate of permanent civil war. Its productive machinery would fall into ruin, unable to dispose of those minimal resources which a predominantly agricultural country would be able to command even under conditions of chaos. 'Although the political revolution is not possible without disorder and confusion, in the same manner the social revolution presupposes the functioning of the productive process. The more fully this is realized, and the more order and tranquillity are consolidated, the greater confidence in the existence of the new régime will be'.[28] As may be seen, Kautsky's central thesis was that the socio-economic development characteristic of an industrialized country determines the forms of the socialist revolution in two senses: 1) there can be no state power unless there is an authority which rests on consent and can thus impose itself democratically on those who disagree with its policies; 2) if the socialist forces are unable to construct the new régime on a basis of democratic consensus, they must have no illusion that they can do so through the violent dictatorship of a minority, since in that event the apparatus of production would be so convulsed that the only result would be to pave the way for the counter-revolution. 'Capitalist industry itself', Kautsky wrote, 'cannot prosper in a phase of disorder. It is based on the division of labour, the mutual dependence of the individual factories, world trade, and credit. Any upheaval, any insecurity, at any of these points triggers a wide-ranging crisis. Even agriculture depends on industry'.[29] If socialism, at the moment when it inherited this apparatus, did not respect its internal laws, then the capitalists would impose them with a reactionary opera-

[27] Ibid., p. 10.
[28] Ibid., p. 11.
[29] Ibid., p. 12.

tion that would appear legitimate and rally wide support.

Having made these methodological points, Kautsky launched his attack on the Spartacists. The latter sought to counterpose councils to parliament, since they had lost all hope of winning over a majority of the population, which was the only method that 'assures our victory and rule in all circumstances'. Indeed, 'there is no institution that could guarantee that we socialists could rule without the majority of the people'. The Spartacists harboured the illusion that the majority they were unable to obtain through universal suffrage could be won through class representation. But what guarantee was there that the councils would not give the majority to other socialist tendencies?[30] In sum, Kautsky repeated, in all cases what was important was the substantive social will of the population, not formal and external institutionism. A socialist majority must not fear confrontation in a representative parliament elected by universsl suffrage, which could surely become the principal instrument of social change.

Any counterposition of a council assembly to the national assembly could only split the ranks of the proletariat between those prepared to support a dictatorship of privileged strata of workers and soldiers and those remaining loyal to the democratic principle that socialism must arise from a constant verification of the majority within a general representative organ of society. The tasks of the German Revolution were essentially two: 1) democratization of the Reich; 2) transition 'in the most rapid possible manner' from the present capitalist mode of production to the socialist.[31] The social organism should be modified, but not destroyed – as the most radical and backward strata of the proletariat and subproletariat linked to the Spartacists were preparing to do. 'In this conception of the further development of the revolution', wrote Kautsky, who was still a member of the USPD, 'we stand in agreement with the majority socialists'.[32] He then proceeded to outline the contrast between the two opposed conceptions of the social revolution thus: 'The further development of the revolution in the social domain is not viewed by the League [the Spartacists] in such a way as to enable one branch of production after another to be socialized, after meticulous preparation, according to the planned intervention of a state power dependent on the workers. Rather, they want the workers, immediately and without plan, through continuous strikes and advanced demands

[30] Ibid., p. 15.
[31] *Das Weitertreiben der Revolution*, n.d. and n.l., p. 4.
[32] Ibid., p. 5.

that cannot be met in all branches of industry simultaneously, to make any production at all impossible'.[33]

Contrary to the opinion of the Spartacists, for whom the revolution required the triumph of the most extreme current over all the other socialist tendencies, the real problem of the German Revolution, Kautsky averred, was to avoid playing into the hands of reaction by unleashing internecine struggles among the masses. The proletariat, he argued, measured its capacity to become a ruling class not according to the logic of radicalization, whose extension would make it impossible to confront the tasks of economic recovery and institutional democratization, but according to the degree of its unity in action. To counterpose a conciliar state to a parliamentary state would plunge the country into civil war, and ensure the victory of internal reaction, which would be strengthened by the collapse of the economy that would inevitably ensue from the civil war itself. To then attempt to project the civil war onto an international plane, in the Spartacist conception of a world revolution independent of the degree of socialist maturation in each individual country, could only result in a war between Germany and the victorious Entente.[34] Kautsky, harking back to his 1910–1912 polemic with Luxemburg and Pannekoek, charged that the strategy of the Spartacists was to give free rein to the 'streets'. The Spartacists had in fact failed to acquire any significant influence at the First Congress of the Councils of Workers and Soldiers, held in Berlin on 16–21 December 1918: of the 489 delegates, 291 belonged to the SPD, 90 to the USPD, and only 10 to the Spartacists. The Congress had decided to refer the whole question of state power to a future national assembly, thus refusing to counterpose councils to representative democracy of the parliamentary type. Kautsky consequently denounced the Spartacists' lack of any firm roots among the masses and hence their need to trust exclusively in 'the streets' and the 'unorganized': 'Disillusioned with the trade unions as well as with parliamentarism, they stake all their hopes on the councils of workers and soldiers. Once their expectations are frustrated in this domain as well, they have nothing left but the "streets". It is in the streets that the new Germany must be built, the new society constructed. The streets: which means those strata of workers who have had nothing to do with any organization up to now. Socialism, the organization of production and democracy, and the reorganization of the state, are not to arise from the workers' organizations; instead, these new structures

[33] Ibid., p. 5.
[34] Ibid., p. 6.

are to be created by those who have had no use for any organization. *The rule of the unorganized over the organized, of the ignorant over the educated, of the selfish over the disinterested: here is where the "further development" of the revolution must lie under present conditions. But this would mean only the degradation of the revolution; and such degradation would merely be the precondition for complete ruin.* For the proletariat can assert itself against the united bourgeois mass only if it too remains united and displays the maximum intelligence, altruism, and organization. A sect of the proletariat which can assert itself only through the destruction of all these elements digs the grave of the revolution'.[35]

Kautsky's verdict on the tragic events of the first weeks of January 1919, which ended with the brutal suppression of the Spartacists and the left of the USPD by Noske's troops in Berlin, was that the far left had fallen victim to a complete incapacity to assess the real relationship of forces in Germany, that its defeat had therefore been inevitable, and that the only political effect of its action had been to strengthen the counter-revolutionary front and shift the entire axis of politics in the country to the right. What had emerged from the struggle, Kautsky wrote, at a time when the repression was still raging, was a shift to the right: 'There can be no doubt about the result. There was no doubt from the very beginning of the movement, at least among those who had preserved the capacity to view the real relationship of forces clearly. On the one side stood a minority of the proletariat, on the other its majority in the Reich and the entire bourgeois world, together with the remains of the apparatus of military power that survived the period of the war'. The socialist government was now weakened; 'its ability to defend itself against bourgeois and military influences, which was slim to begin with, has been further reduced. The bourgeois elements and professional officers have acquired new energy; the danger of counter-revolution is becoming real'. What, then, was to be done? Kautsky's answer was, once again, the unity of the proletariat – henceforward a veritable *idée fixe* for him, for in his view the working class could make no progress without unity. The danger of counter-revolution demanded unity, first of the masses and then of the leaders: 'Whoever desires the constitution of the united front of the proletariat must begin with the union of the masses; the unity of the leaders will follow in a later stage. Only unity can give rise to a second phase of the revolution. The unity of the German proletariat: this is the sign under which we must enter

[35] Ibid., pp. 12–13.

the second phase of the revolution'.[36] Kautsky was to reiterate the same ideas at the Berne Congress of February 1919 which reconstituted the Second International.[37]

Of course, while he hailed the value of unity, Kautsky did not hesitate to lay equal blame on the Spartacists and Noske for scissionism. The Spartacists and Noske, he said, were sons of the same mother: war, with its spirit of violence. Followers of both believed that they had to perpetuate the methods of war. In reality, however, what was needed was precisely a struggle against the spirit of war. The war had ruined the economy, which had to be reconstructed. The war had introduced the 'cult of violence', which had to be combated. 'The spirit with which the Spartacist League is infused is fundamentally that of Ludendorff', although their ends of course were different. 'Noske is the obverse of the Spartacists'.[38] For Kautsky, the task was to unite the proletariat on the basis of two conditions: 1) acceptance of democratic methods; 2) elimination of the two extremisms.

The Second Congress of the Councils, held in Berlin 8–14 April 1919 was attended by 264 delegates, of whom 142 were from the SPD and 57 from the USPD; the newly formed Communist Party, which had not participated in the elections, had no representation. Luise Kautsky read the delegates a report, entitled *Was ist Sozialisierung?*, which had been drafted by her husband, who was ill and could not attend. This document dealt with the timing, modes, and bases of socialization, with particular attention to the role of the trade unions and the workers' councils. By the time the Congress met, the bourgeois character of the new Weimar Republic was already unmistakable. It had also become quite clear that the majority Social Democrats had played a conservative and restorationist role, demonstrating – contrary to the claims of Kautsky, preoccupied primarily with his ideological struggle against the Spartacists – that the aim of the SPD, regardless of its protestations of principle, was to consolidate the bourgeois democratic republic, without any real intention of fostering a process of socialization and workers' power within civil society and the sphere of production. The elections of 19 January 1919 to the national Constituent Assembly had given the majority to the non-socialist parties (the SPD won 37.9% of the vote, the USPD 7.6%; the KPD did not run candidates, but it may be

---

[36] 'Die zweite Phase der Revolution', in *Freiheit*, 13 January 1919.

[37] 'Die Internationale Sozialisten-Konferenz in Bern. Kautskys Rede', in *Arbeiter-Zeitung*, 5 February 1919.

[38] 'Aussichten der Revolution', in *Arbeiter-Zeitung*, 9 April 1919.

assumed that they would have received a very low poll). Together, the two socialist parties had won 45.5%, a high score; but the socialist electorate included currents that were in practice intensely divided over strategy and tactics and could not be considered a politically united force as such. In any event, these elections had dashed the hopes of people like Kautsky, who had argued that the democratic republic would have a socialist majority that would assure the political basis for the socialist transformation of German society. The election of Ebert as provisional President of the Republic on 11 February and the formation two days later of a coalition government headed by the Social Democrat Scheidemann, comprising the SPD, the Liberal Party (DDP) and the Catholic Centre, indicated – despite the Social Democrats' programmatic affirmations that the government should take the road of socialization – less the primacy of the socialists in a coalition with the bourgeois parties, than the organic integration of Social Democracy into the bourgeois republic, the institutional principles of which were codified in the Weimar Constitution.

In his report to the Second Congress of the Councils, Kautsky expressed dissatisfaction at the course events had taken. But once again he put the major share of the responsibility on the Communist left. The 'evil' resulted from the 'division of the proletariat'. Because of this division, the 'government which emerged from the revolution has fallen into dependence on senior bureaucrats, generals, and magnates of capitalism'. If the proletariat had been united, 'the verdict of universal suffrage would have been different, and no Noske or Heine would have been possible'. There is no doubt that Kautsky believed that the actions of the Noskes had been made possible by the destructive attempts of the Spartacists. In his view it was useless and erroneous to denounce the electoral form because of the negative results of the elections themselves. Indeed, the electoral copy had merely mirrored 'the original', namely the reality of social conflicts and the weakness engendered by the division of the proletariat. 'If the proletariat had been united in the revolution from the very outset, it would have had a united government that would have already achieved much in the way of socialization'. Given the division of the working class, exclusive rule by the councils would lead only to the 'dictatorship of *one* section of the proletariat over the others'.[39] Kautsky acknowledged the failure of the Commission on Socialization. He denounced the present coalition government for its lack of desire

[39] *Was ist Sozialisierung? Referat gehalten auf dem 2. Reichskongress der A.-, S.-, u. B.-Räte am 14 April 1919*, Berlin, 1919, p. 26.

to advance socialization and its fear of 'experiments', of 'any new element'.[40] He declared that the Cabinet was issuing mere verbal promises and that 'not a bourgeois-proletarian coalition government but only a purely socialist government solidly based on the unity of the German proletariat' was capable of giving impetus and reality to the process of socialization.[41] But he made no serious analysis of the responsibility of the conservatism of the SPD in provoking the divisions of the proletariat which he denounced so vehemently. This was consonant with the very essence of his position, which, while it led him to denounce the 'weakness', 'timidity', and 'compromises' of the SPD in ideological terms (in other words, in terms of disagreement with its methods), also led him, and with far greater virulence, to brand the Communists as the principal agents of the regression and even ruin of the revolution. Correct the errors of the SPD and drive the KPD out of the ranks of the working class – such was the logical aim of his programme. Regardless of his general theoretical affirmations, Kautsky was thus incapable of grasping the real nature of the subordinate role played by the majority Social Democrats in the social restoration of capitalism in Germany. Nor did he perceive the SPD's determination to confine the proletariat firmly within the framework of a bourgeois democracy, which was the real and sole aspiration of the party and trade union leaders.

Kautsky's report to the Second Congress of the Councils emphasized that in acting to promote socialization the working class had to beware of two dangers: 1) on the one hand, socialization of a wildcat variety, which he defined as 'bankrupt', imposed without preparation, without consciousness of timing or method, in accordance with a simplistic conception of how to overthrow the capitalist order, conducted without any coordination and under the impetus of the most backward masses; 2) on the other hand, a bureaucratic-centralist socialization that would ignore the twofold exigency that must guide any genuinely socialist perspective: material prosperity and workers' 'self-determination'. 'The worker', Kautsky declared, 'wants not only well-being but also self-determination. He opposes capital not only because of starvation wages and inhuman working conditions but also because it treats him as a mere instrument of production, to which he is supposed to conform passively'. This condition of passivity would not be changed, Kautsky insisted, voicing an argument designed to underline the importance of insti-

[40] Ibid., pp. 24–25.
[41] Ibid., p. 29.

tutional mediation and socio-political democracy, 'if the apparatus of state domination, the state bureaucracy, takes the place of the individual capitalist'. In that event there would be an equally negative substitution: 'instead of many employers', the worker would have 'a single employer', and his liberty would consist solely in 'the change of employer'.[42] The problem, then, would not be resolved simply if 'the state power suddenly appropriates all the property of the capitalists'. A genuinely socialist nationalization demanded a social bloc founded on three decisive elements: workers, consumers, and scientists. These three forces for socialization must interpenetrate together, organize themselves democratically, and prevent the sectoral outlook that each would engender if cooperation between them were lacking.[43] The fundamental institution of socialization, Kautsky maintained, was the trade union. But the trade unions could fulfil their task only if they cast off the narrow mentality of corporative and economistic demands acquired under the capitalist system. The positive role of the factory councils lay in a local articulation of workers' initiatives. Born as organs of class combat in the fight for state power against capital, these bodies should in a subsequent phase become means for the mobilization of workers for production and socialization.[44]

2   For the Unity of Social Democracy

A special Congress of the USPD was held in Leipzig from 30 November to 6 December 1919. On 7 November Haase, the president of the party, to whom Kautsky was very close both personally and politically, was assassinated. The USPD congress reflected a process of internal radicalization, which inevitably resulted in the isolation of Kautsky. Disappointed at the violent ideological division and organizational scission among the socialist forces in Germany, and convinced that no progress of proletarian struggle was possible without unity, Kautsky reacted to the decision of the Leipzig Congress of the USPD – now dominated by the left – to explore adherence to the Third International and to adopt a programme based on the dictatorship of the proletariat and the sovereignty of the workers' councils as state organs, by contemplating emigration to Austria, washing his hands of German Social Democracy

[42] Ibid., pp. 23–25, 10.
[43] Ibid., p. 13.
[44] Ibid., pp. 18–19.

in the hope that in Austria he could again become active in a 'united party'.[45]

Later, in 1923, Kautsky did emigrate; but his possibilities of influencing the actual policies of the German labour movement were in any case henceforward drastically diminished. He was now a venerable survivor from the past. Under these conditions, he continued his theoretical work, re-thinking the past and defending the 'classical' tradition of Social Democracy, primarily in polemic against what he now regarded as the greatest threat to the future of the proletariat: the spread of Bolshevism. Kautsky saw the Social Democratic tradition as a powerful call for the national and international unity of the proletariat and for 'democratic methods' as against the malignant incarnation of scissionism and 'despotism' in the barbaric and violent bureaucracy of the USSR. 'All the present socialist parties of Europe', he wrote in 1922, excepting only the British Labour Party, 'have been formed according to the model of German Social Democracy. Under the influence of its example, every split in the socialist movement was overcome, like the last division in France in 1905. Only in the backward economic and political structures of Russia was a pre-Marxist form of party life preserved, with its fragmentation and fratricidal struggles'.[46] To the very end of his long activity, Kautsky continued to maintain that just as the scissionist spirit born of Bolshevism was responsible for the 'lost opportunity' of 1919–1920, so too it was decisively responsible – by weakening the working class – for the rise of fascism in Italy and Germany. In his last full-length work, *Sozialisten und Krieg*, published in 1937 shortly before his death, Kautsky levelled this accusation against the Communists: 'In truth, the Third International was founded not to liberate the workers of the world but to combat the Social Democrats everywhere, especially the non-Communist followers of Zimmerwald. In this domain the Third International has had some success. Perhaps the Social Democrats could have prevented the rise of the bourgeois dictatorships of the Mussolinis, Hitlers, etc. if they had not been paralysed by the Communists in so many states, or drawn into insane adventures'.[47]

Between 1920 and 1922, a period during which the socialist parties in Germany lost ground in national politics, the majority of the USPD unified with the Communist Party of Germany (KPD) and the minority of the USPD reunified with the SPD. Throughout this period, Kautsky

[45] *Das Werden eines Marxisten*, op. cit., p. 147; *Mein Verhältnis zur USPD*, op. cit., p. 14.
[46] *Mein Verhältnis zur USPD*, op. cit., p. 19.
[47] *Sozialisten und Krieg*, op. cit., p. 577.

acted within the USPD as an implacable and polemical advocate of the need for the political unity of the right of the USPD with the left of the SPD. For him this unity was the nucleus of a strategy of comprehensive unification of the proletariat on the basis of democracy and a programme of socialization. But his spirit increasingly yearned for a return to the SPD. He therefore enthusiastically hailed the reunification of the right of the USPD with the SPD when it finally occurred in September 1922.

Kautsky explained how he viewed this unification in an article published in *Freiheit*, the organ of the USPD, in June 1919. What was necessary, he said, was a thorough reconstruction of what he called the 'Marxist Centre' of the pre-war period. Overall unity between the two parties of Social Democracy was not yet conceivable and would now be mechanical, he wrote, since the right of the Social Democratic majority was nationalist and excessively moderate while the left of the USPD was inclined towards the divisive force of communism. 'In my view', he wrote, 'a unification is possible only where there is *intrinsic political agreement*'. 'It seems to me', he continued, 'that the main thing to be achieved is this: to gather together the essential elements of the real spirit of the party, namely the right wing of the USPD and the left wing of the SPD, which genuinely belong to a single whole'. This would mean precisely to breathe new life into the pre-war 'Marxist Centre'. The task of the right of the USPD and the left of the SPD would be to reconquer the masses, reducing the two extremes to marginal critics, without allowing them to 'determine the mass movement'.[48]

A year later, the 6 June 1920 elections to the Reichstag represented a debacle for the socialist parties as a whole (the SPD vote fell from 37.9% to 21.6%; the USPD gained strength, increasing its vote from 7.6% in 1919 to 18.0%; the KPD won only 2.0%) and a strengthening of the conservative forces in Germany. Kautsky now again began to insist on unity, conceived in terms of an *Arbeitsgemeinschaft* composed of the USPD and the SPD, as the only way to prevent the further weakening of the German proletariat. What sort of political cooperation should the USPD and SPD undertake towards this end? Kautsky maintained that socialists must be able to grasp the nature of the new tasks before the workers' parties, disregarding old doctrinaire approaches (including those he had argued himself). The first of these tasks, 'however', was not *an immediate realization of socialism*, but the liquidation of the consequences of the war'. The restoration of an efficient capitalism

[48] 'Kautsky zur Einigungsfrage', in *Freiheit*, 17 June 1919.

was essential, but in a framework of democratic control by the workers' movement. 'The immediate revival of production', Kautsky wrote, 'means primarily the immediate revival of capitalist production. This is a fact of life that even the most energetic socialist desires are incapable of modifying'. It was necessary to fight for a number of socializations, although within the general context of the capitalist mode of production. The function of a socialist government during a transitional period flowed from this objective economic situation. When favourable conditions existed a socialist government could: 1) protect the working class in the capitalist economy better than any other government; 2) take the initiative, when and where the necessary conditions existed, in socializing certain sectors of production (mines, large-scale agricultural property, etc.). But to do all this required a united Social Democracy. Lack of unity merely strengthened the non-socialist or anti-socialist parties.[49]

To lend substance to the democratic strategy for social reforms along the road to socialism, Kautsky developed a particular argument to justify participation by socialist parties in coalition governments with bourgeois parties. He declared that although before the war he had been a fierce opponent of 'ministerialism' and a champion of the 'exclusive rule' of the proletariat, he now felt compelled to draw attention to a number of factors that rendered the participation of socialists in coalition governments desirable. Before the war, he said, he had believed that the crisis of the bourgeois state would be triggered by a Social Democratic conquest of an electoral majority. Now, however, a new situation had arisen. The war, at least in the defeated countries, had thrown the state into crisis without the socialist forces being able to exercise 'exclusive rule'. A choice therefore had to be made among three possibilities: an attempt to establish the dictatorship of the councils based on the power of a minority; participation in a coalition government; or abandonment of all power to the adversary. Kautsky argued that the road of coalition was now the most realistic: 'In Western Europe a dictatorship of the councils is no longer possible; hence, if a socialist régime does not have the support of a majority of socialist voters, it must either resign or adapt itself to a coalition'. Granted, the aim should be not a coalition at any price, but a coalition with democratic, anti-militarist bourgeois elements that favoured a struggle against bureaucratism, agreed to strengthen autonomous local bodies and self-government, and were prepared to accept the socialization of some sectors of production. Since the socialists, Kautsky maintained, found themselves a much stronger force, but not yet a majority on their

[49] 'Was nun?', in *Arbeiter-Zeitung*, 13 June 1920.

own account, a coalition became justifiable. Social Democracy, however, should always remember that it must not enter a coalition in a subordinate position, for that would be suicide. Energetic opposition would then be preferable.[50]

The problems of proletarian unity and coalition government remained the main prisms through which Kautsky was to view the situation in Germany. In October 1920, at its congress in Halle, the majority of the USPD voted for fusion with the KPD. The minority, on the other hand, strengthened by the support of the majority of the party's parliamentary caucus, decided to maintain an independent organization. At this point Kautsky strove with all his might to win support for a reunification of what remained of the USPD with the SPD. He exhorted the members of his party to overcome their lingering hesitancy to endorse the strategy of coalition and to understand that the fundamental question now sounding in Germany was: either a coalition with the participation of the proletariat, or 'the exclusive rule of the worst enemies of the proletariat and the loss of all the gains that have hitherto been made'.[51] He admonished them that only the unity of the two Social Democratic parties could enable the proletariat to release its full energy, and invited them to choose between two conceptions and two types of party: the mass party based on the class struggle, characteristic of Social Democracy, or the conspiratorial party based on a sectarian outlook, characteristic of Communism.[52]

The USPD and the SPD did reunify in September 1922, to the great satisfaction of Kautsky, who throughout the year had hurled harsh accusations at the leadership of the residual USPD, which he charged with not yet having freed itself from the lure of the Communist siren.[53] On 24 September 1922, the day on which 146 delegates of the SPD and 135 delegates of the USPD met in Nuremburg to ratify reunification on the basis of a common 'action programme', Kautsky hailed the event, declaring that the German workers' movement now faced two tasks: 1) to prevent the question of war reparations from leading the nation to catastrophe, and thus to accept 'fulfillment of the peace treaty'; 2) to defend the democratic republic, as the precondition for any success of the workers' movement. With regard to the former, Kautsky insisted

[50] 'Klassenkampf und Koalition', in *Arbeiter-Zeitung*, 18 June 1920.
[51] 'Zum Görlitzer Parteitag', in *Freiheit*, 23 September 1921.
[52] 'Die Frage der sozialistischen Einigung', in *Arbeiter-Zeitung*, 3 January 1922.
[53] Cf. 'Ein offener Brief Kautskys', 28 March 1922; 'Eine Nachlese', 7 April 1922; 'Nochmals die Einigungsfrage', 8 June 1922; 'Koalitionspolitik und Einigung', 17 June 1922. All these articles are in *Freiheit*.

that Germany must struggle for the revision of the financial provisions of the Treaty of Versailles, which, he said, are 'simply deadly'. It would, however, be suicidal to adopt the demand advanced by the nationalists of the right and the Communists for the 'violent abrogation' of the treaty. With regard to the latter, he wrote: 'The second great task of our time is the defence of the democratic republic. Here again the proletariat must stand in the forefront. Among the great classes only the proletariat supports the republic enthusiastically, since it is aware that only under this state form, with an adequate development of capitalist industry, can socialist production arise. . . . To consolidate the republic, the proletariat must collaborate with those bourgeois republicans who maintain a reasonable attitude'. Kautsky ended by emphasizing the necessity to reject the strategy of civil war preached by the Communists, whose adoption would make it impossible to reconstruct the socio-economic order at a level higher than that which had been destroyed during the war.[54]

---

[54] 'Die dauernde Einigung', in *Vorwärts*, 24 September 1922.

VIII

The Ideological Crusade against Bolshevism

1   The 'Renegade' Kautsky?

Although he continued to be involved in party struggles within the German labour movement, after 1918 Kautsky's energies were primarily devoted to an ideological polemic against Bolshevism. Indeed, what may be called his crusade against the domestic and foreign policy of the Soviet state and its leadership was to form the climax of the whole political and ideological career of the man who had seemed during the period of the Second International to so many socialist intellectuals (among them Lenin himself) to be the most legitimate theoretical heir of Marx and Engels. The other aspects of Kautsky's activity during the post-1918 period were simply ramifications and articulations of his struggle against Bolshevism.

This crusade was pursued in an uninterrupted succession of books and pamphlets, the most important of which were: *Demokratie oder Diktatur, Die Diktatur des Proletariats* (both in 1918), *Terrorismus und Kommunismus* (1919), *Die Internationale* (1920), *Von der Demokratie zur Staatssklaverei; Eine Auseinandersetzung mit Trotzki* (1921), *Die proletarische Revolution und ihr Programm* (1922), *Die Internationale und Sowjetrussland* (1925), and *Der Bolschewismus in der Sackgasse* (1930). Even many portions of other works of a general theoretical or historical character, such as his magnum opus of 1927 *Die materialistische Geschichtauffassung* (especially the second volume, devoted to the state) and *Sozialisten und Krieg* (1937), were directly related to the struggle against Bolshevism. In addition, Kautsky's collaboration with the review of Austrian Social Democracy, *Der Kampf*, and with the Berlin journal *Die Gesellschaft* was in large measure devoted to the same theme.

It is well known, of course, that after Kautsky presented, in *The Dictatorship of the Proletariat* (which actually repeated arguments that had already been set down in *Democracy or Dictatorship*) and *Terrorism and Communism*, those theses which were to constitute the ideological arsenal of his polemic against the new Bolshevik régime, the two major architects of the October Revolution, Lenin and Trotsky, both took the field against Kautsky's positions, the former with his celebrated work *The Proletarian Revolution and the Renegade Kautsky* (1918), the latter in his own *Terrorism and Communism* (1920). As indicated by the very title of the former work, both Lenin and Trotsky charged that Kautsky was a 'renegade', in other words, that he had betrayed not only the revolutionary conceptions of Marx, but his own past as well. Lenin wrote that Kautsky had to 'resort to trickery literally at every step to cover up his apostasy', that 'the renegade Bernstein' seemed 'a mere puppy compared to the renegade Kautsky'.[1] Both Lenin and Trotsky counter-posed the revolutionary Kautsky of *Der Weg zur Macht* (1909) to the later 'renegade'.[2] Trotsky in particular reminded Kautsky that in 1909 he had written: 'It was Marx and Engels who formulated the idea of the dictatorship of the proletariat, which Engels stubbornly defended in 1891, shortly before his death: the idea that the political autocracy of the proletariat is the only form in which it can realize its control of the state'.[3]

In reality, by formulating their case against Kautsky in terms of his 'apostasy', Lenin and Trotsky were speaking the political language of party struggle, and not without considerable difficulty. Kautsky had indeed been a protagonist of the theoretical struggle against revisionism. Lenin himself had called him 'the chief of German revolutionaries' and had manifested the most unbounded admiration for Kautsky's method of scientific analysis, in which – he said – 'the method of Marx' lived again. On the other hand, the Bolsheviks considered themselves the only consistent revolutionary Marxists. Compelled now to confront both Kautsky's 'revolutionary' past and his present position as an implacable opponent of the October Revolution and the tactics that had brought the Bolsheviks to power, they sought to 'fracture' the continuity of his work. In support of their political and ideological case, Lenin and Trotsky pointed to the fact that in the past Kautsky had been: 1) a champion of the concept of the dictatorship of the proletariat; 2) a champion of the concept of workers' democracy; 3) a theoretician of the

[1] V. I. Lenin, *Collected Works*, vol. XXVIII, Moscow 1965, pp. 238 and 242.

[2] Lenin, op. cit., p. 289; L. Trotsky, *Terrorism and Communism*, The University of Michigan Press, Ann Arbor, 1961, pp. 17–19.

[3] Trotsky, op. cit., p. 20.

necessity for a class state; 4) an analyst of the inevitable connection between world war and proletarian revolution. Identifying their own conception of the dictatorship of the proletariat, democracy, the state, and the timing and modalities of the revolution with Marxism, and simultaneously registering Kautsky's opposition to Bolshevism, Lenin and Trotsky responded to Kautsky's polemic by denouncing his alleged 'renegacy', abandonment of Marxism, vulgar liberalism, humanitarianism, and pusillanimous democratism. Thus, according to Lenin, the man he had previously considered a peerless master of the Marxist method now became a dreary and mediocre school-master, a Philistine chewer of the cud of counter-revolutionary vulgarity.

In reality, the basis for the charge that there had been an 'apostasy' was exceedingly frail, if indeed it had any basis at all. For the positions Kautsky had developed precisely during the period in which Lenin considered him a 'master' and the 'chief of German revolutionaries' were all such as to lead him inevitably to the sharpest opposition both to the tactics and strategy of the Bolsheviks in the seizure of power and to the manner in which they established their dictatorship after it. It is of course indisputable, as we have shown, that Kautsky's positions did gradually shift in a moderate direction. But it is also undeniable that this shift occurred within the framework of a general conception of socialism, democracy, and the state which was, from the very outset (taking the Erfurt Programme as its fundamental starting point), of such a character as to be irreconcilable with the theory of dictatorship and of the state on which the Bolsheviks acted in 1917. Kautsky could be accused of immobility, but not of having abandoned the fundamental lines of his conception of the revolutionary process, the dictatorship of the proletariat, and the socialist state.

When Trotsky reproached Kautsky with the fact that in 1909 he had still 'correctly' acknowledged the dictatorship of the proletariat, he was in fact misinterpreting a purely verbal formula. Kautsky had indeed spoken of 'dictatorship of the proletariat', of the exclusive power of the proletariat. But he did so in the context of a conception of the revolutionary process that differed qualitatively from that of the Bolsheviks. For Lenin in 1918, the dictatorship of the proletariat was a 'power based directly on force and unrestricted by any laws', 'a rule won and maintained by the use of violence by the proletariat against the bourgeoisie, a rule that is unrestricted by any laws'.[4] For the Trotsky of 1920, 'he who repudiates terrorism in principle – i.e. repudiates measures of suppression and

[4] Lenin, op. cit., p. 236.

intimidation of the armed counter-revolution [here counter-revolution was understood to mean any force that did not accept Bolshevik power, identified with the objective expression of the will of the proletariat; and struggle against counter-revolution to mean the measures directed against all non-Bolsheviks without restraint of law] – must renounce any idea of the political supremacy of the working class and reject its revolutionary dictatorship'.[5] In light of these positions, any reference to Kautsky's supposedly revolutionary and correct ideas of 1909 was based on purely formal analogies, since Kautsky, when speaking of 'dictatorship of the proletariat', associated this dictatorship with a revolutionary dictatorship'.[5] In the light of these positions, any reference by the Bolsheviks. What Kautsky meant by the dictatorship of the proletariat was primarily: 1) power obtained by the working class through the conquest of a majority in parliament, i.e. through the exercise of democratic freedoms in competition with all other parties; 2) the reliance of a purely socialist government, in transforming the social basis of the state, on a parliament that represented all political forces and was controlled by a socialist majority; 3) a régime that would not suppress the political and civil rights of citizens; 4) a régime prepared to verify the basis of popular consent to it in periodic elections; 5) a régime that would use violence only against those advocates of counter-revolution who refused to accept the reality of a socialist majority constituted in a legal government. Ever since 1893, when he had written his book on 'parliamentarism', Kautsky had made it clear that he believed that parliament could be the instrument of the dictatorship either of the bourgeoisie or of the proletariat, that parliament was an indispensable technical agency, and that the dictatorship of the proletariat flowed in substance from the combination of a socialist parliamentary majority and the functional use of this legislative organ. Moreover, in his 1894 essay *A Social Democratic Catechism* he had expounded views on the functions and limits of violence from which he never thereafter deviated and which he reproduced to the letter in *Der Weg zur Macht*. Whatever Kautsky's oscillations in radical or moderate directions may have been, they always remained within a conception of the revolutionary process demarcated by all these points, which were thoroughly incompatible with the Bolshevik conception. Ever since his commentary on the Erfurt Programme, Kautsky had expressed his aversion to the supporters (like Weitling) of a dictatorship of a minority and to the sort of 'barracks socialism' he was later to see in the rule of the Bolsheviks. Lenin accused

[5] Trotsky, op. cit., p. 23.

Kautsky of having abandoned Marxist positions on the state the moment Kautsky refused to acknowledge the validity of soviets as the foundation of a new type of state. But the 'renegade' Kautsky could have retorted, with full justification, that his positions on this question remained identical to those he had elaborated when he was a 'master' of Marxism. For not only in his essay of 1893 on 'parliamentarism', but also in *The Agrarian Question*, he had opposed direct legislation as a utopia that was unrealizable in a great modern state; and he had maintained that socialism would be unable to dispense not only with parliament but also with an efficient centralized bureaucracy, although this bureaucracy should be subjected to public control and flanked by autonomous local bodies subject to direct popular will.

In sum, the Kautsky who launched the crusade against Bolshevism was a Kautsky who had every right to reject the charge of 'renegacy' hurled by Lenin and Trotsky. When Trotsky wrote that Kautsky, 'abandoning the idea of a revolutionary dictatorship . . . transforms the problem of the conquest of power by the proletariat into the problem of the conquest of the majority of votes by the Social Democratic Party in one of the future election campaigns',[6] he was counterposing the image of a fictitious Kautsky to what had always been the real Kautsky. There was never any real 'apostasy' or 'betrayal'. Rather two antithetical conceptions of socialism had taken the field against each other.

2 Democracy and Socialism

A declaration of principle, contained in *The Dictatorship of the Proletariat*, could be inscribed as an epigraph to Kautsky's struggle against Bolshevism: 'Our final goal, correctly understood, consists not in socialism but in the abolition of any form of exploitation and oppression, be it directed against a class or a party, nation, or race (Erfurt Programme)'.[7] If socialists had chosen to be such, Kautsky wrote, it was because they were convinced that socialism was the means by which to achieve that goal:

'We propose the socialist form of production as a goal in this struggle because, given present technical and economic conditions, it appears the only means to attain our goal. If it could be shown that we are mis-

---

[6] Trotsky, op. cit., p. 21.
[7] *Die Diktatur des Proletariats*, Vienna, 1918, p. 4. This work will henceforth be cited as DP.

taken, that the liberation of the proletariat and of humanity in general could be achieved only, or more suitably, on the basis of private property in the means of production, as Proudhon thought at one time, then we would have to reject socialism, without in any way renouncing our final goal, but rather in the very interest of this goal'.[8]

In practice, Kautsky was of course convinced that socialism was indeed the only way to abolish exploitation and oppression. But he was concerned to extricate the idea of socialism from an identification with the pure and simple socialization of the means of production, and to introduce a mediation which he considered essential, namely the 'democratic method' and therewith the 'democratic organization of society'. In his polemic against the Bolsheviks, Kautsky constantly underlined the decisive importance of this mediation: without democratic organization (democracy meaning essentially parliamentarism and political and civil liberties), the socialization of the means of production lost its socialist significance, since its management was then entrusted to a despotically organized minority that annulled the meaning socialization acquired in combination with democracy. To maintain, as did the Bolsheviks, that other than democratic methods could be adopted in the name of socialism was to introduce uncontrolled abuses of power: 'Thus democracy and socialism do not differ in the sense that one is a means and one an end; both are means to the same end. . . . For us, socialism is unthinkable without democracy. By modern socialism we mean not only a social organization of production, but also a democratic organization of society, for socialism is indissolubly linked to democracy. There is no socialism without democracy'.[9]

Two components were fused in Kautsky's approach. One was an ethical-cultural tradition with its roots in liberal humanism, the other a more distinctly political-ideological conception with its roots in an evolutionist conviction that economic development, socialism, and democracy were a sort of indissoluble trinity. The latter was set out, in all its simplicity, in *Democracy or Dictatorship*, Kautsky's first comprehensive essay against Bolshevism: 'The more capitalistic a state is on the one hand, and the more democratic on the other, the closer it is to socialism. The further the development of its capitalist industry, the higher its productivity, and the greater its wealth, the more socialized is its labour and the more numerous its proletariat. The more democratic a state, the better organized and trained is its working class'. The Bol-

[8] DP, p. 4.
[9] DP, pp. 4–5.

sheviks' conception of dictatorship, on the contrary, stood opposed to the Marxist method, which posed a historically necessary link between development and socialism, 'since the dictatorship of the proletariat which they advocate and implement is nothing but a grandiose attempt to leap over necessary phases of development and to eliminate them by decree. They maintain that this is the most painless method to create socialism and to "shorten and lessen its birth pangs". But our experience rather calls to mind, if we want to pursue the analogy, a pregnant woman who leaps madly about to reduce the duration of her pregnancy, which she finds difficult, and thus provokes a premature birth. The result of such behaviour is a baby that cannot survive'.[10]

In fact, according to Kautsky's account, the original sin of Bolshevism was much more serious than a mere premature birth. For Kautsky, it was a necessary condition for a healthy gestation that the proletariat be able to mature in a context of adequate capitalist development and of an experience of struggle seasoned by the exercise of political and civil liberties. Since both conditions were lacking in Russia, Bolshevism was not so much a premature child as an abortion; in other words, it was not an insufficiently mature socialism, but a non-socialism. Indeed, Bolshevism created conditions for the proletariat that were worse than those of capitalism, despite the bright red veneer of the Russian régime. Kautsky maintained that if the proletariat did not possess a sufficient level of organizational and ideological development and socio-political experience or a sufficient numerical strength to assert itself against the other social classes, then socialism could not emerge as a social reality but only as an abstractly voluntarist project. A socialist party that sought to implement such a project could retain power only by a minority dictatorship. A minority dictatorship in turn could be imposed only by methods of bureaucratic and police control. The end result would be a monstrosity – a régime guided ideologically by a radical socialist party, socially unable to establish socialist relations of production and politically organized along the lines of an absolutist-despotic system.

The essential problem of modern socialism, according to Kautsky, was the question of what level of maturity was needed for the proletariat to go beyond the class limits of bourgeois political democracy. Kautsky was convinced that in the advanced countries modern capitalism had now reached the level of development needed for socialization. The problem of power was now a problem of the strength and consciousness of the proletariat: 'There is no reason to believe that in the modern

[10] DoD, pp. 52–54.

industrial states, with their banks and organizations of capitalists, it is not possible today to organize the greater part of production in a socialist manner, through the state, municipalities, and consumer associations. What is of decisive importance is not the material, but the subjective element: Is the proletariat strong and intelligent enough to take this social planning into its own hands? In other words: Does it possess the ability to extend democracy from the political to the economic system?'[11]

Once the necessary economic and social conditions existed, and socialism had acquired its proper foundation in a sufficient expanse of socialist 'will' among the masses, only a 'democratic method' could give voice to this 'will for socialism'.[12] To take power without testing this will – and testing it among the entire population – would be to accomplish a *coup d'Etat* and not a social revolution. Nor was it enough that a desire for socialism be expressed by the majority of the proletariat alone, if that class was still a minority of the population – for then, as in Russia, the proletariat would find itself from the outset in extremely difficult conditions in relation to all other social classes, above all the peasant masses. If the workers constituted a minority, this meant that the level of economic development was insufficient and the will for socialism itself therefore a mere abstract voluntarism. The Bolsheviks mistakenly believed that they were acting in accordance with history, since they had won over the majority of the proletariat, the vanguard class. They thus thought they could establish 'democracy' only for the working class, a 'proletarian democracy', without seeing the general implications of the fact that they could not obtain an adequate consensus from the entire body of society. The result had been to set in motion, independent of any will, a process of degeneration of the entire Bolshevik system of power, inevitably transforming the proletariat into an armed aristocracy incapable of emancipating the rest of society by itself. The dissolution of the Constituent Assembly; the suppression of universal suffrage; the introduction of a system of different weighting of the votes of industrial workers and of peasants; the election of the highest leading bodies through various levels of indirect suffrage; the construction of a bureaucratic-police machine to control the majority of the population, which had been denied any real power in the political system – all these constituted successive steps in a process that had culminated in Bolshevik 'despotism'.

Lenin objected to what he called Kautsky's 'vulgar liberalism',

[11] DP, p. 12.
[12] Ibid., p. 12.

insisting that Marxists, when approaching the question of democracy, could not 'proceed from the relation between the majority and the minority' but from 'the relation between the exploited and the exploiters'.[13] Only by starting from the relationship between exploited and exploiters, Lenin argued, was it possible to understand the necessity for a 'class democracy' and a dictatorship against enemy classes. Hence the opportunist nature of any argument to the effect that democracy was a general method of regulating relations among all classes. Kautsky's opposition to Lenin's approach rested on his contention that in a political system that claimed not to be despotic the character of a government was determined by the relations between those who actually govern and the social forces that are governed, and by the possibility of verifying the degree of consent commanded by the former among the latter. Such consent, even where it initially existed, was not necessarily granted once and for all; its expression required a formal system of control independent of the force to be judged and controlled, namely the government itself. For Kautsky, this was the basis of a democratic system. By contrast, the summary identification of the working class with the Bolsheviks and the Soviet government was an ideological operation designed to legitimize a ruling party without democratic controls, by the false claim that the working class itself was governing in Russia. But could a class itself govern directly? Kautsky's answer was unequivocal: to say that a class governs is nonsense. A 'class can rule, but not govern; since a class is an indeterminate mass, only an organization can govern'. What governs is a party or a coalition of parties. Now, 'a party is nevertheless not the same thing as a class, even though it represents primarily a class interest'.[14] Here there was a further complication. It must be kept in mind that a party represented a class because of a certain policy, that is, it proposed choices and decisions that could be considered positive or negative. 'A class interest', Kautsky wrote, 'or even *the* class interest, can be represented in very different ways by different tactical methods'. Finally, the relationship between classes and parties appeared in its full complexity when it was recalled that 'a class can be divided among various parties' and that 'a party can include members of different classes'. This was what made it possible for the same ruling class to aspire to a change in its governmental representation, when its 'majority believes that the method of the party that has hitherto governed has become unsatis-

[13] V. I. Lenin, *Collected Works*, vol. XXVIII, op. cit., p. 250.
[14] DoD, p. 28.

factory and that of its competitor more suitable'.[15] Only respect for the rules of the contest between minority and majority could satisfy such exigencies. A government like that of the Bolsheviks, which ignored and concealed the problems inherent in the relations between classes and parties by claiming that one revolutionary party objectively represented the interests of the entire working class and therefore that the class itself was governing directly through the party, was inevitably led to mystify its own dictatorship as the dictatorship of the proletariat.

In his reply, Lenin maintained that Kautsky's insistence on the vital necessity to respect the majority-minority relationship was simply a reiteration of the point of view of bourgeois democracy. Yet, when the October Revolution occurred, Lenin himself had indicated the following principles as necessary elements of democracy – albeit within a system of soviets: 1) acceptance of the principle that government parties could be replaced, as one of the rules of the 'democratic' game; 2) transfer of government responsibilities from one party to another in a peaceful manner according to the results of elections in the soviets; 3) therewith acknowledgment that the toiling classes, the workers and peasants, were represented by a plurality of parties. In the Appeal of the Central Committee of the Russian Social Democratic Labour Party (Bolsheviks), dated 5–6 November 1917, Lenin had written that because of the revolution, 'the transfer of government power from one soviet party to another is guaranteed without any revolution, simply by a decision of the soviets, simply by new elections of deputies to the soviets'.[16] Polemicizing in *The Proletarian Revolution and the Renegade Kautsky*, however, he introduced the qualitatively different, objectivist argument that the Bolsheviks constituted the only force genuinely capable of representing the masses and their historic needs. When Kautsky spoke of various Russian parties that could represent the masses in a manner different from the government party, he was thinking primarily of the Mensheviks (which he considered the most authentically Marxist party) and the Social Revolutionaries. According to Lenin, on the contrary, the development of the revolution had demonstrated that the Mensheviks and Social Revolutionaries were socialist parties only in name; in substance they were petty-bourgeois democratic parties. Consequently, Lenin could object that when Kautsky came forward as the champion of the rights of the Mensheviks and Social Revolutionaries, he was 'guided by their *name*, that is, by a word, and not by the *actual place*

[15] DoD, p. 29.
[16] V. I. Lenin, *Collected Works*, vol. XXVI, Moscow 1964, p. 303.

they occupy in the struggle between the proletariat and the bourgeoisie'.[17] It was this real alignment, Lenin argued, that deprived Kautsky's hypothesis of the peaceful transfer of power from one soviet party to another of any significance, for the Mensheviks and Social Revolutionaries had objectively proven themselves non-soviet parties. In sum, the role of the Bolsheviks as the sole governmental force was linked to a conception of the dictatorship of the proletariat as founded on force and independent of any law. (It is clear, in fact, that a representative government, even in the context of a system based solely on soviet parties, would have required that such a dictatorship be founded on law and on the verification of popular consent through contests between majority and minority.)

The situation in Russia led Kautsky to the conclusion that 'the dictatorship of only one of these parties is, in that event, no longer the dictatorship of the proletariat but the dictatorship of one portion of the proletariat over the other'.[18] Furthermore, the dictatorship of a party could not assert itself technically except by relying directly on an organization enabling the minority to rule over a disorganized majority. Thus, Kautsky declared, the only road available to the Bolsheviks was the route of bonapartism: 'to govern by virtue of the superiority of a centralized organization over the unorganized popular masses and by virtue of the superiority of its armed forces'.[19] The inevitable outcome of any use of organized and systematic violence to regulate social relations was a Caesarist structure culminating in a personal dictatorship; then the 'revolution necessarily leads to the rule of a Cromwell or a Napoleon'. As a minority dictatorship marching down the road to Caesarism, the Russian Revolution was assuming bourgeois features.[20]

In Kautsky's view, the explanation for the genesis of the Bolsheviks' conception of dictatorship as coercion exercised by the ruling party lay at once in the very manner of their seizure of power and in the difficulties encountered in the exercise of this power. The Bolsheviks had been able to triumph not because of their own strength, but because of the disruption of the social fabric by the action of an element that was neither proletarian nor socialist: the peasant rabble, which in Russia, unlike the developed countries, still constituted 'an element of rebellion'. However the peasants, having attained their own ends, now represented a politically 'apathetic' force. Thus, favoured by the weakness of the

[17] V. I. Lenin, *Collected Works*, vol. XXVIII, p. 232.
[18] DP, p. 21.
[19] DP, p. 23.
[20] DoD, p. 47.

Provisional Government and by the effects of the War, the Bolsheviks had been able to take power with a *coup d'Etat*. But after the seizure of power, Russian backwardness turned against the Bolsheviks, who found that they now lacked 'all the preconditions for the accomplishment of their own aims'. Having come to power without the consensus of the majority, the Bolsheviks henceforward had to administer power without sufficient popular support or an adequate modern economy. They thus found it necessary to abandon the democratic road, in which they had believed not long ago, and became the theoreticians of dictatorial methods in the normal exercise of power.[21] At this point, however, the Bolsheviks were gripped by an insuperable contradiction: although they were the most radical party of socialism, they could retain power only through the most reactionary bourgeois methods and could not overcome the difficulties engendered by economic and social backwardness. Having come to the forefront of the revolution as the most socialist party, they were condemned to a maximum divergence from their initial promises. But this divorce between theory and practice made it too dangerous for the Bolsheviks to proceed to any verification of popular consent. They therefore adopted the only available alternative: the constitution of a bureaucratic dictatorship, through which they intended to avoid any democratic verification indefinitely. 'The absolute rule of the bureaucracy', Kautsky wrote, 'has its foundation in the hypothesis of rule without end; the violent repression of any opposition is its governing principle'.[22]

Bolshevism, Kautsky declared, departed from socialism the moment it decided to dissolve the Constituent Assembly and imposed, in place of a representative assembly founded on equal, direct, and secret universal suffrage, an assembly founded on 'unequal, indirect, public, and limited suffrage, elected by privileged categories of workers, soldiers, and peasants'.[23] For Kautsky, this not only constituted a violation of universal democratic principles, but also plunged the Bolshevik government into a situation that was intractable even from the standpoint of class democracy. In fact, any class democracy was untenable, he held, because the supression of democracy for enemy classes led inevitably to the construction of a mechanism of authoritarian control that impinged even on the politically privileged classes, within which dissent would be deemed a concession to non-revolutionary points of view. The Bolsheviks

[21] DoD, pp. 6–7.
[22] DP, p. 15.
[23] DoD, p. 9.

had rejected political democracy because they considered it inadequate to liberate the proletariat. They were thereby impelled to consider political democracy itself something to be combated. The Marxist attitude, Kautsky argued, had been and remained quite different: 'Marx and Engels and their students viewed things quite differently. They saw the class struggle of the proletariat as the means to emancipate the workers from bourgeois leadership not only in the economy but also in politics and to render them capable of pursuing an independent policy, guided by an autonomous proletarian party within the framework of a democratic constitution. The first task our teachers found they had to accomplish in order to construct this party of *proletarian democracy* was to destroy the illusions of the bourgeois democrats that the mere existence of democracy was sufficient for the liberation of the working class. When the Communists today deliver interminable lessons designed to prove the same point, they merely triumphantly announce their discovery of America. They are telling us something we have already known for half a century. Except that our conclusion was simply that mere democracy is *insufficient* and not that it is *detestable*. This insufficiency is clear today wherever the proletariat is not ideologically independent. From this it follows that it is necessary to quicken the ideological maturity of the proletariat, but not to reject democracy'.[24]

After the seizure of power, the Bolsheviks found nothing better to do than 'abolish the democracy that had been created, after the destruction of Tsarism, through universal suffrage, freedom of the press, and freedom of association for all'; they replaced this with a 'new aristocracy' 'of the strangest variety', namely a 'proletarian aristocracy' christened 'proletarian democracy'.[25] The justification the Bolsheviks adduced for this régime of a new aristocracy was the urgent need to consolidate the power of the working class. But, Kautsky objected, the classes of the old order, although numerically weak, represented a real social force which no legislative formula could abolish. The only force that could defeat them was a strong and mature working class formed by an advanced economic and social development. In a backward country like Russia, the Bolsheviks were seeking coercive short-cuts and formal guarantees; these, however, would eventually prevent the ideological growth of the proletariat itself, which would be stunted under a system of political and intellectual despotism. Such a system merely corrupted the proletariat into believing

---

[24] 'Demokratie und Demokratie', in *Der Kampf*, XIII, 1920, p. 209.
[25] Ibid., p. 212.

that it could 'assure the power of socialism through purely mechanical measures'.[26]

A genuine dictatorship of the proletariat could only be based on the real strength of the proletariat as a class, democratically verified in society as a whole. Such strength would be evidence that the preconditions existed for the exclusive rule of a united majority class, permitting the real possibility and formal legitimacy of a dictatorship founded on democracy: '*If by dictatorship we mean exclusive rule without compromises, then we mean that form of rule of the proletariat which is determined by social conditions, in contrast with the capitalist class*, which can rule only through compromises with the parties of other classes. . . . Dictatorship in the sense indicated above does not in any way exclude democracy. The democratic republic rather represents the only basis on which a dictatorship of this type can develop and assert itself in conformity with its own goals'. If, on the other hand, a minority dictatorship was established, as in Russia, it would be unable to initiate a new social course. Compelled to construct a militarist-bureaucratic apparatus to defend its own political monopoly, and unable to muster the social forces needed to transform the relations of production, it would have to reconcile itself to ever increasing compromises with the capitalist mode of production and the capitalists themselves.[27]

When he read Rosa Luxemburg's work *Die russische Revolution*, published by Paul Levy, Kautsky saw Luxemburg's criticism of the Bolsheviks on the issue of democracy as substantially similar to his own. Luxemburg, Kautsky wrote, 'most decisively and thoroughly condemns the suffocation of democracy and its replacement by terrorism. What she says in this regard, especially about the degradation of the proletariat which results from this policy, is among the most significant and penetrating of all that has been written about Bolshevism. No one who has concerned himself with Bolshevism, whether for it or against it, can ignore her arguments. They constitute the most important part of the work in question'.

At the same time, Kautsky maintained that the charge Luxemburg had levelled against him in her writings, namely that he understood democracy in 'bourgeois' terms, was without foundation. He said that when she declared that 'dictatorship consists in the *way in which* democracy is *used* and not in its *abolition*', he was in full agreement. Where their positions really diverged, Kautsky said, was in their specific assessment

---

[26] 'Wer ist ein Arbeiter?', in *Der Kampf*, XIII, 1920, p. 450.
[27] 'Klassendiktatur und Parteidiktatur', in *Der Kampf*, XIV, 1921, pp. 279–280.

of the relationship between democracy and its social content in the Russian Revolution. Rosa Luxemburg had rebuked the Bolsheviks for not having made democracy the form of a bold socialist policy, while he, Kautsky, thought that democracy in Russia would necessarily have to respect precisely the impossibility of any such policy, whose preconditions were entirely lacking.[28] According to Kautsky, Luxemburg was caught in an insuperable contradiction, since she separated politics from economics. While Luxemburg reproached the Bolsheviks with not having pursued a sufficiently audacious policy, Kautsky thought that in this respect the Bolsheviks were merely reflecting a historical necessity. His charge against them, on the contrary, was of having suppressed the constitutional form of the democratic republic which alone would have permitted a normal and adequate expression of Russian social limitations and afforded the proletariat conditions in which to advance its own class organization and so to shift those limits back as the economy progressed and the society matured.[29] In fact, although Kautsky was correct to note a point of agreement with Luxemburg in their denunciation of the bureaucratic party dictatorship of the Bolsheviks, he made no mention of the fact that the Polish revolutionary fought for a political order which was not parliamentary but soviet, and which therefore presupposed the breakup of the liberal-bourgeois state machine. In claiming that 'what really counts in the analysis of Rosa Luxemburg is only her impassioned and trenchant defence of democracy',[30] Kautsky was ignoring the importance of the disagreements between himself and Rosa Luxemburg, whose positions he exploited for his own purposes.

Analyzing the origins of the Bolshevik conception of dictatorship as coercion, Kautsky asserted that the task of Social Democracy during the War had been to struggle to restore the possibility of contests between parties. The Bolshevik conception, he continued, was a product of the moral and intellectual degradation caused by the War: 'The World War led to the moral and intellectual debasement of the toiling classes, not only because it brutalized nearly all strata of the population and elevated the least developed section of the proletariat to the vanguard of the social movement, but above all because it aggravated the proletariat's misery enormously, and thus replaced calm deliberation with the most bitter exasperation'. Furthermore, the war induced a section of the working class to withdraw to the conviction typical of the upper classes that

[28] 'Rosa Luxemburg und der Bolschewismus', in *Der Kampf*, XV, 1920, pp. 37–38.
[29] Ibid., pp. 38–39.
[30] Ibid., p. 44.

'force alone constitutes the decisive factor in history and that one can obtain anything one wants provided one commands the necessary force and is prepared to act without scruples'.[31] Polemical zeal led Kautsky to forget the fact that in 1917 he himself had defined the Russian proletariat as a boldly revolutionary class.

Trotsky rejoined that Kautsky's analysis ignored the fact that it was precisely the War which had taught the proletariat a new mentality, for the lesson the workers had learned from the 'imperialist war' was that 'the old criteria were completely useless'. The parliamentary democracy of the Kautskys thus lagged behind the new mentality of the revolutionary working class.[32] Kautsky in turn replied that Trotsky saw the effects of the War from the deformed vantage point of the conditions that prevailed in the defeated countries at the end of the War, and that even so he saw only the short-term and not the longer-term effects. That section of the proletariat which had opted for violence as the road to power, while it could take initial advantage of the consequences of the defeat of the bourgeois state in the War, would be unable – if it did assume power – to pursue the work of reconstruction, which demanded both workers' unity and democracy. The proletariat would thus eventually have to cede power, as in Russia, to the professionals of organized violence.[33] The deeper origin of both the violence of the Bolsheviks and their lack of success in realizing socialist goals lay in the fact that their unbridled subjectivism had violated the limits of immature historical conditions, condemning their programme to be impracticable. The Bolsheviks had then reacted by compounding their initial error and elevating violence to a permanent method of government, reducing their original soviet principles to a 'fig leaf'. But the Bolsheviks, Kautsky said, were not content to apply violence in Russian conditions; perhaps their worst sin was to claim that the 'Russian' case, in reality so exceptional, should be made the rule, that the Bolshevik path to power should become mandatory for all true socialists. In Russia, 'from the autumn of 1917 there arose out of the revolution a dictatorship more centralized, extensive, and unlimited than has ever before been seen. Such a dictatorship is now apparently to be considered not an exceptional case, owing its origin to an exceptional situation, but the form that every revolutionary régime must assume'.[34]

[31] *Terrorismus und Kommunismus*, Berlin, 1919, p. 108. This work will henceforth be cited as TK.

[32] Trotsky, *Terrorism and Communism*, op. cit., p. 16.

[33] *Von der Demokratie zur Staatssklaverei. Eine Auseinandersetzung mit Trotzki*, Berlin, 1921, p. 29. This work will henceforth be cited as VDSS.

[34] Ibid., pp. 51–52.

3 The Model of the Commune and the Soviet State

In *State and Revolution* and later, in *The Proletarian Revolution and the Renegade Kautsky*, Lenin had counterposed soviet proletarian democracy, founded on the principles of the Commune forcefully expounded by Marx, to bourgeois democracy, founded on parliamentarism and the division of powers. Initially, then, the standard of the Commune-state became the banner the Bolsheviks upheld against the opportunists and the 'Kautskyists'.

In his writings against Bolshevism Kautsky dealt with the Commune more than once. He sought to demonstrate that the Commune had in reality represented a form of dictatorship which, since it was based on universal suffrage and a multiparty system, was completely different from the dictatorship of the Bolsheviks, which was founded on restricted and indirect suffrage and on the ever more absolute power of a single party. In the past, Kautsky had taken an ambiguous attitude toward Marx's famous *Address* on the Commune. As all his analyses of the state openly demonstrated, he did not agree that the bourgeois state had to be 'smashed', as Marx demanded, or that the parliamentary system had to be abolished for a fusion of legislative and executive powers, or that the bureaucracy had to be dismantled as a professionally organized apparatus. But he had never dealt openly with the contrast between his own positions and those of Marx, passing in silence over the incompatibility of the two directions of thought, that of Marx and his own. In effect, from the end of the 19th century (when Engels was still alive) to the First World War, Kautsky had engaged in a sort of revisionism on the question of the state that never received a systematic theoretical expression.

In the course of the post-war crisis in Germany, Kautsky utilized Marx's theses on the Commune partially and functionally, to serve his own purposes. (The Bolsheviks did the same, although for opposite ends.) What had to be 'smashed', Kautsky said, was not the parliamentary state but the remnants of the absolutist state, in order to attain the full parliamentarism of the democratic republic. When the Bolsheviks cited the Commune as justification for the structure of the Soviet state, Kautsky polemically emphasized the democratic-pluralistic aspects of the dictatorship of the Commune. Later he denounced what he called Marx's outmoded theses on the abolition of parliamentarism and the division of powers. In marshalling evidence for his case, Kautsky made use of the crisis of sovietism. Historical reality had demonstrated to the

Bolsheviks themselves, he argued, that the Commune-state could not function; this very impossibility had led to an ultra-centralized dictatorship, in complete contradiction with the Commune. Ultra-democratism, he said, an abstraction that was never and could never have been a reality, had paved the way for absolute despotism. The illusion that any impediment to complete popular control of the state could be abolished had led in reality to the abolition of any means of control over it.

Kautsky asserted that although Marx had written, in 1875, that there was a transitional epoch 'between capitalist and communist society' which 'can be nothing other than the *revolutionary dictatorship of the proletariat*', this statement had to be compared to what he had said about the content of such a dictatorship in 1871. At that time, describing the political régime of the Commune, he had spoken of a 'government of the working class' founded on 'universal suffrage', and therefore on the plurality of organizations which was necessarily implied by universal suffrage. In this sense, the dictatorship of the Commune was a dictatorship representing a proletarian majority and founded on democracy. When he discussed it, Marx spoke 'not of a *form of government*, but of a *state of fact*'. In 1891 Engels, explaining the connection between democracy and the dictatorship of the proletariat, effectively ruled out – in the spirit of Marx – any confusion between the dictatorship of the proletariat and the dictatorship of a party: 'The democratic republic is the specific form of the dictatorship of the proletariat'. In sum, it was unthinkable for Marx that the dictatorship of the proletariat, which he said must rest on 'universal suffrage exercised by the entire people', should take the Bolshevik form of a régime founded on the 'right to vote of a particular and privileged class'.[35]

The Bolshevik type of dictatorship would inevitably fail to establish any form of democracy, soviet or otherwise. Without democracy for all, Kautsky argued, the régime would be compelled in practice to elevate repression into a general principle, leaving the ruling group as the sole arbiter of society. But this would destroy democracy even in the ruling party, and even more so in the mere echo-chambers of power which the soviets were condemned to become. 'All governments', Kautsky wrote, 'including revolutionary governments, believe that the opposition is abusing its rights. . . . Scarcely had the Bolsheviks dissolved the opposition of the Mensheviks and the Centre and Right Social Revolutionaries in the soviets when a great struggle broke out between the Bolsheviks and

[35] DoD, pp. 36–39, pp. 20–21.

the Left Social Revolutionaries, with whom the government had been formed. Most of the Left Social Revolutionaries were then also ousted from the soviets. Thus, the circle of those elements of the proletariat who enjoy political rights and on whom the Bolshevik régime is founded is growing ever narrower'.[36] But a party that dispensed with popular consent could base its dictatorship only on loyal military forces. To remain in power it must reduce all social forces to a state of 'complete apathy or complete discouragement', or else prepare to suppress an active opposition left with no alternative but revolt or guerrilla fighting. Such a dictatorship 'perpetually reproduces civil war and is in continual danger of overthrow'.[37] Incapable of allowing space for any position that is not an immediate and instrumental expression of its own power, the Bolshevik régime sought to cancel a dialectical principle of all social, political, and intellectual life, the revolutionary rule that the 'new' always begins as a minority. A political system that rested on the dictatorship of an armed and privileged minority had nothing positive to offer innovating minorities; on the contrary, it feared the emergence and presence of such minorities. Political democracy, by contrast, was the only system capable of regulating this decisive problem of social life. 'It is clear', Kautsky wrote, 'how important the defence of minorities was for the initiators of the Socialist Parties, who everywhere began as small minorities, and for the political development of the proletariat itself. The protection of minorities is of great importance in the ranks of the working class. Any new doctrine, be it theoretical or tactical, is always represented by a minority at the outset. . . . The defence of minorities is an indispensable condition of democratic development, no less important than the rule of the majority'. The fact that the ideas advocated by minorities were not always new or positive was no reason to throw out the baby with the bathwater.[38]

This, then, was the fundamental difference between the experience of the Commune and that of the USSR, which rendered the Bolsheviks' appeal to 1871 purely instrumental. Indeed, Kautsky wrote, 'the Paris Commune was superior to the Republic of the Soviets in one essential respect: it was the work of the entire proletariat. All the tendencies of socialism participated in it, and none stood apart or was excluded from it. The socialist party that governs in Russia today, on the contrary, came to power by struggling against all the other socialist parties and exercises

[36] DP, pp. 37–38.
[37] DP, p. 24.
[38] DoD, pp. 30–33; DP, pp. 16–17.

its rule through the exclusion of the other socialist parties'.[39] In the Commune, it was never contested that 'supreme power lay in the hands of those elected by universal suffrage'.[40] Indeed, the Commune was so democratic that some people saw it as 'a capitulation to anarchism'.[41] With what legitimacy, then, could the Bolsheviks point to the Commune as the model of their own régime? In 1921, pursuing his polemic with Trotsky, Kautsky wrote: 'How can the Bolsheviks today claim allegiance to the Paris Commune and the Marx of 1871?' For the Bolsheviks, he said, reference to the Commune had a purely tactical function – signifying the need to destroy the old state apparatus. It had no strategic value, as a model for the reconstitution of a new state apparatus. Anarchistic in their first phase, in their second phase the Communists became loyal heirs of 'Russianism', the illegitimate scions of the Tsarist despotism against which they had revolted: 'The Commune and Marx demanded the abolition of the old army and its replacement by a militia. The Soviet government began with the dissolution of the old army, but later created the Red Army, one of the strongest military forces in Europe. The Commune and Marx demanded the dissolution of the state police. The Soviet Republic merely dissolved the old police in order to construct the new apparatus of the Cheka, a political police commanding broader, less limited, and harsher powers than those of French Bonapartism or Russian Tsarism. The Commune and Marx demanded the replacement of the state bureaucracy with functionaries elected by the people through universal suffrage. The Soviet Republic has destroyed the old Tsarist bureaucracy but in its place has erected a new, equally centralized bureaucracy with even more extensive powers than its predecessor, since it now regulates all economic life and therefore controls not only the liberty but even the subsistence of the population'.[42] In only one respect had the Bolsheviks remained faithful to the Commune – in their unification of legislative and executive powers, which they treated as a potent instrument of their dictatorship, but one that differed from the Commune even in this regard, since the Commune's unified powers rested on popular representation elected by universal suffrage.[43]

In conclusion, Kautsky argued, the Bolsheviks, after utilizing the example of the Commune during an initial phase in order to destroy the

[39] DP, p. 3.

[40] TK, p. 55.

[41] VDSS, p. 40.

[42] VDSS, pp. 42–43.

[43] *Die proletarische Revolution*, Stuttgart-Berlin, 1922, p. 135. This work will henceforth be cited as PR.

old state apparatus and supersede parliamentarism, had totally abandoned it in a second phase, drawing closer in the construction of their own state to the bonapartist model and to bureaucratic rule. After yielding opportunistically to the radicalism of the backward masses (since this radicalism served to dissolve the old order), they then confronted tasks which these backward masses were unable to resolve in a process of reconstruction. They thereupon fettered the freedom of movement of these masses and suppressed any form of democracy, delegating the solution of tasks that the revolutionary forces were unable in their immaturity to broach to a super-centralized apparatus far from the norms of any sort of socialism.

What, then, was the nature of the new régime? What were the reasons for its survival, despite all the difficulties it encountered? In *Terrorism and Communism* Kautsky formulated a definition he was never to abandon: politically, the Bolshevik régime was a bureaucratic dictatorship; economically, it was a state capitalist order. The reason for the persistence of the Bolsheviks as rulers was precisely that they survived not as socialists but as architects of a bourgeois régime, thereby re-entering the limits of possible economic and social development in Russia, but in such an 'abnormal' and mystified political form as to present a negative pole of comparison to the norms either of a bourgeois régime or of socialism. 'Many western revolutionaries', Kautsky complained, 'triumphantly vaunt the fact that Bolshevism has remained in power so long and remains unshakable even today, at least outwardly, whereas its detractors had predicted, from the very outset of its rule, a rapid collapse. The fact is that this collapse would have come to pass long ago had the Bolsheviks remained faithful to their programme. They have maintained themselves in power only because they have taken one backward step after another, such that they have now arrived at the opposite of what they had attempted to achieve. They began by throwing democratic principles overboard in order to seize power. Then, to maintain this power, they jettisoned socialist principles. In other words, they have succeeded as individuals, but they have sacrificed their principles, demonstrating that they are outright opportunists. Up to now Bolshevism has succeeded in triumphing in Russia because socialism has suffered a complete defeat'.[44]

From the economic standpoint, Kautsky argued, the most the Bolsheviks could achieve was a new type of capitalism which differed from the old in the preponderant role of the state and in the nature of its

[44] TK, pp. 132–133.

administrative stratum, which was not a class of employers but a new bureaucracy. Thus, in 1919 Kautsky laid the basis for an interpretation of the bureaucratic régime as the rule of a 'new class' – a theory that was later to be so often reinterpreted in different variations in the course of polemics about the nature of the Soviet state. Kautsky claimed that because of economic ruin and the absence of democracy, what was emerging in Russia was 'a new class of functionaries that is increasingly appropriating all real power to itself and rendering the liberties of the toilers illusory. . . . The absolute power of the workers' councils has been transformed into the much more absolute power of a new bureaucracy, partially issued of the councils themselves, partially appointed by them, and finally, partially imposed on them. This bureaucracy represents the third and highest of the three classes – the new ruling class, constituted under the patronage of old idealists and communist militants'. Concurrently, a 'new capitalism' was taking shape, 'far inferior to the industrial capitalism of the past'. This capitalism – 'new' in the sense that it replaced private power with the economic power of the state, without leading to any real socialization, in the absence of genuine mechanisms of democratic management – furnished the basis of the most colossal political and social servitude that had ever been seen, even in Russia itself. 'Industrial capitalism has ceased to be private and has become state capitalism. At first the two bureaucracies, public and private, stood opposed to each other in critical, even hostile, manner. The worker had some possibility of forcing at times one, at times the other, to back down. But now the state bureaucracy and the bureaucracy of capital form a single whole; this is the final result of the great socialist transformation wrought by Bolshevism. It is the most oppressive despotism Russia has ever known. The replacement of democracy by the arbitrary power of the workers' councils, which were supposed to expropriate the expropriators, has now led to the arbitrary domination of a new bureaucracy and has reduced democracy to a dead letter'.[45]

In his book *Von Demokratie zur Staatssklaverei*, published in 1921, Kautsky maintained that the character of Bolshevism was now plainly reactionary. Politically, he said, Bolshevik 'state capitalism', established after the failure of the first chaotic experiments, was merely a continuation of the tendencies of Russian capitalism itself. This state capitalism 'represents nothing new, since capitalism in Russia had always existed only by virtue of state power'.[46] Having fused with the past on the terrain

[45] TK, pp. 134–135.
[46] VDSS, p. 122.

of state-bureaucratic capitalism, and having adopted Tsarist methods of political despotism, Bolshevism was inevitably destined to become a reactionary rampart against the struggles of the proletariat subject to its domination. To defend itself, Kautsky prophesied, the bureaucracy would not hesitate to forge alliances with capitalists: 'If Bolshevism', the conclusion of his book declared, 'lasts long enough without backing down, then we could yet witness the spectacle of Bolshevism marching side by side with the capitalists of the West against the Russian proletariat in its struggle for liberty. Then its evolution would be complete'.[47]

Kautsky summed up his controversy with the Bolsheviks over the state and the significance of democracy in a work entitled *Die proletarische Revolution und ihr Programm*, which took the form of a commentary on the programme the SPD had adopted at its congress in Görlitz in 1921. In it he maintained that one of the roots of the failure of the Bolsheviks, who advocated an extreme democracy in principle and an equally extreme despotism in practice, lay in Lenin's simplistic conception of the state. Lenin had started by unrealistically imagining that it was a very simple matter to make a state function; it required, he thought, no more than the transfer of power to the masses. Later, assuming power and registering the collapse of his own illusions, he fell back on a practice that was opposite to his theory. In reality, Lenin and the Bolsheviks had rejected the democratic republic as a framework of power for the proletariat partly because they had not understood that only the democratic republic could allow the state apparatus to be functionally remodelled. Kautsky argued that when Marx spoke of the need to 'smash the state machine' (and here he adapted Marx to his own conceptions), he 'did not at all mean to say that the proletariat was in no case able to exercise its own rule without destroying the apparatus of the existing state. Marx rejected only a *particular form* of this apparatus, the bureaucratic-militarist form, which had attained its extreme expression under the Second Empire in France'.[48] Today, according to Kautsky, there were two great states in Europe in which it was necessary to 'smash' the state machine for proletarian purposes, namely 'France, that empire without an emperor, and, to an even greater extent, Russia, that Tsarism without a Tsar. It is clear from the words of Marx that the destruction of the present state machine in Russia constitutes the indispensable precondition for any progress of the proletariat'. On the other hand, in countries in which a democratic republic existed, the problem was not

[47] VDSS, p. 128.
[48] PR, pp. 117–118.

to smash the state machine but to conquer it and set it to work for the purposes of the proletariat, reforming and correcting it. 'The working class', wrote Kautsky, 'cannot simply take possession of any state machine and use it for its own purposes. A bureaucratic-militarist state machine is useless for this. Only a *democratic republic* can be used for this purpose. Where the victorious proletariat does not possess such a republic, it must create one'.[49] This, then, was the great error of the Bolsheviks: they had jettisoned the democratic republic.

After denying that the Bolsheviks had any right to claim allegiance to any sort of democracy whatever, since they had suppressed all democracy, Kautsky for the first time expressly settled accounts with the attitude Marx had taken toward the elimination of the bureaucratic state apparatus in his *Address* on the Paris Commune. In *State and Revolution* Lenin had accused Kautsky of a 'superstitious belief' in bureaucracy, of not having 'understood at all the difference between bourgeois parliamentarism, which combines democracy (*not for the people*) with bureaucracy (*against the people*), and proletarian democracy, which will take immediate steps to cut bureaucracy down to its roots, and which will be able to carry these measures through to the end, to the complete abolition of bureaucracy, to the introduction of complete democracy for the people'. Kautsky, after observing that no state stood as far from 'proletarian democracy' as that erected by Lenin, acknowledged that it was 'true' that he had 'ignored these challenges up to now'. 'Not, however, out of superstitution towards the bureaucracy, but because I never attached great importance to them'.[50] In reality, there was nothing surprising about Kautsky's admission, given his past analyses of the state and of the significance of its bureaucratic apparatus. Goaded by Lenin's polemic, however, Kautsky now explicitly 'revised' Marx's position on those questions. While claiming that in his writing on the Commune Marx had not devoted more than 'a couple of sentences' to the elimination of the bureaucracy,[51] Kautsky did not content himself with merely limiting the import of Marx's affirmations. He subjected them to a direct critique, emboldened by the fact that not even the Bolsheviks, the most ardent supporters of an anti-bureaucratic state model, had been able to follow the dictates of this model; indeed, nobody had violated them so thoroughly as they. Were Marx's measures realistic, compatible with historical-social exigencies? Discussing the principle

[49] PR, p. 119.
[50] PR, pp. 120–121.
[51] PR, p. 121.

that state functionaries should receive the same wages as workers, Kautsky remarked that of course the proletariat could not leave excessive wage privileges intact, but that 'consequent to the experiences we have had since then [i.e. since the Paris Commune], particularly in Russia, it must certainly be doubted whether it will be possible during the period of transition to socialism to attract all the state officials of the necessary intellectual calibre that are needed, if they are offered only a worker's wage'. As for the demand that deputies be revocable at will, Kautsky asserted that this demand arose 'in an epoch in which the voters still confronted elected officials as a disorganized mass'. 'In the epoch of the Paris Commune this was still the prevalent situation. Once elected, a deputy could do as he pleased. His electors lost any control over him. Hence there emerged the idea that the electors should be able to recall a deputy who had disappointed them'. Kautsky maintained that it was useless merely to repeat formulae, as Lenin did, without situating them in the historic context in which they had arisen. The development of modern political parties had put an end to the disorganization of voters. Since their rise, exemplified by Social Democracy, 'the responsibility of the deputy to his *electors* has increasingly lost ground to his respon-sibility to his *party*'. The deputy was ever more representative of a party, ever less of disorganized voters. 'The individual deputy can no longer do as he pleases in parliament. He is subject to the discipline of the parliamentary caucus of his party, is constantly controlled by his party'. Under present conditions – which no longer corresponded to those of the epoch of the First International and the Paris Commune, when this demand was 'wholly suitable' – the demand for the right of revocability of deputies by single groups of electors would represent a serious step backwards, for if it was implemented (here was an echo of Kautsky's theses of 1893), it would subject the deputies to local and sectoral pressures. 'What was reasonable and revolutionary fifty years ago is now not only wholly unreasonable but has even become reactionary. The deputy who today prefers dependence on a mass of voters lacking any mutual links to dependence on a party, whose unity is based on an idea, is acting in a reactionary manner'.[52]

Another of Lenin's battle cries was Marx's emphasis on the need to unify legislative and executive powers. Once again invoking the criterion of historical specificity, Kautsky maintained that the model Marx prob-ably had in mind was that of the Jacobins, which had been valid for the internal and external conditions under which the Jacobins had to operate.

[52] PR, pp. 125–127.

This model, however, had no relevance to a general theory of the state, of the normal functioning of institutions. On the contrary, there were two fundamental arguments in favour of the division of powers so far as socialists were concerned. The first was that socialism could be built only in a context of internal and external peace (here Kautsky reiterated his positions on the transitional period, which were in complete contradiction with the Leninist view that the dictatorship of the proletariat must necessarily be based on force). Kautsky did not exclude that 'under certain social conditions, war or even civil war could be wholly appropriate, even necessary, for the conquest of political power' (namely when reaction created such conditions through its own violence). He did, however, deny that socialism could be built otherwise than in conditions of normal social peace, in which the democratic method regulated the exercise of power. 'For the period of transition from capitalism to socialism', he wrote, 'we need peace most urgently, not only peace abroad but also at home. Not in the sense of a reconciliation of classes, but rather in the sense of a conduct of class struggle through the methods of democracy and not through the violence of arms. In these conditions there is, in truth, not the slightest reason to unify executive and legislative powers. On the contrary, a multitude of reasons speak against such a measure'.

The division of powers, Kautsky maintained, was above all a progressive expression of the division of labour in the institutional domain: it was not 'an arbitrary phenomenon'. But it was also a democratic necessity. For 'history shows us that an assembly that commands both executive and legislative power does not brook the slightest opposition'.[53] Finally, the division of powers was more functional for the accomplishment of the specific goals of both the executive and legislative powers. It corresponded to the innermost structure of the executive power, whose task was action and whose condition was maximum internal unity, which active opposition indeed tended to paralyze. On the other hand, the legislative power absolutely demanded that every law be born of a confrontation of conflicting opinions; it therefore constituted the proper institutional locus of political divisions. To subordinate the latter to the former or actually to unify them would necessarily be to annul the autonomy of the legislative power, in other words, to confer on the executive the *de facto* ability to establish laws.[54]

[53] PR, pp. 127–129, 132.
[54] PR, p. 132.

Thus, the great doctrinaire, the custodian of Marxist orthodoxy, did not hesitate openly to criticize some of the central aspects of the thought of Marx, accusing Lenin of inability to evaluate Marxism critically in the light of the lessons of history and social change. But if Lenin was such a faithful disciple of Marx, Kautsky went on, if he was so wedded to the unification of legislative and executive powers in the name of Marxist precepts, why then did he refuse to go all the way? Why did he ignore another central aspect of the thought of Marx – namely that the unification of powers was not intended to permit a party dictatorship, but to rest on universal suffrage. 'Of all the institutions of the Paris Commune emphasized by Marx', Kautsky wrote, 'there is only one to which the Bolsheviks remain faithful today: the unification of the executive and legislative powers into a single entity. But the Bolsheviks have not unified these powers into a representative body elected through universal suffrage, like the Paris Commune'. The Bolsheviks, divesting the unification of powers of its basis in universal suffrage, had transformed it into an instrument of their own dictatorship, betraying Marxism even while proclaiming themselves its most assiduous votaries.[55] What was the ultimate and inevitable result of such an attitude? A unified power without controls could never halt at the establishment of the dictatorship of a party, but must end in the dictatorship of the party leaders.[56] Such a dictatorship, however, represented a major obstacle to social development, and to the maturity of the masses which formed the sole guarantee of socialism.[57]

By 1919 Kautsky had reached a drastic conclusion: that the Bolshevik régime, founded on a dictatorship of party leaders, was politically and economically more oppressive for the working class than capitalism itself.[58] Given this premise, it was logical that henceforth Kautsky's sole aim was the overthrow of a régime which called itself revolutionary but was counter-revolutionary in practice. In August 1921, issuing his book *Von der Demokratie zur Staatssklaverei*, Kautsky declared: 'To lift Russia out of the mire into which it now threatens to sink is the most pressing task of the moment, above all for all socialists, since it is in their hands that the destiny of the Russian people lies'.[59]

[55] PR, pp. 135–136.
[56] PR, pp. 135–137.
[57] PR, p. 138.
[58] TC, pp. 134–136.
[59] VDSS, p. 7.

4 The Inevitable Failure of the Third International

'What is the world revolution?' Kautsky asked in *Terrorism and Communism*. He replied: 'It can be conceived in two different ways: either as the development of the socialist idea in the world, accompanied by the strengthening of the proletariat and a simultaneous sharpening of the class struggle, until socialism becomes a motor force of world significance, increasingly determining the fate of all states. Or it can be understood as a revolutionization of the world in the Bolshevik sense, the conquest of political power by the proletariat in all the great states in the very near future (otherwise this world revolution would be unable to save the Russian Revolution), the complete introduction of soviet republics, dictatorships of the Communist Parties, and thus the unleashing of civil wars throughout the globe for a generation'.[60]

Kautsky consistently maintained that the preconditions for the success of the Bolshevik Revolution were lacking in the West. In the West the success of the working class depended on its unity. If it was divided, it could neither take nor keep power. Moreover, in the Western countries, precisely those most important for the world revolution, the strength of the ruling classes remained intact. They had emerged victorious from the World War and possessed armies far more stable than that of Tsarist Russia, whose disintegration had cleared the field for the revolutionaries. The project of civil war was therefore doomed to failure on the very terrain on which it was supposed to operate, that of violence. To have any possibility of success, international Bolshevism would have to exploit in the Western masses the same contempt for the democratic methods characteristic of those who had never known or experienced it. But in the West, Kautsky asserted, 'democracy did not emerge yesterday, as in Russia. It has been won through a series of revolutions and centuries-long struggles; it has become the very flesh and blood of the masses'. Indeed it was the masses themselves who sought to teach the superior classes the rules of democracy. Finally, in the West it would not be possible for the victorious proletariat to reproduce the conditions on which the Bolshevik dictatorship was based: 'here it is quite impossible for entire classes, among them the largest, to be deprived of political rights'.[61] In the West, the very consequences of socio-economic advance made it impossible to imitate the shortcuts

[60] TK, p. 146.
[61] TK, p. 147.

which the revolution had taken in Russia, and which had perverted it: 'Socialism cannot conquer power unless it is strong enough to maintain its own superiority over the other parties within the limits of democracy. This is why socialism has not the slightest reason to repudiate democracy, and it will be precisely the most advanced sections of the proletariat that will certainly not agree to the replacement of democracy by dictatorship, which in practice always eventually becomes a personal dictatorship'.[62]

The inherently mechanistic perspectives of those who insisted on the universal validity of Bolshevism, Kautsky argued, were obvious from their attempt to transform the institutional forms of the Russian Revolution into models to be imitated without taking account of the relationship of class forces and the characteristics under which the Russian forms arose. Anyone considering the developed West, Kautsky said, must first of all note that because of economic development the relations between workers and peasants were radically different from those in the USSR, as were the relations between the masses and the bourgeoisie. What, then, would it mean to generalize the model of the Russian Revolution and attempt to impose its institutions? The Communist International, Kautsky wrote, was 'an International of action', but the action on which it was based was too simplistic: 'There can be no more fatal illusion than the dream of such an International. It is quite true that labour is struggling against capital in all countries; it is likewise true that its goal everywhere is the conquest of state power and the development of production in a socialist direction. But in practice these objectives are transformed into a series of concrete particular tasks which differ in the different countries: one thing in the countries that were victorious in the World War, another in the countries that were defeated; one thing in the countries in which the peasants still have revolutionary aspirations, another in the countries in which the peasants hold conservative positions; one thing where capitalist industry predominates, another where it constitutes a minority sector; one thing in countries in which militarism is strong, another in those in which it is weak; one thing in countries in which the popular masses have been educated in democracy for decades or even centuries, another in those in which these masses are only now beginning to look beyond the limits of the isolated village, etc. Yet they want to create an organization which, despite all these incredible differences, provokes and guides simultaneous

[62] TK, p. 148.

mass actions of the same type!'[63] The attempt to adapt to the West the dictatorship of workers' and peasants' councils that arose from Russian conditions, Kautsky argued, was one of the aspects of the artificial universalism of Bolshevism. In Russia the minority of the workers faced a weak bourgeoisie and a mass of peasants, whom the workers were able to lead because they were revolutionary in the democratic sense, as a consequence of the survivals of feudalism. But none of these conditions existed in the developed capitalist countries: 'In the modern capitalist countries, where the peasants are conservative but also already educated and organized politically, it becomes wholly illusory to view peasant councils within a general council system as a factor acting in a more revolutionary sense, towards socialism rather than democracy. A dictatorship of councils is condemned to the most complete failure'.[64]

Commenting on the foundation of the Third International, Kautsky claimed that an organization that was incapable of evaluating national and socio-economic specificities, issuing external orders to parties that were supposed to provoke the revolution in other countries, could never have any real vitality.[65] In reality, the Communist International was an International in name only. It suffered from an inherent and destructive contradiction: for it conferred the leadership of revolutionary processes not on those who were supposed to realize them, but on those who had already done so; it thus turned those who had to work actively into passive instruments of others who guided their action from outside. In any case, the representatives of the developed countries to which the revolution was to be extended were 'as a rule mere figureheads in the executive committee of the Third International'.[66] Regardless of its intentions, he said, the Third International acted in practice as an 'instrument of the government of one particular country, in which the executive committee resides'.[67] This was evident from the very fact that the Communists of the West were organizationally incapable of standing on their own two feet, but received direct subsidies from the Russian government, facilitating attacks against them and inciting damaging suspicions'.[68]

Dependent on Moscow for their existence – Kautsky wrote in 1925 – the Communist Parties of the West assumed the role of outright 'des-

[63] *Vergangenheit und Zukunft der Internationale*, Wien, 1920, p. 67.
[64] Ibid., p. 73.
[65] Ibid., p. 57.
[66] Ibid., p. 64.
[67] Ibid., p. 64.
[68] Ibid., p. 65.

perados' in the service of their patron, launching systematic and deliberate attacks on 'the proletarian parties outside Russia which do not depend' on the Bolsheviks. This was a permanent objective in a struggle waged by all available methods, including 'lies' and 'deceit'. Indeed, 'for years now the Soviet government has occupied itself primarily with an enterprise designed to enslave, corrupt, debilitate, and stupefy the proletariat inside and outside Russia, rendering it increasingly incapable of liberating itself'. Kautsky eventually came to condemn the Soviet system as even worse than the régimes of Mussolini and Horthy (he was writing in 1925, when the opposition parties and press had not yet been formally suppressed in Italy). 'The Soviet government', he went so far as to write, 'now represents the gravest obstacle to its [the proletariat's] rise in the world. It is even worse than the infamous Horthy régime in Hungary or the Mussolini régime in Italy, which do not yet make any effort at opposition by the proletariat as radically impossible as the Soviet government does'. Hence Kautsky's categorical conclusion: 'This régime today is no longer simply an enemy of all non-Bolshevik parties; it has become the most dangerous enemy of the proletariat itself'.[69] The combination of Social Democratic charges like this with the Communist accusations that the Social Democrats were the principal obstacle to the revolution and therefore the mainstay of bourgeois reaction was a measure of the profound cleavage that now divided the Western workers' movement.

A concrete occasion for Kautsky to denounce Soviet 'Bonapartism' and its congenital inclination to resolve political questions by violence came in February 1921, when the Bolsheviks decided to terminate *manu militari* the existence of the Menshevik republic in Georgia. In September 1920 Vandervelde, MacDonald, and Kautsky himself had visited Georgia, and Kautsky later published a pamphlet, *Georgien. Eine Sozialdemokratische Bauernrepublik*, the final chapters of which were appropriately modified after the end of Menshevism in this region. Kautsky argued that the suppression of the Georgian Republic showed that the internal despotism of the Russian Revolution was also beginning to generate a militaristic imperialism, destined to culminate in Caesarism. He wrote: 'Soviet Russia has entered a new phase of its revolution, one which corresponds to the third phase of the French Revolution – the phase of absolutist police and military power. We may define this phase as that of *Bonapartism*. It is true that the victorious general has not yet made his appearance. In the meantime, Russia today is in its consulate,

[69] *Die Internationale und Sowjetrussland*, Berlin, 1925, pp. 10–11.

282

controlled by the two consuls Lenin and Trotsky'.[70]

In Kautsky's view, the comparison with French Bonapartism was to the disadvantage of Bolshevism. Bonapartism in France had represented a retreat from the preceding phase of the revolution; but it nevertheless represented 'some progress' for the rest of Europe, since it was an expansion of the most advanced state of continental Europe. The imperialist 'Bonapartism' of the Bolsheviks, on the other hand, exported only its own political and social backwardness. 'The present Bonapartism of Moscow is reactionary not only in comparison to the proletarian revolution from which it has emerged, but even more so in comparison to the proletarian movement in the rest of Europe, which it seeks to put in shackles to which no evolved proletariat wants to submit'.[71]

If he compared the Bolshevik to the Bonapartist régime, Kautsky saw Lenin as a sort of 'Bismarck of the proletariat'. When Lenin died, Panski-Solski, the Berlin correspondent of *Izvestia*, rather paradoxically invited Kautsky to write a commemorative article on Lenin for the newspaper of the Soviet government. After overcoming his great surprise at the request, Kautsky did write an article, which was published in *Izvestia* with an editorial note affirming that even 'an open enemy of Leninism' like Kautsky acknowledged 'the greatness of the genius of the proletarian revolution'. In the compass of a text essentially devoted to Lenin as an individual, Kautsky rehearsed the main elements of his attitude toward 'Leninism' as a historical current. In substance, Kautsky considered Lenin a gigantic historical figure, a great revolutionary, who had also proved himself a great statesman, but of a state that had taken the road of 'fire and iron'. While emphasizing and recalling his differences with Lenin, Kautsky saluted him as a 'hero of the proletarian revolution', 'a colossal figure with few equals in world history'. Among the great statesmen of the contemporary era only Bismarck could compare with him. Divided in their historical objectives, the two men were motivated by an equal inflexibility of character and will. Like Bismarck, Lenin 'quite well understood the power of arms in politics, and he could use them without scruples at the decisive moment'. Like Bismarck, however, Lenin also understood the limits of the use of violence and was a 'master of diplomacy, of the art of deceiving his enemies, of surprising them and exploiting their weak points in order to demolish them'. But Lenin had another of Bismarck's qualities as well: the capacity to turn a new page when necessary: 'Lenin, like Bismarck, was always prepared, when he

[70] *Georgien. Eine sozialdemokratische Bauernrepublik*, Vienna, 1921, p. 68.
[71] Ibid., p. 70.

became convinced that the road he had chosen did not lead to his goal, to change direction and take another route. With the same facility with which Bismarck shifted from free trade to protectionism in 1871, Lenin turned from pure communism to the NEP'.

The grave limit of Lenin as a politician and a statesman, Kautsky continued, was his insufficient knowledge of the West, 'even though he lived in the West for many years as an emigré'. 'His policy, which fully corresponded to the specific conditions of Russia, was based in foreign affairs on the expectation of a world revolution, which from the outset appeared illusory to anyone conversant with Western Europe'. Even within Russia, Lenin inevitably succumbed to the historical and social limits of the mass movement of 1917 and was compelled to contradict as a statesman the objectives he had pursued as a revolutionary leader. The masses, powerfully stirred by the war, plunged into motion, and Lenin was supremely able to take advantage of their revolt. But the same masses, while they had the strength to shake the old order, were too backward and lacking in political and organizational experience to be able to construct a new order. Faced with this impasse, Lenin subjected the workers and peasants to a party dictatorship from which the toilers were unable to emancipate themselves. 'Here', Kautsky asserted, 'lie the deeper roots of the success of Lenin, and here also begin my greatest reservations about his system, for the liberation of the proletariat means above all the most limitless independence of its thought and action'. Instead of fostering those conditions which alone could prepare socialism, Lenin chose to exploit the weaknesses of the masses. Kautsky ended his article in commemoration of Lenin by expressing his faith that the Russian proletariat would find the strength to open a second phase of the Russian Revolution, one founded on democracy. For the historical contradiction of Lenin was that he had 'led the proletarian revolution in Russia to victory, but also rendered it incapable of bearing fruit'. Such was the fate of a socialist Kautsky defined as a 'hero' of the proletarian cause, despite their bitter differences.[72]

A year before, Kautsky had written a similar article commemorating the death of Martov, whom he considered the most positive exemplar of Russian socialism. Kautsky defined Martov as 'the leader of those who waged the struggle against Bolshevik Bonapartism even twenty years ago, when Bolshevism was still striving to erect its dictatorship in the party, and not yet in the state'. For Kautsky, Martov was the man who ideally should have triumphed one day, when a new democratic revo-

[72] 'Ein Brief über Lenin', in *Der Kampf*, XVII, 1924, pp. 176-179.

lution had established a 'new proletarian régime' in Russia. Such a revolution, although not immediately predictable, was nevertheless a historic necessity, since the time during which Lenin appeared as the 'messiah of Russia' and Lenin's Russia as the 'messiah of Europe' was now past. The success of Lenin the statesman had laid the basis for the success of Martov the Marxist and socialist leader.[73]

5 Stalinism as Counter-Revolution

The 'fall' of Trotsky in January 1925, climaxing the campaign launched against him in 1924 by the 'troika' of Zinoviev, Kamenev, and Stalin, prompted Kautsky to further sweeping arguments in yet a new work, *Die Lehren des Oktoberexperiments*. This essay attempted an overall balance-sheet of Trotsky's work, similar in substance, if not in form, to the article written about Lenin on the occasion of his death. Kautsky saw the internal conflicts of the Soviet leadership as confirmation of the positions he had maintained up to that time. Had he not asserted that in time the Bolshevik dictatorship would be reduced to a dictatorship of leaders? Had he not argued that without democratic institutions political life would be reduced to a frantic struggle of factions within the leading group, while the proletariat, which according to socialist doctrine was responsible for the political and social administration of the new state, was eliminated from any role in events? Had he not charged that Bolshevism embodied the spirit of violent sectarianism, corrupt and corrupting, incapable of dealing with dissent except in terms of 'betrayal'? For Kautsky, the 'major lesson of the October experiment' was that Bolshevism had created an oppressive machine that was now devouring its own creators. Trotsky, along with Lenin, had certainly been the great hero of the October *'coup d'Etat'*. The essence of the machine was that it functioned according to a single, fundamental rule: deal with political questions through organized violence. Once erected into a system, the machine had acquired a technical independence of its own, and those who now controlled it could massacre those who had initially designed it. 'The despotism of the Bolshevik Party in Russia', wrote the aged theoretician, 'today appears more solid and invulnerable than ever. Nevertheless, its framework is creaking. This has been proven very recently by the fall of Trotsky. At first sight it may seem that his swift

[73] 'Der letzte Gang. Julius Martov zum Gedächtnis', in *Leipziger Volkszeitung*, 11 April 1923.

and smooth liquidation has strengthened the dictatorship to the maximum and has shown that no opposition to it is possible. But precisely the facility with which the opposition was defeated has demonstrated the extent to which Bolshevism has degenerated, for this was not an external opposition, but one that arose in its own ranks, an opposition led by a man who, with Lenin, had created the dictatorship and given it its practical and theoretical foundation, while the greater part of the present bosses of Russia were initially hesitant and uneasy about it, and for good reason'.[74]

How then had 'Zinoviev and company' succeeded in bringing down Trotsky? Kautsky posed a question that was often to be repeated by distinguished historians of Soviet Russia many years later: How was it possible that people so obviously inferior to Trotsky were able 'so rapidly and easily' to defeat a man who, 'for all his weaknesses, stood head and shoulders above his Bolshevik opponents' and who enjoyed the prestige of one who had 'done so much for their state structure'?[75] Kautsky's answer was that the fall of Trotsky was testimony to the internal contradictions of Bolshevism. As an oppositionist, Trotsky had been sacrificed to the machine he himself had played such a great part in creating. It was now quite clear that it was impossible in Russia, even within the Bolshevik leadership, to approach political problems otherwise than in terms of pure force, i.e. the material force that each contending side was capable of mustering. In a state dominated by the bureaucracy and its repressive apparatus, in which it was not possible to wage a struggle for ideas through clashes of opinions as a normal and legitimate method, the only rule was the application within the party and its leading group of the violence that had first been set in motion outside the party, against the other socialist parties, the Mensheviks and Social Revolutionaries. There was no longer any possibility of political initiative by the toiling masses, who had been entirely shunted aside. 'Trotsky himself made the greatest contribution to the construction of that frightful apparatus of domination, which grinds up whoever dares challenge its masters'.[76]

This apparatus was in turn the product of the manner in which the Bolsheviks, guided by Lenin and Trotsky, had conquered power. They had conceived the seizure of power as a *coup d'Etat* conducted according to the rules of military art by a warlike vanguard, elevating the fruit of

[74] 'Die Lehren des Oktoberexperiments', in *Die Gesellschaft*, II, 1925, p. 374.
[75] Ibid., p. 379.
[76] Ibid.

this pre-Marxist technique to an instrument of exclusive domination. 'Lenin and Trotsky', Kautsky wrote, 'propagandized for the armed insurrection of their sect against the other workers' parties – as Trotsky himself admits – initially in conflict with another, significant section of their own followers, who were correctly concerned about this sort of civil war, until they themselves were unable to resist the fascination of power'.[77] Now, a militarized system of power led inevitably – and Trotsky was the greatest exponent of this – to a 'military cretinist' conception of a task that could never be accomplished through violence or military spirit: social construction. Trotsky's was not a parliamentary cretinism but a 'cretinism of a different type: *military* cretinism. Trotsky believes he can resolve all the problems of our time', above all economic problems, 'with the instruments of military force'.[78] Trotsky's attempt, once in opposition, to escape from the implacable consequences of the power structure he himself had so notably contributed to creating was inevitably condemned to failure by the 'contradiction of *nol consente*'. To appeal to the right of criticism, as Trotsky belatedly did, was to recall a reality that he himself had reduced to a phantom when he was in power. 'So far, any attempt on the part of anyone who has fought for the Communist Party to exercise the right of criticism against the government has ended this way: those who have made criticisms have been swept aside and reduced to silence'. The machinery of despotism and repression 'transforms the champions of the ruling party into slaves and cowards'.[79]

As we have already seen, Kautsky was gradually sharpening his polemic against Bolshevism, moving from a critique of Bolshevism as an 'error' and 'deviation' to a position that considered it a plainly and definitively counter-revolutionary force. Already in *Die proletarische Revolution* (1922) Kautsky set forth a 'logic' of the development of the Bolshevik dictatorship which would later serve to explain events like the internal struggle in the party leadership as the demonic triumph of a machine of terror and repression that would turn against the very people who had constructed it. Kautsky claimed that the Bolshevik Revolution was a bourgeois revolution waged by bourgeois methods, namely the struggle of an organized minority against a disorganized majority. In accordance with the historical logic of bourgeois revolutions, it found itself in the inevitable impasse of having to put an end to an abstract and ideological

[77] Ibid., p. 376.
[78] Ibid., p. 374.
[79] Ibid., p. 380.

radicalism which became untenable once real social conditions had re-asserted themselves. The Bolshevik Revolution, however, had been marked by a significant variation with respect to the typical model of bourgeois revolutions. Generally, in past cases, the revolution of the radicals, who then proved unable to keep power, was succeeded by a counter-revolution led by a different, resolutely reactionary party. The historic peculiarity of the Bolshevik régime, however, was that this 'Bonapartist' wave was generated not by another party but by internal forces within the same party. 'Although up to now', Kautsky wrote, 'this process has occurred in all countries through the destruction and dissolution of one party by another, the Bolsheviks have themselves implemented the transition from revolution to counter-revolution. Astonished observers have lauded the vitality of their régime. But this rests not on the vitality of the revolution they have guided, but on the fact that the Bolsheviks, as soon as they noticed that the revolution was heading for defeat, unscrupulously assumed the functions of the counter-revolution themselves'.[80]

As time went by, Kautsky painted his panorama in ever blacker tints. In his 1930 work *Der Bolschewismus in der Sackgasse*, he was still drawing the analogy between Bolshevism and Bonapartism. Shortly thereafter, in 1931, he proceeded to assert that Bolshevism was even worse than Bonapartism. In 1930 his concern was still to combat the view that the Bolsheviks were 'Jacobins', i.e. revolutionaries, possibly bourgeois, but nevertheless progressive (as was maintained, for example, by Kautsky's old Austro-Marxist friends Otto Bauer and Fritz Adler). 'At the outset of their action during the revolution of 1917', Kautsky wrote in this regard, 'the Bolsheviks could perhaps have been compared to the Jacobins, although even then there were great differences. But after their *coup d'Etat*, they departed ever further from their original base, adopting overnight a programme diametrically opposite to their previous one. The Jacobins never made such a turn. They remained faithful to the idea of parliament and universal suffrage. It was thus not the Jacobins, but another party, although issued of the revolution and of Jacobinism, that showed no qualms about throwing their programme overboard as soon as an opportunity to come to power and stay there in this manner arose. This was the party of the "Bonapartists". If one wants to establish parallels between the last Russian Revolution and the first French one, then the Bolsheviks must be compared not mainly to the

[80] PR, p. 98.

Jacobins, but to the Bonapartists'.[81]

In 1931, however, Kautsky announced: 'Bolshevism is not Bonapartism. It is worse than Bonapartism'. For Bonapartism 'was counter-revolutionary only from the political standpoint'; it safeguarded and defended 'the economic basis the revolution had created', and this allowed for the 'economic development of France'. 'Bolshevism, on the contrary, has destroyed not only the political but even the economic conquests of the revolution, has subjugated the trade unions and factory councils, has enveloped the entire apparatus of production in the strait-jacket of a bureaucracy as incompetent as it is corrupt and arbitrary, and has thus condemned the economy to complete ruin'.[82] The essential characteristic of the Soviet régime in the phase of 'Stalinism', was henceforth its 'unlimited arbitrariness'; this was its most 'terrible aspect, which has debased the entire population'.[83] For years Kautsky had been claiming that with its system of suffrage and ideology Bolshevism had transformed the working class in Russia into a sort of 'aristocracy' – in a decisive break with the Marxist programme of using the socialist régime as a weapon to put an end to all class and corporatist privileges. Analyzing the USSR at the end of the twenties, he drew a comparison between Soviet and feudal society. Compared to the great majority of the 'serfs', i.e. the peasants, who were excluded from any influence in the social system and reduced to a mere labour force, the wage workers, although haunted by insecurity and hunger, nevertheless maintained a position of miserable privilege. 'Standing above the workers, as in the countries under a feudal system, there is a high nobility in Soviet society. It is constituted by the Communist Party, which governs the state. Its members enjoy greater freedom of movement than the "subjects"; they can publish newspapers, make money, secure themselves a bourgeois life style. . . . The Communists form the aristocratic class, which commands the rest of the population at will, of which it represents not more than one per cent'. The party rigorously supervised admission into its ranks in order to maintain its control, and 'one is never sure of remaining in those ranks', as was demonstrated by the continual 'purges'. The 'Soviet aristocracy' composed of Communists had in turn only one guarantee of survival: loyalty to an omnipotent leadership, to a 'gang',

---

[81] *Der Bolschewismus in der Sackgasse*, Berlin, 1930, pp. 98–99. This work will henceforth be cited as BS.
[82] 'Sozialdemokratie und Bolschewismus', in *Die Gesellschaft*, VIII, 1931, vol. I, pp. 58–59.
[83] BS, p. 67.

which 'has established itself as the master of the entire Soviet apparatus, namely the army, the bureaucracy, the political police, and consequently dominates not only the trade unions and the soviets but even the Communist Party itself, in a dictatorial manner, i.e. through unlimited arbitrariness'. The law of this absolute power was that it must purge itself ruthlessly. In this sense, 'Soviet feudality' was the embodiment of a much more complete despotism than that which prevailed under classical feudalism. Whereas the feudal lords, who inherited their property and commanded 'considerable rights' against the state, could occasionally constitute a strong and independent opposition, the 'Soviet nobility' was completely subjected to the despotic power of the leadership, while no relations other than those of force existed anywhere among the elements of Russian society. The Soviet Union was a land of unlimited arbitrariness.[84] To those who expressed fears of a danger of Bonapartism in the USSR, Kautsky replied sarcastically: 'What else does Stalin have to do to arrive at Bonapartism? Are we to assume there is no Bonapartism until Stalin has crowned himself Tsar?'[85]

Having identified the Stalinist régime as counter-revolutionary and worse than Bonapartism, Kautsky – viewing socio-political systems through the prism of political and civil rights, of liberty of action for all parties, of full freedom for the organization of the proletariat and of the toiling classes in general – inevitably ended by assimilating Bolshevism to fascism, as practitioners of similar political and governmental techniques. For him Bolshevism could in no way be considered a sort of 'barbaric road' to socialism. The essential point was not that Bolshevism was based on the nationalization of the means of production and fascism on the capitalist mode of production, with private ownership of the means of production: it was rather that both infrastructures served to maintain a régime of despotic power that transformed the proletariat, and with it all society, into a completely subjugated mass. Kautsky's hostility to Bolshevism paralleled his hostility to fascism. In his view there could be no reason to tolerate the former on the grounds that it had a proletarian base. Fascism also, he observed, possessed a significant proletarian component, which could not attenuate opposition to it.[86]

In substance, Kautsky believed that the fate of the proletariat would be the same under a Bolshevik and a fascist régime. But the most serious

[84] BS, pp. 65–69.
[85] BS, p. 101.
[86] 'Das Proletariat in Russland', in *Der Kampf*, XVIII, 1925, p. 380.

charge Kautsky levelled at Bolshevism was that it had served as a school of repressive techniques for fascism itself. 'Fascism', he wrote in *Der Bolschewismus in der Sackgasse*, 'is nothing other than the counterpart of Bolshevism; Mussolini is simply aping Lenin'.[87] To be sure, he acknowledged that fascism was deliberately reactionary, while Bolshevism was reactionary as a consequence of its internal contradictions. Nevertheless, the ultimate results were not different as regards the position of the proletariat. Recalling the judgment he had made of Lenin in 1924, Kautsky admitted in 1931 that 'the *will* of the Bolsheviks is revolutionary', but added that 'their *action* is counter-revolutionary'. He concluded: 'What counts for us in judging a party politically is not only the *will* of its leaders, but also and above all the inevitable *results* of their action'.[88] Thus although Kautsky noted that in 'subjective will' the Bolsheviks differed from the fascists, this did not lead him to abandon his analogy: 'It is true that here [with the Bolsheviks] the starting point was completely different than there [with the fascists]. Fascism shows that Bolshevik methods of dictatorship can be used either to enchain the proletariat or to enchain opponents. But when we compare them, we must note that what is inherent in fascism from the beginning as "intention", namely the suffocation of all the freedoms of the workers' movement, represents the inevitable "result" in the case of Bolshevism'.[89]

From politics Kautsky turned to economics and the relationship between them. One of the roots of the mounting despotism exercised by the Bolsheviks over the proletariat, Kautsky argued, lay in their undemocratic and irrational management of the economy.[90] In 1931, discussing the perspectives of the First Five-Year Plan and the forced-march industrialization of the USSR, Kautsky explained the essence of this irrationality as he saw it. Despite the fact that the Bolsheviks treated the writings of Marx as 'holy writ' and regarded themselves as his only loyal followers, they were adventurers in economic management who flouted all proper procedures. 'As good Marxists', he wrote, 'they ought to be familiar with the second volume of *Capital*, wherein Marx explains that the relationships between the various branches of production must always be determined by the technical and social conditions characteristic of the particular conjuncture; otherwise the entire economic

---

[87] BS, p. 102.
[88] 'Sozialdemokratie und Bolschewismus' op. cit., p. 39.
[89] BS, p. 102.
[90] BS, p. 53.

complex is thrown into disorder. A given quantity of means of production must be devoted to the production of means of personal consumption. Of these, in turn, one portion must serve for the production of foodstuffs, another for the production of cultural goods. A second great group of means of production must serve to produce new means of production, in order both to renovate outmoded means of production and to extend the compass of production itself'.

The Bolsheviks' economic policies, however, were not motivated by social purposes, but only by exigencies of augmenting their military strength. This was the fundamental genesis of the forced industrialization in the USSR, driven forward without regard to economic science or consequent social imbalances. 'Now then, in what does the five-year plan consist? Nothing other than the most gigantic disruption of the proportionality required by the branches of production.... What is valued above all else in Russia are the needs of militarism; the exigencies of production are not taken into consideration in the construction of new industrial complexes. To become independent of foreign industry for purposes of war – this is the greatest concern of the Soviet government in the construction of new industry'. The Bolsheviks sought to achieve this objective regardless of 'economic' and social costs,[91] thereby fully revealing the non-socialist character of Soviet planning. For socialist planning was based on the simultaneous interaction of a number of fundamental variables which could not be divorced from one another: collective property; a high cultural and professional level; democracy permitting the harmonious control of diverse social exigencies; technical-scientific planning. All these were lacking in Russia, save one: the abolition of private property. Thus for Kautsky Soviet 'planning' was not planning in the socialist sense, but merely utilization of an entire state economy in the service of the despotic will and particular interests of a 'new ruling class'. Hence its scarcely 'scientific', capricious empiricism – an inevitable result of the lack of sufficient socio-economic development in Russia. The despotic machine of the Soviet state, however, could afford to take no account of economic, social, or human costs. 'What we are now seeing in Russia', he wrote, 'is not a planned economy but an economy submitted to the uninterrupted alternation of plans, which has characterized Bolshevism ever since its inception. These are often grandiose projects, but every one of them is merely initiated. None is calmly carried through to the end; they are always continually modified, subject to patchwork

---

[91] 'Die Aussichten des Fünfjahresplanes', in *Die Gesellschaft*, VIII, vol. I, 1931, p. 257.

and changes, until they are regarded as inadequate and either "improved" by new projects or laid aside'.[92]

The sort of planning that prevailed in the USSR, then, was completely different from socialist planning, whose condition was the conscious intervention of the toiling masses in the labour process. In the Soviet Union it was a minority that commanded the use of the means of production, a 'new class'. 'When in place of the capitalists', Kautsky wrote, 'there emerges another minority which commands the means of production independent of the population and often in conflict with it, this change in property does not at all mean socialism'. In reality, such a régime had not eliminated the reasons for the struggle of the proletariat, since the working class remained excluded from power under the new régime. In fact, it created greater difficulties for this struggle than existed in the bourgeois-democratic régimes of the West, where the masses enjoyed political and civil liberties enabling them to struggle for change; in the USSR, on the contrary, they were subjected to a far greater oppression and lacked even the possibilities of struggle. Hence Kautsky's drastic conclusion: the new régime and its new ruling class were worse than the capitalist system and the bourgeoisie:

'Thus, what presently exists in Russia is not socialism but its opposite. Socialism can begin to be realized when the expropriators and usurpers who now hold power are themselves expropriated, as Marx said. The popular masses striving for socialism in Russia therefore find themselves facing precisely the same problem as exists in the capitalist countries as far as command of the means of production is concerned. The fact that the expropriators who must be expropriated in Russia call themselves Communists changes nothing. The difference between Soviet Russia and Western Europe is only this: in the developed capitalist countries the workers are already strong enough to impose various sorts of limits on the dictatorship of capital, and the relationship of forces is such that the socialization of important economic monopolies can take effect with the first parliamentary elections favourable to the workers. In Russia, on the other hand, the command of the means of production is not only centralized in a single body to the maximum, but is also supported by a state apparatus which is absolutized to the maximum, while as we have seen the workers are atomized, lacking free organization, a free press, or free elections, and completely incapable of resistance. Soviet Russia has thus certainly wrenched the means of production from the capitalists.

[92] 'Die Aussichten des Sozialismus in Sowjet-Russland', in *Die Gesellschaft*, VIII, 1931, vol. II, p. 442.

Nevertheless, this has occurred in such a way and under such conditions that the capitalists have been replaced with even harsher and more powerful bosses and even greater obstacles have been created to the proletariats's progress towards socialism than exist in the countries of developed capitalism, where democracy is deeply rooted'.[93]

[93] Ibid., pp. 437–438.

IX

The Class Character
of the USSR

1 The Polemic with Bauer, Adler, Dan and Abramovich

Kautsky's increasingly and systematically hostile assessment of Bolshevism and of the prospects of the USSR brought him into conflict
with some of the most distinguished representatives of international
'Menshevism'. Regarding the Soviet régime as economically and
politically anti-proletarian, he concluded that it must be overthrown:
there was no other way forward for socialism in Russia. In other words,
he denied that Bolshevism represented a primitive 'variant' of contemporary socialism, corresponding to Russia's socio-economic backwardness, and therefore one of the 'possible roads' for laying the foundations
of an advanced socialism. He likewise denied that Bolshevism could be
'reformed'. These views led to a direct clash with the Russian Mensheviks Dan and Abramovich and with the Austro-Marxists Fritz Adler
and Otto Bauer. Bauer, the most authoritative of the Austro-Marxists,
had clearly stated his own positions in *Bolschewismus oder Sozialdemokratie?*, a pamphlet published in 1920. In this work he concurred with
Kautsky in rejecting the Bolshevik claim that the Russian model could
be applied in the West, but he parted company with Kautsky in insisting
that there could be different roads to socialism in the East and the West,
equally suitable to the historic mission of the liberation of the local
proletariat. The Bolsheviks, Bauer wrote, had shown 'the working class
a different path to its goal: the violent constitution of a brutally overt
class rule by the proletariat'.[1] The Social Democratic road, on the other
hand, corresponded to the historical and social conditions in countries
that were more developed than Russia.

---

[1] O. Bauer, *Bolschewismus oder Sozialdemokratie?*, Vienna, 1920, p. 4.

Bauer and his fellow-thinkers argued that any insurrection against the Bolsheviks would open the door not to the development of socialism, but to counter-revolutionary action in Russia. They held that despite its 'barbaric' methods, Bolshevism was laying the basis, through its modernization of the Russian economy, for a new rise of democratic socialism in the future. Finally, they believed that for all its negative aspects, Bolshevism remained a genuinely socialist force linked to the proletariat. Kautsky profoundly disagreed with this approach. Having identified the democratic and socialist roads by definition, he denied that Bolshevism had any socialist character whatever. His opponents, pointing to the objective effects of economic modernization and industrialization on the future weight of the Soviet working class, emphasized the socio-economic importance of the proletariat as a class within the Bolshevik party from its very origins. They were convinced that the function of Bolshevism would in the final analysis prove progressive: it could not be equated with reaction and combated as such. Confronted with the depth of this disagreement, Kautsky charged that Bauer and others remained prisoners of a merely economistic and sociologizing analysis. He insisted that any assessment of Bolshevism must be based on a judgment of its political instruments, as the concrete expressions of the system it had created. If socialism employed the same instruments as capitalism, then there was no point in replacing capitalism with socialism. For socialists, a change in the infrastructure was only a means to create new social relations and not an end in itself. If a socialist infrastructure were unable to generate a new pattern of social relations, then the struggle of the working class would lose all meaning. In fact, of course, Kautsky considered Bolshevism worse than the system it had succeeded. It should not be assumed that the development of the productive forces by the new régime would prove in any way superior to the performance of a Russian capitalism, or better yet, an advanced progressive democracy such as the Bolsheviks had extinguished ·by dissolving the Constituent Assembly after their victorious *coup d'Etat*.

Bauer had written that 'the Bolsheviks are undoubtedly a party supported by a section of the Russian proletariat, an unquestionably revolutionary and socialist party', and that for this reason, 'in spite of all our differences', it was necessary to acknowledge a common loyalty to socialism and a 'community of interests' with them. In 1925 Kautsky replied that this had been his own opinion at one time but that he had since been compelled to revise it, for it was now clear that the fundamental feature of the Bolshevik régime was not the static fact that it rested on part of the proletariat, but the dynamic process of its fragmentation of the proletariat as a class and formation of a section of it into the praetorian guard of a government that was anti-proletarian as a whole. This was a most serious crime committed by those who were supposed to lead the entire class in its self-emancipation. Kautsky declared that the conflict between himself and Bauer mirrored the earlier conflict that had divided Martov from the other Mensheviks, like Axelrod.[2]

In 1928 and 1929 Kautsky wrote two articles on the relationship between the goals of Social Democracy and of Communism. His aim was to contest the position officially adopted at the Toulouse Congress of the French Socialists that 'the final goal' of the two movements was identical. Kautsky claimed that the similarity lay merely in word and not in deed: 'It is true that Bolshevism, like Social Democracy, speaks of the liberation of the proletariat. But Bolshevism, contrary to Marx, does not expect that the proletariat will ever attain the capacity to emancipate itself. An elite, namely a workers' "vanguard", must accomplish this task in the name of the entire class' – thereby rendering the working class 'ever less capable of liberating itself'.[3] To provide a foundation for these views, Kautsky turned to the problem of the social nature of the USSR and the significance of its nationalization of the means of production, which could not, he argued, be identified with the socialization proper to Marxism: 'Where the state apparatus is an instrument in the hands of a minority for the subjugation of the great majority of the people, any nationalization of the means of production intensifies the despotism of this minority and enhances servitude of the toiling masses. A process of nationalization undertaken by a state of this type represents the opposite of the sort to which we aspire. . . . Under the model state of Communist Russia, the state . . . is identified not with the nation but with a party that includes not more than one per cent of the population, which is in turn completely dependent on a ruling clique. In effect, then, the means of production have become the private property of this ruling clique, which disposes of them at its will. . . . The nationalization that we seek therefore has nothing in common with that of Bolshevism. What we have in common is only the *word* nationalization, but not the *thing*'.[4]

[2] 'Das Proletariat in Russland', op. cit., pp. 380 and 389.
[3] 'Die Gemeinsamkeit des sozialdemokratischen und des kommunistischen Endziels', in *Tribune*, vol. I, July 1928, no. 3, pp. 73–74.
[4] 'Nochmals die Gemeinsamkeit des sozialdemokratischen und des kommunistischen Endziels', in *Tribune*, vol. I, March 1929, no. 11, pp. 345–46.

Pursuing his polemic with Bauer in 1931, Kautsky emphatically reiterated his conception of democracy and socialism. What was in question, he said, was precisely whether the relationship between the two could be contingent. Was a non-democratic road to socialism conceivable. Kautsky hotly denied the possibility. It was clear that if a thesis like Bauer's became current in international Social Democracy, the entire edifice of Kautsky's position – based on the assumption that an undemocratic road to socialism led not to the preparation of a later democratic revival of socialism, but to its negation – would be exposed to collapse; even more so his conclusion that Bolshevism could not be reformed and so must be brought down by a proletarian revolution aimed primarily at the restoration of political democracy, resuming the brief experiment cut short in October 1917.

In a speech to the Congress of the Socialist International held in Vienna in July 1931, Bauer presented his analysis: 'There are various roads to socialism. They include the road of violence, dictatorship and terror which the world-historical example of the Russian Revolution has rendered enticing to great masses of workers in all countries. Yes, we will not deny that in this manner too it is possible to take the means of production from the capitalists, to break the monopoly of property and education commanded by the possessing classes. We will not deny that the attempt to supplant capitalist anarchy with the planned organization of social production can be undertaken in this way'. Bauer, however, went on to argue that the price of such a 'dictatorial' road was a total political despotism that annihilated individual and collective freedoms, and concluded that it must not be taken in the developed countries: 'This path of violence, of dictatorship, of terror, is not ours. It is not the road that we desire. We do not want to renounce democracy and the political self-determination of the people in the name of socialism; rather, we seek to posit this democracy and self-determination as the very basis for the construction of a socialist society'.

There was something more in Bauer's speech which related to the future strategy of the labour movement in the developed countries. Bauer maintained that the political option of the socialist forces in the West ought to be the democratic road. But at the same time he declared that if the bourgeoisie attempted to enslave the proletariat by the installation of fascism, then the working class would pursue the struggle for socialism 'even through means other' than those of democracy. In sum, although his speech indicated preference for the democratic, it did not exclude an undemocratic, road. Bauer thus lent general strategic legitimacy to the possibility of building socialism with the instruments of 'dictatorship' and therewith sanctioned the socialist credentials of the Bolshevik dictatorship.

Kautsky's reaction was sharp. He did not accept the possibility that there were 'different roads to socialism', some of which violated the obligatory connection between democracy and socialism. For him, there could only be different applications of democracy. Kautsky insisted that the struggle against fascism must be a struggle to reassert the democratic method as essential to socialism, which could never be attained by an undemocratic road. Dictatorship was a too potent medicine that would infallibly destroy not only reaction but also the revolution, paving the way regardless of its intentions for an anti-proletarian régime, since the only mode in which the proletariat could express itself politically was democracy, both under the capitalist system and even more so under a socialist system. Violence could be used only to reconquer democracy. He reasoned that if the proletariat had not been strong enough to prevent the fascist degeneration of the bourgeoisie, all the less would it be strong enough to establish a régime of its own. (This was a variant of the position he had held in the years before 1914 on the possibility of responding to a declaration of war with strikes to paralyze production.)

Such was Kautsky's response to Bauer's 'oscillations' and 'contradictions'. The comrades who shared the position of Bauer, he wrote: 'maintain that there are two roads to socialism, that of democracy and that of dictatorship. We prefer democracy for the countries of Europe apart from Russia. But what is to be done if this road is closed to us? Are we to interpret Bauer's position to mean that in that case we too "will take the road of violence, dictatorship and terror which entices great masses of workers in all countries"? There is no doubt that if we are deprived of democracy as the result of a fascist government we must struggle, and we will struggle, against this régime with all our might. We will meet violence with violence. . . . But towards what aim will we exert all our strength to bring down fascism? Will we act to replace it with another dictatorship through which we can allegedly construct socialism? . . . If we are strong enough to overthrow fascism, then we will command sufficient strength to reintroduce the democracy destroyed by fascism. There is no doubt that we will be stronger in our struggle against fascism if our goal is to replace it with democracy than if our goal is to replace one dictatorship with yet another. A working class that lacks the strength and capacity to hold itself together and reconquer democracy will also be unable to build socialism, which is a much more difficult task than the simple establishment of democracy, in which all the toiling masses have a most passionate interest, even the non-socialist masses. . . . I assert that for us there are not many roads to socialism but only one: that of democracy. When this road is closed to us, we must reopen it before we can take to the road of socialism'.[5]

Kautsky's conflicts with Dan and Abramovich complemented and extended his polemic with Bauer. Since socialism could be achieved only through democracy, the Bolshevik dictatorship was not socialist and could not prepare socialism; it was, on the contrary, an anti-socialist force. Hence Kautsky's refusal to consider the Soviet régime as anything but an enemy to be destroyed. In no case could it be regarded as a reality to be defended, even if only conditionally, against the danger of 'counter-revolution'. 'The disagreement between Dan and myself', Kautsky wrote in 1925, 'centres on the following claims by Dan: 1) an insurrection against the present régime in Russia could favour only the counter-revolution, inevitably damaging the cause of the proletariat; 2) a victorious insurrection against the present régime in Russia is anyway out of the question'. Kautsky rejected the assumption, underlying the first of Dan's theses, that 'the Bolshevik régime today remains, despite all our reservations, a revolutionary and proletarian régime'. Dan arrived at this conclusion, Kautsky said, because he considered the Bolshevik régime a 'child of the revolution'. But the decisive criterion for a realistic and concrete assessment of the régime could not be whether or not it was a child of the revolution. Kautsky did not at all deny Bolshevism's parentage; indeed, he fully acknowledged it. But he maintained that the pertinent criterion of judgment was the evolution and consolidation of Bolshevism. The Soviet régime, he argued, had now been transformed into a repressive bureaucratic apparatus that reduced the proletariat to a 'mass without rights, ruled by a clique commanding a well-disciplined bureaucracy, army, and police'. Bolshevism was therefore no longer to be counted among the revolutionary forces of socialism: it was not even a 'Jacobin' force. Rather it was openly Bonapartist. This was the reality which now had to be confronted. 'The revolutionaries themselves', he wrote, 'have assumed the functions of the counter-revolution'. Under these conditions, there were no grounds to fear that the overthrow of the Bolshevik régime would open the door to the counter-revolution, since the *régime itself* was the counter-revolution. Hence, 'the destruction of Bolshevism can no longer produce a counter-

[5] 'Die Aussichten des Sozialismus in Sowjet-Russland', op. cit., pp. 420–22.

revolution; rather, it can lead much more rapidly to overcoming it'.[6]
In 1925 Kautsky did not exclude the possibility that the Bolshevik
dictatorship could be removed by an internal 'reformist' process, if the
rising tensions within Bolshevism gave the proletariat the strength and
the chance to sustain an opposition determined to alter the status quo
(which was also the hope of Dan). But even at that time he refused to
exclude the option of insurrection, i.e. the 'revolutionary' road, rejecting
the argument that this would necessarily assume a counter-revolutionary
significance. Kautsky wrote: 'I would resolutely oppose any socialist
policy in Russia that took the position: insurrection at any price, only
insurrection can liberate us, any other road is useless. I consider such an
attitude as senseless as the opposite point of view: in no case insurrection,
since it would lead inevitably to counter-revolution. . . . Whoever considers the possibility of a gradual liquidation of the dictatorship in
Russia must also consider the possibility of its unexpected collapse'.[7]

At the beginning of the thirties, when Stalinist power was consolidated
and industrialization and forced collectivization were under way in
the USSR, Kautsky's hostility became even more pronounced. He
declared that he now excluded any possibility of democratization through
a 'reform' within the Bolshevik system effected by an opposition that
would not confront the régime head on. As early as 1921, in his writing
on Georgia, he had pointed to the road of rebellion against Bolshevism
as a third possibility apart from the maintenance of the 'new absolutism'
born of the revolution, or 'reaction' supported by the Entente powers.
This rebellion, he believed, would have to be led by the Mensheviks
and would represent 'the overcoming of Muscovite Bonapartism from
within, through the strengthening of the movement for the liberty of
the proletariat'.[8] Now, however, Kautsky lent this revolt a more precise
content: its necessary mode of operation and expression, he said, was
popular insurrection.

The venerable theorist had never tired of tolling the death knell of
the Soviet régime from its very inception. He spoke of the necessity and
possibility of an anti-Bolshevik revolt because he was convinced that
the collapse of Bolshevism was inevitable in any event. Discussing the
USSR, he now used tones similar to those of his predictions of the
ineluctable end of capitalism during his early 'radical' period. Where in
the past he had counterposed the political and social authoritarianism

---

[6] 'Die Internationale und Sowjet-Russland', in *Der Kampf*, XVIII, 1925, pp. 289–90.
[7] Ibid., p. 295.
[8] *Georgien . . .*, op. cit., p. 71.

of the bourgeoisie to the nascent reality of socialism and democracy, he now set the same ideals against Bolshevik despotism, for he was fully persuaded that only a system of social and political administration different from both capitalism and the Soviet régime could satisfy the pressing needs of humanity. In *Terrorismus und Kommunismus*, for example, he prophesied the 'collapse' of Bolshevism at a time when workers' control and workers' councils had given way to a bureaucratic dictatorship in the economy: 'It is true that the new economic dictatorship functions somewhat better than the economic anarchy which preceded it and which had led even more rapidly to catastrophe. But the dictatorship has merely deferred and not averted this catastrophe, because the new economic bureaucracy is also powerless to organize economic life'.[9] A few years later, in *Von der Demokratie zur Staatssklaverei*, he reiterated this 'prophecy' with its usual combination of certainty and indeterminacy: 'We must count on the collapse of the Communist dictatorship in the foreseeable future. It is not possible to predict the precise date. It can happen overnight or it may be a long time coming, which is more probable. But one thing is certain: Bolshevism has exhausted its possibilities and has entered its declining phase, whose evolution will be increasingly rapid'.[10]

Ten years later, in 1931, when the USSR was advancing towards forced industrialization and the perspectives of the First Five-Year Plan, Kautsky repeated his prediction of economic disaster once again, on the grounds that Russia would be unable to accelerate its development sufficiently without political and social democracy. Kautsky, along with certain Mensheviks, claimed that 'the five-year plan must necessarily fail, since no economic effort can prevail over the terror; on the contrary, the necessary condition for any economic improvement in Russia is greater freedom of movement for the masses through a democratization of the state'.[11]

In his book *Der Bolschewismus in der Sackgasse*, published in 1930, Kautsky traced out a detailed programme for the 'democratic revolution' in Russia and for the prospects of the struggle against Bolshevism. Its general thrust was directed towards two main objectives: 1) the reconquest of the freedom of movement of the proletariat and of political democracy without class limitations; 2) the formation of an economic system that would correspond to the level of productive forces in Russia.

[9] TK, p. 135.
[10] VDSS, p. 77.
[11] 'Eine Ergänzung, in *Arbeiter-Zeitung*, 10 March 1931.

Since Kautsky considered the original sin of the Bolsheviks to have been their voluntaristic violation of the necessary inter-connections between the forces of production, the relations of production, and political and institutional superstructures, he held that it would be indispensable to recompose the unity of these factors by simultaneously broadening the sphere of political and social democracy and restricting the sphere of an irrational and inefficient economic collectivization.

Posing the question of tactics in the struggle against the Bolshevik régime, Kautsky started from the assumption that the slogan of the 'democratization of the soviets', while intrinsically invalid – since democracy was universal or nothing, and sovietism had become the expression of an 'aristocratic' and particularist power – could nevertheless be a useful weapon in the struggle against the arbitrary power of the bureaucracy. 'The democratization of the soviets', he wrote, 'is an absurd idea which cannot replace our demand for democracy for all. Nevertheless, it may still be of some historical importance. Given the mounting bankruptcy of the Soviet system, it might rally a section of the Russian proletariat more rapidly and easily than the demand for universal suffrage. Man is conservative by nature, and even when he acts in a revolutionary manner, he likes, at least when he wants not simply to destroy reality but also to create it anew, to cling to what exists in order to transform it. Thus democratization of the soviets might become one of the levers for bringing the Communist reign to an end. Should such a demand arise spontaneously, it would be useful to support it'.

Kautsky was convinced that the slogan of the 'democratization of the soviets' would in practice, because of its own contradictions, lead to a struggle for democracy without class restriction: 'Its importance lies in the fact that its incoherence would drive it beyond itself, towards total democracy'.[12] Thus: 'If necessary, we can use the demand "democratization of the soviets" as a "transition" to total democracy. But in no case could we accept it as an element to be "substituted" for this democracy'.[13]

But what forces could undertake the struggle against the dictatorship of the Bolshevik party? Because of the tensions generated by forced collectivization, Kautsky considered a peasant revolt possible. But he emphasized the inability of the peasantry to reorganize the social and political structure of Russia as a whole. The most the peasants could do would be to spark off a wider revolt: 'Peasants in rebellion have been

[12] BS, p. 89.
[13] Ibid., p. 91.

able to achieve lasting and important results when they have been allied with the city, but not without the city, and still less against it'. The future of the 'democratic revolution' lay in the attitude of the proletariat, and in particular the capacity of the workers to break with the status of privileged class which the Bolsheviks had conferred on them in order to consolidate their own more extensive and substantial privileges. 'Everything', Kautsky wrote, 'will depend on this: whether the workers understand that their privileges are illusory and deceptive, that the proletariat cannot forge chains for the other oppressed classes without these being used against itself, and that they can create lasting liberty for themselves only by creating it for all. The proletariat in Russia can win only by renouncing its privileges. It is true that these privileges may indeed render the proletariat somewhat less miserable than the other layers of the population in the countryside, but they prevent the end of the general misery which is constantly extended by the soviet system'. It was further necessary, Kautsky continued, that intellectuals unite with workers and peasants, since the wage workers and peasants alone 'are not yet capable of founding a state without intellectuals'.[14]

The common ground of the three classes could only be democracy, as the sole satisfactory method for regulating their mutual relations.[15] The aim, then, of the 'democratic revolution' must be to resume the path that had been interrupted in October 1917: 'Only one perspective can put a rapid end to chaos and immediately assure the Russian masses the peace, liberty, and security for which they yearn: a union of workers of the city, intellectuals of democratic socialist convictions and peasants, to realize elections to a new Constituent Assembly, charged with drafting a constitution for a democratic parliamentary republic'.[16] Kautsky thought that if the 'democratic revolution' occurred in Russia, no force would be strong enough to constitute a government by itself. 'For the establishment of democracy, all the various elements must collaborate in a united manner – or at least the various socialist parties'.[17] The programme of such a coalition government would inevitably have to reflect the fact that Russia was not yet ripe for socialist production and planning. (For Kautsky, of course, Soviet collectivization and planning were signs of socio-economic immaturity, since their despotic apparatus of controls operated by coercion to extract surplus-value through 'state-

[14] Ibid., pp. 112–13.
[15] Ibid., p. 112.
[16] Ibid., p. 117.
[17] Ibid., p. 132.

slavery', for the benefit of a 'privileged caste' of ruling bureaucrats and of military officers who secured the system.) In many respects this programme recalled that which he had outlined for 'Russian democracy' in April 1917, which in turn re-echoed the programme he had drafted during the period of the first Russian Revolution of 1905.

A democratic bourgeoisie could no longer have any real base in Russia, Kautsky said. Weak even before the revolution, it had now perforce disappeared. There remained, he argued, non-socialist democrats who had no 'faith in socialist production' (a scepticism reinforced by the 'failure' of Bolshevism). But it could be assumed that these democrats were not actually anti-socialist and might even be prepared to extend the working class all necessary cooperation on the basis of a realistic economic programme. One of the major faults of the Bolsheviks had been a social policy that was generally inferior to that of the capitalist countries; one of the tasks of Russian democracy would be to bring social legislation and the living standards of the working class up to the level 'of certain countries of the West' in respect of essential consumption and freedom of expression and organization.[18] In industry, Kautsky called for the creation of a mixed economy, partly socialized and partly capitalist, designed to restore creative initiative in its various sectors. This would be a 'new "NEP"'. 'How should a democratic régime treat the large-scale industrial properties that have already been socialized by the Soviet state? Does the democratic programme require that they be purely and simply consigned to capitalists, since Russia is not yet ripe for socialist production?' This, Kautsky replied, 'would be a measure as insane as its opposite, the unplanned and forced socialization undertaken by the Bolsheviks'. Kautsky argued that it was necessary to preserve the socialized sectors; but it was equally necessary to cure them of the irrationality of coercion and of executive passivity. It was therefore necessary to introduce a high degree of 'freedom of economic action'. This could be done by leaving room for the development of competitive enterprises organized in a non-socialist sector, composed of 'free, capitalist, cooperative, and communal enterprises'. 'If these enterprises', Kautsky wrote, 'achieve better results, supply cheaper or superior products, pay higher wages, and so on, then the state enterprises should be abandoned. But not before. The transition to another form of organization, which might possibly even be capitalist, must only occur when and where it is advantageous for consumers and workers'.

[18] Ibid., p. 134.

Kautsky predicted that the state sector would draw great advantage from the emergence of political liberty and 'freedom of action': workers, trade unions, workers' councils, and factory directors would all be able, after bureaucratic domination and control were abolished, to contribute to ensuring that state production profitably embraced a broad sector.[19] At the same time, Kautsky called for the reversion of commerce to private ownership, since 'most branches of trade are not easily adapted to bureaucratic schematization'. In his view the nationalization of trade would not assist 'socialist production', which needed not so much the 'nationalization of the exchange of products as its "replacement" by an organization for circulating products among associations of producers and consumers'. 'Free trade' should also supplant the monopoly of foreign trade, which had exercised 'the most dispiriting effects' on the Soviet economy.[20] On the other hand, there was no reason to transform 'natural monopolies' such as railroads, forests, mines, oil, and similar branches into private monopolies.[21]

Turning to the programme of a 'victorious democratization' for the land, Kautsky maintained that in principle 'we should strive for the nationalization or socialization' of the soil. But he held that this problem could not be resolved in a doctrinaire and formalistic spirit. What mattered in practice was the concrete relationship between human labour and the land itself. Where the soil was worked by peasant labour, small-scale producers must be assured of their right of long-term possession, with no lingering threats of expropriation. For the *sovkhozi* and *kolkhozi*, the question was posed differently. Where labour had assumed a cooperative and collective character, 'the individual labourer is not wedded to his labour on a particular plot of land. The *sovkhozi* and *kolkhozi* can therefore be transformed into social property. In these cases the social ownership of the soil is important; on peasant holdings it is not'. In general, the relevant criterion was not formal categories but effective realities, not juridical status but the actual degree of development of the productive forces and the quality of the organization of labour. Those *sovkhozi* and *kolkhozi* that had been created by pure coercion – whose genesis did not correspond to an 'internal exigency of the toilers and the material conditions' – should be replaced by peasant forms of production. On the other hand, those which were 'technically well-equipped' or which possessed a voluntary labour

[19] Ibid., pp. 136–38.
[20] Ibid., p. 137.
[21] Ibid.

force with an adequate leadership should be maintained as collective property.[22]

The overall direction of Kautsky's programme should now be clear. On the one hand, it sought to 'lower' a collectivization that did not generally correspond to the actual level of the productive forces and relations of production in Russia, but was simply the expression of the 'voluntarist' drive for power of the Soviet bureaucracy – executed without regard for human costs, depletion of social resources, or exploitation of the working class and the peasantry: hence 'irrational' for the collectivity and 'rational' only for the privileged strata of the 'new class', with its despotic machine of political control. On the other hand, the programme was intended to 'heighten' the democratic capacity of all social forces to quicken the economy itself, and so in the long run lay a more solid basis for socialist production, which could be introduced on a large scale once the forces of production had attained much greater maturity.

Kautsky's thesis that Bolshevism could no longer be reformed, that it was now an overtly counter-revolutionary force, which a democratic revolution must overthrow in Russia, provoked further polemics with the Mensheviks Dan and Abramovich. Whereas Kautsky held that the Stalinist régime was a form of consolidated Bonapartism, Dan maintained that Stalinism had not created a conservative-peasant social order and that it was politically more similar to Jacobinism than to Bonapartism.[23] To Kautsky's hopes that forced collectivization might unleash a 'new popular revolution' that would introduce 'full democracy', Dan objected that if anti-Stalinist uprisings occurred in the countryside, they would not take a revolutionary but a particularist, economistic direction. Equally erroneous, Dan argued, was Kautsky's assumption that democratic intellectuals would move toward support of the popular masses, since there were no longer any intellectuals of the type Kautsky imagined in Russia.[24] The only force capable of waging a consistent struggle for democracy in the USSR, Dan wrote, was the working class, which did not want the overthrow of the régime and its replacement by a different order, but rather a transition from 'jacobinism' to socialist democracy – in other words, a political transformation that would not put in question the economic system.[25]

[22] Ibid., pp. 135–36, 138.
[23] Th. Dan, 'Probleme der Liquidationsperiode', in *Der Kampf*, XXIII, December 1930, no. 12, p. 509.
[24] Ibid., pp. 511–513.
[25] Ibid., p. 516.

Abramovich advanced a similar argument. He lucidly delineated two alternatives, Kautsky's position and the Menshevik position upheld by himself and Dan. Those, like Kautsky, who were convinced that the objective preconditions for socialism were lacking in the USSR, would inevitably conclude that the Bolshevik experiment was doomed to failure and therefore that a principled and frontal struggle must be waged against it. Those, on the other hand, who believed that socialism *could* be introduced in the USSR shifted the terrain of discussion to questions of *method*, and struggled precisely against the methods of Stalinism.[26] In sum, for Kautsky the counter-revolution had been victorious in Russia; for the Mensheviks there had been a Jacobin revolution that must overcome its limits and become socialist: 'Whoever is acquainted with the position of Russian Social Democracy as officially expressed in the writings of Martov knows that we, in contrast to Kautsky, consider Russian Bolshevism a Jacobin and utopian revolution. Revolutionary utopianism or Bonapartism? Spurious revolution or genuine counter-revolution? These are the terms of the question, if we are to summarize the antithesis between the conceptions of Kautsky and those of Russian Social Democracy'.[27] 'The Russian Bonapartism of which Kautsky speaks', Abramovich continued, 'is a very special phenomenon, since Bolshevism lacks the social base of Bonapartism. Under Bolshevism there are no classes that could enjoy the fruits of the revolution in lasting manner or could constitute a stable social counterweight'.[28] Finally, Abramovich emphasized that when Kautsky appealed for a general insurrection against the Stalinist régime, he was reckoning without the enemy – in other words, he was underestimating the repressive power of the Soviet state. The only realistic perspective against a centralized machine as highly organized as the Stalinist régime was a link-up of the popular and proletarian movement with one wing of forces engaged in an internal struggle within the dictatorship.[29]

Kautsky replied by explaining the reasons why he considered the perspectives of his 'Menshevik friends' erroneous. The Mensheviks, he wrote, consider the Bolshevik régime 'a revolutionary régime whose methods they do not share but whose overthrow could endanger the entire revolution. For them the problem is to prevent the violent over-

[26] R. Abramovich, 'Revolution und Konterrevolution in Russland', in *Die Gesellschaft*, VII, 1930, Band II, pp. 532–33.

[27] Ibid., p. 534.

[28] Ibid., p. 534.

[29] Ibid., pp. 540–41.

throw of the régime, and to modify its methods in a democratic direction. I, contrary to them, have arrived at the conviction that the apparatus of the Bolshevik government is no longer acting in the direction of the revolution, but rather is proceeding to ruin the conquests of the revolution; it thereby assumes the functions of the counter-revolution'.

So far, Kautsky was merely repeating his traditional views. His conclusion, however, was new. For he now declared that 'the effort to reform the dictatorship in a democratic direction, without a violent uprising of the popular masses, is hopeless'.[30]

In an article published in the Vienna *Arbeiter-Zeitung* in March 1931 Kautsky dealt explicitly with the problem of the political basis of the struggle to realize the programme of the 'democratic revolution' in Russia. His arguments were to provoke another major polemic, this time with Fritz Adler. Kautsky referred to the accusations at the recent Moscow trials against the Mensheviks, repeated in the international Communist press, that the positions he had set out in *Der Bolschewismus in der Sackgasse* represented an active preparation of armed insurrections against Bolshevik state power. Kautsky asserted that this was a deliberate falsification. He had, he said, 'always opposed any state intervention against Soviet Russia and any preparation of armed insurrection in that country'. The question was wholly different. It was not a matter of attempting to promote artificial insurrections, but rather of determining political options in the event that internal social tensions in the USSR spontaneously provoked a popular armed insurrection against Stalinist despotism. This was where real positions parted company: 'What position should be taken in that event?' Kautsky asked. 'Would it then be the duty of the International to call upon Russian Social Democrats to ally themselves against the workers and peasants in revolt against Stalin and his instruments? Is it really true that anyone who revolts against this abominable régime is a "White Guard" or is acting in the service of the White Guards? This is what we are discussing. It is something completely different from whether or not we should advocate foreign intervention and foment insurrections'. Kautsky went on to say that he did not believe, as some of his Social Democratic friends did, that there was any 'possibility of putting an end to the Stalinist terror peacefully', as improvements in the economic situation would someday render it superfluous.[31]

The degree of tension caused by the ideological conflict between

[30] 'Sozialdemokratie und Bolschewismus', op. cit., pp. 54–55.
[31] 'Eine Ergänzung', op. cit.

Kautsky on the one side and Bauer and Adler on the other over their differing assessments of Stalinist Russia was shown in 1933 by the editorial note with which *Der Kampf* accompanied an article by Kautsky entitled *Demokratie und Diktatur*, devoted precisely to the opinions of Bauer and his followers. The journal remarked that some of the judgments of the 'old master', 'especially in regard to Soviet Russia', were 'in quite sharp contrast' to the judgments of the editorial board and of the Austrian Social Democratic Party. In his article, Kautsky reaffirmed his familiar view of the connection between democracy and socialism. He rejected the claim that democracy represented a road to the goal of socialism, but that it did not itself constitute the goal and that a non-democratic road to socialism was therefore conceivable. 'Democracy', he countered, 'is not merely a *road* to the socialist goal but is *a component of the goal itself*'. Equally mistaken, he argued, was another conception that was current in the ranks of Social Democracy, namely that 'true democracy is possible only in a socialist society' whereas 'present democracy is only a fraud, or only formal'. On the contrary, he wrote, democracy, even in a bourgeois framework, was of maximum importance even though it was only partial, since it was only by making use of it that the proletariat could organize itself as a class and attain the strength and maturity necessary to bring democracy to completion by lending it a socialist foundation. Hence, 'democracy is indissolubly linked to socialism at once as the road to the goal and as an element of the goal'.[32]

Replying to this article, Friedrich Adler advanced a series of objections to Kautsky's position which dramatized the divergences within international Social Democracy over the issues of Bolshevism, the USSR, the international Communist movement and especially the urgent question of the united front in the struggle against fascism. In the course of the controversy, Kautsky declared his complete opposition to any united front with Communists guided from Moscow, since it was impossible to forge a united front between 'democracy and dictatorship'. Treating ideological differences as a supreme criterion, Kautsky denied that the common social base of Social Democratic and Communist workers had any political significance whatever. He declared that a united front was possible and desirable only if the Communists in effect adopted Social Democratic positions.

Adler objected that Kautsky's outlook on the USSR and the united front was alien to the Socialist International. Indeed, he argued, Kautsky shared the standpoint of the 'Zarya' Menshevik minority, which the

[32] 'Demokratie und Diktatur', in *Der Kampf*, XXVI, 1933, pp. 45–47.

International had refused to accept into its ranks. What joined Kautsky to the Potressevs and Ingermanns of the 'Zarya' group was not that these people advocated foreign interventions against the Soviet Union (a position which Kautsky did not share), but that they, like Kautsky, did not understand that an uprising against the Bolshevik state (whether internal or external) would create an imminent danger of counter-revolution.[33] The decisive question, Adler maintained, was not whether the Soviet régime was good or otherwise, but whether its existence should be defended or not. Here Adler brought the essence of the conflict into focus. While the majority of the Socialist International accepted the fact of the USSR and sought to favour its transformation in a more democratic direction, Kautsky, convinced of the inevitability and utility of the collapse of Bolshevism, held that it should be abandoned to the condemnation history was about to pronounce on it. The Soviet régime had been born prematurely; on this the Adlers and the Kautskys agreed. But the former sought to aid its survival and development, while the latter judged that it was an abortion to be disposed of as rapidly as possible. Here, Adler wrote, is 'the decisive point, wherein there is but one, inescapable alternative: Despite all that arouses our disgust, despite the abandonment of all illusions, such as the notion that socialism has already been achieved in the Soviet Union or that its achievement is now quite close; in short, *despite all the negative elements*, of which we are well aware and which we have never tried to conceal, do we want to foster the possibilities of survival of the Soviet Union, *to aid it* to the extent we are able, or do we want to abandon it to its fate, i.e. not prepare any blows against it, but also not do anything to prevent such blows from being prepared, because we are convinced of its inevitable collapse?'[34]

Consistent with his positive assessment of the potentially socialist nature of the socio-economic basis of the USSR, Adler condemned Kautsky's call for the return of certain sectors of the Soviet economy to capitalism.[35] Precisely because he believed that the Soviet régime contained genuine germs of socialism, Adler insisted that a 'new civil war' in the USSR could assume no other character than that of an insurrection against socialism, which would involve 'the *danger* of a return of the old

[33] F. Adler, 'Zur Diskussion über Sowjet-Russland. Ein Briefwechsel mit Karl Kautsky'. Adler to Kautsky, letters of 31 December 1932 and 16 January 1933, in *Der Kampf*, XXVI, 1933, pp. 59–60, 64.
[34] Ibid., p. 64.
[35] Ibid., p. 61.

forces, of the constitution of a counter-revolutionary dictatorship' and would certainly not pave the way for a democratic and socialist development.[36] He also rejected Kautsky's 'democratic fetishism' – the claim that there was no other road to socialism than democracy. This fetishism, Adler remarked, was a mere doctrinaire abstraction, parallel to that of the Bolsheviks, who believed that there was no other road to socialism than dictatorship. Finally, Adler indicated that it was possible for Social Democrats and Communists to achieve a united front on the basis of their common interest in socialism, regardless of their conflicts over strategy. Adler's position deserves to be quoted in full, as a forceful expression of the attitude of Austrian Social Democracy to the united front: 'There are two reference points that represent the *minimum basis* for unity between Social Democrats and Bolsheviks, without which agreement is unthinkable. . . . 1) The Bolsheviks must acknowledge that the democratic road to socialism is not excluded, at least in certain countries (Scandinavia, for example). 2) The Socialists must recognize that it is not excluded that Soviet Russia, without returning to private capitalism, may achieve socialism from the starting point of its present situation'.[37]

Kautsky's responses were wholly negative. On the most urgent practical matter of the united front, Kautsky rejected Adler's positions as liable to introduce a cleavage between the theory and practice of Social Democracy. In effect, Adler was asking Western Communists to renounce the very reasons for their existence, in other words, to acknowledge that what had been good for Russia might not be good for developed Europe. He was also ignoring the reality of the incessant struggle between Socialists and Communists, which had certainly not been caused by Kautsky's articles, but reflected an irreconcilable conflict to which Kautsky merely attested. 'I am equally and firmly convinced' Kautsky wrote to Adler on 10 January 1933, on the eve of Hitler's seizure of power in Germany, 'that the formation of a united front is our most important task. If I believed it even remotely possible that my article [*Demokratie und Diktatur*] would prevent this front, I would renounce it immediately [his letter was written before publication of the article]. But in life, as in politics, practice speaks louder than theoretical dissertations. The daily brawls between our people and the Communists are rather greater obstacles to the proletarian united front than is a theoretical article in *Der Kampf*. When our daily press is compelled day after day to stigmatize

[36] Ibid., p. 68.
[37] Ibid., p. 62.

the Communists as deceitful liars lacking any conscience, this has a much greater effect on the masses than my article. There is no future in drawing a line separating Russia from the rest of the world and saying that we want unity with the Russian dictatorship but that we combat the Communists in our own country. Furthermore, I must note once again that my article says nothing new about the International and the Stalinists. That I now say to the Austrians what I have already said to others cannot constitute a fresh obstacle to the united front. I maintain that the proletarian united front is very necessary; but for me this is not tantamount to a united front between democracy and dictatorship. Such a front seems to me neither useful nor possible. The Russian dictators will always reject it. The experiences we have already had in this domain speak for themselves. . . . Only when the dictatorship in Russia is supplanted by democracy will the obstacle that has prevented agreement with the Communists up to now be removed'.[38]

Kautsky reasserted his conviction that a grave crisis could erupt in the USSR in the coming spring because of the enormous economic difficulties there. (This explained one of the decisive aspects of Kautsky's attitude: predicting the possibility of a collapse of the Soviet state, he was not inclined to seek an agreement with an enemy that was about to fall, particularly since he was looking forward, with faith and hope, to a 'democratic' anti-Bolshevik insurrection from within.)[39] Alder had appealed to the resolutions of the Socialist International on the attitude of Social Democracy toward the Soviet Union; the aged theoretician retorted by invoking the right of minorities to dissent. 'You say', he replied to Adler, 'that there is no particular problem about my views on Russia, but that there are clear resolutions of International Congresses. *Roma locuta est, causa finita.* These resolutions express only what the majority thought at the time the resolutions were voted. They do not prohibit discussion of them by the minority'.[40] A few days before these last words were written, Kautsky had declared, again in a letter to Adler, in tones somewhere between arrogance and pathos, that on the question of the Soviet Union and the Communists he was prepared to be the Cassandra of Social Democracy. 'If I remain isolated, then *dixi et salvavi animam meam.* Cassandra remained isolated too. But at least she was not gagged'.[41]

[38] Ibid., p. 2, letter of Kautsky to Adler, 10 January 1933, pp. 65–66.
[39] Ibid., p. 66.
[40] Ibid., 4, letter of Kautsky to Adler, 20 January 1933, p. 69.
[41] Ibid., letter of Kautsky to Adler, 10 January 1933, p. 66.

2 Against the Popular Fronts

Having rejected the united front with the Communists in 1932–1933, Kautsky also rejected the line of the Popular Front, launched by the Seventh Congress of the Communist International in 1935. This was the last battle waged by Kautsky, shortly before his death in 1938. The thrust of his attack was that a 'united front' with the Communists would be possible only if they abandoned the terrain of dictatorship and returned to that of democracy. Otherwise, any unity between Social Democrats and Communists would simply be a contradiction in terms. The orientation of Social Democracy was and could only be opposition to any sort of dictatorship. The struggle against fascism was merely one aspect of such opposition; the second aspect was opposition to the 'red' dictatorship in Russia. Here again Kautsky clashed with his friend Otto Bauer. Agreeing that the problem of a united front between Social Democrats and Communists was critical in combating fascism, he held that the nature of Communism was such as to prevent any solution of it.

In the course of this last sortie against Communism, Kautsky recapitulated his theses on the origin, development, and nature of the Soviet Union, concentrating on his 'twenty-year-long disagreement' with Bauer. The latter, in an article reviewing the recently published book *Staline. Aperçu historique du bolchévisme*, by Boris Souvarine, objected to any assessment of Stalin's role in the Soviet régime that depicted the Russian chief merely as a malevolent 'demiurge'. Responding to Bauer, Kautsky noted that there was no contradiction between an analysis that characterized the apex of power in the USSR as a personal dictatorship and an analysis that emphasized the importance of social conditions. To speak of Stalin's role as an omnipotent dictator did not mean to fall into a sort of idealism. On the contrary, the problem was to correlate the general social and political conditions with the personal dictatorship in Russia. In fact, it had been inevitable that the dictatorship of the Communist Party would be transformed into a one-man dictatorship – not just of any man, but of the man who was the worst of all the top-ranking leaders.

Bolshevism, Kautsky affirmed, was not a historic necessity in Russia. On the contrary, it represented the triumph of one possibility over others. The retrogressive process it represented had been set in motion the moment Lenin had given Bolshevism an organizational configuration which, against Marxism, had reintroduced Blanquism into the workers' movement. Lenin's line had triumphed with the dissolution of the

Constituent Assembly, and was reflected in the dictatorship of the party. If the Communists, Kautsky continued, who now wanted a united front with Social Democracy to combat fascism, had sought a 'united front' at the origin of the Soviet state, then 'Russia would have been spared three decades of civil war and the consequent horrible misery'. 'Without dictatorship, without terror', through the democracy of the workers and peasants, anything would have been possible. Once the road of the dictatorship of an armed minority over the majority had been taken, an inevitable process was set in motion: 'this dictatorship inevitably degenerated from the dictatorship of a party to the dictatorship of an individual over the party and the state'. Which individual? Precisely the man 'who was the weakest intellectually and the most brutal morally, the least guided by conscience, even though he was also the shrewdest and most cunning'. Stalin had been the true subjective interpreter of the objective conditions created during the period prior to his rise to power. Exploiting the degradation of democracy that had already occurred during the Leninist period, Stalin had possessed the brutality and acuity needed to demolish the facade of popular power and lend the substance of despotism its appropriate form. That form was precisely a personal dictatorship. He had thus been able simultaneously to interpret and to sublimate the contradictions of Leninism in a new synthesis.[42]

Bauer had written that whatever the reservations to be made about its political methods, Soviet industrialization had undeniably been a great historical success. Kautsky reproached Bauer for having halted economistically at the objective fact of industrialization, and then arbitrarily imparting a progressive significance to it, as an advance towards socialism. The procedure, Kautsky charged, was gratuitous. There was no reason to hail industrialization in itself, he said. It must be kept in mind that the 'constructive programme implemented under Stalin is not at all unprecedented' and that its antecedants, given the forms in which the programme had been realized, were those of capitalist industrialization. Stalinist, like capitalist, industrialization had been realized through the indiscriminate exploitation of the broad masses. To confer on Soviet industrialization the label of socialism, albeit of a violent and brutal variety, as Bauer did, was to be deluded by an ideological nominalism. From the standpoint of socialism, technical and economic innovations had to be viewed in relation to their human and social consequences. 'Bauer', Kautsky wrote, 'sees only the construction of plants and collectives, but fails to grasp *the rise of a new aristocracy that controls*

[42] 'The United Front', in *The New Leader*, 4 January 1936.

these new means of production and exploits them for its own purposes', an aristocracy of which Stalin was the natural chief. Now, Kautsky sarcastically observed, 'Otto Bauer considers this the rise of a classless society'. Could a greater blunder be imagined? The point of view of Bauer and those who followed him was not Marxist. Lecturing Bauer in Marxism, Kautsky denounced objectivist materialism as a fetishism of technique, which had nothing to do with Marxism. Those who concentrated their regard on technique alone and thought that the installation of machinery amounted to the introduction of socialism were close to ideological bankruptcy. 'Marx knew that the human factors are decisive in society', that technique is significant for socialism only when it develops under specific and appropriate social relations. Soviet industrialization was a process of primitive accumulation of capital at the expense of the masses, primarily the peasants; the political and social relations of that accumulation took the form of a violent despotism. Marx held that socialism must be the product of the workers; Bauer, on the other hand, thought that socialism could be the automatic product of industrialization. Marx maintained that freedom and democracy were simultaneously the preconditions and the necessary form of socialism; Bauer claimed that in the USSR these could be the final products of a despotic state.[43] The leader of Austrian Social Democracy had thus completely lost sight of the 'nature' of the Soviet-Stalinist régime. It was not a Jacobin government preparing socialism and liberty, but the rule of a new class. 'The fruit of Bolshevism as we have outlined it', Kautsky wrote, 'has been the establishment of a new class régime' with a purely instrumental relationship to socialist ideology. All those Bolsheviks who opposed the construction of this class régime have been physically eliminated. 'Not the abolition of all classes, but the replacement of the old classes by new ones – this has been the outcome of the Bolshevik Revolution of 1917, just like the French Revolution of 1789. . . . The militarized, highly concentrated economy of the Soviet state is certainly radically different from the private capitalist economy, but it is no less different from the objective of the emancipation of the toiling classes from any exploitation and servitude'.[44]

What sort of unity was possible in the West, then, between the Socialists on the one hand and the Communists who saw the Soviet régime as their model on the other hand? What common strategy could there be between those who strove for socialism with democracy and

[43] 'The United Front', in *The New Leader*, II, 11 January 1936.
[44] 'The United Front', in *The New Leader*, III, 18 January 1936.

those who strove to reproduce in the West the sort of régime characteristic of Stalinism? Up to now, Kautsky asserted, the results of the frenzied struggle the Western Communists had waged against the Socialists had been favourable only to the rise of reactionary dictatorships which imitated the political methods of the Stalinist régime. 'These are the "successes" the working class of the entire world owes the Communist dictatorship in Russia'.[45] Kautsky's attitude to the united front was in consequence exceedingly rigid. He held that Communists and Socialists could find no common ground of agreement and particularly that the masses of the two wings of the workers' movement could not conduct common struggles, laying their differences aside as 'secondary' compared to the 'principal' conflict between the workers' movement and fascism. The fact is that Kautsky did not at all consider the conflicts between Communists and Socialists 'secondary' and that he clearly lent greater importance to organizations than to relations among the masses. In his old age, the 'principal' contradiction for him was between democracy and dictatorship. Hence he denied any validity to a united front between Communist supporters of dictatorship and democratic Socialists. The practical implications of the divergence between Bauer and Kautsky were evident. For the former, the 'barbaric' socialism of Stalin awaited a future redemption and the Communists were therefore potential allies. For Kautsky, Stalin's régime was a despotism of a new variety; indeed, it was the statal variant of modern despotism, of which fascism was the capitalist variant. The idea of an agreement between Socialists and Communists was a contrivance proposed by the latter on the orders of their master in Moscow, vitiated by the fact that the Communists conceived of unity not as an autonomous value but as a tactical exigency. The Communists, Kautsky wrote, 'do not intend to respect the will of the movement as a whole, but reserve for themselves the right to turn away to separate action at any moment, whenever they want'. 'The Communists of all countries are the disciplined praetorian guard' of Moscow; 'for the present rulers of Russia, Communism has become what pan-Slavism was for the Tsars'. In conclusion, what the Communist International was proposing was not the autonomous 'cooperation' of workers seeking a strategy of their own, but the instrumental 'cooperation' of the Socialist International with 'the world's strongest dictatorship'. Having said all this, Kautsky did not absolutely reject any unity with the Communists whatever. But he imposed rigid conditions. The sort of collaboration that should be

[45] 'The United Front', in *The New Leader*, I, op. cit.

established between Socialists and Communists, he said, could only be a limited one for specific goals, such as, for example, support to Stalin against Hitler 'in the event of war'. What was completely excluded was any strategic alliance between Socialists and Communists.[46]

Two years later, in late 1937, Kautsky took up the same arguments again, this time with reference to the development of the Popular Fronts and the foreign policy of the Soviet Union, which was then increasingly seeking military agreements with France and Britain against the threat of Nazi militarism. His hostility to the Communists and the USSR had not diminished in the slightest. Indeed, it culminated in a prophecy: he warned the European workers' movement that the shift of the Communists and their 'rehabilitation' of democracy was merely a manoeuvre dictated not by any modification of their principles but once again by obedience to the wishes of their master in the Kremlin, who now required international accords. So much so, Kautsky declared, that it was not to be excluded that if agreements with France and Britain were not forthcoming, there could be a new volte-face ending in the aberration of a direct Nazi-Soviet understanding and Communist denunciation of the war-mongering imperialism of the bourgeois-democratic countries of the West as the main enemy.

The USSR and the Communists, Kautsky wrote in one of the last essays of his life, with their contempt for democracy (need it be recalled that by this Kautsky meant parliamentarism and political and civil rights), had decisively contributed to weakening the workers' movement in many countries, which then fell prey to fascism. Ultimately, this created menacing conditions even for the security of the Soviet state itself, which 'is now compelled to appeal for aid from democracy outside Russia'. The USSR, acting through the Third International, had thus given the Communist Parties the word: halt the frenzied attacks on democracy and Social Democracy and advance proposals for the constitution of a 'united front'. Despite everything, this could be grounds for satisfaction. 'But our satisfaction is somewhat diminished by the fact that this change in the Communists is not a modification of principles but merely a tactical manoeuvre. They defend democracy only where they are in opposition. They annihilate it and enforce the most merciless suppression of popular liberty wherever they are in power'. Was the USSR seeking allies in the West because there were democratic powers there? On the contrary, the Soviet Union was taking a new attitude towards democracy because the allies it needed 'can be found only in

[46] 'The United Front', in *The New Leader*, III, op. cit.

the democratic states of the West'. Thus precisely because the 'democratic' turn of the Comintern was rooted not in any shift in principles but solely in the exigencies of the foreign policy of the USSR, it was necessary to prepare for further surprises: 'In the event that the Soviet rulers come to an agreement with Germany and Japan, the Communists everywhere will become supporters of fascism'. Kautsky said that he did not consider an agreement between Hitler and Stalin 'probable', since too many differences between their two countries militated against this. But he did insist that the possibility should not be discounted, since the supreme criterion of Soviet policy was the pursuit of power uncurbed by any obstacle of principle or ideology. The same could be said of Nazism. 'We must reckon with such changes in Russia as much as in Germany'. Despite all this, Kautsky concluded with an expression of hope that a strategic change might occur in the attitude of the Communist movement to the importance of democracy for the socialist struggle; then the proletarian united front could become a reality: 'We have no need of a new programme, nor of a new theory of socialism. What we need is a rise in the strength of democracy, a powerful rise that depends only on the Communists, one they could realize overnight if their leaders were willing. Struggle for democracy in Soviet Russia! This is the slogan for a stable and irresistable united front of the proletariat'.[47]

---

[47] 'Communist Swing Far to Right in New Tactical Manoeuvre', in *The New Leader*, 27 November 1937.

X

Proletarian 'Dictatorship' or Proletarian 'Rule'?

1 The Question of 'Coalition Government'

The struggle first against Bolshevism and Leninism and later against Stalinism constituted the principal focus of Kautsky's theoretical activity after the October Revolution. As we have seen, he viewed Bolshevism as the failure of a practical and theoretical rebellion against a premise of Marxism central since the time of the First International, when it had superseded all pre-Marxist conceptions: that 'the liberation of the proletariat' was first possible only in 'the most developed countries'.[1]

Kautsky's commentaries on the road travelled by the workers' movement in the Western countries between the end of the First World War and the advent of the Nazi régime in Germany were initially marked by the conviction that the proletariat was capable of profoundly influencing the capitalist system and of laying the basis for the transformation of the social system in a socialist direction. Later, when the reactionary, national fascist danger began to take threatening shape on the horizon, Kautsky maintained that, at least in a country like Germany, the strength of the toiling masses would be sufficient to guarantee the preservation of political democracy.

It is significant that Kautsky saw Nazism as a lethal force, but one ultimately incapable of conquering power. In this respect he evinced a personal incomprehension that was characteristic not only of the SPD but also of the KPD in Germany. The roots of this failure were not to be found in the inability of the Social Democrats and Communists to perceive the function of fascist violence for the big bourgeoisie (this they correctly understood), but rather in their incapacity to see that fascism might penetrate the body of society as a whole. In other words, they

[1] 'Vergangenheit und Zukunft der Internationale', op. cit. p. 26.

grasped the nature of reaction as a static phenomenon, but not its dynamic possibilities of development. For his part, Kautsky analyzed the social bases of reaction with great acumen, but was convinced that political democracy had been too firmly consolidated in Germany, that the proletariat was too strong and well organized, to allow Nazism to come to power. Indeed, he held that developed industrial society in general was incompatible with a stable reactionary régime. Thus, when Italy fell under fascist rule, he claimed that fascism had been able to take root in that country because Italy was still socially and economically backward. Again, when fascism emerged in its Nazi form in Germany, he considered it a grave yet transitory lapse. In either case, even with regard to Nazism – this was, in a certain sense, his political testament – he held that Socialists must not fall into the irrational temptation of allowing the degeneration of the bourgeois political system into Nazism to lead them to the conviction that democracy as a system had failed and therefore had to be supplanted by a class dictatorship. Such failure as there was, he said, was due to the insufficient strength of the movement for democracy; hence, the task of the Socialists was precisely to reconquer and reinforce democracy. Confronted with the reality of the Nazi state, Kautsky finally relinquished what had been one of his central and constant assumptions throughout the inter-war period: his overestimation of the virtues of the Weimar constitution of 1919, which he had once proclaimed a valid framework for the transition to socialism. Thereafter he noted the weaknesses and ambiguities of this constitution from the standpoint of bourgeois democracy itself. But what he did not do (a failure consubstantial with his past incomprehension of the rising strength of Nazism) was to analyze the real malady of the Weimar Republic: the chasm between a bourgeois-democratic political facade and an authoritarian socio-economic system, unaffected by the institutions of parliamentary democracy.

In his writings on 'ultra-imperialism' Kautsky had grasped, more lucidly than any other Marxist of his time, the possibility of the survival and development of capitalism as a productive system. But he had imagined that this survival would be accompanied by the political democracy characteristic of an industrial economy and by advances of the proletariat as a class. He further believed that these two elements would suffice to establish the candidacy of socialism to the succession of capitalism without social upheavals, on the basis of an enormous development of the productive forces, which simply needed to be managed in a more efficient, rational, and human manner for the good of all society and with the aim of the abolition of class divisions. However, on the basis of his assumption that the choice between 'ultra-imperialism' and 'imperialism' lay in the hands of the capitalist bloc and depended on the relationship of forces within the ruling classes, Kautsky had not excluded the opposite possibility, namely a revival of a reactionary and militarist imperialism inspired by financial speculators, senior bureaucrats and military officers. Such a course, he argued, would result in the inevitable ruin of bourgeois society. It is important to note that Kautsky was convinced that both in the event of ultra-imperialism and in the event of a revival of imperialism, the rise of the proletariat could not be halted, precisely because of the role it had now definitively acquired in the industrial system of production itself.

In the period between the end of the First World War and the great crisis that erupted in 1929, marked by the forceful emergence of US capitalism onto the world economic scene, accompanied by an economic upswing and 'democratization' in West-Central Europe (with the exception of the Italian 'incident', the historical significance of which he vastly underestimated), Kautsky thought that a phase of capitalist internationalization of the 'ultra-imperialist' variety was taking shape. His faith in the effects of the combination of democracy, socialism, and economic development thus remained substantially intact (although he did detect threatening signs). After the crash of 1929, on the other hand, when drives towards economic isolationism and political authoritarianism gained the upper hand, the latter sweeping Europe and above all Germany, he was confronted with a prospect that had been wholly alien to his outlook (indeed, not only his, but also that of Social Democracy in general, as well as of the Comintern): a very deep crisis in the political efficacy and combativity of the workers' movement. Along with all other Marxists, whether of the right or the left, he was obliged to register empirically, without available categories to interpret the phenomenon, that the contemporary historical epoch in the developed countries (even those which remained 'democratic') was an age not of social revolution but on the contrary of capitalist counter-offensive and counter-revolution. Kautsky reacted to this disconcerting situation by calling for a struggle to defend or where necessary reconquer the conditions of existence of the workers' movement as a political force – above all democracy, relegating socialism once again, as in the epoch prior to the First World War, to a distant historical future rather than any proximate perspective.

In the years immediately after the Armistice, Kautsky had postulated the following international processes: 1) a supersession of imperialist conflicts and an interpenetration between democracy and economy at home and abroad (hence his enthusiasm for the League of Nations); 2) a growing influence of the United States and introduction into Europe of advanced American technology, favouring the struggle for socialization in the Old World, where technological progress was hampered by the inadequacy of capitalist relations of production; 3) a trend towards reunification of reformists and revolutionaries in the ranks of Social Democracy, with the 'return' of the English labour movement, the great 'separate brother' of the Second International, to the fold of continental socialism; 4) an acceptance by Socialists of governmental responsibilities, even when they did not command a majority in parliament.

In *Die Wurzeln der Politik Wilsons*, written in 1919, Kautsky had stressed his conviction that imperialism did not constitute an iron necessity for capitalism, and entrusted his hopes for peace and for democratic renovation in Europe to the creation of a League of Nations resting on two pillars: 'the strength of that part of the proletariat whose sentiments are internationalist and . . . the strength of America and its president, Wilson, the supporter of the idea of a League of Nations in the bourgeois world'.[2] A democratic peace, Kautsky wrote further in the same essay, 'is possible on the basis Wilson proposes. It will accompany the victory of American arms, certainly due in no small measure to US industrial methods, and the victory of the political principles and methods so far supremely represented by the United States. Coming decades should therefore introduce an epoch of ever greater socialization and simultaneously increasing Americanization of the world'.[3]

Kautsky's hopes were thus founded on a *pax americana*, which would usher into Europe both ultra-modern productive methods and a more advanced political democracy, together with the guarantee of a League of Nations. The old imperialist wolves of Europe would finally have to yield to a capitalism of a different type, accepting an advanced democratic framework which in European historical and political conditions would favour the action of the socialist proletariat. 'Woodrow Wilson was elected in his capacity as an enemy of imperialism and finance capital. . . . Even Wilson was compelled to allow finance capital to survive. But to allow a class to survive does not mean to submit to it'.[4] Thus, a series of factors would combine to create a more advanced and

[2] *Die Wurzeln der Politik Wilsons*, Berlin, 1919, p. 4.
[3] Ibid., p. 40.
[4] Ibid., p. 26.

modern basis for social and class relations in Europe: international peace, League of Nations, political democracy, revival of production, international reorganization of the working class, assumption of governmental responsibilities by Socialists to sustain this framework, abandonment of imperialist policies abroad and of reactionary policies at home. In 1921 Kautsky again reaffirmed his 'philosophy of progress': 'The idea of democracy, the self-determination of nations, is inseparably linked to modern economic development and becomes irresistable by virtue of it'.[5]

At the same time, Kautsky held that conditions existed for the re-unification of international socialism. Observing the ferment developing in the English working class and prophesying a rapid decline in the influence of Bolshevism, he expressed the hope in 1921 that international socialism would be renovated in keeping with the premises of Marxism: international unity, socialism as the ideology of the working class in the developed countries, supersession of the conflict between reformism and revolution. The English workers, he wrote, were again becoming 'the front-line fighters of the modern working class', such that 'in this new situation of international socialism, the old contradiction, customarily termed a conflict between reformism and revolutionism, has been overcome. The English manner of thought is becoming ever more concordant with that of the socialists of the rest of Western Europe. . . . But the Marxists of Eastern Europe will also, once the bankruptcy of the Bolshevik experience as a method of introducing socialism becomes fully clear, unanimously return as before to Marxist principles, according to which "the most industrially developed country shows the less developed ones the image of their own future" (Preface [by Marx] to the first edition of *Capital*)'.[6]

On many occasions during the last two decades of his life Kautsky insisted that his antagonistic dispute with revisionism had been overcome in the course of time. In 1925, in an article celebrating Bernstein's seventy-fifth birthday, Kautsky drew a balance-sheet of the history of his past controversy with Bernstein and of what remained of it. On this occasion he laid the old conflicts to rest. To begin with, he acknowledged the fecundity of the controversy and of Bernstein's main themes. Because of the debate, he noted, 'I was led to pay attention to the weak points of our doctrine which I had hitherto neglected. Now I had to study them more closely and profoundly and perceive them more clearly'.[7] Further-

[5] *Rasse und Judentum*, Stuttgart, 1921, p. 92.
[6] 'Rosa Luxemburg, Karl Liebknecht, Leo Jogisches', op. cit., p. 20.
[7] 'Eduard Bernstein zu seinem fünfundsiebzigsten Geburtstag', in *Die Gesellschaft*, II, 1925, vol. I, p. 14.

more, he admitted that Bernstein's activity after the great polemic at the end of the 19th century had clarified the true meaning of his phrase 'the goal of socialism, whatever it may be, is nothing to me; the movement is everything'. Kautsky now wrote: 'This phrase, with which he launched the critical movement we defined as "revisionism", did immense damage to Bernstein in our ranks and raised doubts whether he was still really a socialist. But Bernstein's entire subsequent behaviour has proved that this unhappy phrase meant no more than Marx's famous statement that one step forward by the real movement was worth more than a dozen programmes, or his other dictum, that the working class does not seek to realize an ideal, but only to emancipate the elements of the new society'.[8] Those differences that still remained, Kautsky concluded, were not such as to involve practical divergences.[9]

Kautsky repeated this assessment in 1932, in an obituary of Bernstein published in *Vorwärts*. With scant fidelity to history but close correspondence to his present outlook, he strove to minimize the significance of the great theoretical-political controversy that had divided him and Bernstein at the end of the 19th and the beginning of the 20th century. This polemic, he now claimed, even though it lasted 'not a few years', was nevertheless 'only an episode'. He and Bernstein had come together 'during the World War', and thereafter, on the issues of the War, of revolution, and of the evolution of Germany and of the world, there was no longer anything 'to divide us'. On all questions, he said, 'we have always adopted the same point of view'.[10]

Thus when he pronounced his final, formal word on the old controversy between revisionist and revolutionary perspectives, Kautsky had already buried the main reasons for the conflict. In his earlier criticism of Bernstein, Kautsky had championed the organizational autonomy of the proletariat, and insisted on the need to eschew any 'ministerialism', to reject any prospect – even tactical – of coalition government with progressive bourgeois forces: state power could be won only through the exclusive rule of socialist forces, prior to which state institutions could not be 'democratized'. At that time, democracy for him meant first the independent struggle of the proletariat for the conquest of the state and later the acts of a socialist government itself. Kautsky continued to maintain these positions during the immediate post-war period. But then his disappointment with the electoral results

[8] Ibid., p. 17.
[9] Ibid., pp. 20–21.
[10] 'Abschied. Karl Kautsky über Eduard Bernstein', in *Vorwärts*, 22 December 1932.

of 1919 and 1920, and his new-found conviction that the Social Democratic parties should support the beleaguered democratic republic of Weimar even though they had not succeeded in winning a majority in parliament, led him to declare that it was now necessary for socialists to participate in coalition governments. Confronted with the practical implementation of this line by the SPD (to which he had again drawn close, despite his nominal adherence to the USPD), Kautsky not only accepted it but developed a theoretical justification for it that brought him substantially closer to the old 'ministerial' positions of Bernstein and the revisionists (even though he continued to reject 'mini-ministerialism', i.e. participation in coalitions in a subordinate position). He now argued that since the democratic republic had been won, only the entry of the socialists into government could assure its defence and safeguard the living conditions of the toiling masses – thereby improving the conditions for the conquest of political power by the proletariat, which he expected imminently. In accordance with his typical inclination, Kautsky strove to weave a cloak of 'rationality' for what had already become the practice of Social Democracy, which after 1919–1923 was thoroughly embarked on a policy of participation in governments alongside non-socialist parties.

In *Die proletarische Revolution*, his commentary on the new programme adopted by the SPD at its Görlitz Congress in 1921, Kautsky analyzed the conditions for the formation of a coalition government with socialist participation, maintaining that this might become the best means to achieve the goal of a purely socialist government. In so doing Kautsky openly revised not only what had once been his own position but also – and explicitly – some aspects of the thought of Marx that he had earlier diligently interpreted in a fully 'orthodox' manner. 'Rejection in principle of any coalition in all circumstances', he wrote, 'corresponds to a conception of the class struggle which regards all the bourgeois parties, without exception, as a single reactionary mass, a view which no one combated more strongly than Marx, since it fostered class obtusity more than class consciousness'.[11] Following Otto Bauer, Kautsky distinguished two 'types of coalition government'. The first was the 'reformist' type, which was to be rejected, for in it bourgeois power clearly predominated and utilized socialist participation as a political cover. In such a case, the socialists in the Cabinet became 'responsible for a purely capitalist governmental policy'. The second type corresponded to a situation in which 'the proletariat has become so strong

[11] PR, p. 102.

that there is an equilibrium between classes'.[12] The latter form of government, Kautsky argued, answered to the need to fortify the foundations of the democratic republic, although it could not accomplish directly socialist tasks, for that required a purely socialist government. 'The enemies of a coalition policy in our ranks', he wrote, 'generally counterpose the advantages of a purely socialist government to it. But such a comparison is senseless, since no socialist would prefer a coalition if a purely socialist government were possible. Only the latter can open the door to socialism; it alone is able energetically and systematically to proceed to the socialization of capitalist production. There is no question about this. What we confront, however, is a stage in which the proletariat does not yet command sufficient strength to form and sustain a purely socialist government, but does command the strength to rule out a government that adopts an overtly hostile attitude toward the proletariat. In this stage the question can only be: coalition government or bourgeois government by grace of the proletariat'.[13]

At this point, after deducing his defence of coalition government from Marx's hostility towards the theory of the 'single reactionary mass' (a theory which Kautsky himself had upheld in the past, it will be recalled), he openly proceeded to a revision of Marx's central thesis that a dictatorship of the proletariat was the specific political form of the transition from capitalism to socialism. Against the Bolsheviks and their interpretation of the nature of their dictatorship, Kautsky had initially contrasted dictatorship as a 'state of affairs' to dictatorship as a form of government, in other words a state power founded on democracy to one founded on violence. He now introduced a new variant: coalition government as characteristic of the phase between the end of the purely bourgois system and the advent of socialist state power. The political form of the period of transition was no longer a dictatorship of the proletariat, however understood, but coalition government. 'In the stage in which the capitalist countries now find themselves', Kautsky explained, 'the idea of coalition government will increasingly take root despite all the resistance to it and will increasingly dominate working-class policy, not as an element replacing the proletarian revolution, as has so often been maintained in the past, with results clearly unfavourable to the propagation of the idea of coalition, but rather as the inauguration and preparation of this revolution; in other words, of the exclusive rule of the working class exercised by a purely socialist government, sustained by the

[12] Ibid.
[13] Ibid., p. 104.

superiority of the proletariat. In his famous article *Zur Kritik des sozialdemokratischen Parteiprogramms*, Marx said: "Between capitalist society and communist society there is a period of revolutionary transition from the one to the other. This is accompanied by a period of political transition under which the state can be nothing other than the revolutionary dictatorship of the proletariat". On the basis of the experience of recent years, we can now alter this formulation as far as the government is concerned, and rephrase it as follows: "Between the epoch of the purely bourgeois state and the epoch of the democratic state erected on a purely proletarian basis there is a period of transition from the one to the other. This is accompanied by a period of political transition, which will as a rule take the form of a coalition government". This will occur wherever the conquest of power proceeds on a democratic basis; it represents the normal road to this goal after the collapse of the great military monarchies. Whoever continues to reject the policy of coalition as a matter of principle is blind to the signs of the times. Such people are incapable of accomplishing their tasks'.[14]

Furthermore, Kautsky justified this new theory of transition in such a way as to cast the positions of his past 'radical' period, or at least the period prior to his acceptance of coalition governments, in a rather unfavourable light. Previously, he had tenaciously rejected the idea of a coalition government (save for a few exceptional, transitory cases) on the grounds that a government always represents an indivisible political unity and that participation in the cabinet of another class would necessarily signify the subordination of one side to the other. Now he posed the entire question on a different plane, appealing to the greater maturity the workers' movement had attained: when the proletariat was in a position of weakness, it was necessary for propaganda purposes to uphold the idea of a purely socialist government. Having attained maturity, however, the proletariat could no longer subsist on propaganda, but must abandon self-satisfying myths and realistically assume its own responsibilities within the given constellation of forces. It must therefore be prepared to enter a coalition government. 'The World War', Kautsky wrote in *Die marxsche Staatsauffassung* in 1923, 'along with its consequences, has put the socialist movement of the more developed countries in a new situation. It is now at the stage in which the necessity for propaganda gives way to the need to take part in the life of the state, not simply from the critical standpoint of an opposition

[14] PR, pp. 105–106.

but primarily from the positive vantage point of government – if not yet as the sole government party – either by participating in a coalition or by preparing itself to assume governmental power in the foreseeable future. Thanks to the incessant rise in the strength of the proletariat, this stage must sooner or later become a reality in every country with a capitalist industry'.[15]

The change represented by this shift in Kautsky's position was sweeping. But it nonetheless was still traceable to the Kautskyist conception of the state. In the past he had defined the winning of a majority in parliament as the prerequisite for the assumption of governmental responsibilities by socialists, branding as 'ministerialism' any attempt to 'anticipate' in government what had not yet matured in society and in class relations. Now, maintaining that the conquest of the democratic republic and the bourgeoisie's inability to govern without socialist participation had created a new terrain for the action of the proletariat, he had arrived at a theory of the 'phase of transition' which viewed 'coalition government' as a necessary step towards 'purely proletarian government'. A profound hiatus was thus introduced between the past and the present, one which Kautsky justified in the terms we have summarized above. But it is not difficult to see the ground on which this hiatus had arisen. Kautsky had always regarded the parliament and administrative machine characteristic of the bourgeoisie as institutions that could and should be adapted to the needs of the proletariat, without being 'smashed'. Had he agreed with Pannekoek in the famous polemic of 1912 that a workers' state must emerge from the struggle of the proletariat against the bourgeois state apparatus and model itself on qualitatively different norms (a position shared, although with various differences, by Lenin and Luxemburg), Kautsky would never have been able to substitute a theory of 'coalition government' for the 'dictatorship of the proletariat'. But since he held a parliamentary conception of the state, he was inexorably led to consider coalition government a necessity once a situation was created in which the socialist parties were strong enough to prevent the exclusive rule of the bourgeoisie at the parliamentary level, but were not strong enough to render possible the exclusive rule of the proletariat. Discussing the Weimar Constitution, the Görlitz programme had declared: 'the Social Democratic Party . . . considers the democratic republic to be the unalterable state form bequeathed by historical development; any attack on it is a threat to the vital rights of

[15] *Die marxsche Staatsauffassung*, Jena, 1923, p. 5.

the people'.[16] Kautsky himself commented in 1922: 'despite its imper-
fections, the Constitution of the Reich, issued of the revolution, affords
the socialist proletariat sufficient possibility to conquer political power
through the peaceful road'.[17]

Almost ten years later, just as the final crisis of the Weimar Republic
was rapidly unfolding, Kautsky pursued the same arguments, going so
far as to claim that 'political revolution' had now become useless. 'The
political tasks of the proletarian parties', he wrote, 'have been fundamentally altered by the revolution [of November 1918] and its consequences.
The state in which we are living is no longer a military monarchy but a
democratic republic, which finds its certain salvation from the menace
of reaction only in the proletariat. To preserve the republic – in other
words, the existing state – and not to overthrow it, is currently our
function. To this extent Social Democracy ceases to be revolutionary and
becomes conservative. Not in the sense that it abandons any of the goals
for which it strives, but in the sense that it has realized an essential part
of them. It is not Social Democracy that has changed, but the state.
Once the political revolution has occurred, the idea of a political revolution loses all meaning. But although we defend the democratic republic,
it is nevertheless far from having assumed the forms for which we strive,
not to mention our goal of a socialist organization of production. It
constitutes only the starting point. The proletariat has the greatest
interest in the further development of the republic, a task it cannot con-
sign to the bougeois parties alone. But at the same time, the proletariat
has registered such an expansion, has acquired such force, that it has
achieved at least parity with the bourgeois parties, although not yet
preponderance over them. A socialist party cannot yet govern alone,
but it no longer has to remain in irreducible opposition to any government, to any party. This is the case wherever its task of winning the
proletariat from the bourgeois parties and uniting it in a class party has
been essentially accomplished. Wherever the socialists have not yet
achieved this goal, they continue, it is true, to remain in irreducible
antagonism to the radicals. For all these reasons, after the revolutions
that followed the World War, the socialists everywhere find themselves
compelled to renounce their principled aversion to occasional coalitions
with other parties, an aversion which has guided them up to now and

[16] 'Programm der SPD (Mehrheits-Sozialdemokratie). Beschlossen zu Görlitz 1921',
in Abendroth, *Aufstieg und Krise der deutschen Sozialdemokratie*, Frankfurt/M, 1969,
p. 103.
[17] PR, p. 84.

was correct in the light of the political tasks of the proletariat under past conditions. The fourth and final stage of the struggle for socialism will begin from the moment that we win a majority large enough to constitute a strong government alone and to stamp its legislation with our imprint'.[18]

In theorizing the new function of coalition governments, Kautsky insisted on the general necessity of replacing the term 'dictatorship of the proletariat' with 'rule' of the proletariat, precisely because the term dictatorship had now acquired a connotation too closely linked to the Bolshevik experience. In 1921 he wrote in this regard that the Social Democrats now had every reason 'to renounce use of the expression "dictatorship of the proletariat", which was always a source of mis-understandings and, up to 1917, played a role only in polemical and not in agitational literature. The language of the *Communist Manifesto* can and must be wholly satisfactory for us, and this document speaks not of the *dictatorship* but rather of the *rule* of the proletariat on the basis of the democracy for which the revolution fights'.[19]

2 The World War and the Roots of Counter-Revolution

Virtually down the fatal crisis of 1933, as we have seen, Kautsky con-tinued to believe that the Weimar Constitution could pave the way for the conquest of political power by the proletariat, because it rested on those democratic principles to which Social Democracy clung as a conservative force. It was necessary to preserve democracy against the forces that sought to overthrow the parliamentary and multi-party system, namely reactionary nationalists and Communists. Surveying the dangers threatening the republic from the right, Kautsky analyzed with acuity some of the elements that favoured reactionary subversion; but never, until Nazism finally triumphed, did he ever believe that fascism represented anything more than a malignant presence within an institutional framework strong enough to resist it. From this angle, like the German Social Democrats in general, he evinced a deep lack of understanding of the expansionist dynamic of reaction – a failure shared by the Communists. To the extent that he entertained the hypothesis of a national-militarist-bureaucratic assumption of power, he seemed quite convinced that the proletariat as a class was now too strong to

[18] BS, pp. 130–131.
[19] VDSS, p. 84.

allow a reactionary government to be anything but a brief and transitory episode: it would represent a lost battle for the workers' movement, but not a lost war.

In January 1924 Kautsky wrote a noteworthy essay dealing with this problematic. The article reflected the deterioration of the political and economic situation in Germany after a series of events: the fall of the Wirth government in November 1922; the formation of the Cuno government, on a strongly conservative basis; the crisis triggered by the French occupation of the Ruhr; the exceptional wave of speculation concomitant with galloping inflation; the crisis of the trade-union organizations; the crisis in the SPD itself; the counter-revolutionary manoeuvres in Bavaria; the dissolution of the left coalition governments in Thuringia and Saxony; the failure of the insurrectionary attempt in Hamburg in October 1923; the attempted National Socialist *putsch* in Munich in November; the fall of the Stresemann government and the formation of the new government of more intensely conservative colouration headed by the Catholic Wilhelm Marx. Under the direct influence of this process, Kautsky published *Die Aussichten der Gegenrevolution in Deutschland*, in *Der Kampf*. This article began, significantly, with the words: 'We find ourselves in the midst of counter-revolution'.[20]

In his analysis, Kautsky traced the responsibility for the deterioration of the situation to the division of the proletariat. He began from the assumption that the German revolution of 1918 could in no way be considered a bourgeois revolution and that it had been, on the contrary, a proletarian revolution. In his view the internal contradictions and the consequent weaknesses of the revolution had resulted from its lack of organizational unity and political leadership, the essential responsibility for which devolved on Bolshevism, which had exerted strong influence on broad masses and yet possessed no adequate strategy for the developed industrial countries. 'The war had divided Social Democracy', he wrote. 'Only as a united body could the latter have asserted itself in the revolution. But the Russian Bolsheviks, not content to persecute Social Democrats and Social Revolutionaries in their own country, had sworn the most implacable enmity against the Social Democrats of all countries. The grandiose phenomenon of the Russian Revolution had created the conditions for them to exert profound influence on the workers of all countries. They used this influence to drive the socialist workers away from Social Democracy everywhere. What thus occurred was this: the German revolution, instead of putting an end to the split of Social

[20] 'Die Aussichten der Gegenrevolution in Deutschland', in *Der Kampf*, XVII, 1924, p. 1.

Democracy, deepened it even further, at a time when only close-knit unity could have enabled the proletariat to preserve the rule that had fallen into its hands as a consequence of the military collapse of the old order'.[21] Hence, the workers' movement suffered from a destructive internal malady. It was the only force into whose hands power could have fallen at the end of 1918, but at the same time, because of its divisions, it proved to be too weak to assume power in stable fashion. 'Because of its unfortunate division, the proletariat was wholly unable to obtain from its revolution what it could have won on the basis of united strength. Its revolution led only to this result: the capitalist class was temporarily cowed and lastingly embittered, but its instruments of power were not reduced'.[22]

Kautsky linked this analysis of the weakness of the political movement of the German workers to an account of the internal transformations of the capitalist class. Before the war, he said, the bourgeoisie had organized exploitation on the basis of intensive industrial labour; but the war had profoundly changed it. Kautsky's description of this mutation was very similar to Lenin's, except that he limited it to Germany and argued that it was not necessarily organic and definitive. German capital, he said, had assumed an increasingly speculative character; the weakening of the state was its supreme goal. One of its tactics was to fish in the troubled waters of a swollen sub-proletariat, recruiting thugs for its purposes. In the meantime, the crisis of industrial production and the consequent general weakening of the proletariat favoured the 'adventurers' of capital. 'The old class of capitalists no longer exists. War, inflation, and constant insecurity have steadily reduced the possessing classes' interest in industry compared with speculation. The dominant elements within the capitalist class are no longer the industrialists, but the speculators, for the most part uneducated *parvenus* lacking any sense of responsibility, any comprehension of the workers, and any respect for labour. The state, as it was constituted after the revolution, is no longer *their* state, and their fundamental objective is to weaken it'.

Speculators and landowners, Kautsky argued, had no intention of footing the fiscal bill for any financial reconstruction. Indeed, they considered it their 'political duty' to hasten the 'bankruptcy of the state'. Thus, the only forces still prospering in Germany were the speculators and the sub-proletarians, swelled by the economic crisis and recruited from all classes. This sub-proletariat was acting in the pay of the

[21] Ibid., p. 3.
[22] Ibid., pp. 3–4.

'ambitious chiefs of speculation'. Under these conditions, 'the greater the disorder and general insecurity, the better things are for the business' of the speculators.[23] The proletariat confronting this alignment of forces was weak. In full accordance with his strategic conceptions over the past years, Kautsky did not see the social and economic crisis in Germany as a springboard for the intensification and radicalization of the class struggle, and thereby the political strengthening of the working class. On the contrary, he maintained that these conditions depressed the proletariat economically and thereby weakened it politically. The crisis of 1923 had stricken the trade unions and the SPD, drastically reducing the number of their members. Even the eight-hour day had been challenged and the workers were incapable of offering effective resistance. Kautsky believed that the proletariat had reached the low point of a process that had been initiated with the World War. 'Against these forces of the counter-revolution, which are becoming ever stronger', he wrote, 'stands a proletariat that for nearly a decade, ever since the out-break of the War, had been waging a constant struggle against hunger, poverty, and the threat of death, and, in recent years, has been increasingly afflicted by the scourge of unemployment. Exhausted and weakened, it has nevertheless succeeded in barring the path of the counter-revolution so far. The latter is among us, but does not yet dominate uncontested. How much longer will its pressure last?'[24]

The sort of answer Kautsky advanced to this question reveals the limits of his analysis. He clearly believed that at that time the counter-revolution had no lasting and organic prospects in Germany. The inter-national situation was unfavourable, since the victorious powers would not tolerate a nationalist dictatorship in Germany. The internal organiza-tion of the counter-revolutionary forces was also deficient, for they did not possess sufficient centralization or leadership and lacked an acknowledged chief.[25] All these elements of the situation in 1924 were real, and correctly indicated. But Kautsky also maintained that a dynamic expansion of reaction as a system, by a fusion of the anti-proletarian struggle and the exigencies of the rule of big monopoly capital, was impossible. He considered Italian fascism, for example, a reactionary episode possible in an organic and lasting form only in a backward agrarian country. He believed that in the long run modern capitalism was incompatible with reaction in any developed industrial country. Thus in his analysis reaction

[23] Ibid., pp. 5–6.
[24] Ibid., p. 5.
[25] Ibid., p. 6.

appeared as a degenerate tendency reflecting a contingent situation of crisis. In sum, he could not credit that reaction would become a comprehensive strategy of the ruling classes in a country like Germany, where he thought that the proletariat, although weakened, nonetheless constituted an adequate guarantee of the defence of democratic parliamentary institutions.

Assessing the experience of the German proletariat since the revolution of November 1918, Kautsky generally inclined to an optimistic perspective. He held that the pressure of common class interests would foster the recomposition of the political unity of the proletariat, either in the form of organizational reunification or in the form of a loss of influence by scissionist minorities. In short, he had faith in a perspective which the subsequent course of German history was to belie completely. He thought that it was probable that a solid proletarian united front would be constituted (the very front that he would later reject as unrealizable because of the persistence of a separate organization of the Communist proletariat). 'Thus', he wrote, 'we must expect that the proletariat will emerge from the defeat of the counter-revolution stronger and more mature than it entered the past revolution'.[26] Kautsky's optimism, which rendered him incapable of conceiving the potential force of a fusion between political reaction and big monopoly capital, culminated in the conviction that an eventual triumph of the counter-revolution would itself expose the profound incapacity of that counter-revolution to survive much beyond the time of its initial, contingent success. 'Thus, we must expect that the counter-revolution . . . even if it succeeds in asserting itself . . . would give rise to a régime of frightful misery, complete decay, and the deepest national humiliation; it would inevitably fail rapidly. We must expect that if it came to this, a new socialist régime would arise out of its fiasco, with a greater unity and a clearer comprehension of its tasks than prevailed in November 1918'.[27]

3   The Heidelberg Programme of the SPD

In 1925, on the occasion of the congress of the SPD held in Heidelberg on 13–18 September and in reference to the new programme adopted at this congress, Kautsky outlined the tasks of socialism in the current historical situation. He had made a substantial contribution to the

[26] Ibid., p. 9.
[27] Ibid., p. 10.

preparation and drafting of this programme. (In September 1922, at the Nuremburg congress that reunified the SPD and USPD, Kautsky had been president of the programme commission.) The congress approved, with only a few votes against, a draft presented by Kautsky. Thus, the third programme of German Social Democracy, like the first, bore the imprint of the sage of the movement. Indeed, in many respects the text of the Heidelberg programme paralleled that of the Erfurt programme, above all in its analysis of economic development and the role played by the proletariat within it. The new element was that the forward march of the proletariat was no longer proceeding within the framework of a military-bureaucratic state but in that of a democratic republic, which the proletariat was now called upon to defend as the indispensable basis for the struggle for socialism.

The text of the programme began with the statement that economic development had led with iron logic to the domination of great capitalist enterprises in industry. This had granted a few magnates a 'monopoly' over the 'decisive means of production in the economic domain'. It further asserted that 'only through constant struggle' could the workers improve their conditions and oppose the objective tendency of capitalism to deprive them increasingly of their share of social wealth. Since there could be no reconciliation of interests between capitalists and proletarians (because of the exploitation to which the former subjected the latter), and since 'finance capitalism' was constantly provoking the danger of war (because of its imperialist aims), the conflict between the two classes was becoming 'increasingly bitter' and the class struggle 'increasingly aggravated'. Hence, 'the goal of the working class can be attained only through the conversion of capitalist property in the means of production into social property'.

What differentiated the socio-economic analysis in the Heidelberg programme from that of its Erfurt predecessor was its central attention to the development of the layer of white-collar workers and intellectuals, which it related to the rising importance of large-scale enterprises: 'Concurrent with the rise of the large enterprises in the economy, the number and weight of white-collar workers and intellectuals of all varieties is growing'. Nevertheless, there was no deep analysis of the socio-political role this stratum might play; indeed, it was assimilated, on the basis of strictly economistic criteria, to the masses of workers *tout court*: 'With the rise in their numbers they increasingly lose any possibility of acquiring privileged positions, and their interests therefore increasingly coincide with those of the other workers'. There was only brief mention of the problem of unemployment, so fraught with consequences for political struggle in periods of capitalist crisis. Unemployment was merely cited as a concomitant aspect of the 'insecurity of existence' that threatened the workers in such periods.

Finally – and this position was typical of both the SPD and Kautsky after the November 1918 revolution – the programme declared that the democratic republic constituted a 'stable form, the defence and reinforcement of which is an indispensable necessity for the working class'. It was the only form that could enable the working class to assume power and introduce the 'socialization of the means of production'. In keeping with all this, and in an obvious polemic against the road to power of the Bolsheviks and the state structure they had created, the section of the Erfurt programme committing Social Democracy to struggle against the oppression of any class, party, sex, or race was reproduced in full.[28]

As in the case of the Erfurt programme and the Görlitz programme, Kautsky wrote a 'commentary' on the Heidelberg programme. There were two central elements to his analysis. On the one hand, he asserted that capitalist development was in no way able to respond to the needs of the toiling masses and that any project of an 'integrated' capitalist society was therefore anti-historical, since insofar as the bloc in power succeeded in halting the workers' struggle, it must thereby damage the interests of the proletariat. On the other hand, he called upon the toiling masses to defend political democracy intransigently against the undemocratic tendencies of both big finance capital and the Communists, who scorned democracy as a bourgeois historical form. Indeed, the 'spirit' of Kautsky's commentary on the Heidelberg programme was set precisely by his discourse on the significance of democracy, the only terrain of growth for the struggle for socialism and the only way to lend a socialist content to the collectivization of the means of production.

In this text, written during a period when capitalist stabilization was taking shape in Germany, as in other countries, after the period of post-war crisis, Kautsky vigorously upheld a fundamental historic optimism as to the prospects of German Social Democracy. The latter, he said, had become the strongest political party of the Reich, and 'despite all the ups and downs, it is coming closer to the moment at which it will have the majority of the German people behind it and will win full political power'.[29] Such optimism was founded on his view that demo-

---

[28] Cf. 'Sozialdemokratische Partei Deutschlands, auf dem Heidelberger Parteitag 1925 beschlossenes Programm', in Abendroth, op. cit., pp. 107–108.

[29] 'Grundsätzlicher Teil', in *Das Heidelberger Programm. Grundsätze und Forderungen der Sozialdemokratie*, Berlin, [1925], p. 5.

cracy constituted the form of economic development that would guarantee the political growth of the toiling masses. In this respect the tranquillizing function of the analysis he devoted to the 'new middle class' was very significant: it was manifestly intended to justify the programme's assertion that this layer could not act autonomously. Kautsky began from the correct observation that 'under present conditions no social stratum is growing as rapidly as that of the self-employed and white-collar workers, the mental labourers, the "intellectuals", groups that are classified as the new middle class'. But he then went on to maintain that because of its economic situation, this new middle class, growing even more rapidly than the proletariat, was generally acquiring features characteristic of the mass of wage workers. It was nonetheless true, he noted, that a portion of this layer was throwing itself into the arms of the ruling classes in an attempt to win privileged positions. But there was no economic possibility of such positions becoming generalized. Hence the hopes of those bourgeois politicians who believed they had found in the new middle class a conservative mass stratum to act as a 'counterweight' to the proletariat were fated to be disappointed. Politically, Kautsky claimed, the destiny of the 'new middle class' was wholly analogous to that of the 'old middle class': 'The new middle class, like the old, will divide into two groups, one of which, the majority, will lean towards socialist feelings and ideas'. The minority group, on the other hand, would evolve towards fanatical reaction and become the champion of brutal violence.[30]

Kautsky stated that the opinion current among many bourgeois politicians and economists that the capitalist system was capable of 'softening' class conflicts was wholly erroneous.[31] There were, he said, only two ways to 'put an end to the class struggle'. One was indeed capitalist, but it was not at all that of the integration of the proletariat into the system in the context of peaceful bourgeois hegemony. On the contrary, it was the method of unbridled violence, which 'aims at handing the proletariat over to its exploiters bound and gagged'. This, however, was a road which, even if it succeeded, could only be transitory, for such success 'would signify not the end of the class struggle but on the contrary its exacerbation in the direction of civil war'.[32] This was an important comment, because, as we shall see, it represented a preparation for Kautsky's interpretation of fascism as an interlude, an 'anti-historical phenomenon', whose attempt to conciliate the capitalist mode of pro-

[30] Ibid., pp. 10–12.
[31] Ibid., p. 13.
[32] Ibid., p. 19.

duction with the suppression of the class struggle was historically impossible. The other method, that of the proletariat, on the contrary conformed to the real and rational direction of history. It was the only way to put an end to the class struggle, for it deprived that struggle of its foundation by eliminating its cause, namely private property in the means of production. The proletarian way was 'the only method' capable of putting an end to the class struggle 'radically and for good'. The capitalist method, 'even if it succeeded, would lead only to the complete ruin of society'.[33] (It should be noted, however, that at the time Kautsky considered such a possibility purely theoretical, since it was 'ruled out by the power the proletariat has already acquired'.)

Turning to the relationship between the class struggle and democracy, Kautsky insisted that precisely to the extent that big monopoly capital tended to restrict, or eventually eliminate, democracy, the proletariat must support democracy with all its might. Democracy, of course, had been born of the struggle of the capitalist bourgeoisie against the aristocracy and the absolutist state. But it was no accident that once the bourgeoisie had won class democracy for itself, it had sought with all its might to prevent the extension of this democracy. Hence, full political democracy had been the product of the struggle not of the bourgeoisie but of the proletariat against all the conservative strata allied against it. Those people (and here Kautsky was clearly alluding to the Communists) who maintained that democracy 'is a capitalist invention and an instrument of the power of capital' because it was the bourgeoisie that had originally waged the struggle for democracy did not realize the extent of the confusion to which they had fallen victim. After all, even the class struggle of the proletariat itself was generated and strengthened by capital and was the product of it.[34] 'Full democracy is therefore a conquest of the proletariat. . . . The democratic rights we possess today are primarily the product of the struggles of the last three or four generations of the working class. Born of the strengthening of the proletariat, each of these rights, through a continuous process of interaction, becomes the premise for a new rise in the strength of the proletariat, of its capacity for organization, of its clarity and consciousness of its own goals, of its experience in the administration of the state and the municipalities, of its knowledge of the decisive political and economic forces in its own country and throughout the world. *The most complete form of democracy is that which is realized under the democratic republic*'.

[33] Ibid., p. 19.
[34] Ibid., p. 15.

Naturally, in and of itself the democratic republic in no way guaranteed the victory of the proletariat. Indeed, 'in certain circumstances' it could even 'serve the aims of the great exploiters'. But what the democratic republic could guarantee better than any other institutional form was the most ideal terrain for the class struggle of the workers. It thus represented *'the indispensable precondition for the victory of labour over capitalist exploitation'*. Even before this victory, it provided the most favourable conditions for the defence of the living and working conditions of the workers.[35] But that was not all, Kautsky declared. Democracy was not only the best form for the defence of liberty and the conquest of new rights for the proletariat under the capitalist system; it also represented the necessary terrain of continuity of this process with that of the construction of socialism. Indeed, only political democracy could prevent the degeneration of socialization into bureaucratic nationalization, since without political democracy, the popular control and organizational growth which were preconditions for a socialist society would be impossible: 'for Social Democracy, the only nationalization that is socialist is one that occurs in the framework of a completely democratic state with a proletariat that is strong and independent, ideologically and organizationally'.[36] The criteria for socialization to be found in his commentary on the Heidelberg programme repeated the list Kautsky had set out in 1919 and 1920: gradual progress; compensation for former owners; confiscation of the goods of capitalists who conspired against the state; respect for small-scale enterprises and their peaceful transformation over time by methods of cooperation; dialectical organization of the relations between producers and consumers.[37]

[35] Ibid., p. 16.
[36] Ibid., p. 20.
[37] Ibid., pp. 21–24.

XI

Fascism and Democracy

1 Industrial Society, Socialism and Fascism

Kautsky believed that the economic stabilization which followed the
Dawes Plan confirmed that a revival of production would create the
preconditions for a rise in the strength of the democratic republic and
for a recovery of political initiative by the socialist forces, and not only
in Germany. In 1927 he explicitly expressed the conviction that what had
happened in Italy could not occur in Germany. The preceding historical
period, he declared, had been characterized by the ability of the ruling
classes to stem the expanding thrust of the socialists. Hence, 'we have
already been in the midst of the period of counter-revolution for years
now'. But in the industrially advanced countries, and therefore in Germany, this counter-revolution was not of such a nature as to lead to the
extinction of political life. 'Only in Italy has it succeeded in achieving
the complete oppression of the opposition that has been the characteristic
of every counter-revolution up to now'. In the countries in which the
proletariat was sufficiently strong, Kautsky asserted, voicing an illusion,
'this strength compels the counter-revolution to assume a form different
from that typical of the past or of those states where development is
scant. Here the counter-revolution takes the form not of a subjugation
and enslavement of the proletariat, but rather of an interruption of its
march to power and of its defensive need to fight not to conquer new
positions but to preserve those already won'. In any event, Kautsky held
that the decline of the 'days of reaction' had begun.[1]

Kautsky's confidence in the future was due to his conviction that
economic recovery would permit the reinvigoration of democracy as the
normal political rule of modern industrialism. Linking external imperialism to internal reaction, he extended his analysis of the former as a

[1] 'Revolution und Gegenrevolution', in *Vorwärts*, 1 June 1927.

340

contingent and pathological phenomenon contrary to the long-run interests of capital itself; the latter was the domestic facet of the same 'irrational' tendencies. He reiterated that the institutional form most natural to industrial society was democracy. In *Die materialistische Geschichtsauffassung* (1927) he wrote: 'Not only the proletariat, but all the industrial classes, along with the peasantry, have an interest in democracy' and in the political and civil system inherent in it. Above all, they had an interest in a government subject to parliamentary control.[2] Kautsky reasoned that in a developed capitalist country, if the 'capitalists should ever attempt a violent assault against democracy', their problem would be to amass 'an armed force sufficient' to carry out such a task. It is clear from all his subsequent writings that Kautsky remained wedded to an excessively formal-institutional analysis that blinded him to the real strength and influence of the 'separate bodies' within the German capitalist state. He viewed the Weimar Republic as comparable to the long-established Anglo-Saxon bourgeois democracies, to whose institutional pattern Germany – with moreover a major presence of proletarian organizations – now apparently conformed. He failed to grasp the overall relationship of class forces in Weimar Germany, beyond the parliamentary arena. To launch an attack on the democratic republic, Kautsky observed, the capitalists would have to appeal to the army. But in a democratic country in which the armed forces were composed predominantly of workers, the soldiers would not rally to a reactionary plot. For democracy was 'important to all the broad strata of the population, even those which have no proletarian or socialist outlook. In a modern industrial country, and it is only with such countries that we are dealing here, the entire toiling population, the overwhelming majority of the inhabitants, would support the preservation of democratic rights. Under these conditions, an attempt by the capitalists to use an army based on compulsory military service to destroy democracy would be most dangerous precisely for those who perpetrated it'.

Nor did Kautsky believe that an army composed of professional soldiers or even a militia directly in the pay of the capitalists could achieve any more success. He was convinced that what had happened in Italy could not be repeated in Germany, because of the effects of economic recovery on an industrialized society. 'The fascists today', he wrote, 'have become the paid executioners of popular liberty. They are certainly dangerous, but fortunately only in particular circumstances which cannot be summoned by their capitalist overlords at will. To have

[2] *Die materialistische Geschichtsauffassung*, vol. II, op. cit., p. 509.

a political impact, the fascists must possess substantial numerical strength (in Italy, with 39 million inhabitants, there are about 500,000 of them). In Germany they would have to number a million to achieve the same proportionate weight. But in an industrial country it is not possible to amass such a large number of young vagabonds as capitalist tools. In Italy the conditions for doing so were unusually favourable'.

Kautsky's comparison of Italy and Germany was based on a narrowly sociological and economistic approach, insensitive to the dynamic force of big monopoly capital in contemporary class conflicts. He imagined fascism to be a phenomenon specific to economic backwardness. Recalling the persistence of 'displaced' elements in Italian history, which had variously produced first banditry and later anarchism and finally flowed together into Mussolini's squads under the protection of big capital in the aftermath of the World War, Kautsky emphasized the limits of industrial development in Italy and the negative consequences of the division of the working class caused by Bolshevism. He concluded that the conditions that had brought fascism to power in Italy were 'limited to a particular country during a specific phase and will not be easily repeated'. Kautsky also underestimated the functional significance of fascism for the maintenance of 'capitalist order'. Indeed, he even thought there was a fundamental incompatibility between fascism and orderly economic development: 'Capitalist production and accumulation are possible only when complete security of property and person prevails. These conditions of capitalism have now been completely eliminated in Italy. The *Duce* would be astonished at what would happen if he tried to recreate them'. Kautsky saw in fascism only the civil war and disorder unleashed during its seizure of power; he failed to perceive the dynamic of its counter-revolutionary dictatorship and the connection between the victory of political reaction and the general reorganization of big capital. In effect, hypnotized by its petty-bourgeois scum and systematic terrorism, he viewed fascism merely as the long arm of anti-proletarian struggle, rather than as a new system capable of stabilizing its own order. Hence he believed that progressive economic recovery in Germany after the war would strengthen parliamentary democracy, and that any possible fascist success would be ephemeral, because incompatible with the conditions of modern capitalist society. 'From year to year', he wrote, 'the further we move from the World War and the sort of soldateska it created, the more the processes of production return to their normal channels, and the less becomes the number of destitute and unemployed, then the lower are the chances that the violent faction within the capitalist class could arrest the rise of the proletariat within democracy by un-leashing civil war and by annihilating democracy itself. But even if such a project were to succeed under particular conditions in this or that state, it would be a Pyrrhic victory. For over time the advance of democracy in the modern state cannot be halted'.[3]

The advance of democracy was irresistible, according to Kautsky, because the modern state depended on an accurate representation of classes and social groups of the type assured by parliamentary institutions. In sum, observing the German scene during an ebb of the Nazi movement, Kautsky underestimated the unitary political and social drive of big monopoly and finance capital, and its capacity to establish in certain circumstances a stable totalitarian control over the whole of civil society. He therefore failed to perceive the potential dynamism of a fusion of fascism with big capital. Deeming fascism an 'irrationality', he never discerned the type of rationality it nonetheless possessed for reaction. Similarly, but antithetically, he failed to appreciate the possible longevity of the Soviet régime, the inevitable crisis of which he never tired of predicting on the grounds of its incompatibility with a 'rational' demo-cratic representation of social forces. For Kautsky, fascism and Bol-shevism alike remained exceptional governments incapable of developing into organic systems of political-social management.

2   1929: the Terminal Crisis of Capitalism?

Since he regarded democratic progress as the most effective political, and therefore most rational social, form for the development of the forces of production – indeed the only form in which the transition from capitalism to socialism could occur – Kautsky came to view capitalist reaction and Bolshevik dictatorship as two opposite yet complementary variants of degeneration, born of inadequate and irrational 'responses' to the problems of contemporary society. His analysis of bourgeois 'counter-revolution' and Bolshevik 'sectarianism' was based on a series of theoretical assumptions which may be summarized as follows: 1) the capitalist mode of production does not necessarily generate a collapse that renders it technically and materially unable to function; 2) the proletariat has an interest in conducting its own class action within a perspective of economic development and not 'catastrophe'; 3) the root of the class conflict between capitalists and workers lies in the

[3] Ibid., pp. 476–478.

relationship of exploitation itself, which cannot be eliminated under capitalism; 4) the class struggle between capital and labour therefore has a permanent economic basis; 5) the contest between capitalism and socialism concerns the model of development – which capitalism strives to channel in the direction of private interests, while socialism seeks the general social interest; 6) the proletariat must defend democracy if it is won and reconquer it if it is lost, since democracy alone permits the working class to build its own organizations and to prepare for the administration of society; 7) dictatorial forms are least suitable for the development characteristic of industrial society and represent stable and 'normal' solutions neither for capitalism nor for socialism, retarding both economic development and the growth of the proletariat; 8) fascism is a futile attempt to halt that rise of the working class which is a concomitant of social development itself; Bolshevism is an unsuccessful bid to accelerate a historic cycle which can be run through only when the relations between capital and labour have reached an advanced level of maturity – its political installation therefore inevitably acquires the guise of a mystified 'socialism'; 9) any ruinous paralysis of capitalist forces of production would lead not to socialism but to the cancellation of its material possibility, since the genesis of socialism can only lie in the contradiction between the economic development and social exigencies generated by the most numerous class in industrial society, and the failure of capitalism to respond to them adequately; 10) the aim of the proletariat must therefore be not the destruction of the productive forces of capitalism, but rather a different 'model' of their management, which can be worked out only amidst the broadest political democracy.

In *Die materialistische Geschichtsauffassung* Kautsky formulated the 'law' of the rise of socialism in contemporary industrial society thus: '*The more prosperous and expansionary the capitalist mode of production, the better are the prospects for the socialist system that will succeed it*'.[4] He counterposed this thesis (largely a repetition of one of the traditional themes of revisionism) to the claim of the theoreticians of 'catastrophism' (from Lenin to Bukharin or Trotsky) that a revolutionary process inevitably involved a sharp if temporary decline in production. He must have had in mind the lines Trotsky had written precisely in his polemic against Kautsky: 'Palace revolutions, which end merely by personal reshufflings at the top, can take place in a short space of time, having practically no effect on the economic life of the country. Quite another matter are revolutions which drag into their whirlpool millions

[4] Ibid., p. 591.

of workers. Whatever be the form of society, it rests on the foundation of labour. Dragging the mass of the people away from labour, drawing them for a prolonged period into the struggle, thereby destroying their connection with production, the revolution in all these ways strikes deadly blows at economic life, and inevitably lowers the standard which it found at its birth. The more perfect the revolution, the greater are the masses it draws in; and the longer it is prolonged, the greater is the destruction it achieves in the apparatus of production and the more terrible inroads does it make upon public resources'.[5] Trotsky's solution was to ensure that the phase of civil war, with its negative consequences on production, was as brief as possible, by maximum concentration of revolutionary action and therewith coercion against the enemy force. Kautsky held that this strategy, if applied in an industrialized country, would bring the masses to their knees and destroy the material and the moral possibilities of socialism, leading directly to counter-revolution. Commenting on the 'law' he had formulated, Kautsky remarked: 'This may sound paradoxical to those who believe that socialism will arise from a "collapse", from the "failure" or the "bankruptcy" of capitalism. But it does not conflict with the conception that expects the victory of socialism not from the economic decadence of capital, but from the growth in numbers and the increase in moral, intellectual, and political strength of the proletariat'.[6]

The sequel to Kautsky's argument is revealing of the origins of his view that the revolutionary process was dependent on the 'state of health' of capitalism, and of the way in which he was to apply it during the post-war crisis. He recalled that in 1899, when he wrote his book against Bernstein, he was still 'of the conviction that the capitalist mode of production had economic limits which it could not surpass'. At the same time, however, correctly identifying the most creative element in the Marxist tradition, he had advanced the hypothesis that the class struggle could bring the system to an end before capitalism had entered the phase of its 'chronic crisis', of constant over-production.[7] Now precisely this second element was the real Ariadne's thread that had led him definitively to the conclusion that socialism would be born only of the intellectual and moral maturity of the working class in the framework of a developed political democracy. In 1933, a fatal year for German

[5] Trotsky, *Terrorism and Communism*, op. cit., p. 7.

[6] *Die materialistische Geschichtsauffassung*, vol. II, op. cit., p. 591. On this point see also the similar formulations in 'Phasen und Zeitschriften des Marxismus', in *Die Gesellschaft*, I, 1924, p. 25.

[7] *Die materialistische Geschichtsauffassung*, vol. II, op. cit., p. 591.

Social Democracy, and also the fiftieth anniversary of the death of Karl Marx, Kautsky wrote that nothing was more damaging to socialism than the mechanical theory of collapse – especially since any 'collapse' of the productive system would furnish a basis not for socialism but merely for a management of misery. 'If capitalism stands near collapse', he wrote, 'would that not mean the victory of socialism? Not at all, in fact. When the mechanisms of capitalist production stagnate, the result is first and foremost a stagnation of production *tout court* and certainly not a furtherance of it in socialist forms. We must refrain from interpreting the materialist conception of history in an automatic and mechanistic sense, as if historical development inherently proceeded in a virtually pre-determined direction. Men make history, and its course is necessary only in the sense that on the average men necessarily react in the same manner to the same stimuli when they occur under the same conditions. As I pointed out in 1899 in my writings against Bernstein, Marx did not expect the victory of socialism to result from capitalist collapse. He expected this victory to result from the rising strength and maturity of the proletariat'.[8]

Naturally, Kautsky did not deny or underestimate the actively anticapitalist effects of the economic crises of the system. But he insisted that if they were to become forces for socialism, these would have to be reflected in an increase in the organizational and intellectual vigour of the proletariat, expressed in its capacity to influence the outcome of economic crises. What he resolutely rejected was the notion that crises constituted the specific and necessary basis for the proletarian revolution. Indeed, he insisted that if anything, crises had always depressed the proletariat as a class, dividing the employed from the unemployed,[9] impelling the former towards a defensive corporatism and the latter towards a rebellious desperation. Kautsky held that the task of socialists was rather to contribute, as an active and independent political force, to the reconstruction of the fabric of production, while advancing a critique of capitalism designed to modify the relationship of class forces gradually in their favour, within the framework of democracy. In effect he advocated a strategy of reforms rooted simultaneously in the prosperity of the productive system and the power of the organized proletariat within it. He did not believe that capitalist prosperity could abolish social contradictions and therefore durably integrate the proletarian class into the system; at the same time he was confident that democracy, the only

[8] 'Marx und Marxismus', in *Die Gesellschaft*, X, 1933, p. 197.
[9] *Die materialistische Geschichtsauffassung*, vol. II, op. cit., p. 594.

political system that effectively expressed the relations between the fundamental classes, would inevitably acquire a socialist content in the long run. Economic prosperity, he argued, was needed if the state was to acquire 'the means necessary to introduce great changes in the interests of the masses'. It was 'during periods of prosperity' that 'decisive reforms' could be 'imposed' on the capitalists, such as the shortening of the working week, measures favouring public health, etc. It was also during periods of prosperity that new enterprises 'moving towards socialization' could be created.[10] The precondition for the success of this reformist strategy was obviously a constant increase in the growth of a powerful democratic-socialist movement.

Kautsky's attitude toward the crisis of 1929 and its consequences was very revealing. In 1931, in a preface to the third edition of *Die proletarische Revolution*, he 'read' the crisis through the optic of a theory that the internal evolution of the recession would cyclically lead to a recovery, accompanied by a new rise in the strength of the workers' movement. He rejected the idea that the crisis of 1929 heralded a collapse; on the contrary, he held that its resolution would create the preconditions for a great advance by the proletariat and lay the basis for the socialist revolution. Kautsky expected anything but the possibility that the exit from the crisis in Germany would take the form of a Nazi seizure of power. The Communists believed it necessary to intervene in the economic crisis by leading a radicalized proletariat into an assault on capitalism and the bourgeois state, clearing the revolutionary road to the dictatorship of the proletariat. Kautsky, on the other hand, held that the proletariat should intervene in the economic crisis by remedial measures through democratic parliamentary institutions. Both, however, saw a historic victory for socialism at the end of the road; neither had any adequate notion of a counter-revolutionary capitalist management of the crisis. This was Kautsky's analysis: 'The present distressing situation is primarily the product of frightful unemployment. On the basis of Marxist economic analysis, we know that periodic crises are inevitable, that every era of prosperity is inevitably followed by one of stagnation and unemployment, accompanied by dreadful misery. We also know, however, that this situation is by no means eternal but must in turn give way to a new upswing of production. Nothing entitles us to think that it will be otherwise this time. In truth, the crisis may last a long time, since it has not only asphyxiated industry but stricken agriculture. The same occurred during the long crisis that racked Europe after

[10] Ibid., p. 595.

1873. . . . Nevertheless, it is wholly possible that the present crisis may be overcome in the near future. The more the various states can agree to overcome their political and economic divisions, the sooner this could happen. . . . But whatever its starting point may be, the advent of a new phase of prosperity is inevitable. Equally inevitable, however, is a powerful rise in the political and economic strength of the proletariat of the great industrial countries. The situation of class equilibrium which now exists in these societies will cease as the proletariat acquires a rapidly increasing supremacy. The principal cause of the division of the masses will disappear with the end of unemployment, and the proletariat will take government power alone. . . . At present, the conditions do not exist for socialist measures to resolve the crisis. But we have every reason to expect that the coming period of prosperity will give rise to an era of lasting well-being and security, of rapid adaptation of the productive process to the needs of the toiling classes, an era which we should define as that of the proletarian revolution'.[11]

In an article published in *Vorwärts*, also in 1931, Kautsky repeated that he expected the crisis to be overcome 'within the framework of capitalism'. The question was by what means, for there were various possible solutions. 'Given the present crisis of capitalism', he declared, 'our task' is 'to study these means' and to fight against the obstacles to economic recovery. He did not think that the crisis itself would be overcome by socialism, but he did think that the workers' movement would be able to strengthen itself by its intervention in it.[12]

3   The Fascist 'Interlude' and the Way Forward

Even while cultivating this optimistic theory of how the capitalist crisis would be overcome, Kautsky could not fail to note the rising tide of Nazism in Germany. The NSDAP scored an unprecedented success in the 14 September 1930 elections. After obtaining only 810,000 votes (2.6%, 12 deputies) in the elections of May 1928, it garnered 6,410,000 votes (18.3%, 107 deputies) in 1930. The economic crisis was now immensely sharpening social and political conflicts in Germany. Great masses of unemployed, disappointed in the republic and the party system, which they blamed for their own misery, were flocking to the

[11] 'Die proletarische Revolution', in *Der Kampf*, XXIV, 1931, p. 297.
[12] 'Um die Einheit', in *Vorwärts*, 11 October 1931.

banner of the swastika. The Nazis were now arrogantly breaking out of the political isolation in which they had been confined during the period of capitalist stabilization (1924–1928); they were now the centrepiece of the bloc of social and political forces resolved to close the interlude of the democratic republic and opt for systematic reaction. Of course, the die was not yet cast. The role of the Nazis in a future restructuration of state power was not yet clear. But that they were about to become a decisive component of the counter-revolutionary bloc in Germany was demonstrated by the pact reached by the Harzburg Front, which sealed the alliance of the rightist forces determined to stifle the Weimar Republic.

Kautsky's attitude toward the Nazi threat was a blend of anxiety and of faith in the strength of the workers' movement – tempered by the fear that its internal division could pave the way for Nazism. 'There is no greater imaginable danger to the rise of the German proletariat, indeed to the German people in general, than the constitution of a "Third Reich"', he wrote in May 1931. The only way to confront this danger was to unify the proletariat and reach agreements with those bourgeois forces prepared to oppose Nazism.[13] A few months later, in an article outlining the 'tasks of Social Democracy' for the new year, 1932, Kautsky asserted that if Germany fell into the coils of Nazism, the country would fall into 'a slime of blood and filth'. But he still harboured his old illusions. He held to the delusion (to which he would cling even after 1933) that the gravity of the German economic crisis would rapidly exhaust Nazism if it did seize power, since the Nazis would prove unable to solve the complex problems of managing industry and society. Mussolini, Kautsky declared, had taken power in more favourable times and circumstances. Hitler would have to seize it in the midst of a frightful crisis. Furthermore (here he repeated one of his most tenacious convictions), the German proletariat 'is much stronger and better disciplined and organized' than the Italian. At the same time, he continued to sound his warnings: 'if the proletariat of the Reich was united, it would undoubtedly determine the character of the state'. The responsibility for its lack of unity lay with the Communists, who were conducting a suicidal policy 'on the orders of the potentates of the Kremlin in Moscow', and with those misguided sub-proletarians who served as Hitler's praetorians. 'Without unity we are lost'.[14]

Even as the Nazi seizure of power drew close, Kautsky advanced an

[13] 'Was ist zu tun?', in *Leipziger Volkszeitung*, 30 June 1931.
[14] 'Die Aufgaben der deutschen Sozialdemokratie im kommenden Jahr', in *Arbeiter-Zeitung*, 1 January 1932.

analysis of the historic roots of German fascism which emphasized its 'irrational' character. Pursuing his theory that imperialism, of which fascism was the most brutal incarnation, was not a necessary result of capitalism but merely one of its degenerate variants, the product of a 'bad policy', Kautsky described the following elements of the soil in which the evil weed of fascism had taken root: 1) the conditions created by the senseless provisions of the Versailles Peace Treaty; 2) the national particularism engendered after the war (the breakup of Austria-Hungary, creation of a multitude of small states in Europe), which had embittered international economic relations, thus damaging German industry; 3) the rise of an unbridled finance capitalism seeking abnormal profits; 4) the complete distortion of free trade, which had never been more necessary for economic recovery. 'So long as these tendencies of private monopolism prevail', he concluded, 'it is extremely difficult to expect an improvement in the economy'. Having said this, however, he immediately added that he believed these factors of rampant irrationality were not 'necessarily linked to the natural laws of the capitalist economy'.[15] His hope was that 'rationality' would prevail over 'irrationality'.

It was not long before the Brown Shirts were to inaugurate a reign of terror in the country with the strongest Social Democracy in the world and the strongest Communist Party in Western Europe. The triumph of Nazi reaction in Germany demonstrated that fascism was not something that could take root and bear fruit only in economically backward countries where industrialization was limited. The myth, shared by the Social Democrats and Communists, that the strength of the organized German proletariat was a fortress the Nazis could never conquer, collapsed. All the defects and weaknesses of the Weimar Republic were laid bare. The November Revolution of 1918, which had brought the 'democratic republic', had not represented the point of no return Kautsky had believed. In *Terrorismus und Kommunismus* (1919) he had written that neither a 'red' nor 'black' dictatorship could ever consolidate power in Germany. That confident assertion, ringing with the pride of a certain stage of German Social Democracy, was one Kautsky was to continue to repeat even after the Nazi seizure of power. It now appeared more as a profession of faith than as a comprehension of reality. 'Less than ever before in Western Europe', Kautsky had written, 'can the call for a dictatorship of the proletariat in Germany result in the establishment of a genuine, lasting, effective, and energetic dictatorship capable of spreading throughout the country. The population is too advanced for

[15] 'In schwerer Zeit', in *Arbeiter-Zeitung*, 25 July 1931.

this. All the attempts by isolated elements of the proletariat to institute such a dictatorship can attain only temporary and local success and will lead to this common result: the aggravation of the economic and political ruin of the state and the strengthening of the tendencies towards a counter-revolutionary military dictatorship. But neither could this variety of dictatorship attain durable and generalized power. In the long run, it is no longer possible to govern against the workers in Germany'.[16]

When the political catastrophe of Weimar Germany occurred, Kautsky summarized the terms of his analysis in several essays which constitute the last pronouncement before his death on a major turning point of European and world history. The most important of these writings were: *Die blutige Revolution* (1933), *Der Zusammenbruch der deutschen Sozial-demokratie* (1933), *Die Ausrottung der Besten* (1933), *Neue Programm* (1933), *Was tun?* (1934), *Grenzen der Gewalt. Aussichten und Wirkungen bewaffneter Erhebung des Proletariats* (1934). In them Kautsky explored the factors that had generated the victory of reaction in the socio-economic and politico-institutional arenas in Germany, while at the same time reaffirming his faith in the future of democracy and socialism as the only basis for progress. He expressed his conviction that the countries with a long-standing history of parliamentary democracy could never fall victim to fascism. This was an important, even decisive point, for it represented the last-ditch refuge of what remained of his theory of the indissoluble connection between modern industrial society and parliamentary democracy. Kautsky would not yield up this connection. But he was now compelled to admit that the Germany of the November Revolution and the Weimar Constitution had not definitively attained the goal of parliamentary democracy, contrary to what he had believed. For Kautsky, the theoretical model remained valid, but the compass of its application had now to be narrowed, for certain conditions of economic and social development characteristic of 'advanced' states had been wanting in Germany, driving the country into the clutches of the most aggressive form of capitalism. 'Fascism', he wrote, 'will not cross the Rhine or the North Sea. In France, England and America it will remain the folly of a handful of braggarts of no political significance'.[17] In the general history of Europe, Kautsky argued, fascism would necessarily remain a parenthesis in the onward march of humanism and social progress, a lapse that was grave but passing. Kautsky's theory of fascism as a 'parenthesis' was very similar to that of Benedetto Croce (particularly

[16] TK, p. 220.
[17] *Neue Programme*, Vienna-Leipzig, 1933, p. 45.

in his *Storia d'Europa*), although the two thinkers employed different conceptions of civic progress as criteria for the condemnation of fascism; for Kautsky progress was represented by Social Democracy, for Croce by freedom as an immanent force of history. Kautsky wrote: 'The rise of dictatorship in some states signals a local, transitory interruption of a process that has been under way for more than a century in the entire civilized world. It is a consequence of the World War. We must not fear that it may become so general and persistent as to lead to the "decadence of the West" that has been prophesied by one of the leaders of National Socialism'.[18]

The claim that fascism would be transient had its complement in the view that a 'red dictatorship' would also be unable to take root in those countries in which liberty was of longer and stronger standing: 'The idea of a socialist dictatorship will have no better fate in these countries'.[19] This, of course, was a repetition and adaptation of the theses of *Terrorismus und Kommunismus* in 1919. But its geographic compass had shifted, from Germany to the 'Western democracies'. In the course of this shift, Kautsky jettisoned one fundamental prior conviction – that the strength of the workers' organizations in Germany constituted an insuperable barrier against 'dictatorship'. Kautsky's 'geography of dictatorship' had been transformed by the collapse of the SPD and the German labour movement and the debacle of the Weimar Constitution, which he had always presented as the authentic expression of a sturdily democratic parliamentary system. The claim he had maintained so tenaciously that in a country in which the industrial proletariat had attained the level of development it had in Germany, 'red or black dictatorships' would face a virtually insurmountable obstacle, had now lost all credibility.

Once the Nazis had conquered power, Kautsky reposed his hopes for resistance to fascism essentially in the countries with older democratic-parliamentary traditions. At the same time, he persisted in his conviction that fascism would be ephemeral in Germany, that it could not become a 'system', still maintaining that industrial development and political democracy were ultimately equivalent. He now, of course, had to modify his prediction that the 1929 crisis would be followed in Germany as elsewhere by a recovery of production accompanied by an increase in the political and organizational strength of the proletariat, culminating in the unification of the labour movement and the advent of the socialists

[18] 'Die Ausrottung der Besten', in *Arbeiter-Zeitung*, 15 October 1933.
[19] *Neue Programme*, op. cit., p. 45.

to power. Elements previously considered 'secondary', such as the counter-revolutionary drive of the most aggressive sectors of capital and the manipulation of sub-proletarians and unemployed by reaction, now occupied the front of the stage in Kautsky's account, which recalled much in his earlier analyses of the 'imperialist' tendencies that had culminated in the First World War: 'After the great world crisis that erupted in 1873 and lasted almost two decades', Kautsky wrote, 'capitalism itself increasingly came to doubt the advantages of free competition and freedom of trade. It sought to replace them with the organization of production in private monopolies. For this purpose it required high customs tariffs and other measures. These were placed at its disposal by the state, which simultaneously became dependent on capital. The latter no longer combated state power but instead made use of it. Towards this end it forged links with large landed property, towards which it had previously been hostile. In order to monopolize the internal market, it strove to achieve similar monopolization of foreign markets. . . . During this period heavy industry came increasingly to the forefront, while light industry declined in importance. But heavy industry has an interest in armaments. Rearmament assumed insane proportions. . . . The proletariat was compelled to bear the costs of this entire development. The spirit of violence that flowed from it was directed primarily against the toiling classes. This spirit was exacerbated by the fact that the capitalists lost the conviction that their mode of production was the most advantageous for the well-being of all nations and became convinced that it could preserve and assert itself only if it guaranteed them the freedom to exist through violence. Now they saw the victorious advance of the idea that the socialization of production in ever more numerous branches of activity within a democratic state would create a mode of production superior to capitalism. The capitalists are ever less able to combat this idea theoretically, which is acquiring ever greater force as the proletariat grows not only numerically but also in ideological independence and capacity for mass organization. The violent destruction of workers' organizations and of democracy, within the context of which these organizations develop, is thus increasingly becoming the objective of the capitalists, whose previous liberalism is fading from view'.[20]

Kautsky's analysis here posited the rising strength of the proletariat as a determinant of the crisis of democratic institutions. In the past he had, of course, emphasized that democracy did not abolish the class struggle; but, at least after the creation of the Weimar Republic, he had

[20] 'Die blutige Revolution', in *Der Kampf*, XXVI, 1933, p. 353.

held that it was quite possible for the proletariat to wage the class struggle within the framework of representative institutions. Now he was compelled to note that class conflict during an economic crisis had plunged political democracy itself into crisis. At this point, however, Kautsky studiously avoided embracing the position, which he had bitterly combated in the past, that the abolition of representative parliamentary democracy and the creation of the proletariat's own political dictatorship became inevitable once class conflict reached a certain pitch of intensity. His perspective remained substantially unchanged: When democracy was suppressed, the proletariat must struggle to reconquer it, since the proletariat is the only class that cannot advance without democracy. It was unthinkable, he argued, that the overthrow of the 'black' dictatorship could lead directly to the 'red' dictatorship, since a class that had been too weak to defend democracy would be unable to establish any dictatorship other than that of a clique.

Reviewing the factors that had permitted the triumph of National Socialism, Kautsky centered his account on the struggle between capital and labour: the Nazi dictatorship originated in the imperialist tendencies of finance capitalism and was a régime championed by influential sectors of big business. However, Kautsky also analyzed the composition of the social bloc that had made the 'bloody revolution' of Nazism possible, calling attention to the quest of many intellectuals, who 'did not believe' in the victory of the proletariat or who 'feared it', for 'a position of privileged monopoly', founded on violence, amidst rising intellectual unemployment. Such elements poured into the columns of those who promised these privileges to them.[21] Another subordinate stratum massively manipulated by capital was the sub-proletariat of desperate unemployed who, deprived of any 'normal' prospects, readily succumbed to the bribes and promises of big business.[22]

Moreover, Kautsky was well aware that the fascist dictatorships had to be considered a new chapter of world history, that they were not a simple repetition on a broader scale of previous phenomena. He wrote that 'the modern dictatorships [among which he definitely included the Bolshevik state] are something new, never before seen in world history'.[23] Speaking of an 'epoch of dictatorships', he sought to identify their ideological accoutrements as well as their class constituents. The World War, he argued, had acted as a breeding-ground for powerful germs of

[21] Ibid., p. 353.
[22] Ibid., p. 354.
[23] Neue Programme, op. cit., p. 30.

'ethical-political' degeneration. The economic effects of the war, spreading unemployment and proletarianization among broad petty-bourgeois layers, had fused with these political and ideological effects. Within the working class, the war and the slump had interrupted the education in discipline and consciousness instilled by Social Democracy and significantly increased the weight of 'undisciplined, disorganized elements' prone to infantile radicalism. 'All these factors', Kautsky argued, 'militated against those conditions of freedom and equality, of democracy, that had arisen in the European states east of the Rhine for the first time after the end of the war. The most decisive force supporting the new states was the most advanced section of the proletariat, the thinking portion of Social Democracy. The monopoly capitalists and intellectuals sought to substitute for these conditions a method of dealing with political and social contradictions based on war, or more precisely on civil war: a civil war which, unlike the English revolutions of the 17th century and the French Revolution of the 18th century, would lead not to the conquest and defence of liberty and equality – in sum, to democracy – but rather to the privation of rights and the subjugation of those defeated in the civil war, and therefore to unfreedom and to inequality, which in the particular conditions of the centralized state take the organizational state form of dictatorship'.[24]

The virulent ideological degradation insinuated by the effects of the war among those social strata converted to violence, Kautsky argued, had been contained until the outbreak of the great crisis, so that in 1928, on the eve of the crash, the Nazis had won only 12 seats in the legislative elections. But the collapse of 1929 liberated the 'germs' of anti-democratic violence and furnished the most brutal capitalist forces an opportunity to act against the republic, by exploiting the desperation of the least advanced masses, those who reasoned 'in military and not economic terms' and believed they could improve their lot by smashing the existing institutional order and throwing themselves into the arms of a capitalist dictatorship.[25]

At this point, Kautsky argued that the example the Bolsheviks had set the capitalists had also contributed to the dissolution of the fabric of democracy. The Communists were not the most consistent enemies of fascist dictatorship but its 'fraternal adversaries'. They had constructed a model of dictatorship in Russia which the capitalists had

[24] 'Die blutige Revolution', op. cit., p. 357.
[25] 'Einige Ursachen und Wirkungen des deutschen Nationalsozialismus', in *Der Kampf*, XXVI, 1933, p. 238.

studied to apply for their own purposes. Their influence had converted sectors of the proletariat to the methods of dictatorship, though they lacked the strength ever to achieve it, and had weakened the sectors of the proletariat committed to democracy, thereby clearing the path for the opposite dictatorship, which triumphed because of the ideological and organizational division of the working masses. 'Bolshevik methods', Kautsky wrote, 'were closely studied and imitated not only by the Communists but also by the capitalists and reactionaries. The techniques of oppression first developed over the course of years by the Bolsheviks, techniques which not even Mussolini had found ready-made, have now been completed and utilized with maximum intensity by the National Socialists'.[26]

Kautsky was concerned to defend Social Democracy against the charge that it had failed to move against the reactionary forces with the necessary determination at the time of its greatest strength, in 1918 and 1919. Could not Germany have been spared the Nazi dictatorship if Social Democracy had established a proletarian dictatorship after the war? Kautsky contested the validity of the question, both because he held that such a dictatorship was incompatible with an advance towards socialism and because he regarded it as an unrealistic option purely in terms of the political balance of forces. A proletarian dictatorship in Germany, Kautsky maintained, would have been merely a prelude to reactionary dictatorship: 'If Social Democracy had pursued a policy of terror in 1918 and 1919, the only result would have been that the isolation of Germany and the paralysis of its economic life now accomplished by Hitler, would have occurred a dozen years earlier, under even more unfavourable conditions, in a "white" and sanguinary Germany'.[27] Thus, if there was to be talk of responsibility, Kautsky said, the focus must lie elsewhere. The proletariat could have opened a new road in Germany and the paralysis of its economic life, now accomplished by cleavages and within the framework of democracy. But the most radical elements, the Liebknechts and Ledebours, rejected the necessary co-operation. Then the election results of January 1919, which gave the bourgeoisie a majority, made the path of the working class even more difficult. An immediate and general socialization introduced when Social Democracy held power alone, without the necessary preparation and consensus, would have brought on catastrophe. Reconstructing the main

---

[26] 'Die blutige Revolution', op. cit., p. 358.
[27] Ibid., p. 360.

features of the immediate post-war situation and surveying the factors that had prevented a more complete renovation of German politics and society, Kautsky wrote: 'The German Reich had fallen into collapse during the war. It was necessary to accept an armistice, which made it indispensable to bring the enormous army back across the Rhine as rapidly as possible. Millions of soldiers had to be demobilized. In addition, stagnant production had to be revived and the war economy reconverted for peace. At the same time, a hungry population had to be fed, in spite of the continuing blockade. The various currents of Social Democracy did not work together in attempting to solve these enormous problems, but stood opposed in mutual hostility. Karl Liebknecht and Ledebour were asked to become members of the Council of People's Commissioners. They refused, and even combated the Council as much as they could. The Central Committee of the Workers' Councils could have unified all the forces of the German proletariat. But the leftist elements separated themselves from it, because they did not have a majority in the Workers' Councils. These were the conditions under which the socialization of the great enterprises would have had to be carried out – a question that was thrust to the background by the most pressing daily problems, absorbing every energy, from demobilization to the provision of food to the defence of the government against armed uprisings'. The Council of Commissioners did what it could, introducing the eight-hour day, factory councils, and measures to aid the unemployed. 'Socialization requires the most careful preparation. The Commission on Socialization was constituted at the end of November [1918] for just that purpose. But the elections to the National Assembly in January 1919 resulted in a bourgeois majority and thus put an end to any attempt at sweeping socialization. One might think that Social Democracy should have introduced socialization immediately, when it held power alone. Those who hold this view should recall the example of Hungary'.

For Kautsky, the fate of the Hungarian Commune constituted the classic example of a radical political acceleration that did not correspond to real possibilities of stabilizing a new model of social management. It thus resulted in violent reaction. Germany, of course, was not Hungary, but even there a radical course, given a disunited proletariat and a bourgeois majority in parliament, would not have permitted a broad socialization with the proper technical and political preparation. 'A hurried and unprepared socialization serves for nothing. But the Social Democrats did not remain in power in Germany long enough to gain the necessary time for preparation'.[28] Kautsky's whole approach, of course, rested on the assumption that the Bolshevik model had no validity. He viewed the Russian experience as economic and social 'adventurism', the product of a political radicalism that responded to its own inevitable failure to achieve impossible goals by subjecting society to siege and plunder. Its backward, authoritarian and hierarchical forms of social organization were even worse for the working class than those of capitalism.

Having rejected the charge that Social Democracy had not acted with sufficient determination during the immediate post-war period, Kautsky also asserted that neither could Social Democracy be condemned, after the catastrophe, for its conduct during the final crisis of the German Republic. What had Social Democracy done, given the weakness of republican and democratic institutions? It had done its utmost to defend them. In the circumstances, Kautsky wrote, 'two types of policy were open to us. Either that of the lesser evil or that of the Communists, which amounted to paving the way for the greater evil. Our policy at least involved the *possibility* of averting the greater evil, namely the dictatorship of Hitler. Had we united behind the policy of the Communists, we ourselves would have put Hitler in the saddle'.[29] In his analysis of the factors that had led to the collapse of the Weimar Republic,[30] Kautsky emphasized the 'defects' of the constitution he had once considered an appropriate instrument for the conquest of political power by the proletariat. He now maintained that when it was drafted in 1919 this constitution had not 'broken' sharply enough with the past. This was manifest above all in the excessive power it conferred on the President of the Republic, who commanded prerogatives superior, for example, to those of the French President, not to mention the British King. Directly elected by the people and not by parliament, the German President confronted the latter 'as an independent power' invested with supreme command of the army and disposing of the right of temporary suspension even of the validity of some of the articles of the constitution (Kautsky was thinking of article 48 and particularly of the use Hindenburg made of it). Hence, 'the President of the Reich attained a position similar to that which the constitution of the French Republic of 1848 conferred on its President, who crowned himself Emperor in 1852. The

---

[28] *Neue Programme*, op. cit., pp. 13–14.

[29] 'Der Zusammenbruch der deutschen Sozialdemokratie', in *Tribune*, VI, 1933, p. 333.

[30] *Neue Programme*, op. cit., p. 9.

experiences of that epoch were ignored by the fathers of the German constitution of 1919'. In this sense, it was fatal that the drafters of the constitution had tried to imitate the figure of the President of the United States, taking no account of the relationship between the presidency and the general structure of the state, which was radically different in the two countries: 'In Weimar the delegates were thinking primarily of the Constitution of the United States, which grants the President much greater powers than those now held by the President of the French Republic. But one fact was forgotten: in America they could grant the President such sweeping powers with respect to popular representation without endangering the Republic, because the United States does not have a strong centralized state administration and the population has been accustomed for centuries to a spirit of independence from authority. Moreover, the federal army is of modest proportions'. Precisely because of the role attributed to the President by the German Constitution, 'the struggle against Hitler culminated, in the final analysis, in the alternative Hindenburg or Hitler. In that alternative dictatorship had already prevailed over democracy'.[31]

What were now the prospects? What were the programmes and methods needed to struggle against the new dictatorship? Kautsky posed the question of whether or not Hitler's victory required a revision of the fundamental principles on which Social Democracy was based, in particular the democratic road to the conquest of power. Kautsky's anxiety was that the collapse of the parliamentary system in Germany could appear to confirm the validity of the violent and 'dictatorial method' of conquering the state. For the problem seemed to be posed whether the Bolshevik and the Nazi methods, which had succeeded, should not be considered more realistic options than a Social Democratic strategy which had failed. Should a future perspective for Germany be based on the use for socialist purposes of the methods the Nazis had employed for their own ends? Kautsky's reply was an emphatic negative: he saw 'no reason' to revise the traditional strategy of Social Democracy.[32] Rejecting the 'new dictatorial current' that had emerged in the SPD (supported by Bienstock and Irlen),[33] he argued that it was necessary to distinguish the struggle for the reconquest of democracy from the struggle for socialism, whose precondition was democracy and whose

---

[31] Ibid., pp. 51–52.
[32] 'Die blutige Revolution', op. cit., p. 346.
[33] *Neue Programme*, op. cit., p. 28.

establishment was incompatible with dictatorship as a form of state organization.[34] It was certainly true that the struggle against Nazism on occasion demanded illegal, conspiratorial, and violent methods, for the very conditions imposed by the fascist régime left no other road of struggle available to its opponents. It was not this that was under dispute, but the strategy of the phase subsequent to the overthrow of the reactionary dictatorship. 'The struggle against fascism', Kautsky wrote, 'necessarily requires illegal, secret organizations. If we want not merely to make propaganda but also to prepare uprisings against the dictatorship, then these organizations must engage in conspiracies. Such conspiracies, like wars and even civil wars, require dictatorial powers of command. War and conspiracy have always been little favourable to democracy. This may be deplorable, but it must not prevent us from resorting to effective methods in the struggle against fascism, even when their employment is possible only through dictatorial and undemocratic means. In this sense it would be highly inconsistent to reject any dictatorship *a priori*. All of us in the party agree on this. The open question is what political goal we intend to call for in the struggle against fascism: the conquest of democracy or a "Marxist dictatorship"? These are two very different questions: what *means* we must use in the struggle against Hitler and what political *goal* we must pose beyond him'.[35]

Those who argued that the Nazi dictatorship should be supplanted by a 'Marxist' dictatorship were the same people who held that the proletariat could never take power in a democratic state because of the economic, social, and cultural domination of the bourgeoisie over the working class. Hence they advocated the violent road not only for the reconquest of democracy but also for socialism. To them Kautsky objected that if a class like the proletariat was unwilling to cast a majority of its votes for the socialists, its lack of ideological maturity would be even more evident if the socialists called upon it to join a violent and mortal struggle against the ruling class. If such a struggle erupted in any event, then the working class would find itself not in the most favourable but in the most unfavourable conditions, since it could not hope for a degree of military preparation that would enable it to challenge the repressive machine of the bourgeois state: 'A socialist party that, despite these obstacles [the economic superiority of the bourgeoisie, its command of greater means of communication and propaganda, etc.], is

---

[34] Cf. 'Die Diktatur des Proletariats', in *Der Kampf*, XXVI, 1933, in which Kautsky repeats the arguments of his writings of 1918–1919, especially pp. 437–38, 440, 446.
[35] *Neue Programme*, op. cit., p. 31.

unable to win over the majority of the population in an electoral struggle conducted under complete democracy will be all the less able to win over the majority of the people in an armed struggle or a general strike, for in that case the instruments of power in the hands of the enemy have even greater efficacy against us than they do in a democratic electoral battle'.[36]

Democracy, Kautsky insisted, was the most suitable mirror of the relationship of class forces. If democracy revealed a weak proletariat, it was illusory to think that breaking the mirror could lend it strength. If the proletariat was weak and democracy was weak, it was essential to be lucid. 'What now appears as the weakness of democracy is actually the weakness of the proletariat. A working class that does not possess the strength to defend democracy has no chance, until the relationship of class forces changes, of being able to defend itself against the exploiters through violence. Where we lose democracy, our first and more important duty is to reconquer it'.[37] The Bolshevik experience, Kautsky asserted, could in no way negate 'the role of democracy in the modern state'. To begin with, the Bolsheviks, a minority of the proletariat, took power as the consequence not of a direct clash with the state, but of a series of conditions the 'repetition' of which was unthinkable: the destruction of the army by German militarism; the state of 'complete anarchy' in the country; the favourable opportunity for an armed minority.[38] Thereafter, when constructing a new order after its seizure of power, Bolshevism did not proceed to build socialism but instead reproduced traditional patterns, 'with the construction of a new army and a new bureaucracy'.[39]

In the hour of doubt and of temptation to counterpose a Marxist dictatorship to the fascist dictatorship, Kautsky stubbornly reiterated his exhortations to remain faithful to democratic ideals: 'The proletariat today has become the strongest bastion of democracy everywhere. Whoever asserts that democracy has failed asserts that the proletariat itself is not yet capable of liberating itself. . . . The first condition for overcoming the new dictatorships is to overcome those factors which have dragged broad sectors of the proletariat to such a low moral and intellectual level. . . . But one thing we can do above all and in all circumstances: *remain faithful to ourselves*. We must not become worshippers

[36] Ibid., pp. 32–33.
[37] Ibid., p. 34.
[38] Ibid., pp. 35–36.
[39] Ibid., p. 36.

of the success of the moment; we must not at one stroke jettison the ideals for which so many workers and socialists of all countries have placed their lives and liberty in jeopardy for a century, just because in special conditions our enemies have done a brisk political business in the past few years with opposite methods and goals'.[40] So far as the future of Germany was concerned, Kautsky insisted on the need to modify the state apparatus 'profoundly'. Just as he criticized the 'limits' of the Weimar Constitution, he now also admitted that the state apparatus that arose from the November Revolution had conserved too much of the machinery of the monarchy from which it had emerged. 'The revolution of 1918 and the republic issued of it', he wrote, 'insufficiently remodelled this apparatus'. In support of his argument, Kautsky recalled Marx's letter to Kugelmann of 12 April 1871, in which he had spoken of the need to 'smash' the 'bureaucratic military machine'. But Kautsky used it to counterpose his own conception of democracy to the theoreticians of dictatorship who wanted to use a centralized-despotic machine for socialist purposes. Glossing the letter of Marx, he wrote: 'This is exactly the opposite of what the supporters of a Social Democratic dictatorship want. They would like to "transfer" Hitler's "bureaucratic military machine" from his hands to ours, in order, with the aid of that machine, to complete the "real popular revolution", i.e. to put an end to capitalist rule'.[41]

The real meaning of Marx's analysis, Kautsky held, pointed in a direction contrary to those who argued the necessity of dictatorial rule as a state form on the grounds of the alleged weakness of democracy and of the need for a strong dictatorship to assure the transition from capitalism to socialism. In reality, all the weaknesses of Social Democratic governments, or of governments in which Social Democrats had participated, had been rooted in a frailty not of 'form' but of 'content': 'it was not *democracy* that impeded them but the fact that they did not command a solid *socialist majority*'.[42] Reiterating this argument, Kautsky insisted: 'Democracy and the rise of socialism will be guaranteed only when a particular condition prevails. That condition is the existence of a proletariat which is organizationally advanced and ideologically and politically experienced. When it is lacking, democracy cannot lead to socialism; indeed, democracy itself is threatened. *When such a proletariat*

---

[40] *Grenzen der Gewalt!*, Karlsbad, 1934, pp. 49, 50.
[41] *Neue Programme*, op. cit., p. 54.
[42] Ibid., p. 38.

is absent, there is no other road that can lead to socialism', for 'anti-capitalism' must not be confused with socialism. Bolshevism, for example, was anti-capitalist but not socialist. When capitalism was overthrown without democracy being preserved, the result was only 'a nationalized economy founded on state slavery'; in other words, 'a mode of production which is economically disastrous and atrophies all the energies of the workers'.[43]

So far as the changes to be made in the state apparatus were concerned, Kautsky rehearsed the traditional Social Democratic demands for the replacement of the army with a militia, the necessity for the broadest liberty for the trade unions, cooperatives, parties, etc. But the central problem remained the bureaucracy. Here he repeated that it was impossible to abolish bureaucracy either in the state or in modern large-scale industry. Indeed, he wrote, 'the victory of Social Democracy cannot reduce the tasks of the state', whose realization would demand the use of a bureaucratic machine. Social Democracy could not ignore the fact that 'no great undertaking is possible without an extensive administrative apparatus, a "bureaucracy"'. What could and should be done was to deprive the bureaucracy of powers of autonomous command, rendering it a strictly executive instrument, and at the same time to limit it to the extent compatible with the efficient centralization of the state, by the creation of a broad and independent network of municipalities, provinces, and *Länder* – while ensuring that the latter did not become states within the state, as had happened in the case of Prussia and Bavaria in the Reich. Finally, the decisive guarantee of control over 'bureaucratic power' lay in the juridical existence and active exercise of civil and political liberties. In the economic arena, meanwhile, socialists must never lose sight of the fact that Marx and Engels spoke of 'socialization' and not 'statification'; nationalization should never be confused with socialism.[44]

4 The Invincibility of Democracy

Just as he did not believe that Bolshevism could resolve the problems of building socialism, denouncing its failure to meet the civic, social, economic, and intellectual needs of the proletariat and its lack of 'ration-

[43] Ibid., pp. 70–71.
[44] Ibid., pp. 52–56.

ality' in the field of production, so Kautsky now asserted that Nazism was an abnormal phenomenon that would inevitably fail to answer the exigencies of capitalism itself. The premise of these twin predictions was that only democracy could assure the maximum development of the forces of production and that there was a necessary and inseparable link between industry and democracy, whether under capitalism or socialism. To rupture this link, Kautsky held, was to unleash irrationality, decadence, and ruin. He did not doubt that the forces of progress, objectively rooted in social classes, would eventually prevail, restoring democracy to society wherever it had been destroyed.

It is clear that Kautsky, who had often noted that his masters, Marx and Engels, consistently erred in their estimation of the tempo of the crisis and end of capitalism, himself committed an analogous mistake in his assessment of fascism and Bolshevism, which he deemed incapable of creating stable systems of power. He was convinced not only that Bolshevism and fascism were incapable of establishing a 'just' and 'rational' order in the countries which they ruled, but also that they could not consolidate their 'own' orders either. He thereby proved that he had not understood what a potent means of control and domination the state could represent once a political force had taken totalitarian possession of it and bent the economy to its goals. He, who had so thoroughly assimilated the 19th century values of 'humanity' and 'justice' from a liberalism that had been directly absorbed by Social Democracy, regarded them as principles definitively established in the advanced industrial countries. He did not imagine that they could suffer a profound eclipse.[45]

Thus the aged 'master' of German and European Social Democracy sounded the death-knell of fascism in the name of history and humanity, at the very moment when the Brown Shirts were celebrating their victory in highly developed Germany. He pronounced the same sentence on the Bolshevik 'dictatorship', from which the fascists had learned an accursed lesson: 'What forms this end will assume', he wrote in 1933, 'and how the dictatorships will fall is something that cannot be predicted. In an epoch of constant economic development, like the epoch of capitalism, especially an epoch of continual disorder and insecurity, like that initiated by the World War, any dictatorship must end in catastrophe. . . . Those who believe that the militarization of the economy is a means to provide for the well-being and freedom of the proletariat are mistaken.

[45] Cf., as regards Germany: 'Was nun?' in *Tribune*, VII, January 1934, p. 10.

It is no less erroneous to aim at a dictatorship in order to combat the dictatorship of the enemy and as a means thereafter to introduce democracy. It is an equally fatal error to grant the proletariat a privileged position in state and society and reduce the other classes of the population to the condition of pariahs in order to introduce socialist equality for all. But it would be particularly abominable to attempt to found the reign of humanity on bloody brutality, for a genuine socialist community is impossible without humanity. Socialism must be the realization of the banner of the French Revolution, on which is inscribed liberty, equality, fraternity. The dictators can torture and kill us, but they will not succeed in demoralizing the spirit of our movement, in inducing it to renounce its will to live and the purpose of its being. Our cause will win despite everything, for today, in both politics and economics, only communities and organizations of free men gladly collaborating can develop their fullest possibilities of participation and achievement. Apart from these, any community, any organization, that rests on coercion and maintains itself through bloody violence against its members will eventually be left behind and sink into decadence. . . . We remain, under all conditions, advocates of democracy and humanity'.[46] With these words Kautsky concluded his essay *Die blutige Revolution*, in which he had analyzed the significance of the rise of Nazism. In an essay published the following year, devoted to illustrating the 'limits of violence', Kautsky proclaimed his tenacious faith in the future of the proletariat as a class: 'The proletariat can never be annihilated, for all society rests on its labour. . . Never and in no country can the workers' movement be durably suppressed. It can be paralyzed only temporarily'.[47]

He ended another essay devoted to revolutionary strategy, *Neue Programme*, the last of the many programmes he drafted in the course of his long activity as a socialist theoretician, by reaffirming once again that political democracy for all society was the necessary form of the rule of the proletariat, whose general maturity and influence were the titles to its socialist mission. These were his words: 'The ideology of dictatorship is the ideology of the commander of a horde, which reduces the masses to a flock of ignorant and stupid sheep. Whoever accepts this ideology may desire socialism as passionately as he likes, but he expresses only his own moral bankruptcy. We who believe in the capacity for development and the future of the working class put our full faith in democracy. The

---

[46] 'Die blutige Revolution', op. cit., p. 361.
[47] *Grenzen der Gewalt!*, op. cit., p. 42.

toiling masses have been struggling for democracy for a century and a half now. Many have been their defeats, but they have never been demoralized. Those who have fought for democracy have never lost faith in it; democracy has always been reborn. . . . A single defeat must not induce us to abandon this embattled front, which alone can lead our party to victory and liberate toiling humanity forever'.[48]

[48] *Neue Programme*, op. cit., p. 70.

Biographical Note

Main Dates in the Life of Karl Kautsky

16 October 1854	Born in Prague.
1875	Joins Austrian Social Democracy while a student in Vienna.
1880	Moves to Zurich, where he works, under Bernstein, on *Der Sozialdemokrat*, published in Switzerland because of the Anti-Socialist Laws in Germany.
1881	Meets Plekhanov in Paris, before going to London, where he meets Marx and Engels.
Late 1881	Returns to Vienna.
1882	Moves to Stuttgart; works for Dietz Verlag.
1883	Creation, in Stuttgart, of *Die Neue Zeit*, of which Kautsky remains editor until 1917.
October 1883	Moves to Zurich, along with *Die Neue Zeit*.
1885–1890	Resident in London, where he collaborates with Engels and continues to edit *Die Neue Zeit*.
1890	Abrogation of Anti-Socialist Laws; moves to Stuttgart; *Die Neue Zeit* becomes a weekly.
1891	Plays major role in drafting the Erfurt Programme of German Social Democracy.
1893	Polemic against direct legislation.
1896–1898	Polemic with Bernstein on revisionism.
1899	Publication of *The Agrarian Question*.
1902	Publication of *The Social Revolution*.
1909	Publication of *The Road to Power*.
1912	Polemic with Luxemburg and Pannekoek.
1914	Supports vote for German war credits after his

	proposal for abstention rejected in Social Democratic parliamentary caucus.
1917	Formation of the USPD; drafts founding statement of the new party.
1918	Publication of *Democracy or Dictatorship* and *The Dictatorship of the Proletariat*; beginning of the polemic against Bolshevism.
1918–1919	Edits archives of German Foreign Office after November 1918 Revolution, publishing secret documents concerning origins of First World War.
1919	*Publication of Terrorism and Communism.*
1920	USPD majority fuses with Communist Party of Germany; Kautsky remains outside with USPD right wing.
1921	Publication of *From Democracy to State Slavery*; continuation of polemic with Trotsky.
1922	Publication of *The Labour Revolution*, continuation of anti-Bolshevik polemic.
1923	Reunification of right wing of USPD with SPD.
1924	Emigrates to Vienna; renews literary collaboration with Austrian Social Democracy.
1925	Publication of *The International and Soviet Russia*.
1927	Publication of *The Materialist Conception of History*.
1930	Publication of *Bolshevism at a Deadlock*.
1934	Emigrates to Prague after Dolfuss *coup* in Austria.
1937	Publication of *Socialists and War*.
1938	Emigrates to Holland just before Nazi invasion of Czechoslovakia.
17 October 1938	Dies in Amsterdam.

Bibliographical Note

Very few of Kautsky's writings are readily available in English. Some major works, *The Agrarian Question* and *The Materialist Conception of History*, for example, have never been translated. In many cases, translations date from the early years of the 20th century and are archaic at best and inaccurate at worst. In the translation of the present book, the original German editions have therefore been relied upon whenever these were available. For the information of readers who may want to consult translations, however, there follows a list of works by Kautsky that have been published in English, copies of which may be found in libraries. Those titles still in print are marked by an asterisk.

Communism in Central Europe in the Time of the Reformation,
    London, 1897.
The Social Revolution and on the Morrow of the Social Revolution,
    London, 1909.
The Road to Power, Chicago, 1909.
The Class Struggle (being the 'commentary' on the Erfurt Programme),
    Chicago, 1910 (re-issued by W. W. Norton, inc., New York, 1971).
The Dictatorship of the Proletariat, Manchester, 1918 (re-issued by
    Ann Arbor Paperbacks, University of Michigan Press, 1964).
Terrorism and Communism, London, 1920.
Georgia, a Social Democratic Peasant Rupublic, London, 1921.
The Economic Doctrines of Karl Marx, London, 1925.
Foundations of Christianity, London, 1925 (re-issued by Monthly
    Review Press, New York, 1972).
The Labour Revolution, London, 1925.
Are the Jews a Race?, London, 1926.
Thomas More and His Utopia, London, 1927.
Bolshevism at a Deadlock, London, 1931.

Index

373